Lecture Notes in Computer Science 4674

Commenced Publication in 1973
Founding and Former Series Editors:
Gerhard Goos, Juris Hartmanis, and Jan van Leeuwen

Editorial Board

Yuhua Luo (Ed.)

Cooperative Design, Visualization, and Engineering

4th International Conference, CDVE 2007
Shanghai, China, September 16-20, 2007
Proceedings

 Springer

Volume Editor

Yuhua Luo
University of Balearic Islands
Department of Mathematics and Computer Science
07122 Palma de Mallorca, Spain
E-mail: dmilyu0@uib.es

Library of Congress Control Number: 2007934910

CR Subject Classification (1998): H.5.3, H.5.2, H.5, H.4, C.2.4, D.2.12, D.4, H.2.8

LNCS Sublibrary: SL 3 – Information Systems and Application, incl. Internet/Web
and HCI

ISSN   0302-9743
ISBN-10   3-540-74779-6 Springer Berlin Heidelberg New York
ISBN-13   978-3-540-74779-6 Springer Berlin Heidelberg New York

Springer is a part of Springer Science+Business Media

springer.com

© Springer-Verlag Berlin Heidelberg 2007
Printed in Germany

Typesetting: Camera-ready by author, data conversion by Scientific Publishing Services, Chennai, India
Printed on acid-free paper   SPIN: 12119080   06/3180   5 4 3 2 1 0

Preface

This year the CDVE conference celebrated its fourth annual event in an exciting city—Shanghai, China. The cooperative design, visualization and engineering community sensed the economic pulse of a new giant economy where cooperation is vital for its success.

This year we received a large number of papers from all over the world. In addition to many submissions from Europe, we received more papers from Asia and China this time. Many authors from key Chinese research centers and national projects presented their papers, which gave us insight into the progress of research and development in this giant economy.

From a technical point of view, as a major trend in cooperative design, visualization, engineering and other applications, advanced Web-based cooperation technology stands out by itself. Many papers reflect the research in this aspect with very convincing results.

Web-based cooperative working applications have been emerging strongly since the wide availability and accessibility of the WWW. It is a form of sharing and collaborating by its nature. It is suitable for the cooperation of a much wider range of users.

In the field of cooperative engineering, new findings and new results were presented. Among all, work flow technology was recognized as a key element for successful cooperative engineering. According to these new findings, only Web-based cooperation tools and shared databases are not enough for cooperative engineering. Workflow-based methodology should be introduced to guarantee the integration and coordination of the whole life cycle process of products.

This year we had many papers concerning other aspects of cooperative applications. Knowledge management for cooperative work, grid and distributed architecture etc. were some of them. To give users an "anytime, anywhere" cooperation possibility was also one of the areas of focus. Multiple platform applications are developed that use all possible communication networks, including interactive digital TV, mobile phones and mobile devices etc.

I would like thank all the authors who submitted their papers to the CDVE2007 conference. It is their enthusiasm and hard work that made this conference unique. I would also like to express my thanks to our Program Committee, our Organizing Committee for reviewing the papers and doing conference organization work on top of their very heavy daily workloads. I would like to express my special thanks to many volunteer experts for reviewing our papers and providing a great help to raise the quality of the papers of this conference.

This conference aims to promote technologies for cooperation. I believe all of our efforts will contribute to the research and development of this field very positively, and to a better cooperation and mutual understanding in our international community.

September 2007   Yuhua Luo

Organization

Conference Chair   Yuhua Luo
Math and Computer Science Department
University of Balearic Islands
Spain

International Program Committee

Program Chair   Dieter Roller
University of Stuttgart
Germany

Members

Peter Demian	Francis Lau	Miguel Sales Dias
Susan Finger	Jos P. Leeuwen	Weiming Shen
Ning Gu	Kwan-Liu Ma	Ram Sriram
Ivan Jelinek	Mary Lou Maher	Chengzheng Sun
Matti Hannus	Bjorn E. Munkvold	Carlos Vila
Mikael Jern	Moira C. Norrie	Nobuyoshi Yabuki
Irina Kondratova	Benoit Otjacques	Xiu-Tian Yan
Larry Korba	Wolfgang Prinz	

Organizing Committee

Chair   Qiyan Li
Tongji University
China

General Secretary   Guofeng Qin
Tongji University
China

Members

Huoyan Chen	Alex Garcia	Qunsheng Peng
Tomeu Estrany	Shaozi Li	Guofeng Qin
Xin Fan	Yingwei Luo	Rongqiao Wang

Table of Contents

Integrating Advanced Collaborative Capabilities into Web-Based Word Processors

Haifeng Shen, Steven Xia, and Chengzheng Sun

School of Computer Engineering
Nanyang Technological University
50 Nanyang Avenue, Singapore 639798
{ashfshen,stevenxia,czsun}@ntu.edu.sg

Abstract. With the development of new web technologies, web-based collaborative applications, exemplified by office applications, are emerging to take advantage of web's attractive features. We propose to plug a collaborative engine into web-based office applications so that advanced collaboration capabilities can be seamlessly integrated without compromising or modifying their conventional capabilities. This engine lies on application-independent data addressing and operation models to be reusable for a wide range of diverse applications without being modified. In this paper, we present a data addressing model for web-based word processors, which complies with the model used by the engine and shall lay a good foundation for investigating data addressing models for other web-based applications.

1 Introduction

Web-based (or essentially web-browser-based) applications have been an alternative to desktop applications since the emergence of WWW and are becoming more and more attractive owing to its advantages like no installation, easy-to-use, ubiquitous accessibility, platform agnosticism, low risk of data loss, and more important, sharing and collaboration. Representative niche web-based applications include Internet applications such as web-based email, bookmarks, discussion boards, blogs, wikis, and search engines; e-Business applications such as e-Bay and Amazon; and various MIS (Management Information System) and ERP (Enterprise Resource Planning) applications. These applications use standard web and database technologies to provide a lightweight solution to average end-users who possess limited or fair set of skills of using computers.

Recent development of new web technologies exemplified by Ajax (Asynchronous Javascript And XML) and Web 2.0 is making it possible to port some widely-used desktop applications onto the web. These web-based applications have similar user interfaces, features, and functions as those offered by their desktop counterparts. Although their functions are relatively limited and not comparable with their desktop counterparts at the moment, they do provide essential functions that satisfy the majority of average end-users, and more importantly, these web-based applications have so many attractive advantages that do not exist in their desktop counterparts.

Y. Luo (Ed.): CDVE 2007, LNCS 4674, pp. 1–8, 2007.

Such applications are represented by various web-based office applications such as web-based word processors (their most influential desktop counterpart is *Microsoft Word*): *Google Docs* [1], *FCKeditor* [2], *Zoho Writer*, and *ajaxWrite*; spreadsheet authoring tools (their most influential desktop counterpart is *Microsoft Excel*): *Google Spreadsheet*, *Zoho Sheet*, and *ajaxXLS*; and slides authoring and presentation tools (their most influential desktop counterpart is *Microsoft PowerPoint*): *Zoho Show* and *ajaxPresents*.

Sharing and collaboration are two characteristic features of these web-based office applications. All of them support sharing of documents on the web in that a document can be accessed with nothing but a web browser by anyone authorized, at anytime, from anywhere. Some (e.g., *Google Docs & Spreadsheet*, *Zoho Writer & Sheet*) come with built-in collaboration functionality that allows multiple users to view and edit shared documents in real time. However, the collaboration functionality in these applications is limited in that it is either based on a sequential interaction paradigm, where only one user can modify the shared document at any instance of time, or based on a Copy-Modify-Merge paradigm (supported by an *html diff* and an *html merge* algorithm) , where concurrent conflicting changes will be aborted.

We propose to plug a collaborative engine into web-based office applications so that advanced collaboration capabilities, such as fast local response, concurrent work and unconstrained interaction, relaxed WYSIWIS (What You See Is What I See) [3], collaborative undo, and detailed workspace awareness, can be seamlessly integrated without compromising or modifying their conventional capabilities. This engine uses application-independent data addressing and operation models to underpin advanced collaborative techniques so that it can be plugged into a wide range of diverse applications without being modified.

As different applications use their own data addressing and operation models to reference and manipulate internal data objects, an application-dependent adapter middleware is required for the engine to be plugged into an application, which essentially bridges the gap between the data and operation models used by the application and engine. Therefore, we choose to study the data addressing and operation models for web-based word processors in order to explore a data addressing model and an operation model that rigidly comply with the models used by the collaborative engine. In this paper, we present a data addressing model for the adapter of web-based word processors, which complies with the model used by the engine and shall lay a good foundation for investigating adapters for other web-based applications (e.g., web-based spreadsheet authoring tools, web-based slides authoring and presentation tools). This model has been implemented in the adapter for an open source web-based word processor, which, when the collaborative engine is plugged in via the adapter, supports advanced collaboration capabilities.

The rest of the paper is organized as follows. The next section describes the cornerstone of the collaborative engine. After that, we present a data addressing model for web-based word processors. Finally, the paper is concluded with a summary of major contributions and future work.

2   Cornerstone of the Collaborative Engine

Advanced collaboration capabilities lie upon a cornerstone technology called Operational Transformation (OT) [4] for supporting unconstrained interaction, i.e., to allow any user to modify any data object consistently at any time without imposing any restrictions on users' actions. OT uses an application-independent data addressing model called *XOTDM* [5], which consists of a hierarchy of addressing groups, where each group consists of multiple independent linear addressing domains. Inside each addressing group, independent linear addressing domains are identified by their unique names within that group.

A data object is mapped to a position in a linear addressing domain only if it has the position number as its address in this domain. Consequently, the address used by an operation is a vector pair, i.e., a vector of (n, p) pairs, where n is the name of a linear addressing domain in this group, and p is the object's position in this domain. More precisely, an addresses has the format of $addr = \langle (n_0, p_0), (n_1, p_1), \ldots, (n_i, p_i), \ldots, (n_k, p_k) \rangle$, where $addr[i] = (n_i, p_i)$, $0 \le i \le k$, represents one addressing point at level i.

3   An OT-Compliant Data Addressing Model

Documents used by web-based word processors are in the format of HTML or its extensions such as XHTML (eXtensible HTML). To investigate an OT-compliant data addressing model, we first need to study how data objects can be referenced in an HTML document. The Document Object Model (DOM) is a platform and language neutral Application Programming Interface (API) for representing a structured HTML and XML document and for accessing and manipulating the elements (such as HTML tags and strings of text) that make up that document.

An HTML document has a hierarchical structure that is represented in the DOM as a tree structure. The nodes of the tree represent the various types of content in the document. The tree representation of an HTML document

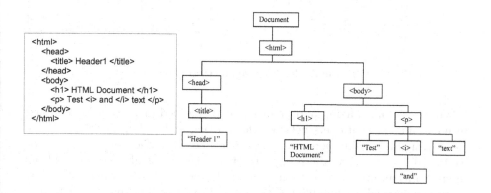

Fig. 1. The DOM tree for an HTML document

primarily contains nodes representing elements or tags such as ⟨body⟩ and ⟨p⟩ nodes representing strings of text. Figure 1 is a simple graphical representation of an HTML document with respect to a DOM tree. The DOM tree structure is represented as a tree of various types of Node objects. The Node interface defines properties and methods for traversing and manipulating the tree. One way to access a data object in an HTML document is to traverse its DOM tree by recursively using the *childNodes* property of a node until the object is found. DOM also provides a number of ways to access specified nodes, for example, *getElementsByTagName("tagname")*, *getElementsById("id")*, and *getElements-ByName("objectname")*. However, none of these ways matches the data addressing model used by OT.

3.1   The Range Object

Our further investigation led to the discovery of the **Range** object in DOM. A Range object represents a contiguous range of document content contained between specified starting and ending points. The starting and ending points of a range are each specified by a pair (*node, offset*), where *node* is typically a *text*, *document*, or *element* object, and *offset* is the position between the children of the *node*. For example, an offset of 0 will represent the position after the first child and before the second. When the specified node is a *text* node, the offset represents a position between two characters in the text node. For example, an offset of 1 represents the position between the first and second characters.

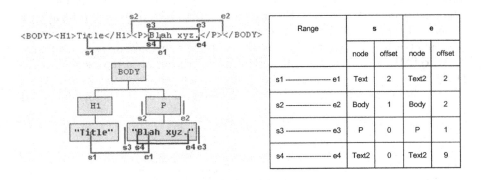

Fig. 2. The **Range** object in DOM

With both the starting and ending points specified, a range will represent all nodes and/or characters between the starting and ending positions. When the starting and ending points of a range are the same, the range is said to be "collapsed". In this case, the Range object represents a single position, and can be viewed as an insertion position within a document. The starting and ending points can even fall within different nodes, and can therefore span multiple (and fractional) *elements* and/or *text* nodes. Figure 2 shows examples of four different

text ranges, where **s#** and **e#** denote the starting and ending points of range#
respectively. For Range 2, the starting point s2 = ($\langle BODY \rangle$, 1) because it is
in the $\langle BODY \rangle$ element and is immediately after the first child $\langle H1 \rangle$ element
and before the second child $\langle P \rangle$ element. In particular, the starting and ending
points of Range 3 and Range 4 are the same, although Range 3 and Range 4 use
different representations. Moreover, the starting and ending points of Range 1
fall in different nodes (starting node $\langle H1 \rangle$ and ending note $\langle P \rangle$) and the range
spans two different text nodes to return a string of characters.

3.2   The TextRange Object

Every range is contiguous because it must include all nodes and elements specified by the starting and ending points. The **Range** object looks somewhat
relevant to the XOTDM model in that elements seems to be addressable with
their offsets in a contiguous range. However, it is difficult to address every data
object with a unique offset in a document due to 1) offsets may not be unique
because offsets are relative to the starting and ending points of a range and multiple arbitrarily related ranges may exist in a document, and 2) if a single range
is created to encompass the whole document, tags and data objects are mixed
in the range and consequently offsets are non-deterministic because lengths of
tags and objects may not be deterministic. For example, the length of an $\langle img \rangle$
tag depends on the path of the image source.

Although the data addressing model based on DOM's *Range* cannot directly
be mapped to XOTDM, it has inspired us to continue our investigation along
this line, which results in the discovery of the **TextRange** object. TextRange is
based on DOM's Range and is available in the Dynamic HTML (DHTML) object
model, which is built upon DOM. As the name implies, DHTML is particularly
useful to deal with dynamic content such as searching, and manipulation of text
content such as characters, words, sentences, and even paragraphs.

Similar to a DOM's Range, a DHTML's TextRange object consists of, and
is bounded by its starting and ending points and a created TextRange object
in DHTML must also be contiguous. What remains different in DHTML is the
fact that although a TextRange object must be finite, it is not always necessary
to explicitly specify starting and ending positions. Instead, they can be defined
by using a container tag (i.e. $\langle body \rangle$). In other words, creating a TextRange
object over the $\langle body \rangle$ element would automatically position the starting and
ending points at the beginning and the end of the textual content of the $\langle body \rangle$
tag. With this functionality, the entire contents of a document can be set as a
single TextRange object, and more importantly, only data objects are included
in the TextRange (i.e., tags are excluded) and the length of every data object is
deterministic. Therefore, every data object can be addressed by a unique offset
in the TextRange. In the following paragraphs, we will discuss how different
types of data objects are addressed in a TextRange.

Text, presented as a string of formatted characters, is the main object type in
HTML and its extensions. Each character (excluding its formatting tags) occupies

(a) TextRange before inserting the new text

(b) TextRange after inserting the new text

Fig. 3. Text object in the TextRange

a unique position in the TextRange. As characters are inserted or deleted, the TextRange will expand or shrink accordingly.

The TextRange in Figure 3(a) was created for the HTML document shown on its left side, where every character can be identified by a unique offset value. For example, character 'o' in the word "report" can be addressed by offset 11. When the word "my" and a space are inserted between words "is" and "report" (as shown in Figure 3(b)), the TextRange is expanded in that the offsets of characters after the word "is" are all increased by 3. At this moment, to address character 'o' in the word "report", the new offset 14 must be used.

Object, exemplified by an image, checkbox, radio button, dropdown list, textfield, texarea, button, hidden input, or a horizontal rule, occupies a single position in the TextRange. A shown in Figure 4, when the image and a space are inserted between words "this" and "as", the TextRange is expanded in that the offsets of characters after the inserted images are all increased by 2.

Table, consisting of multiple cells, occupies a sequence of positions in the TextRange. To be more precise, each empty cell occupies one position and every character or object within a cell also occupies one position in the TextRange. As

```
<HTML>
 <BODY>
  show this as eg
 </BODY>
<HTML>
```

0	1	2	3	4	5	6	7	8	9	10	11	12	13	14
S	h	o	w		t	h	i	s		a	s		e	g

(a) TextRange before inserting the image

```
<HTML>
 <BODY>
  show this <img src="find.jpg"> as eg
 </BODY>
<HTML>
```

0	1	2	3	4	5	6	7	8	9	10	11	12	13	14	15	16
S	h	o	w		t	h	i	s		<img>		a	s		e	g

(b) TextRange after inserting the image

Fig. 4. Image object in the TextRange

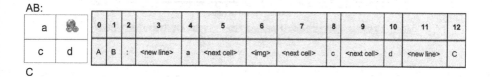

Fig. 5. Table object in the TextRange

shown in Figure 5, when a table is created, it has to be placed in a new line (i.e., it cannot be inline with other text or objects). The new line object ⟨new line⟩, which can be a break, new paragraph, or a page break, occupies a single position in the TextRange. An empty cell object ⟨next cell⟩ or a character/image object also occupies a single position in the TextRange.

In conclusion, an OT-compliant data addressing model for web-based word processors can be a single linearly addressed domain *TextRange*. Every data object can be addressed with its unique index (offset) in the domain. For example, to reference character 'o' in the word "report" in Figure 3(b), the address to be used is ⟨(TextRange, 14)⟩; to reference the image in Figure 4(b), the address to be used is ⟨(TextRange, 10)⟩; and to reference character 'c' in the table in Figure 5, the address to be used is ⟨(TextRange, 8)⟩. This data addressing model is generally applicable to any web-based word processor that is based on DHTML.

4   Conclusions and Future Work

Web is evolving from an one-to-many information sharing medium to a many-to-many collaboration locus, where people interact to jointly fulfill tasks. With the development of new web technologies, collaborative applications, mostly available on the desktop platform, are emerging as web-based collaborative applications to take advantage of web's attractive features. However, collaboration functionality in these web-based collaborative applications, exemplified by web-based office applications, is limited. Our proprietary collaborative engine offers a set of advanced collaboration capabilities based on the OT core technology. To seamlessly plug this engine into web-based word processors, we contribute an OT-compliant data addressing model, which shall also lay a good foundation for investigating adapters for other web-based applications.

The data addressing and operation models have been implemented in the adapter for *FCKeditor* - an open source web-based word processor. When the collaborative engine is plugged into *FCKeditor* through the adapter and turned on, *FCKeditor* is functioning as a collaborating web-based word processor. Figure 6(a) shows a web-based collaborative document repository manager for user *qz*, where there are five shared documents and document *doc2* is being edited by user *qh* and *eric*. A collaborative editing session is set up by invitation. Figure 6(b) shows the collaborative *FCKeditor* for user *qz* (doing error-correction) in a collaborative editing session for document *doc2*, which involves other two users *qh* and *eric* (doing brainstorming).

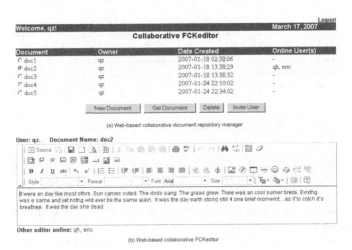

Fig. 6. Collaborative FCKeditor

The current adapter is based on the TextRange data addressing model, which only works on web browsers that support DHTML. At this moment, DHTML is only fully supported by Internet Explorer. Other browsers such as Firefox, Opera, Safari, only partially or do not support DHTML at all. To make the adapter available across different browsers, we are still working on a data addressing model that is purely based on the low level DOM structure.

Acknowledgment

The work is partially supported by an ASTAR IMSS grant (P0520094) and an ASTAR PSF grant (062-101-0034), Singapore. The authors wish to thank Seow Ching Soh and Yong Hock Goh for the prototype development.

References

1. Google: Google Docs and SpreadSheets, Create and share your work online, http://docs.google.com/
2. FredCK.com: FCKeditor - The text editor for Internet, http://www.fckeditor.net/
3. Stefik, M., Bobrow, D.G., Foster, G., Lanning, S., Tatar, D.: WYSIWIS Revised: Early Experiences with Multiuser Interface. In: Proc. of ACM Conference on Computer Supported Cooperative Work, December 1986, pp. 276–290 (1986)
4. Sun, C., Ellis, C.: Operational transformation in real-time group editors: Issues, algorithms, and achievements. In: Proc. of ACM Conference on Computer Supported Cooperative Work, November 1998, pp. 59–68 (1998)
5. Sun, C., Xia, S., Sun, D., Chen, D., Shen, H., Cai, W.: Transparent adaptation of single-user applications for multi-user real-time collaboration. ACM Transactions on Computer-Human Interaction 13(4), 531–582 (2006)

A Peer-to-Peer Based Communication Environment for Synchronous Collaborative Product Design

Lirong Wang [1,*], Jiacai Wang [1,2], Lixia Sun[1], and Ichiro Hagiwara[1]

[1] Department of Mechanical Science and Engineering, Tokyo Institute of Technology, Tokyo, Japan
[2] School of Mechanical & Vehicular Engineering, Beijing Institute of Technology, 5 South Zhongguancun Street, Haidian District, Beijing 100081, P.R. China
{wanglr.aa,wangjc.aa,sun.aa,hagiwara}@m.titech.ac.jp

Abstract. Efficiency and timeliness of collaborative communication among geographically distributed design teams are vital to collaborative product design for synchronous exchange of product design information and faster product availability. This paper introduces a preliminary research work about P2P&VRML-based collaborative communication environment that attempts to support synchronous collaborative product design in the way of WYSIWIS (What You See Is What I see). A prototype with communication means of document co-sharing & editing, draft co-drawing, instant message and VRML-based visualization space is developed on the basis of JXTA platform. Collaborative model modification is performed by cooperation between document co-editing space and VRML visualization.

Keywords: Collaborative design, P2P, VRML, CSCW.

1 Introduction

Nowadays, market globalization is increasingly driving industry to be highly desired for synchronous collaborative product design environment to perform multi-sited product design cooperation with partners around the world. During design processes of complex product, such as automobile and airplane, accuracy, timeliness and efficiency of product design information co-sharing and co-operating among geographically distributed design teams are essential for companies to reduce design failure-rate as well as design iteration loops, to shorten lead-time for faster product availability, and to keep dynamic enterprise group competitiveness to market. With the expansion of internet and development of web-based technologies in the past decade, collaborative product design to support CE (concurrent engineering) has attracted more and more attention in the research field of CSCW (computer supported cooperative work), which is promising to get satisfied solution with highly synchronous collaborative capability to enhance enterprise group competitiveness and to make full use of resources in enterprise group. Synchronization and interoperation are the emphases for a collaborative product design system to ensure real-time interactions among distributed work teams. Establishment of a synchronous communication environment to make cooperation working in the way of WYSIWIS (What You See Is What I see) is a well-know problem in CSCW research field.

Y. Luo (Ed.): CDVE 2007, LNCS 4674, pp. 9–20, 2007.

Up to now, many collaborative design systems somehow supporting collaborative design activities, such as collaborative model annotation and visualization, are developed on the basis of C/S (client/server) or B/S (browser/server) network architecture. C/S or B/S is also relative common network architecture in almost all database, web, business, and communication applications. However, in C/S or B/S collaborative design environment, all the system grouping, operation, and communication have to rely on central server, single point bottlenecks always rise because of limited bandwidth, and system maintenance cost is very high as well. Bidarra, R. et al [1] developed a C/S based collaborative feature modeling system, named WebSPIFF. Fat server generates selection model with a set of feature canonical shape in VRML format; thin client directly visualizes VRML model under Java3D based scene; real time interactive model manipulation is performed by collaboration of feature shape selection on client side and feature parameter modification on sever side. Li W.D. et al. [2] developed a manipulation-client/modeling-server infrastructure to accomplish feature-based collaborative design environment, in which light face-based representation on the client side supports interactive visualization and manipulation, a heavy representation with features and part information on the server side provide primary feature-based modeling functions, and a distributed feature manipulation mechanism is presented to facilitate efficient information exchange for larger size 3D (3-dimensional) model. CollabCAD^{TM} [3] is a modeling-client/communication-server based commercial collaborative framework developed by using Java3D and RMI. Many open sources and standards have been adopted to achieve inter-application operability, e.g. Open CASCADE for 3D modeling engine, JPython/Jacl for client-side scripting, STEP for product data exchanges, XML (Extensible Markup Language) for geometry data storage and database connectivity, VRML for preview, and CVW (Collaborative Virtual Workspace, from Mitre Corporation) for collaborative functionalities like video, voice, text, and white-board conferencing. Event-transmission collaborative mechanism for one participating site to observe what is happening on the other site by executing received events individually is employed. Whereas, its collaboration environment is not heterogeneous since the same kind of sophisticated design capability is set up to all sites, and computing resources are not utilized efficiently due to the same execution process be repeated at different sites. OneSpace.net^{TM} [4] is another commercial collaborative product with manipulation-client/modeling-server to support multi-party 3D CAD design reviewing and engineering data sharing. However, its modeling ability is limited because of lacking sophisticated geometric kernel in server.

P2P (Peer-to-Peer) network closely mimics collaboration among persons in society. In P2P network, any computer or device, which can be connected with each other through network, is generally called peer; and peer acts as both client and server, that is, it is not necessary to have an intermediary or a centralized repository like server for communication between peers. P2P network technology has advantages, which C/S or B/S lacks, such as convenient direct exchange of data between peers to minimize workload on servers and maximize overall network performance, sufficiently utilization of large scalar resources from any other peer, and flexible and dynamical structure to enable join in and leave in voluntary and convenient way. In contrast with C/S or B/S architecture, P2P has the more promising potential to provide synchronous collaborations for large-scale distributed involvers in the way of WYSIWIS. P2P technology has proved successful in resource-sharing, file-sharing, messaging application, and distributed computing. However, research on P2P-based collaborative design system is relatively young. Recently, some researchers attempted to adopt P2P network technology in building up collaborative engineering design platform. Alda S et al. [5] developed an integrated multi-agent and peer-to-peer software architecture for supporting collaborative civil structural design process. Component-based P2P model for the flexible integration of heterogeneous software in a co-operation and agent-based workflow modeling for collaborative design process were presented. Chen H.M. et al. [6] presented a P2P-based synchronous collaboration design prototype for civil engineering named ROCCAD. This prototype developed by OpenGL and Java provides mutual graphic or drawing interchange, and adopts Application level multicast (ALM) scheme to improve communication efficiency.

This paper presents a preliminary research work in establishment of P2P-based collaborative communication platform. Management of peer & peer group, multicast message propagation and event-transmission collaborative mechanism are built up into P2P network. Synchronous communication environment with document co-sharing & co-editing, instant message, draft co-drawing is developed. VRML visualization interface with stand alone and co-visualization workspaces is built up to display geometry gesture for private use and for synchronous sharing respectively, which is able to reduce redundant collaborative operations and increase collaborative efficiency. File co-editing based collaborative model modification is established among peer group members to realize WYSIWIS collaboration.

2 Platform of Collaborative Communication Environment

2.1 Architecture Overview

Fig. 1 shows the architecture of the developed prototype of P2P&VRML-based collaboration communication environment. This P2P application is able to independently reside on any machine to connect with other peers in distributed places. It includes main four functionalities of GUI (graphics user interface), Peer collaborative space, VRML visualization and P2P network platform. GUI provides the interface for user to login/ logout as a peer with certain peer ID under security authentication in password. Peer collaborative spaces supports communication space among group peers. VRML visualization and parameter editor provides workspace for scene-graph manipulation and model modification of product 3D data. P2P network platform is developed on the basis of protocols in JXTA platform [7], and is responsible for connection with physical internet and provides network services.

2.2 Introduction to JXTA Platform

JXTA is an open-source project initiated by Sun Microsystems, Inc. to provide a platform with the basic protocol functions for building up P2P application. As shown in Fig. 1, six protocols of peer discovery, information, resolver, pipe binding, endpoint routing and rendezvous protocols are used for peer discovering, advertising,

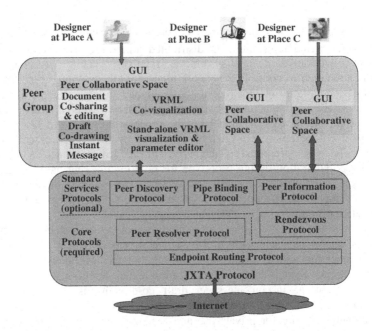

Fig. 1. P2P&VRML-based collaborative communication environment

messages routing, communication and so on. JXTA technology enables developers of P2P network architecture to concentrate on their own applications without worrying about low-level details of the interior P2P technology in JXTA.

In JXTA, a peer is a device that implements one or more JXTA protocols to communicate and exchange data with others over a network. Each peer is assigned a unique identifier as peer ID after registering JXTA configuration setting, and belongs to one or more peer groups. As shown in Fig.2, peer has three abstract layers: Application layer contains logic and GUI of individual applications; Service layer provides common library-like functionality like a CMS (Content Management System) service; Core layer is responsible for managing JXTA protocols, creating an addressing space separate from IP addresses by providing each peer a unique peer ID,

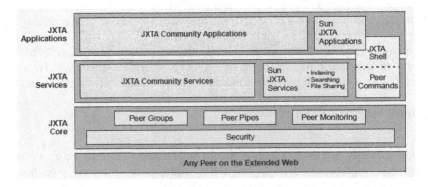

Fig. 2. JXTA platform

providing boot-strapping mechanism for peer grouping, locating peers in a secure/authenticated manner, and opening a pipe to another peer or group of peer. By publishing advertisements that are encoded in XML format, communication between peers is established, and messages are exchanged. Peers communicate with each other using pipe.

In JXTA, pipe is virtual peer connection with endpoints available to the connected peers for sending and receiving network messages. When two peers communicate with each other, one peer's sending endpoint as pipe input would be linked to the other peer's receiving endpoint as pipe output to establish a unidirectional, virtual connection. Peer group is essential boundary for pipe connectivity. Each group provides its own pipe service. Endpoints have to be located within peer group in order to be mutually resolved, and hence peers have to join the same group to establish a connection. All peers are natural part of the standard NetPeerGroup of JXTA, and all the other peer groups can be regarded as a sub-group of NetPeerGroup. In one peer group, a pipe service is used to resolve group pipe, and security properties and authentication of the group is defined among the group peers. The process of finding other peers is called discovery, and can be put forth on any JXTA resources like other peers, peer group, pipe, advertisement, and other resources. Discovery occurs within a peer group. Resources are made available through pipe advertisement mechanism.

2.3 P2P Network Platform

The functionalities of P2P network architecture are to manage state of peer and peer group, to monitor occurring changes and to transfer the changes to other peers in synchronous interaction mode. The whole architecture is mainly comprised of peer & group manager, message manager, event controller, and collaborative spaces.

(1) Peer & peer group manager. The functionality of peer & peer group manager includes creation of group, definition of group membership, join in/leave group, status monitoring and refreshment, and demonstration of peer & group information.

(2) Event controller. Event Controller is to listen, capture and exchange event information on peer communication spaces and GUI. Event-transmission collaborative mechanism is adopted to let other peers to know the event at the same time. As shown in Fig. 3, event controller consists of three components, event source, event listener and event handler. Event source is the object that generates event like components in peer communication spaces and GUI. Event listener is responsible for event monitoring, sensing and capturing. Event handler dispatches the captured event information to the corresponding performers to invoke corresponding actions.

(3) Message Manager. Message Manager is responsible for message transportation by using discovery and propagation mechanism of pipe for multicast communication in a peer group. Propagate pipe is adopted due to its efficient ability of multicast propagation in a group. As shown in Fig. 3, message manager consists of sender and receiver modules. When message manager receives event information from event handler, sender module takes action in three steps: firstly message separator classifies event message according to its source; then, message encoder packages the message in JXTA message format; and finally, pipe allocator dispatches the message to input and output pipe endpoints. The Message will be published to all peers in the same group through pipe. Correspondingly, receiver module also has three action performances: pipe listener monitors and receives the discovery message; message decoder takes out message from the encoded discovery; and finally, message adapter classifies the decoded message and transfers to event handler to invoke corresponding event in peer collaborative spaces.

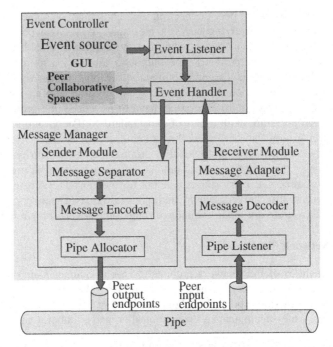

Fig. 3. Configuration of message manager and event controller

2.4 Visualization and Collaborative Modification of Product 3D Model

Visualization and visibility are important attributes of web based collaborative design environment for user to perceive, immerse, and interact in collaborative design process. Capabilities and functionality of multi-user 3D co-viewer environment mainly includes aspects like view control, collaborative model modification, product 3D data format for web transmission, and transmission mode for synchronous sharing of model update.

(1) **View control.** Co-visualization and stand-alone visualization are the two visualization means. Co-visualization is to enable distributed users to synchronously share the same visualization. Stand-alone visualization is the workspace of private manipulation site to foster individual interest. Coexistence environment with co-visualization and stand-alone visualization is able to collect group opinion in the sharing workspace and to conduct personal creation in the private workspace at the same time, which helps to reduce abundant communication and to increase collaboration efficiency among multi-users.

(2) Collaborative model modification. File co-editing based collaborative modification, geometrical parameter co-editing based modification and geometry visualization based modification, are three kinds of approaches to be implemented in practical environment. File co-editing based collaboration is the simplest mode in interactive mechanism; however, it requires user to have a high understandability to modeling expression. Parameter co-editing based collaboration provides user a more friendly collaborative interface than the former one does, whereas it is necessary to build up a suitable bridge to connect model expression and geometry parameter editor. Geometry visualization based collaboration support the most convenient collaborative interface; however, interactive mechanism to map visual geometrical properties and the topological feature of original geometry is complex to be built up.

(3) Product 3D data format for web transmission. Many kinds of product 3D data formats in existed CAD (computer aided design) and CG (computer graphics) fields are available. Data format for web transmission mainly depends on the geometrical modeling kernel in a collaborative product design environment. VRML (Virtual Reality Modeling Language) [8] is a standard file format for representing 3D interactive vector graphics, which is designed particularly to support large-scale web-based virtual environments. VRML format written in text file format is adequate and effective to be transmitted through web. In addition, 3D model can be saved in VRML format by many commercial softwares; thus VRML is an obvious conversion tool to connect current CAD system. Moreover, Extensible 3D (X3D) [9], a format for integrated 3D graphics and multimedia, succeeds VRML with new features. Currently, X3D becomes a software standard for defining interactive web- and broadcast-based 3D content integrated with multimedia to support shared virtual worlds. X3D standard is usually implemented and used through the XML file format [10], which is an ideal standard for a large range of 3D description and scene-graph manipulation features, routes, scripting, and event passing. Beneficial advantage of X3D covers needs of web based visualization, including scene-graph handling, hierarchical node-structures that can be parsed, basic expression of 3D geometries and text, and networking adaptability.

(4) Data transmission mode. Model duplication and progressive transmission are the two typical transmission modes. Model duplication transmission sends replicates of the whole modified model to others. Whereas transmission efficiency and collaboration efficiency are low due to limited network bandwidth, when product model data is large. Progressive transmission mode only sends the changed part. For large product model, transmission and collaborative efficiency is higher than duplication mode does; however, it is necessary to develop geometrical mapping mechanism to distinguish topology feature relationship during model updating progress.

3   A Developed Prototype

A preliminary prototype of P2P&VRML-based collaborative communication environment is developed. This prototype is developed by using JAVA JDK 6.0, and can be run under windows system. Its collaborative functionalities are demonstrated

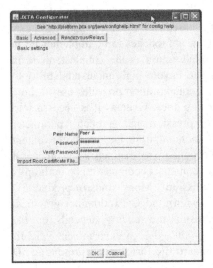

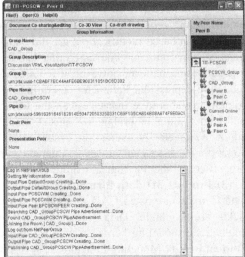

Fig. 4. Register into JXTA configuration

Fig. 5. Screen snapshot of peer & peer group information

through an example with a peer group named CAD_group including three joined peers named Peer A, B and C in the following sections.

3.1 GUI

Any designer is able to conveniently login/logout into the P2P platform in a self-defined peer name and password when registering into JXTA configuration, as shown in Fig. 4. A registered peer can create group, and join in/leave group, and communicates with group members through co-sharing spaces. Fig. 5 shows a peer GUI. On the right side of the GUI, peer information tree list shows peer name, group name, and status information about current-online peer & peer group. Operation of group creation, join in/leave group and information refreshment can be carried out by the right-click on group icon on the tree list, which can also be conducted by the top menu of Oper. On the left side of GUI, panel of Group Information demonstrates group name, group description and ID, and name and ID information of the group pipe. The bottom panels record the history of current-online peer, group and console operation.

3.2 Peer Collaborative Space

Peer collaborative space provides communication workshop for distributed and synchronous collaboration in the way of WYSIWIS. Up to now, collaborative spaces of document co-sharing & co-editing, draft co-drawing, VRML co-visualization and instant message are developed. In document co-sharing & co-editing space, peer can share a document by open an existed document, co-edit the document, and save the modified document into a new file. As shown in Fig. 6, a VRML file is opened by Peer A and is shared by Peer B. In draft co-drawing space, peer can draw a draft by using color pen on the toolbar. The draft can be saved into file or be cleared from draw panel, as shown in Fig. 7. Instant message enables peers to have a real time chat in text communication with other group peers. Pop-up widows shown in Fig. 7 illustrate instant message chat between Peer A and C.

(a) Screen snapshot of Peer A   (b) Screen snapshot of Peer B

Fig. 6. VRML file sharing & editing

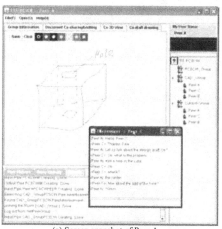
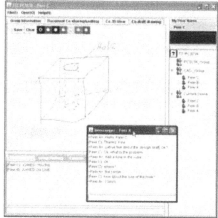

(a) Screen snapshot of Peer A   (b) Screen snapshot of Peer C

Fig. 7. Draft co-drawing and instant message chat

3.3   VRML Based Visualization and Collaborative Model Modification

An existence environment with VRML based co-visualization and stand alone visualizations is established, when considering web data transmission and data exchange

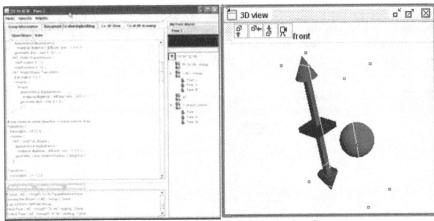

(a) VRML model is read and viewed by Peer C

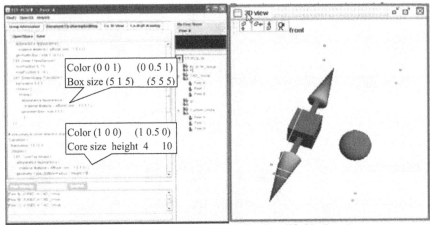

(b) The shared VRML model is shared and modified by Peer A

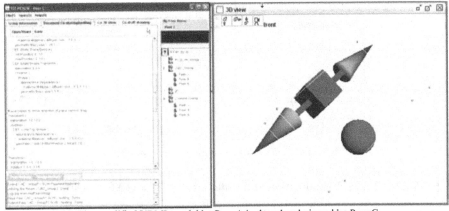

(c) The modified VRML model by Peer A is shared and viewed by Peer C

Fig. 8. VRML visualization and collaborative model modification

with existing CAD system. Such visualization environment is also valuable to be easily extended into X3D to achieve more large networking capability in the future research as well. The research into collaborative model modification begins with co-editing file based collaboration. Progressive transmission mode is adopted into P2P network architecture.

Fig. 8 demonstrates a collaborative model modification process of a simple 3D product data with a sphere, two cone and two boxes in VRML format. Peer C reads the VRML model and co-sharing it on document co-sharing & co-editing space with other two peers, as shown in Fig. 8 (a). Then, Peer A modifies the parameters of the VRML model by changing size and color property of a box and a cone respectively color, as shown in Fig. 8 (b). These changes are updated on document co-sharing & co-editing spaces of Peer A synchronously, and the updated VRML model is visualized, as shown in Fig. 8 (c).

4 Conclusion

This paper presents a solution of P2P&VRML-based collaborative product design environment. JXTA based P2P network communication platform with document co-sharing & co-editing, draft co-drawing, co-3D visualization and instant message chat is developed. Multicast based message mechanism and event-transmission collaborative mechanism are adopted in network architecture, enable convenient and synchronous collaborative interaction among distributed peers by sharing object and communication service in the way of WYSIWIS.Coexistence of VRML-based stand alone and co-sharing visualizations provides flexible workspace and interface structure for collaborative interoperations of modeling, viewing, and modifying. File co-editing based collaborative model modification environment is built up. However, current research is just a preliminary study into collaborative product design environment. Much more research, such as tele-/video communication, collaborative control mechanism in P2P network architecture, mapping algorithm between feature based CAD model and VRML model, and visualization based collaborative modification of 3D product model, will be investigated to enhance synchronously collaborative capability among distributed multi-users in the future.

Acknowledgments

This research is supported by Industrial Technology Research Grant Program of 06A11010a from New Energy and Industrial Technology Development Organization (NEDO) in Japan.

References

1. Bidarra, R., Eelco, V.D.B., Bronsvoort, W.F.: A Collaborative Feature Modeling System. Transactions of the ASME 2, 192–198 (2002)
2. Li, W.D., Ong, S.K., Fuh, J.Y.H., Wong, Y.S., Lu, Y.Q., Nee, A.Y.C.: Feature-based design in a distributed and collaborative environment. Computer Aided Design 36, 775–797 (2004)

3. CollabCAD^{TM}, National Informatics Centre, India, http://www.collabcad.com
4. OneSpace^{TM}, CoCreate Inc., http://www.onespace.com
5. Alda, S., Cremers, A.B., Bilek, J., Hartmann, D.: Integrated Multiagent and Peer-to-Peer based Workflow-Control of Dynamic Networked Co-operations in Structural Design. In: Proceedings of the 22nd International Conference Information Technology in Construction (CIB-W78), Dresden Germany (2005)
6. Chen, H.M., Tien, H.C.: Application of Peer-to-Peer Network for Real-Time Online Collaborative Computer Aided Design. Journal of Computing in Civil Engineering 2, 112–121 (2007)
7. The JXTA Project, http://www.jxta.org
8. VRML, http://www.web3d.org
9. X3D, http://www.web3d.org/x3d.html
10. XML, http://www.w3.org/XML/

VICA: A Voronoi Interface for Visualizing Collaborative Annotations

Yue Wang, James Shearer, and Kwan-Liu Ma

University of California, Davis
yuewan@ucdavis.edu, jjshearer@ucdavis.edu, ma@cs.ucdavis.edu

Abstract. Large-scale scientific investigation often includes collaborative data exploration among geographically distributed researchers. The tools used for this exploration typically include some communicative component, and this component often forms the basis for insight and idea sharing among collaborators. Minimizing the tool interaction required to locate "interesting" communications is therefore of paramount importance. We present the design of a novel visualization interface for representing the communications among multiple collaborating authors, and detail the benefits of our approach versus traditional methods. Our visualization integrates directly with the existing data exploration interface. We present our system in the context of an international research effort conducting collaborative analysis of accelerator simulations.

Keywords: multiple location collaborative design applications, information visualization, user interaction, cooperative visualization.

1 Introduction

Many human endeavors require the combined intellectual horsepower of multiple collaborators. Frequently several collaborators work from geographically disparate locations, and less convenient means of communication are necessary. The ubiquity of networked computers has provided a variety of electronic communication methods to address this need. One interesting technique for remote collaboration is the "post-it note" method for collaborative annotation. Using this method, collaborators can attach annotations to points of interest in a data set within the primary investigation tools.

Despite their obvious utility, collaborative annotations have some drawbacks, primarily due to their typical presentation in the user interface. Most often, annotations are shown as a textual list of titles, perhaps augmented with size information, authorship, or a time stamp. As the investigator works within the collaborative software, the list changes to reflect the currently selected data. This presentation method fails to effectively illustrate underlying annotation patterns. For example, it is difficult to determine which data points are discussion "hotbeds," to identify heavy contributors, or to understand the overall temporal evolution of the annotations. This lack of clarity contributes to collaborator information overload, which can impede a discovery available only though

Y. Luo (Ed.): CDVE 2007, LNCS 4674, pp. 21–32, 2007.

combined thinking. Visually separating the annotations from the data places an unnecessary navigation burden on the user, particularly when a large number of annotation operations are necessary.

We propose VICA, a novel visualization interface which clearly illustrates the collaborative annotations, and greatly simplifies the navigation of these documents. VICA presents far more annotation information than traditional display methods. The interactive mechanisms offer even more annotation information, including overall temporal evolution of annotation creation. The visualization is integrated directly with the existing data set displayed in the investigator's tool. With VICA, collaborators can now effectively and efficiently answer questions such as "Where have my co-workers been recently focusing the most attention?", "Which annotations by Maria contain the most content?", and "Which data points have substantial annotations written by Andrew?". These types of questions could only be answered with great difficulty using traditional displays, yet VICA answers them at a glance.

The impetus for our work came from the ModeVis project, an existing online collaboration system. Our data sets come from the International Linear Collider (ILC) project [1]. Researchers from SLAC (Stanford Linear Accelerator Center), KEK (High Energy Accelerator Research Organization) in Japan, DESY (Deutsches Elektronen Synchrotron) in Germany, and various U.S. national labs use ModeVis explore data from the ILC project. In ModeVis, a data set consists of a group of points displayed on a two-dimensional area, and both the horizontal and vertical axis carry meaning for the scientists. Figure 1 shows the ModeVis interface. A key component of ModeVis is the collaborative annotation feature. Our goal was to keep the visualization intuitive and conceptually simple, so that the myriad of presented information would not overwhelm the utility. Though ModeVis drove our initial design, our system could benefit any collaborative system with a 2D data navigation mechanism in which the relative point positions are important.

2   Related Work

Viégas [2] et al. presented the history flow visualization, a technique for effectively presenting the collaboration of many authors on a wiki article. Their work focus primarily on visualizing the evolution of a single, co-authored document. Document visualization drives much research, of which [3], [4], and Granitzer's InfoSky [5] are examples. The Galaxy of News [6] also presents a means of navigating and understanding large, interconnected document collections.

Space partitioning visualizations are a widely used type of information display. Balzer [7] describes the use of voronoi diagrams to augment previous treemap algorithms. Heilmann [8] provided a space-filling technique which used rectangular partitions. Our method also utilizes space partitioning using voronoi diagrams. However, our visualization is integrated with an existing 2D information display, and the data points in this display constrain our partitions.

Weber [9] described Spiral Graph, a technique for the visualization of time series. Shanbhag [10] used a tree ring visualization to present temporal ordering of data. Growing Polygons, presented by Elmqvist [11], graphically represent the causal relations and information flow in an interactive processing system. Yang [12] proposed a radial hierarchy visualization which supports and extensive set of user interactions, and includes multi-focus distortions, interactive hierarchy reconfiguration, and various forms of selection. Our system also uses rings, yet we vary the width to carry another dimension of information.

ThemeRiver [13], presented by Havre et al., is a visualization which can depict how a collection of documents varies thematically over time by using a river metaphor. ThemeRiver could be considered complimentary to our technique, as VICA does not consider thematic content of the document collection.

VICA aims to provide not just a visualization of the document set, but to do so within the context of another, position-constrained data set.

3   Voronoi Interface

Displaying the annotations for a point separately from the data only increases the interaction burden on the users, as it requires visual re-orientation and semantically separates data which should be strongly visually connected. A better approach, which we use, is to combine the data and associated annotations into one view. In the exploration display, each point is surrounded by concentric voronoi growth rings, one for each annotation. The total area of the surrounding rings is proportional to the total annotation content size, so that points with proportionally more annotations are given more space during partitioning. The voronoi rings have variable width, with larger annotations having proportionally thicker rings. Ring color coding denotes annotation authorship, and each point is colored using the heaviest contributor's color. These basic features are shown in Figure 1 right. Note the clear visibility of larger content annotations, and how the concentricity of the voronoi diagrams servers to emphasize the point positions.

3.1   Partition Generation

In order to integrate the annotation visualization with the existing data navigation area, we required a method for assigning each data point an area within which we could represent its annotations. We wanted to completely utilize the space, both overall and within each point's assigned region, while avoiding any overlapping. Further, we wanted a method which would dovetail with our use of growth rings. Circular or elliptical regions fit the latter criteria, but violate the former in that they leave gaps in the resulting visualization. Rectangular partitioning succeeds in maximal space-filling, but does not produce a visually pleasing result when combined with growth rings. Voronoi partitioning delivers on both requirements – it utilizes all available space while producing convex shapes that handle the growth-ring concentricity nicely.

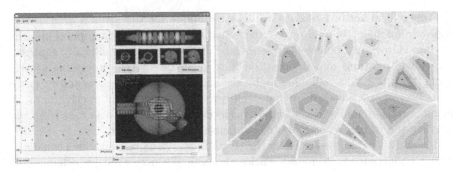

Fig. 1. The left image is the ModeVis interface. VICA's deals primarily with the point display area on the left. The right image is an overview of a ModeVis data set with 50 points.

VICA uses a simulated annealing (SA) algorithm to adjust the point positions so that the area of the generated voronoi cells reflect the proportion of annotation content for each point. Simulated annealing is a global optimization method named for a metallurgical technique in which a material is subjected to controlled temperature changes in order to reduce defects. Increased temperature frees atoms and allows them to naturally wander through various states of energy. Subsequent controlled cooling eventually "freezes" the atoms into an improved state with lower internal energy. Likewise, SA optimization involves incremental adjustments of the overall arrangement towards the desired goal. Simulated annealing is tolerant of small, non-optimal changes as long as the *overall* change progresses towards the optimal solution. In our case, we wanted the size of the cells to be proportional to the amount of annotation content relative to the whole data set. Our acceptance test not only checks for progressively improved voronoi area, but also ensures that the relative positions of all points remain unchanged.

3.2   Growth Rings

Growth rings are a space-filling visualization for intuitively representing time-ordered data. This technique derives directly from nature, adapting the concept of the annular rings found on tree cross-sections where the innermost rings represent the earliest "events." VICA represents each annotation with a growth ring centered on the related point, using creation time for ordering. This trivializes the task of locating annotations for a given point. The time endpoints, both starting and ending, could be adjusted either automatically or by the users to refine the amount of presented information. For example, using last login time as the earlier endpoint would likely fit most real-world usage patterns, in which users are most interested in recent developments. However, it's important to allow user adjustment to the presented timeline, so that they can revisit interesting past annotations as necessary.

Each author in the system is assigned a unique color, and annotation authorship typically dictates ring color. However, the user can choose to interactively change the basis of ring color.

In our system, we desired an easy way to quickly identify annotations of greater length, based on the assumption that these are the most likely to be interesting. For example, one can imagine a substantive, interesting annotation that inspires several short and relatively meaningless responses. Without some differentiation, a user would have to look at each note in turn, even when few are of interest. We already partition our display space such that the most-annotated points are given more ring space, so to identify the longest annotations, we need only vary the internal ring widths in proportion to relative annotation length. Note that using voronoi diagrams and the basis for growth rings, different portions of a ring can have different thicknesses. However, if one imagines a radial line traced from the center point to the edge of the outermost ring, it's clear that width proportions remain constant in all sections. No matter what path a user's eyes take, she will see an appropriate representation of relative annotation lengths. With VICA, it's quite easy to pinpoint the longest annotations.

Saturation. We utilize growth ring color saturation in four ways in our visualization, three of which highlights distinct properties of the visible annotations. Two of these views use the concept of *baseline saturation*, which is simply the lowest saturation utilized at a given time. Baseline saturation is interactively adjustable, as described below in Section 3.3.

In the default "hill" view, we use saturation to emphasize those points with many annotations, thus identifying data points which have generated relatively more "conversation." We achieve this emphasis by using the baseline saturation for the outermost ring of each point. Saturation increases with each step towards the center, as in Figure 2 left. Therefore, points with many annotations will have more saturated centers, giving them a pronounced, hill-like appearance.

Hit count is the number of total annotation views for a point since a specified time. A point with a high hit count is likely of interest other users, so we provide a second use of saturation to highlight such data. The point with the lowest hit count is assigned the current baseline saturation. Figure 2 right demonstrates this use.

We also utilize saturation to provide an overview of the relative creation times of the visible annotations. This feature facilitates the immediate identification of the most recent annotation activity, useful for highlighting the data that has recently captured the interest of other users. The saturation scheme is similar to that employed in our "hit count" mode. The oldest annotation in the entire set is assigned the baseline saturation, and other annotations are proportionally more saturated depending on their creation time. (Figure 3 left).

3.3   Interactive Features

While a static picture using our technique conveys a substantial amount of annotation information, user interaction presents even more possibilities.

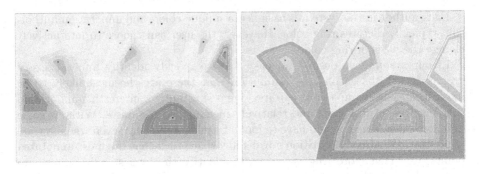

Fig. 2. An example of "hill" saturation (left) and "Hit count" saturation (right)

Fig. 3. In the left image, saturation is used to represent the global creation time of the annotations. The right image is an example of author subset selection.

Saturation Adjustments. We noted above in Section 3.2 that our system provides various usages of saturation, and each produces a different coloring of the annotation data while leaving the size, placement, and ring thickness intact. These saturation functions all represent useful and interesting information for system users.

The baseline saturation is a key parameter in our visualization. Because our visualization coexists in the same display space as the original data, it's imperative that our visualization remain unobtrusive. In this case, a lower baseline saturation is preferable as it produces a visually "quiet" image. However, low saturation might impair the investigator's ability to accurately determine annotation authorship, or count the rings around a data point. Essentially, certain situations call for different settings, sometimes significantly so. Therefore, a prominent control is the baseline saturation adjustment slider. It allows the user to set baseline saturation to any point on the entire available range (0 to 255). We have found that exploration with this control in the various saturation views (hill, hit count, global time) produce useful, uncluttered, and visually pleasing results for a variety of users and display methods.

Annotation Navigation. As the user mouses over the region assigned to a given point, the associated annotations are drawn with uniformly high color saturation. Double-clicking on an annotation's ring causes the associated text to appear in a floating window superimposed over the main display area. By presenting the text close to both the data point and the ring, we reinforce the user's mental association between the annotation and the location. Later, if the user attempts to locate a remembered annotation, but cannot initially recall the associated data point, this spatial reinforcement would likely prove useful.

Author Focus. It's likely that in a large collaborative effort, people will naturally gravitate into efficient subgroups of compatible individuals. Or perhaps certain authors produce more insightful, more useful data set commentary. What if an user simply wants to easily see all data points on which he has worked, and those he has accidentally missed? In all of these scenarios, users need the ability to prominently display annotations authored by specific people. VICA delivers this ability by allowing the selection of one or more authors via a special interface control. Annotations written by any members of the selected subset are shown with full color saturation, as depicted in Figure 3. If the user does not want to adjust the baseline saturation away from some otherwise optimal position, we provide a toggle-able option to render annotations by non-selected authors in grayscale.

Temporal Evolution. VICA also allows users to interactively animate the evolution of annotation creation over a given time period. At time zero, all annotations are completely de-saturated; only the data points are visible. Using a slider control, the user can advance and "rewind" time. Annotations are rendered with progressively more saturation as their creation time arrives and then passes. At the exact moment of creation, annotations are surrounded by a bold red border, so that they briefly flash as they appear and disappear. The end result of this interactivity is an interesting animation in which annotations grow outward from the points in clearly visible spurts. It's easy to see which points piqued researcher interest early in the investigation, which were revisited, which produced rapid conversations, and which were essentially ignored.

3.4 Scalability Issues

For our system to have real-world utility, it must scale. The first litmus test of scalability is the general overview picture. Does it retain its illustrative properties when displaying significantly more data points? To answer this question, we tested VICA using a data set approximately ten times the size of a typical ModeVis data set.

Point Display. We immediately noticed that while the visualization still worked well on the large data set, the data points had become a distraction when working with the background annotation display. However, we also noticed that the use of voronoi rings centered at the data points obviated the need for points at this level of scale. We added a control to selectively enable and disable the display of points, and images with and without points are shown in figures 4.

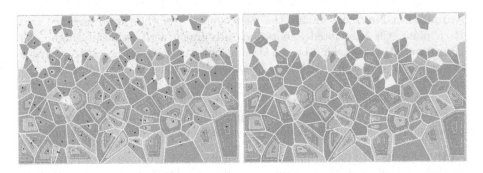

Fig. 4. A 298-point data set with point display enabled (left). The same 298-point data set with point display *disabled* (right). For large data sets, this can serve to clarify the overall visualization, while still showing the general point locations.

Zoom. When a large number of rings surround one point, the relative thickness, author coloring, and saturation can easily be lost in the noise. Sensible selections for the represented time range can greatly reduce the threat of this problem, and a range slider with adjustable endpoints could serve as a time filter. Zooming provided an intuitive solution to both issues.

If the user mouses over a point's annotation region which falls below a given threshold, then system uniformly scales that region to an acceptable size. Rather than deform the neighbor's regions during presentation of a scaled region, the system temporarily allows the scaled region to overlap its neighbors. Once the user navigates to another point, the region returns to its normal size and the neighbors are uncovered. This aspect of zooming effectively addresses large data sets. To more specifically deal with the "many rings" scenario, we allow a user to select a point's voronoi region with the mouse and keyboard, and manually scale it to an arbitrarily large size as in Figure 5 left. At any zoom level, the user can interact with the modified region. With this feature, even regions with large numbers of annotation rings become visually legible and surrender their information. When a user manually selects a zoom level, her choice is saved. As she continues to mouseover other regions, they will be zoomed to the same level. Not only does this help with UI continuity, but we felt that situations in which one region had sufficient rings to warrant manual zoom would like have many more. Saving the user-chosen manual zoom level prevents the user from repeatedly finding the "best" level for the current data set.

Focus+Context. We have added a simple focus+context feature to our system to further cope with the above-mentioned problems. Using the mouse, a user can select a vertical slice of the display area. She can then horizontally stretch the area, which pushes neighboring points aside and widens the vertical portions of the region's voronoi rings. This feature, like zooming, can help users handle a single data point with many annotations. But unlike zooming, it can also clarify a densely populated region of points, as demonstrated in Figure 5 right. VICA allows users to use zooming and focus+context in concert if desired.

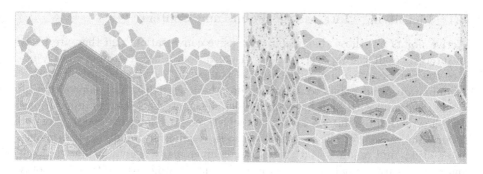

Fig. 5. An example of user-defined zoom size (left). Focus plus context used to disambiguate a populous region (right).

Grouping. A large number of authors, all represented by a different color, could cause our visualization to devolve into a rainbow of confusion. The author focus features can help mitigate this problem in cases where all authors are unrelated. Usually, however, some natural grouping of these authors (e.g. organizational affiliation) exists. For these cases, we have developed author grouping features in our system. We assign each group a base color, and assign authors within that group a slightly hue-shifted variation of that color. Annotation ring coloration, saturation, and subset selection behave exactly as described for individual authors. For situations with many group-affiliated authors, this presentation greatly reduces apparent clutter, and can provide a more useful overview. Further, it allows an investigator to understand the annotation authoring behavior of entire participating organizations. Combined with the timeline animation described in Section 3.3, grouping could also serve to demonstrate how a particular organization's participation grew as more affiliated authors joined the collaborative effort. Figure 3 right shows an example of group selection.

4   Discussion

Highlighting the advantages of our voronoi interface is best accomplished through comparison against a more common method of displaying annotations. We briefly describe such a method in Section 1. In this example system, annotations for a selected data point are listed in a separate UI control. Each item of the list contains the annotation author, size, creation time, and hit count. As with most common UIs, this list can be sorted by each attribute by clicking on the appropriate column header. As in ModeVis, this system has some way to alert users to the presence of news annotations. The following sections identify several annotation navigation tasks we have found to be of interest to users. For each scenario, we discuss the interface gymnastics necessary with the traditional text view, and show how VICA improves the situation.

4.1   Identifying "Interesting" Points and Content

Active points are those that inspire extensive conversation, and they are likely of interest to all system users. In our visualization, a user can immediately notice the points with many rings, yet the traditional system requires on-by-one examination of all points to see which has the longest list. The same situation holds for points with high hit count, which designate heavily-read annotations. We show high hit count via saturation, which requires only that the user switch saturation views. Yet the text-based system requires seemingly endless mouse interaction, and requires that the user remember many counts for mental comparison. If a user is only interested in high-content annotations, they need only click the thickest rings they see. Perhaps they want to examine only the most recent annotations. Again, our visualization (using the time saturation view) offers this with almost not user effort. For almost any definition of interesting, our visualization offers a low-effort, high-information-yield view. The seemingly endless clicking, re-orientation, and processing required by the traditional system is frustrating, particularly when it's an unavoidable part of daily research.

4.2   Identifying Under-Annotated Points

The traditional display shows annotation-free points well – they are designated with a different color. But it does not show *under*-annotated points. VICA highlights these points in a variety of ways: relative partition size, low saturation in the "hill" view, and via low ring count.

4.3   Identifying Interesting Authors

Similar to the above scenarios, it's possible to discover interesting authors using the hit count saturation view. If the most-saturated rings in the display are all of a single color, then that author is frequently read, and is likely quite interesting. This task has no obvious workflow in the traditional display. Mentally juggling listed hit counts while switching between points would work, but is likely far too difficult to be realistic.

4.4   Selecting Preferred Authors

Users will likely want to read (or avoid) annotations by certain authors. In the traditional system, a user can find a specific author's annotations easily, but only for one point at a time. The overview we provide again proves invaluable, as it clearly distinguishes all posts by the selected authors for every data point. Author selection is particularly effective for this task when combined with the ability to temporarily de-saturate all other authors.

4.5   Uncovering Collaboration Patterns

By selected different subsets of authors, users can discover patterns of annotation authorship (Figure 3 right). Perhaps two people frequently work on the same data points because they have compatible ideas, work habits, or simply because they inspire each other. Our visualization highlights such patterns easily, while they are essentially invisible using the traditional view.

4.6 Examining Data Analysis Evolution

Other than directly comparing annotation time stamps between all time points, the annotations lists provide no facility for understanding the *overall* evolution of the data analysis. Our time slider animates the progress of annotation creation in intuitive manner.

These examples serve to highlight the versatility of our visual interface, the power of which clearly derives from overview it provides. Because we place the annotation rings around the associated point, a user never need look away from the main navigation area to examine their collaborator's contributions. Because we provide the ability to adjust the baseline saturation, the user can tailor the overall visualization so that it works on diverse displays and fits a wide range of user preference.

5 Conclusion

We have presented VICA, a novel interface for visualizing collaborative annotations. We discussed how VICA's overview, combined with its specific interactive features, provide significantly more information than traditional list-based displays. Little to no user interaction is required to uncover the most interesting annotations, authors, and conversations. We have shown how VICA can assist in understanding how the exploration of a particular data set evolved, and how it can illuminate patterns in author (and group) collaboration.

We designed this visual interface with the requirements of real-world collaborative scientists in mind, and VICA will soon be used daily by the ModeVis researchers. Though the needs of the ModeVis user base drove our initial design, we have much hope for the broader application our our system. With further research, we expect to generalize this technique to a wider range of applications, such as online discussion forums.

References

1. Ko, K.: The international linear collider. SciDAC Review 1, 17–20 (2006)
2. Viégas, F.B., Wattenberg, M., Dave, K.: Studying cooperation and conflict between authors with history flow visualizations. In: CHI '04: Proceedings of the SIGCHI conference on Human factors in computing systems, New York, NY, USA, pp. 575–582. ACM Press, New York (2004)
3. Bier, E., Good, L., Popat, K., Newberger, A.: A document corpus browser for in-depth reading. In: Proceedings of the 2004 Joint ACM/IEEE Conference on Digital Libraries (JCDL) (2004)

4. Fekete, J.-D., Dufournaud, N.: Compus: visualization and analysis of structured documents for understanding social life in the 16th century. In: Proceedings of the fifth ACM Conference on Digital Libraries, pp. 47–56. ACM Press, New York (2000)

5. Granitzer, M., Kienreich, W., Sabol, V., Andrews, K., Klieber, W.: Evaluating a system for interactive exploration of large, hierarchically structured document repositories. In: Proceedings of IEEE Symposium on Information Visualization (INFOVIS'04), pp. 127–134. IEEE Computer Society Press, Los Alamitos (2004)

6. Rennison, E.: Galaxy of news: An approach to visualizing and understanding expansive news landscapes. In: ACM Symposium on User Interface Software and Technology, pp. 3–12. ACM Press, New York (1994)

7. Balzer, M., Deussen, O.: Voronoi treemaps. In: Proceedings of IEEE Symposium on Information Visualization (INFOVIS'05), IEEE Computer Society Press, Los Alamitos (2005)

8. Heilmann, R., Keim, D.A., Panse, C., Sips, M.: Recmap: Rectangular map approximations. In: Proceedings of IEEE Symposium on Information Visualization (INFOVIS'04), pp. 33–40. IEEE Computer Society Press, Los Alamitos (2004)

9. Weber, M., Alexa, M., uller, W.M: Visualizing time-series on spirals. In: Proceedings of IEEE Symposium on Information Visualization (INFOVIS'01), IEEE Computer Society Press, Los Alamitos (2001)

10. Shanbhag, P., Rheingans, P., desJardins, M.: Temporal visualization of planning polygons for efficient partitioning of geo-spatial data. In: Proceedings of IEEE Symposium on Information Visualization (INFOVIS'05), IEEE Computer Society Press, Los Alamitos (2005)

11. Elmqvist, N., Tsigas, P.: Causality visualization using animated growing polygons. In: Proceedings of IEEE Symposium on Information Visualization (INFOVIS'03), pp. 189–196. IEEE Computer Society Press, Los Alamitos (2003)

12. Yang, J., Ward, M.O., Rundensteiner, E.A.: Interring: An interactive tool for visually navigating and manipulating hierarchical structures. In: Proceedings of IEEE Symposium on Information Visualization (INFOVIS'02), pp. 77–84. IEEE Computer Society Press, Los Alamitos (2002)

13. Havre, S., Hetzler, E., Whitney, P., Nowell, L.: Themeriver: Visualizing thematic changes in large document collections. IEEE Transcations on Visualization and Computer Graphics 8(1), 9–20 (2002)

14. Kirkpatrick, S., Gelatt, C.D., Vecchi, M.P.: Optimization by simulated annealing. Science, Number 4598, 13 May 1983 220, 4598, 671–680 (1983)

15. Okabe, A., Boots, B., Sugihara, K.: Spatial Tessellations: Concepts and Applications of Voronoi Diagrams. Wiley, New York (1992)

16. Metropolis, N., Rosenbluth, A.W., Rosenbluth, M.N., Teller, A.H., Teller, E.: Equations of state calculations by fast computing machine. J. Chem. Phys. 21, 1087–1091 (1953)

Innovative Visualization Tools to Monitor Scientific Cooperative Activities

Benoît Otjacques[1], Monique Noirhomme[2], and Fernand Feltz[1]

[1] Public Research Center – Gabriel Lippmann
Department ISC – Informatics, Systems and Collaboration
41, Rue du Brill
L-4422 Belvaux, Luxembourg
otjacque@lippmann.lu, feltz@lippmann.lu
[2] University of Namur (FUNDP)
Computer Science Institute
21, Rue Grangagnage
B-5000 Namur, Belgium
monique.noirhomme@info.fundp.ac.be

Abstract. This paper describes how information visualization techniques can be used to monitor a web-based collaborative platform and to support workplace awareness by providing a global overview of the activities. An innovative prototype is described. Its originality relies on using some enclosure-based visualization methods in the context of activities monitoring, which is rather unusual. In addition, a new layout is described for representing data trees. The use of the system is illustrated with the case of a EU-funded Network of Excellence.

Keywords: Information visualization, collaborative platforms, treemaps, ellimaps.

1 Introduction

More than a decade ago, Dourish and Belloti [5] introduced the concept of awareness that they defined as '*an understanding of the activities of others, which provides a context for your own activity*'. Ellis [6] argued that '*the philosophy of groupware is to encourage cooperation by making it known and instantly apparent to all who is sharing what with whom*'. Since the emergence of the awareness concept, numerous works have stressed its importance in the domain of Computer-Supported Cooperative Work (CSCW). Greenberg [10] refined the concept and identified many forms of awareness. Workspace awareness, which will be under focus in this paper, includes awareness of people, how they interact with the workspace, and the events happening within the workspace. Otjacques et al. [14] proposed another classification that distinguishes Workspace Individual Awareness (WIA) and Workspace Global Awareness (WGA). WIA refers to the notification of information relating to a specific resource or user within the workspace. WGA concerns high level information that relates to the general level of activities in the workplace.

Y. Luo (Ed.): CDVE 2007, LNCS 4674, pp. 33–41, 2007.

In this paper, we focus on workspace awareness in the Greenberg's taxonomy. In Otjacques et al.'s classification, we include some elements relating to both WGA and WIA but with a special interest for the global overview. In other words, the purpose of our research consists in providing the supervisors of a collaborative platform with some global information about what happens in this workplace. Graphics have proven to be of high value for conveying information efficiently and rapidly. We have then chosen to investigate how information visualization can support collaborative platform monitoring.

2 State-of-the-Art

2.1 Visualization of Cooperation

Numerous approaches have been proposed to visualize information related to a cooperative context. In this domain, the electronic communications are probably the data that has been the most intensively studied. For instance, the '*Mat'Graph*' [13], '*Themail*' [24] or '*Correspondent Treemap*' [15] prototypes focused on how to extract and represent useful information from mailboxes or e-mail log files. Other researchers explored the visualization of chat conversations (e.g. '*Crystalchat*' [22], '*Fugue*' [18]) or discussion groups (e.g. '*Newsgroup Crowds*' [25]). The graphical representation of the presence of actors in a shared environment has been under examination too (e.g. '*Babble*' [7] or '*Tower World*' [16]). The research in visualization also focused on the actions on shared resources (e.g. '*LifeSource*' [9], '*ArchiChronos*' [17]). Finally, some researchers have also tackled the representation of calendars (e.g. '*Availability Bars*' [8], '*DateLens*' [1]).

In the discipline of information visualization, the dataset and its basic properties (e.g. structure, size) have a major influence to choose the appropriate graphical representation. Therefore, we propose to examine the data associated to a collaborative platform from this perspective. Shneiderman's seminal taxonomy [19] distinguishes networks, trees, temporal, multidimensional, 1-D, 2-D or 3-D data. Considering this classification, we note that collaborative data may take many of these forms. For instance, the communications within a group are typically organized as network data and the actions on shared objects are often represented as temporal data. We have chosen to concentrate on another datatype: hierarchical data. Indeed, this structure also appears regularly in collaborative platforms. For instance, a workplace defined as a combination of sub-workplaces; a project broken down in work packages; and a set of documents organized in directories illustrate how often hierarchies may be encountered in the context of collaborative platforms.

To sum up, the purpose of our research is to explore how workspace awareness can be supported by innovative techniques visualizing data structured as hierarchies.

2.2 Visualization of Hierarchies

The visualization of hierarchies is well documented in the literature. Nevertheless, most of the techniques rely on only two basic visual properties: *enclosure* and *connectivity*.

Connectivity means representing the nodes of the hierarchy by punctual objects (e.g. points, icons) and the parent-child relationship among them by lines (e.g. straight lines, curves). The vertical tree used in numerous applications is a typical example of this kind of techniques but some researchers also proposed more original approaches (e.g. *Disk Tree* [3], *Hyperbolic Browser* [11]).

Enclosure consists in representing the nodes by geometrical shapes that are successively inscribed one into each other. Shneiderman's treemaps [20] [21] are probably the most famous technique of this kind. This recursive algorithm keeps the size of the display space constant, whatever the size of the dataset. In addition, the treemaps offer the advantage that the area of the nested rectangles visualizes the relative weight of the nodes. This very useful feature makes it easy to realize the relative 'power' of each node.

From a global viewpoint, the visualization of hierarchies faces a specific challenge: finding the right trade-off that maximizes the perception of the data structure and minimizes the proportion of lost area in the display space. Moreover, it is sometimes also required to represent the weight of the nodes. In general, connection-based approaches perform well in terms of structure perception and enclosure-based techniques are very efficient to use the display space. However, it must be noted that some improvements have been proposed to tackle the weaknesses of both types of representation (e.g. [23] for treemaps).

3 Use Case

The use case considered in this research project is a Network of Excellence (NoE) funded by the European Union. A NoE is essentially a group of research, academic and commercial organizations that join together to form a virtual research community. It is an ideal case study as it consists of a wide range of organizations, in this case around thirteen and in turn a diverse group of participants, such as professors, research assistants, students, administrators and technical staff. The main outputs are reports, academic papers and other printed or online materials, the members also meet regularly. The NoE discussed here also trains new scientists in the field via a PhD school.

The NoE has a website that aims to bring people together and encourage communication and the creation of ideas. This collaborative platform contains a number of key features, such as the ability for people to submit information or files, a news page as well as a mailing list.

In order to determine the most suitable actions to be undertaken to promote and support this platform, the persons responsible for its animation expressed a need for an efficient and easy-to-use monitoring tool. They were looking for a way to rapidly realize what happens on the platform. In practical terms, this can be expressed by issues like which workspaces are active, what are the largest spaces in terms of the total size of the stored documents or what is the relative importance of the topics considering the number of people joining the discussions. Such questions typically relate to workspace awareness. To tackle this issue, graphical tools rapidly appeared to be a suitable answer.

4 Prototype

The web platform is built upon the usual PHP/My SQL couple of technologies. The data about the platform activities are then stored in a relational database. This information can be exported as XML files and imported into our visualization system.

Our prototype, called *Platform Monitoring System* (PMS), is basically composed of two modules: the Data Provider Module (DPM) and the Visualization Tool (VT). The DPM module is responsible for accessing the data stored on the platform and for providing data to the VT. This dataset is formatted as an XML file (e.g. size of the sub-workplace is set as an attribute of the sub-workplace node), which is transferred to the VT tool handling the interaction with the user. The modular architecture of the PMS system implies that the VT module is completely independent from the DPM module. In other words, the PMS system could easily be extended to interact with a collaborative platform running on another technology.

The PMS user interface includes three different views of the dataset: a classic tree, a treemap and a new approach called ellimap. The first two techniques are well known and do not require further explanation. The latter is, however, totally new and requires a specific description.

The ellimap is a new generic approach that we developed to visualize hierarchies. Providing the details of the algorithm goes beyond the purpose of this paper and will be described in a future dedicated paper. Nevertheless, the basic idea is described in this paragraph. In a few words, we replaced the rectangles by some ellipses in a treemap-like recursive algorithm. Each node is then associated to an ellipse. The children of a given node are represented as smaller ellipses inscribed into the ellipse corresponding to the parent node. In addition, the area of each ellipse is proportional to the relative weight of the corresponding node. The resulting picture shows the hierarchical structure as a set of nested ellipses. The relative importance of each node also appears clearly. The purpose of the ellimap technique is to highlight the nested structure of the dataset in an intuitive way. Some preliminary evaluations have shown that some users without any previous experience in information visualization rapidly understand the ellimap representation.

The prototype offers then one technique based on the connectivity property (i.e. the classic tree) and two others relying on the enclosure principle (i.e. treemap and ellimap). This mix is intended to combine the advantages of the three techniques. The drawbacks of a given view can be counterbalanced by the advantages of another one. Indeed, as Blythe et al. [2] showed many years ago with an experimental study, *'they may be no single [graph] drawing that best highlights every characteristic [of the dataset].'* The combination of multiple views appears then to be a reasonable strategy because the dataset characteristics and the tasks to be carried out influence the relevance of a layout in a given situation.

The tree view is especially efficient to visualize the structure of the hierarchy. Moreover, as Lee et al. [12] explain, *'interaction with and interpretation of node-link tree structures poses little difficulty for novice users and therefore interactive tree visualizations can be used for a large audience'*. In comparison, the treemap allows representing a large amount of data and visualizes the node value. It is *'appropriate when showing the attribute value distributions is more important than showing the graph structure'* [12]. The ellimap offers a rather good trade-off between structure perception and node value representation. Unfortunately, the lost space is higher than for a treemap. However, the informal feedback collected from the pilot users seems to show that the perception of the structure of the dataset might be better in the ellimap than in the treemap. This preliminary result remains to be confirmed by a rigorous experimental evaluation, which is planned in the future.

The PMS prototype is completely generic in the sense that every hierarchical dataset can be visualized by any of the three types of view (tree, treemap or ellimap) and several combinations of these views (e.g. tree + treemap, tree + ellimap). In addition, when a combination of views is displayed, the components are dynamically coupled. The user can navigate through the data via the view that he or she prefers or via the view that best suits the ongoing task. PMS also includes various advanced interaction features. We mention three of them for illustration purposes. The data tree can be displayed up to a given level of depth via a dynamic query. This feature is useful when the user wants to see an overview of the platform data without being overwhelmed by information details. Second, a tool tip showing the detailed data of a given node can be displayed when the cursor is moved upon the node. Third, the user can dynamically select which information is used as label in any of the views. For instance, he / she can choose to label the treemap with the nodes weight and the tree with the nodes identifier. This mechanism is also active for every combined view.

5 Visualization of the Workplace Activity

In the previous section, we propose a generic description of the views included in the PMS prototype. Now we explain how it is used to monitor the collaborative platform.

First, the number of clicks on the website pages, which is a very common indicator, is represented on a treemap calendar (cf. Figure 1). In this view, the displayed time period is broken down as a tree. Each node is associated to a given day. The number of clicks by day is used to weight the corresponding node in the treemap view. A period with intense activity appears as a sequence of large rectangles.

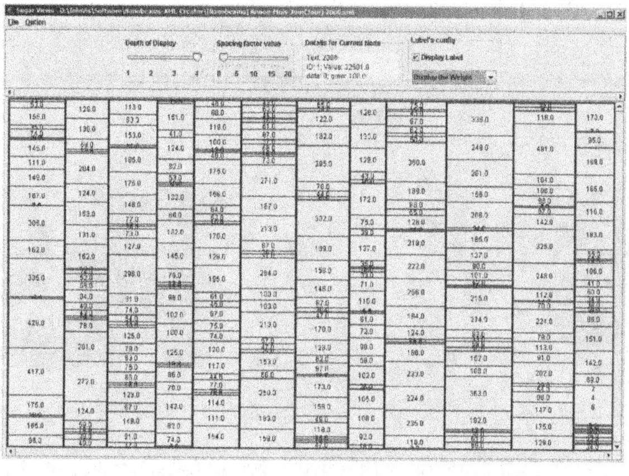

Fig. 1. Treemap calendar displaying the daily frequency of clicks

Second, two views can be used to show the size of the groups of users (i.e. user affiliation) and the activity of each group. The former (cf. Figure 2, left) highlights which institutions stimulate the most their employees or students to register on the platform. The latter (cf. Figure 2, right) points out how the usage of the collaboration platform is distributed among the institutions. In these cases, we believe that the ellimap view is appropriate as it relies on the usual representation of groups as nested ellipses. In Figure 2, the ellimap is combined with a tree view (cf. left panel).

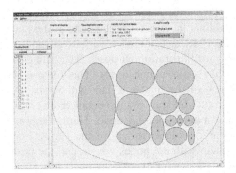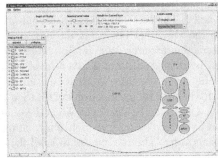

Fig. 2. Groups of users: size vs. activity

The number of interactions (e.g. uploading document, posting news…) by user also provides useful information for the platform supervisors. It can be combined with the date of the last interaction in which each user was involved. This information shows how recent is the activity of each user on the platform. A specific view displays this combined dataset (cf. Figure 3). The ellipses of the deepest level represent the users and they are weighted according to the number of interactions that these users were involved in.

This view uses a specific feature of the visualization module that allows coloring the ellipses associated to the leaves of the data tree. In accordance to the opponent process theory [26], the 'red-green' channel can be chosen to map time and a two-colors scale. The red color is associated to old interactions and green is linked to

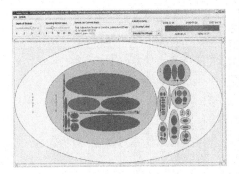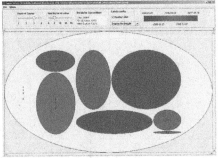

Fig. 3. Activity of the users of a given group (quantity and newness)

recent ones. The attention of the platform supervisor is then drawn to the inactive users (colored in red) that might require a specific initiative to encourage them to use the platform. When it better suits the semantics of the data, the PMS system also permits the user to choose a monochromatic scale to visualize the data range.

The first screenshot in Figure 3 (left) shows the global overview of the platform. The group and the actors that are involved in many interactions can be rapidly identified. The second screenshot (right) is focused on a specific group (semantic zoom). The actors profile appears clearly, showing on the same picture which actors are active both in quantitative and in newness terms.

The PMS system also includes a view (Figure 4) that shows the distribution of interactions on the platform aggregated by group of users (cf. affiliation) and by type of collaborative tool (e.g. events manager, news, document management system…). In this view, each discrete value of a given attribute of the tree leaves (i.e. type of collaborative tool in the example) is mapped to a given color. It must be noted that this mechanism differs from the range color mapping where the attribute takes continuous value. For instance, the Figure 4 points out which tool is preferably used by the users of each institution.

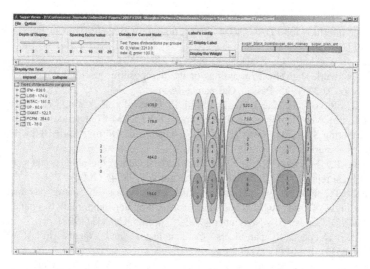

Fig. 4. Types of collaborative tools used on the platform

To sum up, the PMS prototype can visualize any kind of hierarchical data about the collaborative platform. In addition to the structure of the dataset, it can also visualize the relative weight of each node as well as the value of a given property of the leaves, should it be continuous or discrete.

6 Conclusion

To the limit of our knowledge, few examples have been reported in which some enclosure-based visualization methods have been used for monitoring a collaborative platform. The PMS system illustrates however the potential of such approaches to provide a global overview of a workplace and to visualize some metrics of the activities carried out in such cooperative environments.

For the future, we consider two directions to extend the research presented in this paper. First, we are investigating new visualization techniques to display other metrics of the platform activity. Second, we plan to extend the system to interface it with platforms running on different technologies.

Acknowledgements

The findings reported in this paper have been supported by a grant of the National Research Fund (FNR) of Luxembourg. The authors also thank Pierre Collin and Xavier Gobert for their contribution to the development of the prototype.

References

1. Bederson, B., Clamage, A., Czerwinski, M., Robertson, G.G.: DateLens: A fisheye calendar interface for PDAs. ACM Transactions on Computer-Human Interaction 11(1), 90–119 (2004)
2. Blythe, J., McGrath, C., Krackhardt, D.: The effect of Graph Layout on Inference from Social Network Data. In: Proceedings of the Symposium on Graph Drawing (GD '95), September 20-22, 1995, Passau, Germany (1995)
3. Chi, E.H., Pitkow, J., Mackinlay, J., Pirolli, P., Gosswiler, R., Card, S.K.: Visualizing the Evolution of Web Ecologies. In: Proceedings of the ACM Conference on Human Factors in Computing Systems 1998 (CHI'98), Los Angeles, California, April 18-23, 1998, ACM Press, New York (1998)
4. Demian, P., Fruchter, R.: Finding and understanding reusable designs from large hierarchical repositories. Information Visualization 5, 28–46 (2006)
5. Dourish, P., Belloti, V.: Awareness and coordination in shared workspaces. In: Proceedings of the ACM Conference on Computer-Supported Cooperative Work (CSCW'92), October 31 - November 4, 1992, Toronto, Canada (1992)
6. Ellis, C.: Keepers, Synchronizers, Communicators and Agents. In ACM SIGOIS Bulletin 15(3), 10–14 (1995)
7. Erickson, T., Halverson, C., Kellogg, W.A., Laff, M., Wolf, T.: Social translucence, designing social infrastructures that make collective activity visible. Communications of the ACM 45(4), 40–44 (2002)
8. Faulring, A., Myers, B.A.: Availability Bars for Calendar Scheduling. In: Proceedings of Conference on Human Factors in Computing Systems (CHI'06), Montréal, Canada, 22-27 April 2006, pp. 22–27 (2006)
9. Gilbert, E., Karahalios, K.: LifeSource: Two CVS Visualizations. In: Proceedings of ACM Conference on Human Factors in Computing Systems 2006 (CHI'06), Montréal, Canada, 22-27 April 2006, ACM Press, New York (2006)
10. Greenberg, S., Gutwin, C., Cockburn, A.: Awareness Through Fisheye Views in Relaxed-WYSIWIS Groupware. In: Proceedings of the Graphics Interface 1996 Conference, May 22-24 1996, Toronto, Canada (1996)

11. Lamping, J., Rao, R.: Laying out and Visualizing Large Trees Using a Hyperbolic Space. In: Proceedings of 7th annual ACM symposium on User interface software and technology (UIST'94), Marina del Rey, California, 2–4 November 1994, ACM Press, New York (1994)
12. Lee, B., Parr, C.S., Plaisant, C., Bederson, B., Veksler, V.D., Gray, W.D., Kotfila, C.: TreePlus: Interactive Exploration of Networks with Enhanced Tree Layouts. IEEE Transactions on Visualization and Computer Graphics 12(6), 1414–1426 (2006)
13. Otjacques, B., Feltz, F.: Representation of Graphs on a Matrix Layout. In: Proceedings of the 9th International Conference on Information Visualization (IV'05), 6-8 July 2005, London, United-Kingdom (2005)
14. Otjacques, B., Noirhomme, M., Gobert, X., Feltz, F.: Cooperation Indexes to Support Workplace Awareness. In: Proceedings of the 12th International Workshop on Groupware (CRIWG 2006), 17-21 September 2006, Valladolid, Spain (2006)
15. Perer, A., Smith, A.: Contrasting Portraits of Email Practices: Visual approaches to reflection and analysis. In: Proceedings of the working conference on Advanced Visual Interfaces (AVI 2006), 23-26 May 2006, Venice, Italy (2006)
16. Prinz, W., Pankoke-Babatz, U., Gräther, W., Gross, T., Kolvenbach, S., Schäfer, L.: Presenting Activity Information in an Inhabited Information Space. In: Snodown, et Frécon, C. (eds.) Inhabited Information Spaces. CSCW Series, Springer, London (2004)
17. Riendeau, S.: Space-Time Navigator for Architectural Projects. Electronic Journal of Information Technology in construction (ITCon) 11, 1–15
18. Rosenberger, S.T., Vankleek, M., Vicente, A., Smith, B.K.: Fugue: A Computer Mediated Conversational System that Supports Turn Negociation. In: Proceedings of the Hawaii International Conference on System Sciences (HICSS 2000), 4-7 January 2000, Hawaii, USA (2000)
19. Shneiderman, B.: The Eyes Have It: A Task by Data Type Taxonomy for Information Visualizations. In: Proceedings of the IEEE Symposium on Visual Languages, Boulder, USA (1996)
20. Shneiderman, B.: Tree Visualization with Tree-Maps: 2-d Space-Filling Approach. ACM Transactions on Graphics 11(1), 92–99 (1992)
21. Shneiderman, B.: Treemaps for space-constrained visualization of hierarchies, University of Maryland. In: Human – Computer Interaction Lab (accessed 25 January 2007), Internet address: http://www.cs.umd.edu/hcil/treemap-history/
22. Tat, A., Carpendale, S.: CrystalChat: Visualizing Chat History. In: Proceedings of the Hawaii International Conference on System Sciences (HICSS 2006), USA, 4-7 January 2006, Hawaii (2006)
23. van Wijk, J.J., van de Wetering, H.: Cushion TreeMaps. In: Proceedings of the IEEE Symposium on Information Visualization (InfoVis 1999), San Francisco, California, 24-29 October 1999, IEEE Computer Society Press, Los Alamitos (1999)
24. Viégas, F.B., Golder, S., Donath, J.: Visualizing Email Content : Protraying Relationships from Conversational Histories. In: Proceedings of Conference on Human Factors in Computing Systems (CHI'06), 22-27 April 2006, Montréal, Canada (2006)
25. Viegas, F.B., Smith, M.: Newsgroup Crowds and AuthorLines: Visualizing the Activity of Individuals in Conversational Cyberspaces. In: Proceedings of the Hawaii International Conference on System Sciences (HICSS 2004), 5-8 January 2004, Hawaii, USA (2004)
26. Ware, C.: Information Visualization, Perception for Design. Morgan Kaufmann Publishers, San Francisco, USA (2004)

Workflow Methodology for Collaborative Design and Manufacturing

Carlos Vila, Antonio Estruch, Héctor R. Siller, José V. Abellán,
and Fernando Romero

Department of Industrial Systems Engineering and Design,
School of Experimental Sciences and Technology, Universitat Jaume I,
Av. de Vicent Sos Baynat s/n. 12071 Castellón, Spain
vila@esid.uji.es

Abstract. During product development processes, collaboration has become a common practice between different departments and companies that are involved in their activities. Product Lifecycle Management (PLM) tools can facilitate collaboration among distributed teams within the context of an extended enterprise, but the efficient use of them is still hard to achieve. In this work, we propose a workflow based approach in order to implement product development collaboration, focusing the discussion on a case study of the integration of design and manufacturing activities, using workflow functionality offered by PLM software.

Keywords: Workflow Management, Collaborative Engineering, Extended Enterprise, Product Lifecycle Management.

1 Introduction

In the age of the extended enterprise, the quick expansion of the Internet provides the infrastructure by which information can be simultaneously available to all those involved in product lifecycle activities from product design to product recycling. Collaboration has become the mainstay of product and processes development but it must not end just with engineering design activities, it should continue with other activities such manufacturing process planning, manufacturing, production and those that concern the product lifecycle [1, 2].

It is obvious that collaboration is needed in all the activities of the product lifecycle (Fig. 1.) and if there is any problem within two activities of the chain it will affect all the others. In this scenario we would like to pay attention to the problems between product design and manufacturing.

Today, computer aided tools enable collaboration among marketing department, product designers and manufacturing engineers to avoid manufacturing problems and decrease lead times in product development. Typically, these tools integrate the product development data within a Web shared database [3]. Nevertheless, real practice is far away from total collaboration [4].

In the framework of the extended enterprise, where companies collaborate and compete, designers need to know the exact capacities of the processes used by the

Y. Luo (Ed.): CDVE 2007, LNCS 4674, pp. 42–49, 2007.

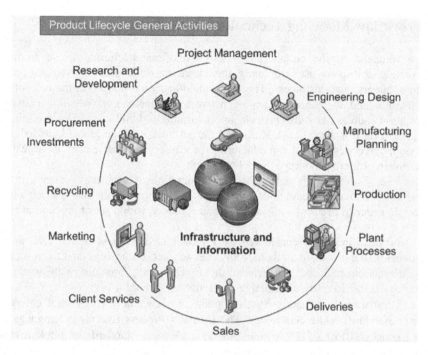

Fig. 1. Collaboration across Product Lifecycle

enterprises responsible for product manufacturing in order to make an efficient process planning which is the bridge activity between design and manufacturing [5].

Although collaborative engineering (CE) depends on the use of modern web based collaboration, the real situation of many CE implementations reminds us that, by simply adopting the required technology, it does not ensure the success. Therefore, it is needed not only a web-based tool for collaboration (Product Lifecycle Management, PLM, or Computer Support for Collaborative Work, CSCW) but also a workflow based methodology that enables the integration and coordination of products life cycle processes and the information exchange between all the people involved [6,7].

Literature reports some research efforts in the direction of collaborative manufacturing and distributed networks [8-10] with applications based on the Information and Communication Technologies (ICT) through the Internet.

With this aim, the research presented in this paper is part of a project conceived for collaborative design and manufacturing within a manufacturing cluster, where workflow models support and coordinate the information sharing and the management of the product development activities. We present a particular case study, in which we propose a framework for the coordination of the design, process planning and manufacturing activities, through a workflow model and its implementation in a commercial product lifecycle management tool (PLM).

2 Workflow Modeling Technologies and Tools

The advantages of the collaborative design and manufacturing derive from an enterprise's ability to use efficiently the entire network of employees, supplier, vendors, buyers, and customers. The flows of information that lie at the core of the coordination and collaboration among network members, not only link disparate information sources, they also provide an opportunity to build knowledge-based tools [7]. Therefore, it is necessary to define all the activities and the global knowledge of the cooperative design and manufacturing processes and implement them with a workflow in order to encourage the collaboration.

The term "*workflow*" is defined as the automation of a business process in the course of which documents, information or tasks move from one participant to another in order to perform some action, in accordance with a set of procedural rules [11].

A workflow model is considered as a model of a process in the real world. Components of a process may include all necessary actions or steps, and the resources and information required to perform them. The main problem with workflow technology is the diversity of available standards.

From Software Information Systems point of view, there are several emerging industry standards and technologies. The Business Process Execution Language for Web Services (BPEL) [12] is emerging as a *de-facto* standard for implementing business processes on top of Web services technology. Numerous workflow platforms support the execution of BPEL processes. However, BPEL modeling tools do not have the necessary level of abstraction required to make them usable during analysis and design phases of high complexity processes like collaborative product development process. On the other hand, the Business Process Modeling Notation (BPMN) [13] has attracted the attention of business analyst and system architects as a language for defining business process blueprints for subsequent implantation. The BPMN is a graph-oriented language in which control and action nodes can be connected almost arbitrarily. Also supported by numerous modeling tools, none of these can directly execute BPMN models, but only few support the translation of BPMN to BPEL in order to execute the model. XML Process Definition Language (XPDL) [14] is a process design format that represents the "drawing" of the process definition that enables to save and exchange the process diagram. Last XPDL 2.0 contains extensions in order to be able to represent all aspects of BPMN.

Workflow technology has found its way into mainstream application development tools and application integration middleware. We can now use workflow technology in e-commerce to coordinate the interaction with customers and inter-enterprise processes or in packaged applications as a means of customization.

The skills and level of abstraction, required by the users of software products involved in the product design and manufacturing, force software suppliers to hide all the above considerations and provide embedded workflow engines and specific modeling tools with graph-oriented workflow designers, with specialized activity nodes that can be used for customization of process workflow models.

Common PLM tools does not use any of the mentioned emerging standards and use instead proprietary workflow modeling methodologies and execution technologies that have been adopted and accepted by their users and do not fit easily with new standards without important changes. Perhaps, when those new standards, allow the accomplishment of the increasing required levels of interoperability with external systems like ERP (Enterprise Resource Planning), software vendors will be forced to adopt and support all of them.

In this research a PLM software, with an embedded workflow engine and modeling user interface, is used in a case study to support a collaborative environment for the design and manufacturing in an extended enterprise context, in which a main organization interacts with several suppliers for product development.

3   A Case Study: Design and Manufacturing in a Collaborative Environment

Usually, the collaboration in product development can be found among marketing, conceptual design, detailed design and prototyping. This collaboration can be inside or outside the organization but it always imply sharing knowledge and data. In the field of manufacturing, internal resources and external suppliers are required to perform specialized operations, which increase the complexity of the collaborative environment.

The context of our case study involves several geographically distributed companies, members of an extended enterprise dedicated to the design and manufacture of a discrete product that requires metalworking operations. One of these companies is the owner of the product to manufacture, that works in close collaboration with other enterprises dedicated to different tasks of the design process like for example detail design and engineering analysis. The definitive manufacturing contract is assigned to one of the rest members of the supply chain that compete each other for it. In order to integrate this distributed environment, is proposed a methodology for collaborative product development, focused on product design and process planning activities.

As mentioned above, process planning is a critical activity in the transition from design to manufacturing, especially when exists outside participants. In order to facilitate the interaction between them, three levels of manufacturing process plan activities can be establish: meta-planning, macro-planning and micro-planning [5]. Meta-planning is performed to determine the manufacturing process and the machines that fit the shape, size, quality and cost requirements of the parts that have been designed. In macro-planning the equipment is selected, the minimum number of assemblies needed to manufacture the part is determined and the sequence of operations is established. Micro-planning is concerned with determining the tools to be used, the stages they have to follow during the manufacturing process, and the parameters associated to shop floor operations so that productivity, quality of the parts and manufacturing costs can be optimized.

The methodology proposed here is divided in three mainstays: description of the collaborative environment, definition of the product lifecycle phases, and design of the workflow required to enable the collaboration.

3.1 Description of Collaborative Environment

PLM tools are used for product data management during its lifecycle and for organizing, controlling and accessing related information. PLM predecessor, known as PDM (Product Data Management), are limited to store CAD/CAM files, text files and other document formats [15]. PLM add functionalities to manage the complete product lifecycle and organize activities performed by all involved participants through workflow enactment (definition and execution). The collaborative environment proposed here make use of a PLM tool (Windchill by PTC), a CAD/CAM application (Pro-Engineer Wildfire 3.0) and Internet tools. With the aid of these resources, the extended enterprise members interact as shown in Fig. 2.

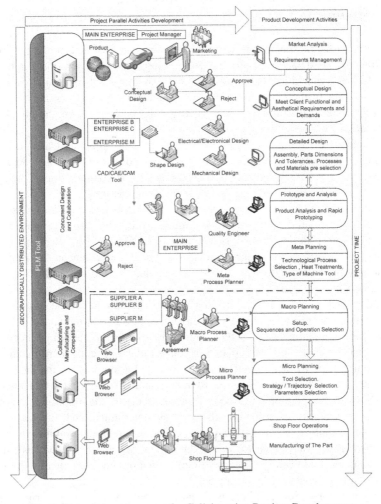

Fig. 2. Proposed environment for Collaborative Product Development

3.2 Definition of the Lifecycle Phases and the Workflow

The workflow automates the running of tasks that allow the product development to move on from one stage to another during its lifecycle. The modeled workflow is a global composition of several workflows linked each other in order to be launched consecutively (Fig. 3).

The definition of product lifecycle phases is essential for correct workflow definition and design. This case study involves the following phases of product development: conceptual design, detail design, proposal for manufacturing, quotation, planning and manufacturing. Each of these stages is delimited by approval "gates" that determine the transition from one stage to another, as the tasks set out in the workflow are completed.

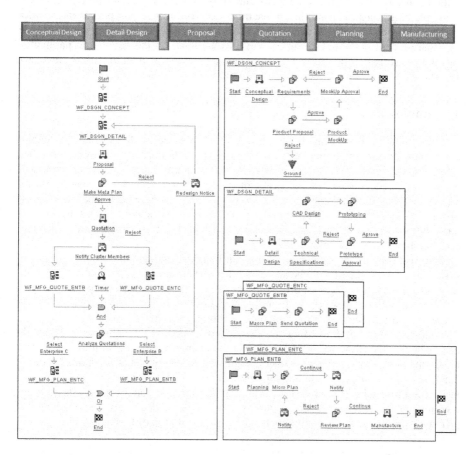

Fig. 3. Workflow Deployment across Collaborative Product Development

3.3 Workflow Execution

The activities carried out by workflows are explained as follows. The main enterprise coordinates all product development activities and manages workflow enactments.

Also performs market analysis and 'conceptual design' stage activities like realization of virtual mock ups that meet aesthetical and functional requirements. Interacting within the PLM tool, enterprises dedicated to detailed design work in technical specifications like material selection, geometrical dimensioning and tolerancing (GD&T), etc. Once the product model is finished, it is ready for product analysis and rapid prototyping as the conclusion of the detail design stage.

Meta-planning is the trigger activity of the 'proposal for manufacturing' stage, performed by the purchasing department of the main enterprise, for technological process selection and for sending quotation requests to the right sub-contractors. Once quotation requests are received, macro-planning activities need to be done by supplier's technical department in order to make cost estimation in the quotation stage. After the main enterprise receives quotations and selects the best supplier, the technical department of the supplier is authorized to begin micro-planning activities, in the planning stage. During this, a machine operator provides shop floor information to the micro-process planner, in order to incorporate the real machine capabilities in the final process plan, and to correct any inconsistence in the machining parameters calculations. Finally, the product development ends with the manufacturing stage, and all generated files were stored in the PLM database for further use.

4 Conclusions

The research work presented here has been developed with the aim of helping companies in the implementation of web-based collaborative environments. The effort for studying a PLM deployment in an extended enterprise, has forced us to make a detailed analysis of the problem of distributed design and manufacturing, especially when external enterprises are involved and compete each other. As a result of this analysis, we have enumerated all the required participants and activities that must be incorporated in a workflow model that must be implemented to help collaborative product development.

The workflow approach exposed here can be taken into account as a guide for the systematic execution of collaborative product development tasks and it allows the controlled interaction between different members of the extended enterprise.

Furthermore, the use of a friendly workflow designer tool can help to the straightforward definition of the suitable collaborative scenario.

The success of implementing the developed workflow depends not only on the acquisition of the PLM software but also in the overcoming of the cultural barriers of the cooperative work among product designers, process planners, manufacturers and external participants, all of them geographically dispersed. The next steps of this pilot project are to establish metrics for evaluating the organizational impacts in short and medium terms, and to prepare a survey that helps to determine the readiness of different supply chain environments for the implementation of this approach.

Acknowledgements

The research team would like to acknowledge the main support of the Caja Castelló-Bancaixa Foundation and Universitat Jaume I. Particular thanks go to the Programme Alßan: European Union Programme of High Level Scholarships for Latin America (scholarship # E04D030982MX).

References

1. Camarinha-Matos, L., Afsarmanesh, H.: Collaborative networks: a new scientific discipline. Journal of Intelligent Manufacturing 16, 439–452 (2005)
2. Perrin, O., Godart, C.: A model to support collaborative work in virtual enterprises. Data & Knowledge Engineering 50, 63–86 (2004)
3. Xu, X.W., Liu, T.: A web-enabled PDM system in a collaborative design environment. Robotics and Computer Integrated Manufacturing 19, 315–328 (2003)
4. Ming, X.G., Yan, J.Q., Lu, W.F., Ma, D.Z.: Technology Solutions for Collaborative Product Lifecycle Management – Status Review and Future Trend. Concurrent Engineering Research and Applications 13, 311–319 (2005)
5. Ahn, S.H., Sundararajan, V., Smith, C., Kannan, B., D'Souza, R., Sun, G., Ashish, M., Wright, P.K., Kim, J., McMains, S., Smith, J., Sequin, C.: Cybercut: An Internet-based CAD/CAM System. Transactions of the ASME 1, 52–59 (2001)
6. Maropoulos, P.G., Bramall, D.G., Chapman, P., Cheung, W.M., McKay, K.R., Rogers, B.C.: Digital Enterprise Technology in Production Networks. International Journal of Advanced Manufacturing Technology 30, 911–916 (2006)
7. Ho, C.T., Chen, Y.M., Chen, Y.J., Wang, C.B.: Developing a distributed knowledge model for knowledge management in collaborative development and implementation of an enterprise system. Robotics and Computer-Integrated Manufacturing 20, 439–456 (2004)
8. Sun, Q.L., Gramoll, K.: Internet-based distributed collaborative engineering analysis. Concurrent Engineering-Research and Applications 10, 341–348 (2002)
9. Tian, G.Y., Yin, G.F., Taylor, D.: Internet-based manufacturing: A review and a new infrastructure for distributed intelligent manufacturing. Journal of Intelligent Manufacturing 13, 323–338 (2002)
10. Huang, C.Y.: Distributed manufacturing execution systems: A workflow perspective. Journal of Intelligent Manufacturing 13, 485–497 (2002)
11. Workflow Management Coalition.: Terminology & Glossary. WfMC-TC-1011 (1999), http://www.wfmc.org
12. Web Services Business Process Execution Language Version 2.0. Working Draft. WS-BPEL TC OASIS (2005)
13. Business Process Modeling Notation (BPMN) Specificaction Version 1.0. OMG (2004), http://www.bpmn.org/
14. XML Process: Definition Language (XPDL) Specification Version 2.0. WfMC (2005), http://www.wfmc.org/standards/xpdl.htm
15. Van Den Hamer, P., Lepoter, K.: Managing Design data: The Five Dimensions of CAD Frameworks, Configuration Management, and Product Data Management. Proceedings of the IEEE 84, 42–56 (1996)

Cooperative Reinforcing Bar Arrangement and Checking by Using Augmented Reality

Nobuyoshi Yabuki[1] and Zhantao Li[2]

[1] Department of Civil Engineering and Architecture, Muroran Institute of Technology,
27-1 Mizumoto-cho, Muroran-shi, Hokkaido, 050-8585, Japan
yabuki@news3.ce.muroran-it.ac.jp
[2] Division of Civil and Environmental Engineering, Graduate School,
Muroran Institute of Technology

Abstract. In this research, a bridge product model named New IFC-BRIDGE was developed to represent entities of various types of bridges in a standardized manner. To solve problems identified in planning and design of reinforcing bar works, a cooperative reinforcing bar arrangement support system using Augmented Reality technology was developed. In this system, multiple users can move tangible markers that represent entities of reinforcing bars and that are linked to computer graphics images represented from the New IFC-BRIDGE product model data. A prototype system was developed by deploying head mounted displays with video cameras. Furthermore, to enhance the reinforcing bar checking task at construction sites, a cooperative reinforcing bar checking support system was developed by using AR technology. The test of the prototype system showed the practicality of the system, and some problems were identified for future study.

Keywords: Product Model, Reinforcing Bar, Augmented Reality, IFC, IFC-BRIDGE, Collaborative Work.

1 Introduction

Reinforcing bar arrangement and checking are very important because they are directly related to the strength including earthquake resistance of concrete structures such as buildings, bridges, tunnels, etc. Currently, reinforcing bar arrangement is done by construction site workmen based on 2D drawings which can show only minimal information of reinforcing bars. Thus, workmen usually draft many large drawings and discuss with their colleagues how to arrange reinforcing bars sequentially if the reinforcing bars are complex or to be laid out densely. Otherwise, they will be in trouble at construction sites. However, it is often difficult for inexperienced workmen to visualize the reinforcing bar arrangement and sequence in their minds. Furthermore, inspectors often find it difficult to check whether reinforcing bars are arranged correctly in accordance with the drawings by using tape measures because it is almost impossible to measure all distances and spaces of reinforce bars in a short time. In addition, it is also difficult for inspectors to find time to visit the construction site from their distant offices by car or on foot for checking.

Y. Luo (Ed.): CDVE 2007, LNCS 4674, pp. 50–57, 2007.

Therefore, in this research, a cooperative engineering environment for reinforcing bar arrangement using augmented reality (AR) is proposed. In this environment, multiple workmen wear head mounted displays (HMDs) with video cameras, which are connected with their computers. They grab and move markers, each of which is linked to 3D model data of reinforcing bars, and represented by newly developed IFC-BRIDGE product model schema. By using an AR tool called ARToolKit [1], users can view the virtual reinforcing bars represented by computer graphics on their HMDs. They can discuss how to arrange reinforcing bars by moving the markers in a virtual 3D world. A prototype system has been developed, and students used it for review. The prototype showed the feasibility of this methodology.

In addition, a new framework consisting of an AR system at a construction site and a viewing and controlling system at a remote office, connected via the Internet, has been developed. This framework intends to facilitate the inspection process more efficiently so that inspectors do not have to visit construction sites.

2 New IFC-Bridge Product Model

Much effort has been seen in developing product models for building design and construction in order to enable the interoperability among heterogeneous application systems and software packages such as CAD, analysis, conformance checking, cost estimation, construction scheduling, for more than two decades. Recently, Industry Foundation Classes (IFC) of International Alliance for Interoperability (IAI) [2] seems to be considered as a de facto standard for building product models. However, as for bridges, each CAD and design software company, nation, or organization has been developing its own product model, and there is little interoperability among those models and application systems.

The authors have developed a bridge product model for prestressed concrete (PC) bridges by expanding IFC in collaboration with Japan Prestressed Concrete Contractors Association [3]. In parallel, a steel girder bridge product model was developed by the similar method [4]. These two bridge product models were merged into one, which is called J-IFC-BRIDGE.

Around the same time as this model was developed, IAI French Speaking Chapter developed a bridge product model called IFC-BRIDGE based on the IFC and OA-EXPRESS, which is a bridge product model developed by SETRA, French governmental technical center for roads and highways, and it has been open to public since 2002 via the Internet web site [5].

Both Japanese and French groups did not know their efforts in developing bridge product models each other by 2002, although their approaches were quite similar. Both Japanese and French groups decided to integrate the two product models and have proposed New IFC-BRIDGE by merging their product models by the support of IAI. Reinforcing bars of bridges can be represented by using the New IFC-BRIDGE product model.

3 Augmented Reality Technology

Augmented Reality technology provides a facility to overlap real video images with virtual computer graphics images. This can be done by showing a special marker to the video camera attached with a HMD worn by the user. The marker is linked with a designated object and the system shows the object image on the marker of the video screen. The similar thing can be done by wearing see-through glasses with a video camera.

In this research, the authors used ARToolKit, which is a set of open source libraries for AR, developed by Kato et al. [1]. If a 2D square marker is shown on the video screen image, the system measures the location, inclination, etc. and inspects the pattern of the marker, and displays real time the 3D computer graphics image corresponding to the marker on the video display, as shown in Fig. 1. The computer graphics images are created from the New IFC-BRIDGE product model.

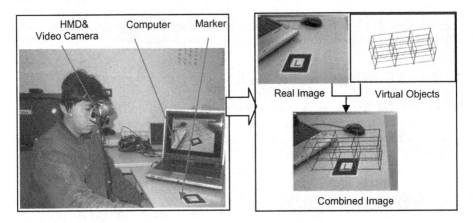

Fig. 1. Augmented reality using a HMD, video camera, markers, and ARToolKit

4 A Cooperative Reinforcing Bar Arrangement Support

As described before, experienced workmen are necessary in order to arrange reinforcing bars appropriately at construction sites. The knowledge needed to construct reinforcing bars is usually embedded in construction workmen's minds and has not been explicitly represented. Thus, on-the-job training is usually employed to transfer the knowledge from senior workmen to juniors. And a trial-and-error approach is often used for planning the sequence of reinforcing bars by drawing and modifying many plans. Consequently, cooperative environment would be necessary to arrange and construct reinforcing bars adequately. To solve such problems, the authors propose a collaborative system where multiple users can move tangible markers each of which represents single or a set of reinforcing bars in an augmented reality environment as shown in Fig. 2.

To demonstrate the feasibility and practicality of the proposed AR approach, the authors developed a prototype system and tested it in their laboratory. A set of five reinforcing bars comprising a section of a prestressed concrete bridge girder was selected and represented by using New IFC-BRIDGE product model. As shown in Fig. 3, five markers, A, B, C, D, and E, were scattered on the table. Two graduate

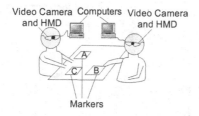

Fig. 2. Cooperative environment using AR technology

students majoring in civil engineering, simulating workmen X and Y, wore HMDs with video cameras. Fig. 3 shows that the worker X was moving the marker C, while the worker Y was moving the marker B. They discussed the sequence of arranging the five reinforcing bars. The two workers looked at the same 3D virtual reinforcing bars from different angles and discussed many possible sequences, moving the markers intuitively. The test showed the efficiency and effectiveness of the system over the traditional pencil-and-eraser method.

5 A Cooperative Reinforcing Bar Checking Support

The traditional method for checking whether reinforcing bars are arranged and set correctly and conform the design by using tape measures and 2D paper drawings is time-consuming and error-prone. Thus, the authors proposed and developed a reinforcing bar checking support system by using augmented reality technology and New IFC-BRIDGE product model. In this method, reinforcing bars are represented by New IFC-BRIDGE and its computer graphics image is linked with a marker. The marker is placed in front of the reinforcing bars at its designated location, and a user wearing a HMD with a video camera looked at the marker and the reinforcing bars. The user can check whether the reinforcing bars are correctly arranged or not by checking the overlapped computer graphics image over the actual reinforcing bar image on the HMD monitors. The user can vary the viewing direction and angle by simply moving his or her head freely (Fig. 4).

To check the feasibility of this method, an indoor test was performed. Two small wood frames were crafted. One was made just as designed while the other was made poorly with errors. As shown in Fig. 5, the good craft model on the left was overlapped properly with the computer graphics image, while the poor model on the right was not overlapped with the virtual reinforcing bar image.

As the indoor test was successfully done, an on-site experiment was executed at a construction site near Muroran, Japan. A part of a prestressed concrete bridge girder was selected and was represented by IFC-BRIDGE product model. As shown in Fig. 6, an inspector wore the HMD with a video camera and looked at the marker attached to the reinforcing bars. The image that the inspector viewed is shown in Fig. 7. As the figure shows, there was not big difference between the virtual computer graphics and the real reinforcing bar images. Therefore, the actual reinforcing bars could be judged as properly constructed.

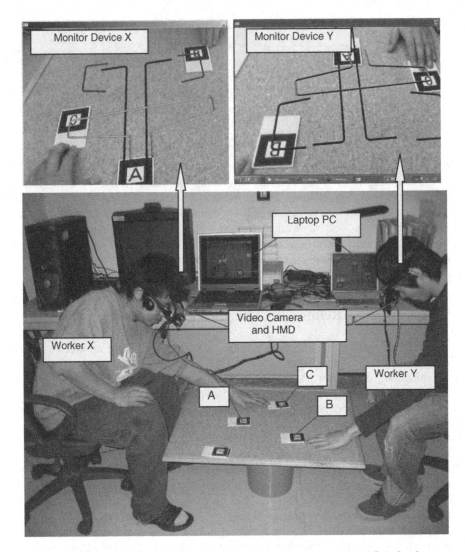

Fig. 3. Cooperative reinforcing bar arrangement support system using AR technology

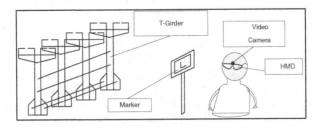

Fig. 4. Reinforcing bar checking support system using AR

Fig. 5. A well crafted wood model and poorly made one overlapped with CG images

| Video Camera and HMD | Marker | Laptop PC |

Fig. 6. Inspector is checking reinforcing bars   **Fig. 7.** Inspector's monitor image

However, four problems were identified. Since there exists strain in lenses of video cameras and there are subtle errors in positioning the marker, it was difficult to overlap the real and virtual images completely. Next, as the amount of data for representing reinforcing bars increased significantly compared to the wood craft models made for the indoor test, the response for renewing images became very slow. The third problem was that the quality of the combined view was not stable enough, particularly when the on-site light changed considerably, the real world could not be seen clearly. The fourth problem was that only one marker was used in the field experiment, which made the scope of the inspector's view narrow. These problems can mostly be solved technically. The fourth one can be solved by placing multiple markers at the site, as shown in Fig. 8.

Other problems in checking of reinforcing bars include that inspectors are usually very busy with other work and their offices are tend to be far from construction sites.

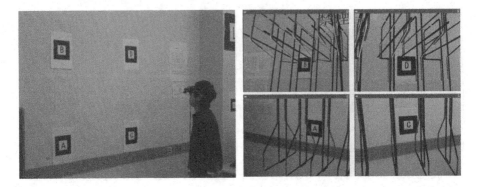

Fig. 8. Multiple markers representing different parts of reinforcing bars and CG images

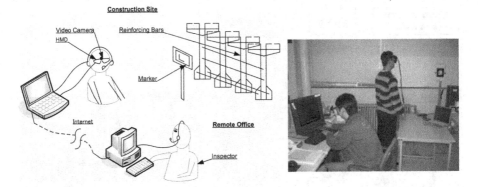

Fig. 9. Inspector at his office can check reinforcing bars at a construction site via the Internet

To solve this problem, a prototype of remote cooperative reinforcing bar checking system was developed by using AR technology and NetMeeting. As shown in Fig. 9, the inspector at his remote office can view the actual and virtual reinforcing bars at the construction site just as the workman wearing the HMD and a video camera there is looking at.

6   Conclusion

In this research, a bridge product model named New IFC-BRIDGE was developed by merging the authors' J-IFC-BRIDGE and French IFC-BRIDGE to represent entities of various types of bridges in a standardized manner, based on the object-oriented paradigm. The product model enables the interoperability among heterogeneous applications.

Next, problems in planning of reinforcing bar arrangement were identified. To solve the problems, a cooperative reinforcing bar arrangement support system using Augmented Reality technology was developed. In this system, multiple users can move tangible markers that represent entities of reinforcing bars and that are linked to computer graphics images represented from the New IFC-BRIDGE product model data, while discussing. A prototype system was developed by deploying HMDs with video cameras. The test performed indoor by students imitating workmen showed the feasibility of the method and the system.

Furthermore, the authors identified problems in checking reinforcing bar arrangement at construction sites. It is virtually impossible to completely check reinforcing bars by using measures and 2D paper drawings. Thus, a cooperative reinforcing bar checking support system was developed by using AR technology. In this system, the inspector wearing a HMD with a video camera compares and checks whether reinforcing bars set at a construction site overlap the computer graphics image generated from the New IFC-BRIDGE product model data. This system was tested both indoor and at a construction site. Although the tests showed the practicality of the method, several problems related to errors and computer performances were identified.

For further study, the authors intend to enhance the AR supporting systems and quantify and compare the cost and benefits by using these systems.

Acknowledgments. This research has been partially supported by the Japan-France Bilateral Research Project, SAKURA, of the Japan Society for the Promotion of Science (JSPS). It is also partially supported by the Japan Construction Information Center (JACIC).

References

1. ARToolKit: http://www.hitl.washington.edu/ artoolkit/
2. IAI International: http://www.iai-international. org/
3. Yabuki, N., Shitani, T.: Development and Application of an IFC-based Bridge Product Model. In: Proceedings of the Ninth International Conference on Civil and Structural Engineering Computing, Egmond aan Zee, the Netherlands, Paper No.93 (2003) 14pp (CD-ROM)
4. Yabuki, N., Kotani, J., Shitani, T.: A Steel Bridge Design System Architecture using VR-CAD and Web Service-based Multi-Agents. In: Proceedings of the Xth International Conference on Computing in Civil and Building Engineering, Weimar, Germany (2004) 8pp (CD-ROM)
5. IFC-BRIDGE: http://www.iai-france.org/bridge/

A Virtual Interactive Community Platform Supporting Education for Long-Term Sick Children

Pieter Jorissen[1], Fabian Di Fiore[1], Gert Vansichem[2], and Wim Lamotte[1]

[1] Hasselt University
Expertise Centre for Digital Media - IBBT
Transnationale Universiteit Limburg
Universitaire Campus, BE-3590 Diepenbeek, Belgium
{pieter.jorissen, fabian.difiore, wim.lamotte}@uhasselt.be
http://www.edm.uhasselt.be
[2] Androme NV
Wetenschapspark 4, BE-3590 Diepenbeek, Belgium
gert.vansichem@androme.be
http://www.androme.com

Abstract. Analysis of existing ICT-based solutions for the education of long-term ill children reveal several weaknesses with respect to social and cooperative involvement, cost of development, and mobility issues. We present a scalable and affordable solution that supports both the social needs and learning process of these children. An educational platform was created based on the concepts of 3D networked virtual environments and Virtual Interactive Communities. In this work we describe the system architecture, network setup and protocols, and how we implemented the educational support. Our solution incorporates innovative hardware, software and connectivity features, set in a user friendly user interface based on networking and 3D technologies. It helps to establish high quality involvement of the long-term sick children in a communication based scenario between the place where the child stays/has been moved and their original classroom learning setting.

Keywords: Cooperative Learning Environment, Edutainment, E-Health, E-Learning, Virtual Interactive Communities, Social Networks.

1 Introduction and Motivation

Health care is becoming less hospital-centric; the hospitalization periods are much briefer and treatments are increasingly carried out at home. This shift has mediated medical, social and economic reasons and consequences. Furthermore, in the case of long-term and chronically ill children, this shift has a major impact on their education. The responsibility to provide education, is transferred from the hospital to the school which the children attended before their absence. Regular schools, however, are hardly able to set up high quality instruction for

Y. Luo (Ed.): CDVE 2007, LNCS 4674, pp. 58–69, 2007.

their home-based pupils. As a result, the socialization opportunities offered by schools are no longer available for them and friendships between the ill child and fellow pupils become more and more disintegrated [1,2].

In this work, we present a cooperative, community-based, E-Learning platform that aims at re-establishing the communication link between the place where the child is staying and the original school setting in view of supporting high-quality instructional scenarios. Analysis of existing ICT-based solutions, for educating long-term sick children ([3,4,5,6]), reveal weaknesses including the absence of social involvement, high development costs and mobility issues. Furthermore, although scientific publications have been written about several ICT-solutions, most of them focus on the results rather then giving a clear insight into the development process or the technical details.

The solution we propose, is based on the concepts of 3D networked virtual environments (NVEs) and Virtual Interactive Communities (VICs). It has to be stressed that we do not aim on the development of a new electronic learning environment (ELE) such as there are: Blackboard, WebCT, Anywize, etc. or a content management system (CMS). In contrast, we concentrate on a solution that can be linked to or used in cooperation with existing ELEs and CMS applications. The platform we present, does not focus on developing content, is based on concrete user needs, is educationally sound and relevant, and offers a scalable and affordable solution. The communication provisions build on audio and video (A/V) links, using standardized protocols, and help to support educational scenarios that support learning processes. Regarding the entire process, five interactive steps were undertaken: (i) analysis of user needs, user characteristics and context factors, (ii) design, (iii) development, (iv) evaluation, and (v) delivery. The focus of this work is on the more technical aspects of the design and development processes. More specifically we will give an insight on system architecture, network setup and protocols, consistency maintenance and visualization.

In the following section we elaborate on related research in the fields of E-learning solutions and VICs. Thereafter, we will give a brief overview of the required functionality. Section 4 discusses the details of how this functionality was implemented. In the fifth section, we will give some preliminary results. Finally, we give some concluding remarks and future research directions.

2   Related Work

2.1   ICT Solutions for E-Learning

To date, several ICT-based solutions have been proposed in order to support education for children with health impairments. The most remarkable probably is the PEBBLES project (Providing Education By Bringing Learning Environments to Students). It comprises an advanced prototype solution developed in the USA and Canada [3,6]. It was launched as the worlds first fully functional telepresence application: a social and technological solution that virtually places a child within the classroom by putting a robot which replaces the sick child in the regular classroom. The robot is connected through a high-speed Internet line to the tools in the hospital. Major advantages are stated to be the remote control opportunities and the possibility to create an authentic learning setting because of two-way video, audio and document transmission possibilities. The PEBBLES solution enables a strong synchronous and authentic presence of the sick pupil in the original classroom setting. An advantage for the school/teacher perspective is the scant investment of extra time and energy to develop alternative solutions for these children. In addition to these advantages, it is possible to determine some problems of the PEBBLES-solution. For example, no documentation can be found on what happens when the sick pupil is unable to follow lessons synchronously due to health related problems such as tiredness, lack of concentration or therapies scheduled during the lessons. As no information can be found in articles or on the Internet, we assume that this solution lacks backing-up functionalities for missed classes. Furthermore, there is the issue of mobility of the ICT-based solution. Moving to another hospital room or classroom, moving back and away from hospital or home may cause interruptions or even an impossibility to continue the instructional experience. Another critical issue, hardly mentioned in the literature, is the high cost of developing and maintaining the PEBBLES-provision.

Another solution is STARBRIGHT World (SBW), a safe and secure online community where these children can connect to each other. Children on SBW can chat, read and post to bulletin boards, email, search for friends with similar illnesses, participate in fun events and contests, surf pre-screen Web sites and play games [7]. Further analysis of the available papers on the use of SBW, however, pointed out that the communicative possibilities were seldomly used by the children: only 3% to 15% of the time was spent on communication [5]. Another downside of this project is that it does not support educational scenarios.

In Flanders, the Dutch speaking part of Belgium in which our research project is carried out, a type of video phone is already in use to support long-term sick children to stay in touch with their family and peers at school [4]. However, hospital personnel has experienced some problems with these tools: there is an asynchronous delivery of sound and images, they offer basic video connection capabilities of rather low quality and if it is often used, it is a rather expensive solution because of the payment per minute of talking. In addition, each use of a video phone involves extra costs. For these reasons, the video phone has ended up in a closet in most of the hospitals we visited. Besides the use of this video phone device, ELEs through which the school, parents and pupils get in touch more regularly, are increasingly promoted. However, these tools build heavily on text-based input and communication and are therefore less suited for pupils of elementary school age. Also, they create a less authentic setting and hardly support the active and interactive involvement of the sick children.

2.2 Virtual Interactive Communities

We define Virtual Interactive Communities (VICs) as 3D virtual environments (VEs) in which (groups of) people sharing the same interests or ideas can easily communicate and interact with each other. Over the past decade, VICs have evolved tremendously. Undoubtedly the most popular VICs, nowadays, are the Massive Multiplayer Online Role-Playing Games (MMORPGs) with millions of subscribtions worldwide. Second Life [8], World of Warcraft [9] and Knight Online [10] are some examples. What these VICs have in common, is the fact that they build on high-end PCs with permanent broadband access to the Internet. Also, most of them rely on text chat as their primary means of communication (although some also supports voice communication, usually with added costs). In most VICs the users are represented by virtual animated characters, usually referred to as *avatars*. These represent the location and the actions of the user in the virtual world. In [11,12] we proposed an extension to these avatars. We presented a framework for networked 3D VE applications that incorporates real-time video communication between avatars. We strongly believe that the combination of 3D worlds and live video streaming is perfectly suitable for this work, since it results in more explorative and fun learning environments than present-day solutions. Moreover, our aim is to work with children of elementary school age, which are assumed to prefer non-abstract environments with a limited amount of textual cues.

3   Requirements and User Needs

Our goal is to re-establish both the communication link between the sick child and its classroom and allow it to follow the class activities with fellow pupils. By providing the involved parties (child, teacher and fellow pupils) with access to a VIC that allows for A/V communication, we can already solve some aspects of our goal, however it is far from sufficient. From our observations and functional analysis ([13,14]) we learned that in order to fully achieve our goal, our learning platform should support:

1. *Synchronous lessons*, including two way A/V stream so both sides can see and hear each other, a high resolution view the chalkboard and the possibility for the child to draw the class' attention.
2. Digital versions of the *diary and timetable.*
3. *Asynchronous lesson possibilities*, as the sick child will not be able to follow all classes due to tiredness, treatments or sickness.
4. Exchanging *homework, exercises, tests and markings* both for synchronous and asynchronous lessons.
5. *Social functionalities*, since the involvement in informal activities at school are at least as important as being involved in formal activities. In particular, children indicated they miss the socialization opportunities offered at school.

In the next section we discuss how our platform supports these functionalities.

4   Approach

4.1   The VIC Learning Platform

The virtual learning environment that we propose is based on our earlier experiences with VICs [11,12]. This includes support for various synchronous communication components into the 3D VE such as audio conversation, video conferencing, text chat and video-based avatars. We have extended this work with community support functions like buddy lists, authentication and authorization functionalities, rich presence (showing who is on line, which mood, what kind of activities one is pursuing), media publishing (diary, timetable, exercises), and file exchange.

Using this platform, we built a VIC application implementing the required functionality to achieve our goals. A logical overview of our platform is shown in Fig. 1. Here, we also see that our solution consists of several components, which all play an important role: (i) the virtual school environment, its functionality and how it is displayed, (ii) the underlying network supporting it and (iii) the hardware. The platform is programmed in C++ and runs on most Windows based systems. This was chosen so most home computers will be able to run the software.

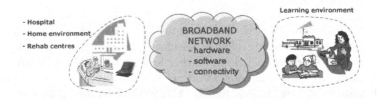

Fig. 1. Overview of the Virtual Learning Platform approach

4.2   The Virtual School Environment

The VE of our test application is a 3D modeled environment that is rendered using the Ogre 3D open source graphics engine [15]. Taking into account that the community is children-oriented, all its objects are created in cartoon style and interaction is kept as intuitive and natural as possible (by clicking easily understandable icons). Our system, however, is not restricted to a specific 3D environment. Instead, each school is free to choose the look of the VE. Navigating in this virtual world happens by means of an animated avatar that is controlled through the arrows on the keyboard. This corresponds to navigating in present-day games and on-line communities like Ice Age 2 and (Teen) Second Life. The looks of the avatars is also adjustable by the participants (type of character, colors of clothing, hair,...).

The virtual playground (Fig. 2 (a)) is the starting position of the user in the VE. Therein, the child can navigate, meet its friends and teachers and communicate through video avatars (Fig. 2 (b)). When it is time for class, the pupil can enter the virtual classroom, which is a 3D scene containing the most important elements of the real classroom environment: a live video A/V stream of the class (top, left), a high resolution captured image of the chalkboard (middle), the pupils school desk containing his diary, homework book and school timetable (bottom), and the pupils personal bookshelf (top, right). A view of the virtual classroom is shown in Fig. 2 (c). In the real classroom, the teacher and fellow students, have a similar view. Only here, the video stream of the child is displayed instead of the class' video. Furthermore, several function buttons allow the users (child, teacher, fellow student) to quickly launch specific tasks such as: scanning and transmitting documents (with automatic printing), capturing the chalkboard and drawing/granting attention. Finally, the user is also able to switch to a close-up view of classroom elements by simply clicking them to get a better look, and get a view of its own video. Virtual books (Fig. 2 (d)) can be used to store documents, scans (of homework, tests,...) and pictures and can be accessed at any time. Furthermore, teachers can add recorded lessons (webcam feed and slideshow of the chalkboard images), in case the sick pupil could not attend a lesson. This way, he can view these at later.

Before we discuss the details on how the functionality works, we take a closer look into the network architecture.

Fig. 2. Views of the school environment: (a) the virtual playground, (b) video avatars, (c) the virtual classroom, (d) a close-up of the class diary with scanned pages

4.3   The Network Architecture

The network architecture that supports our virtual community consists of several servers, each with their own responsibilities. In order to be as general and interoperable as possible, we used standardized protocols as much as possible. The division into the different servers is not necessary physical; in practice several servers can be run on a single machine. Due to the desire to be compatible with existing standards and the dependency on communication services a substantial part of the architecture is inspired on the IP Multimedia Subsystem (IMS [16]). With the Session Initiation Protocol (SIP [17]) being the key technology behind the IMS, the client application incorporates the Intellivic SDK [18], a toolkit for integration SIP-based video telephony into an application. On the network side this choice also implies the presence of elements from the IMS architecture like session management and communication services.

The first server used, is the *Session Management Server*. It takes care of and authenticating users and logging users on and off. In addition, it is also being used to initiate A/V communication sessions. In order to communicate and manage these sessions, SIP is being used. A second server is used for communication. Although peer-to-peer communication is possible when only two parties are involved (e.g. sick child and classroom). When more parties become involved, it is desirable to use the *Communication Server*, since the setup of peer-to-peer connections between multiple parties is impossible due to bandwidth limitations. The solution is to send a single stream to the communication server, which relays it to the different parties. This way every participant only has to send a single A/V stream instead of one for every participant. It is the Session Server that is responsibility to indicate clients which communication server to use (in case more than one is available). Due to the real-time nature of the A/V streams the Real-Time Transport Protocol (RTP [19]) is the obvious choice for the underlying protocol. Other possibilities for even more efficient A/V stream transmission would be to use multicasting as was done in [11,12]. However, since multicasting is not yet fully available in practice, it could not be used during our field trials. In order to not exceed the 128 kbps (or 256 kbps) upload bandwidth limitation, that is available in most Flemish homes, we need to compress our A/V streams. Currently we use mpeg4 80kbit QCIF compression for video and speex_narrowband 15kbit compression for the audio. These parameters can be remotely configured to provide the desired quality and exploiting the available bandwidth optimally. Managing synchronization and persistence of the 3D VE is the responsibility of the *VIC Server*. This involves transmitting the world itself, synchronization of object and user states, and managing and storing a persistent world state. Apart from location, user states also include information on its mood and actions. File transfers are done using the File Transfer Protocol (FTP [20]) and update messages for objects and clients are sent using ENet [21], a thin, simple and robust network communication layer on top of UDP. Finally, The *Data Server* is used for two categories of data. On the one hand, it stores configuration files of the users containing personal information such as A/V parameters and address lists of the community. On the other hand, the server makes it possible to transmit and store (shared) media and other data files such as shared virtual books. Underlying protocols used are FTP and Hypertext Transfer Protocol (HTTP [22]). An overview of the network architecture and the used protocols is given in Fig. 3.

4.4   Providing Education

Since we are working with children and teachers who usually have little computer knowledge, we want to hide as much of the technical details as possible and provide intuitive interaction methods. All user data and configuration settings are set up in advance and saved in an XML file that is parsed on startup of the application, and backed up on the data server. Logging on and off via SIP is done completely transparently on startup. The user data, webcam and audio settings are read from file and used to log on to the session management server. Immediately, the user can see which other participants are in the environment and in

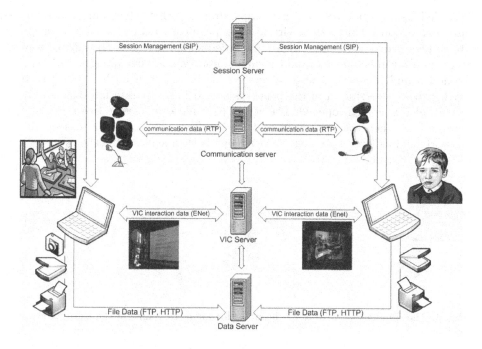

Fig. 3. Overview of the network architecture and the necessary client hardware

what mood they are in. When other users are encountered on the playground, an A/V session is set up automatically. Also, when both the sick child and classroom are logged in and have entered the virtual classroom (which is done simply by clicking the door of the classroom in the virtual school environment) an A/V session is started automatically. The video images are incorporated in the 3D classroom using video textures.

Apart from synchronous A/V communication, the most important functionality is the easy *exchange of documents* (drawings, tasks, exercises or tests). We have also kept this task as simple as possible for the users. The different steps of synchronous exchange of a scanned document are shown in Fig. 4. Note that the user only has to perform step 1 and 2, the rest is done completely automatically. An example of the use of this functionality is when a teacher hands out a page of exercises to his students. He can put the sick pupil's page in the scanner and send it to him with a single button click. On the other side the document is automatically downloaded and printed. The child can then fill in the exercises and send his results in the exact same manner for correcting and/or grading. Taking *pictures of the chalkboard* happens in a similar way. The only difference is the final step. Instead of automatically download and printing, the picture is integrated in the virtual 3D scene. In order to take these pictures, the classroom must be equipped with a digital camera that can be controlled by software. More details on the hardware are given in the next section. The *virtual books* also use the same principle and can, besides the diary and time table, be used for storing recorded lessons, pictures from field trips, drawings that fellow pupils made or just digital notes. Currently a virtual book page can contain: a scanned image (text, photo, drawing,...), a video, a recorded sound or a link to a file or web page. Books can be opened from the virtual library, and virtual pages can easily be added and removed. The data server contains a list of all books and each book (with a description of the pages) is stored in a separate file that is only downloaded when it is opened. The actual page data (images, videos,...) is only downloaded when the page is viewed for the first time, in order to keep the network load as low as possible. A local copy is then kept on the client.

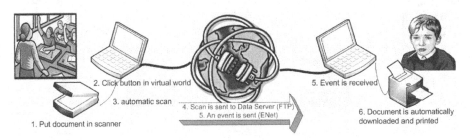

Fig. 4. The different steps of a synchronous document exchange in the learning environment

4.5   Hardware and Network Requirements

One of our initial objectives was to develop an affordable solution. Therefore, we tried to exploit commodity hardware as much as possible. The hardware that is necessary at the pupil's and the classroom site can be seen in Fig. 3. At first, we have the PC/laptop that runs the software, this can be a commercial off-the-shelf machine; it only needs to have a 3D accelerator graphics card in order to fluently visualize the 3D environment. Most Flemish households have a home PC that fits these requirements, so only the software installation is required to run our E-learning platform. In our current setup we use Pentium 4, 2.4 GHz PCs with 1 GB of RAM in the classroom and Pentium 4, 3.06 GHz portables with 512 MB of RAM for the pupil's setting. Furthermore, both sides need A/V hardware. Tests pointed out that a resolution of 320 x 240 suffices to have a decent view and frame rate (25fps), so off the shelf webcams can be used. Concerning audio, the pupils can make use of a headset or a microphone that is integrated in most available webcams. The classroom on the other hand is equipped with a wireless microphone together with a set of speakers. This requires the need for acoustic echo cancellation (AEC), which may be integrated in the microphone or in the software. Furthermore, both sides need a printer and a scanner. Since we use Windows Image Architecture (WIA) for scanning and printing to the default printer, most available printers/scanners can be used. Finally, in the classroom, a digital camera is employed in order to take snapshots of the chalkboard. During the test phase, results indicated that we should use a minimal resolution of 1600 x 1200 pixels (i.e. 2.1 Mpixel) for readability, (ii) to avoid using the flash,

(iii) that colors look better on a green chalkboard than on a marker whiteboard. In our current setting, we use Canon Powershot A620 cameras controlled in our software using the Canon PowerShot Remote Capture SDK [23]. This allows to control the camera's settings (resolution, zoom, flash,...) and permits taking pictures which are automatically loaded onto the PC.

Regarding bandwidth, the real bottleneck is the streaming live audio and video. In the Flemish setting, most people and schools own a xDSL or cable connection (download speed: 4.4Mb, upload: 128 to 256kb). These connections can easily handle the streams of the resolution and frame rate mentioned here, using the compression techniques mentioned in section 4.3. Even far better quality can be used when 256 kbps upload is available.

5   Results

In order to evaluate our system, several field trials have been set up with a realistic target audience (i.e. sick children and their schools) and within authentic settings (i.e. at home or at a hospital). The authentic setting required a diversity of preparatory work: methodology, installation, establishing connectivity, introduction of the package, planning front-office support, data analysis and reporting. Although at the time of writing not all field trials have finished, current tentative data are significant enough to conclude that our solution provides the functionality that we proposed and that the current hardware requirements are able to support it. With regards to usability, we can already conclude that the users, especially the children, are really pleased with the approach of a VIC for both the learning and social aspects of attending class. All users state that the social bond between the sick child, his fellow pupils and friends and the teacher has dramatically improved. To completely evaluate the fulfilling of concrete user needs as indicated by the needs analysis, the data of the individual case studies will need to be combined. These complete results of the user needs are not yet available however. In order to give a more complete image of our learning platform, a video of a lab test and some field trials can be found on http://research.edm.uhasselt.be/pjorissen/CDVE2007/.

6   Conclusions and Future Work

This work presents a cooperative, community-based, E-Learning platform based on the concepts of 3D NVEs and supporting VIC functionalities. While our goal was not to develop an ELE or CMS, we showed how, based on concrete user needs, our platform can be used to support educational scenarios that support learning processes. We described the underlying network architecture and the employed protocols, that support the communication provisions through which the communication link between the sick child and its original classroom and friends was restored. Our system offers a scalable and affordable solution, it utilizes standard hardware and is adjustable to most home network setups.

Tentative results show that our solution functions well and is technically sound. Currently more in-the-field trials are being conducted. The investigation of how our platform will socially and educationally influence long-term ill children will be subject of our future work. More specifically, it is recommended to investigate the effects of using user-based ICT-solutions on several relevant outcomes such as the experiences of children when reentering their school, the academic achievement and psychosocial outcomes (e.g., well being, coping and social adjustment).

Acknowledgments. This study was conducted in view of the ASCIT-project (Again at my School by fostering Communication through Interactive Technologies for long term sick children) financed by the Flemish Interdisciplinary institute for Broadband Technology (IBBT) and following partners: Androme, Alcatel, Artec-Electronics, Televic, Vlaams Patiëntenplatform, Hospital School Gasthuisberg (Leuven), Bednet vzw, and Vlaamse Liga tegen Kanker. We gratefully express our gratitude to the European Fund for Regional Development (ERDF) and the Flemish Government which are kindly funding part of the research at the Expertise Centre for Digital Media. Many thanks go also to Xemi Morales for his artistic contribution.

References

1. Prevatt, F.F., Heffer, R.W., Lowe, P.A.: A review of school reintegration programs for children with cancer. Journal of School Psychology, 447–467 (2000)
2. Fels, D.I., Shrimpton, B., Robertson, M.: Kids in hospital, kids in school. In: Proceedings of EdMedia, pp. 2358–2363 (2003)
3. Weiss, P.L., Whiteley, C.P., Treviranus, J., Fels, D.I.: PEBBLES: A personal technology for meeting educational, social and emotional needs of hospitalized children. Personal and Ubiquitous Computing, 157–168 (2001)
4. Jonge Kamera v.z.w. Jonge kamera, http://www.jongekamera.be
5. Battles, H.B., Wiener, L.S.: Starbright World: Effects of an electronic network on the social environment of children with life-threatening illnesses. Children's Health Care, 47–68 (2002)
6. The PEBBLES project. http://www.ryerson.ca/pebbles/
7. Starlight Starbright children's foundation. Starbright World. http://www.starbrightworld.org
8. Second Life. http://secondlife.com
9. World of Warcraft, http://www.worldofwarcraft.com
10. Knignt Online, http://www.knightonlineworld.com
11. Quax, P., Flerackers, C., Jehaes, T., Lamotte, W.: Scalable transmission of avatar video streams in virtual environments. In: Proceedings of the 2004 IEEE International Conference on Multimedia and Expo (ICME 2004), pp. 631–634. IEEE Computer Society Press, Los Alamitos (2004)
12. Quax, P., Jehaes, T., Jorissen, P., Lamotte, W.: A Multi-User Framework Supporting Video-Based Avatars. In: NETGAMES 2003. Proceedings of the 2nd workshop on Network and system support for games, California (2003)

13. Lombaert, E., Veevate, P., Schuurmans, D., Hauttekeete, L., Valcke, M.: A special tool for special children: creating an ICT tool to fulfill the educational and social needs of long-term sick children. In: Proceedings of the International Conference on Multimedia and Information and Communication Technologies in Education (mICTE) (2006)

14. Lombaert, E., Valcke, M.: Education for Long-Term Sick Children: Towards an Integrated IT-Solution. In: Computer Assisted Learning conference (CAL '07) (to appear, 2007)

15. Ogre 3D, http://www.ogre3d.org

16. SIP Centre on IMS.
http://www.sipcentre.com/sip.nsf/html/IMS+IP+Multimedia+Subsystem

17. Rosenberg, J., Schulzrinne, H., Camarillo, G., Johnston, A., Peterson, J., Sparks, R., Handley, M., Schooler, E.: SIP Session Initiation Protocol, RFC 3261. Technical report (2002)

18. Androme Intellivic SDK, http://www.intellivic.com/

19. Schulzrinne, H., Casner, S., Frederick, R., Jacobson, V.: RTP: A transport protocol for real-time applications, RFC 3550. Technical report (2003)

20. Postel, J., Reynolds, J.: FTP: File transfer protocol, RFC 959. Technical report (1985)

21. ENet: http://enet.bespin.org

22. Fielding, R., Gettys, J., Mogul, J., Frystyk, H., Masinter, L., Leach, P., Berners-Lee, T.: HTTP/1.1: Hypertext transfer protocol, RFC 2616 Technical report

23. Canon's European Developer Programmes,
http://www.developers.canon-europa.com

Pro-active Environment for Assisted Model Composition

Sascha Opletal, Emil Stoyanov, and Dieter Roller

Institute of Computer-Aided Product Development Systems
University of Stuttgart
{opletal,stoyanov,roller}@informatik.uni-stuttgart.de

Abstract. Automatic testing and learning methods are of great benefit in many engineering areas. They provide the possibility for training without the need of personal communication and eliminate related barriers that hold up project progress. As most technical systems include components that are related to each other and need to form a properly working system, a knowledge base which allows to retrieve the relations of a component to others regarding its properties and targeted functionality can support this task in many ways. Our system for assisted model composition forms a highly structured documentation system, based on model semantics. An important aspect of our system is the combination of user activated information retrieval and pro-active model composition assistance. The model semantics define specialized dependency annotations that can be attached to selected parts of the model, and with the help of which relevant guidelines for related processes, such as model couplings, and belonging remarks about materials, integration oddities, exceptions and other dynamically defined properties, can be brought to the designer's attention.

Keywords: Knowledge Management, Cooperative Learning, Error-Reduced CAD.

1 Introduction

Whenever a new component is designed, it has to meet certain requirements and constraints such as quality, cost and fitness for the intended purpose. The task is to find the optimal ratio between all those factors in order to succeed on the market. A large set of technical requirements and product specifications determine the projects technical characteristics which the designer has to consider when working on particular elements.

The product development as a whole is highly dependent on how well participating parties handle these requirements, the speed of the development and re-usage of accumulated experience and knowledge [2].

This work presents a system that addresses effective re-usage of accumulated designer experience in a collaborative manner and as a result improves speed of development while being able to follow project specifications. The described system is implemented on top of a semantic network, which in itself acts as a foundation to store and semantically link knowledge.

Y. Luo (Ed.): CDVE 2007, LNCS 4674, pp. 70–79, 2007.
© Springer-Verlag Berlin Heidelberg 2007

1.1 Knowledge

The concept of knowledge is not easy to grasp and is still open to philosophical debate, as a few exemplary definitions show:

"Information combined with experience, context, interpretation, and reflection. It is a high-value form of information that is ready to apply to decisions and actions." T. Davenport et al., 1998

"Explicit or codified knowledge refers to knowledge that is transmittable in formal, systematic language. On the other hand, tacit knowledge has a personal quality, which makes it hard to formalize and communicate." I. Nonaka, 1994

A tacit knowledge is one that exists purely in the mind of people, while explicit knowledge is communicated through the exchange of modeled information in the collaborative environment. A key to a more efficient work flow is to include the tacit knowledge into the design process as much as possible and make it available as expertise on a problem domain. A system can only access the knowledge that is modeled and captured. This process can be assisted through special developed tools that can catch semantics and intentions of the users and links to where the expertise can be found. This leads to two major aspects that we need to cover with our semantic expertise sharing and acquisition environment:

- Methods for description of expertise such as conflicts, solutions, workarounds, etc.
- Enabling pro-active assistance for the distribution of knowledge

Currently, by no means, shared documentation is used for rapid learning rather than spending resources and time on absorbing the documentation individually. An expertise sharing would support rapid learning with the ability of the designer tools to extract knowledge automatically in the development process, as well assist for its proper import to the knowledge base system.

The used active semantic network (ASN) [7][9] implements a knowledge-representation technique that allows for modeling of complex geometric entities, team organization, document flow and processes in the product development model. These information entities are linked by semantic relations which provide as well a means to organize information as well as to establish connections between relevant information types and augment the information beyond the actual content.

1.2 Proactive Assistance

The process of design requires the designers to be aware of a large number of parameters related to the project specification, techniques of composition, design practices, conflict resolution, etc., with knowledge-base approaches described briefly in section 1.1 that address aspects like semantic representation and retrieval. However, this information has to be retrieved in the appropriate moment, considering the designer's role, current task and progression to deliver meaningful and helpful information that can be consumed immediately. Traditional ways of information retrieval assume that the designer himself searches for documentation on demand, which costs him time and distracts him from the concrete details of the problem and the task itself. A pro-active system that assists in the process of design, delivering information about critical issues at the appropriate time and according to the current context may have a direct impact on the quality of the end-product, and reduces the time of development, thus saving costs.

Pro-activeness of a system can be defined as the ability of a system to act and re-act by demand or autonomously in order to improve the experience of its users in aspects related to its functional purpose. In the case that is described in this paper, pro-active behavior is assisting the users/designers with delivery of information related to the process of model design.

2   Related Work and Motivation

An efficient knowledge management has the power to strip down the development cost and time to market by letting the single designer benefit from the input of a design team in a collaborative environment. In such an environment, all informational aspects of the product development process are shared between the involved designers [5]. Our goal is to use an active and efficient knowledge base to connect the designers in a stronger, more pro-active way than they are used to work in. Such a pro-active approach, structured for the efficient support of construction tasks, is very convenient to be used in teaching environments to educate inexperienced designers. A system that uses a highly abstract way to input information can be used as a learning tool because it eliminates detailed knowledge needs for the designer and provides him with means to solve the problem to be encountered.

Aspects of this procedure are covered in several systems:

A distributed collaborative design tool was developed by [3]. It enables remote parties to come together in a virtual environment and discuss and modify a common product model represented in VRML. While this environment takes care of synchronization and integrity, the aspect of learning was not emphasized.

Another system was established by [8] that covers aspects like distributed product models across non-trusting enterprises. The main focus is on how to organize and maintain a decentralized product model and keep the transactions isolated. Other conventional tutoring systems focus on simple problems to educate students. [1] uses neural networks to select lectures driven by the progress of the students.

3   Components and Work Flow Requirements

Designers need to coordinate their work in an efficient manner. This means that tools for the design work flow are needed. Also the domain of expertises are usually overlapping. Why not try to share and integrate them? A sharing model would relate expertises to already developed products. The models can then provide expertise references to their creators. The designer would learn faster, and could communicate with other creators and get additional knowledge.

Sharing of knowledge provides the following benefits:

- Knowledge propagation
- Automated context help
- Knowledge re-use

Automated knowledge propagation and context-related assistance may help the designer to be informed in advance about potential problems and associated workarounds in the process of his work. Means of finding the right resource/person to help can be provided by the system and this way support on-topic discussions. Expertise sharing adds value to the product development supporting system by relating problems and solutions in a distributed manner.

A system supporting this functionality faces the following challenges:

- Context Extraction – the modeling environment has to be able to provide information about the current activities of the user
- Expertise Modeling and Traversal – the system should be able to retrieve information relevant to the context
- Knowledge Distribution – relevant information has to be communicated to the user
- Knowledge Integration – the system should allow newly acquired expertise to be added dynamically to its knowledge repository and be made available for re-use by other participants in the process

The advantages of modular designs are used in many fields, e.g. software development, or product configuration [6]. The representation of our system forms a

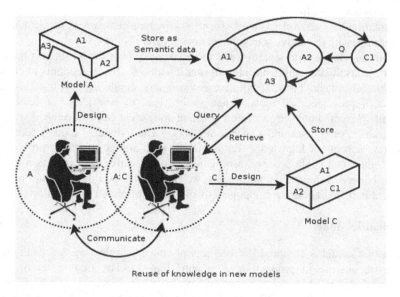

Fig. 1. Sharing of coupling expertise between designers in collaborative environment with the help of a semantic network as knowledge-base

highly structured documentation system, based on model semantics. It uses a knowledge base to retrieve information about elements relative to the context of the designer's work and brings them to the attention of the user.

Figure 1 shows a typical definition of expertise inside a shared knowledge base. In this sense, an expertise knowledge contains information about different problems in certain conditions. That is why a model for expertise sharing necessarily defines means for description of problems and solutions (workarounds). In the following scenario we consider two aspects of problem and solution definition. The first aspect covers the way a problem and solution relate to the elements in the model. The second aspect covers the relation of the problem/solution to the expertise provider.

The common understanding of the term *expertise* is the possession of knowledge for the completion of a certain task. However it is important to note that the completion of a task is a process containing chains of problems and solutions. While the first is important for the acquisition of experience by designers with problems containing composite elements, the second is essential for locating the expertise provider and respectively other expertise and solutions. (Table 2) includes the additional concept mapping for the scenarios.

4   Structure of the Pro-active Environment

To target the discussed issues in cooperative design support, we designed a model for expertise sharing. It consists of two elements each covering the desired functionality: a semantic model and a pro-active knowledge delivery framework. The semantic model covers the way expertise sharing can be achieved using a simple extension of knowledge base representation mechanisms, such as semantic nets. The layer of pro-active assistance addresses the pro-active behavior of the system and its implementation in a networked environment. As a reference example we demonstrate the integration with the active semantic network (ASN) [7] [9].

A good knowledge representation and the associated tools should support the need to acquire, consolidate, and distribute information among involved clients to create a measurable advantage. The collaborative environment should support this through a collection of processes and tools, which should lead to new ideas, processes and techniques. Several knowledge modeling techniques have been developed over the years – frames, ontologies and semantic networks. The individual models take focus on different aspects of knowledge, ontologies as such are e.g. suited to provide and organize additional CAD process information in an effective way [4]. As a general approach is needed to cover more aspects, we have developed the semantic network further and included an active component to support information propagation.

4.1   Semantic Model

The semantic model is composed of two sets of concepts reflecting the requirements of expertise sharing in product development (Fig. 2). The first set is the Core Expertise Model (CEM) and is composed of six basic concepts - CEM_Element, CEM_Expertise, CEM_TypeOfExpertise and CEM_ExpertiseProvider. We introduce containment concepts CEM_ElementCollection and CEM_ExpertiseGroup. Every concept possesses properties targeted mainly as input fields in the documentation form for a selected element. It is important to note that the semantic model is a description (meta-) model on top of a semantic network and not a concrete representation of the actual elements that it associates.

- CEM_Element represents an element of a model that can be described in a documentation.
- CEM_Expertise represents the actual expertise record, regarding certain know-how, for example coupling of elements, solving of problems and workarounds. Its properties are related only to the abstract representation of the way elements are interacting or coupled.
- CEM_TypeOfExpertise determines the concrete type of expertise associated with a coupling element. It serves as a basic connection to the rest of the elements in the semantic model.
- CEM_ExpertiseProvider serves as association of a human resource or other expert resource responsible for providing knowledge related to a certain expertise. Its properties are directly associated with concepts such as developers/designers, other knowledge bases or literature.
- In a complex environment it is necessary to take into consideration that a collection of elements has to be treated in a different way than a sum of the single elements. A composite element may provide additionally capabilities or filter such in a way to form itself as a separate component. The CEM_ElementCollection represents a composite element as an aggregation of multiple CEM_Element but at the same time has its own values in the set of properties provided by CEM_Element.
- CEM_ExpertiseGroup serves a similar purpose, but regarding to a common knowledge aggregated by participators in a team working on a common product.

The second set are concepts in the Extended Expertise Model (EEM). It extends the core model with concepts related to narrowed expertise areas such as coupling of components, solving conflicts, applying workarounds, etc. EEM is a demonstration of the way CEM can be applied for expertise sharing. Currently the number of these concepts is limited for reasons of keeping the system simple and relevant to the model's application in consistency support.

In order to demonstrate the capability of the model to relate shared expertise we look at the simple examples of modeling a stored expertise for coupling of elements (Fig. 3a), problem description and a possible workaround for the problem (Fig. 3b).

In the presented scenarios designer D2 tries to construct composite element AD2, that consists partially from elements that are already being coupled by designer D1 (AD11-12). In this case the ability to define expertise related not only to atomic elements (AD11, AD12, AD21) but also to composite elements (AD1, AD2) is vital.

This is done using CEM_ElementCollection which inherits the properties of atomic elements but represents its collection of CEM_Elements as a single component that can be used by the expertise. D2 reuses the shared coupling expertise of D1 and constructs element AD2 by adding his expertise of coupling AD1, AD21 in the shared knowledge base.

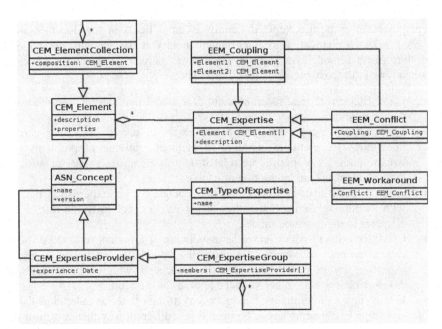

Fig. 2. The Core Expertise Meta-Model – enabling description of expertise relations in project knowledge-bases

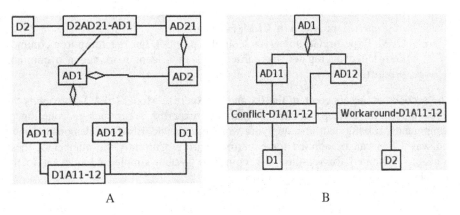

A   B

Fig. 3. Concepts representing relations between conflicts and workarounds filed by different designers

The first scenario involves the ideal case where no problems are experienced. The second scenario illustrates the definition of a problem and corresponding workaround as shared knowledge. (Table 1) shows the mapping of real to semantic entities (concepts) inside the knowledge base.

Problem (or conflict) representation is similar to the way a successful coupling is related to a set of elements. A conflict in coupling of two elements AD11 and AD12 is illustrated in Fig. 3. After a conflict has been discovered it is associated to an

Table 1. Map of entities for utilization

Real Entity	Entity Type	ASN Concept
Designer D1	CEM_ExpertiseProvider	D1
Designer D2	CEM_ExpertiseProvider	D2
Composite Element Type AD1	CEM_ElementCollection	AD1
Composite Element Type AD2	CEM_ElementCollection	AD2
Atomic Element Type AD11	CEM_Element	AD11
Atomic Element Type AD12	CEM_Element	AD12
Atomic Element Type AD21	CEM_Element	AS21
Expertise of Coupling AD11 and AD12	EEM_Coupling	AS11-12
Expertise of Coupling AD1 and AD21	EEM_Coupling	D2AD21-AD1

Table 2. Expressing conflict/solution entities

Real Entity	Entity Type	ASN Concept
Conflict in coupling elements A11 and A12	EEM_Conflict	Conflict-D1A11-12
Solution to the problem of coupling A11-A12	EEM_Workaround	Workaround-D1A11-12

expertise provider. In case a workaround is found it is also filed with its expertise provider. Linking of conflict record to solution record and their respective providers allows, additionally, notification of the designer(s) who has experienced the problem with a concrete coupling of the elements.

4.2 Pro-active Knowledge Delivery

A key advantage of knowledge bases is that they are extensible. Adding functionality to the core semantical meta model is prone to incompatibility or incomplete semantics on the level of the model. That is why the current integration into the semantic network is realized by extending its (ASN) concepts in a natural way and treating the model as an instance of descriptive objects.

This approach does not lead to broken dependencies on the implementation level. A major benefit of this approach is that at the same time queries involved with the concrete instances of the knowledge base artifacts can co-operate with queries targeted at the concepts.

As discussed the model targets context sensitive knowledge navigation in the process of design for better learning experience and communication. The entities are stored using the ASN persistence mechanism (Fig. 4). While the process of storing of ASN concepts does not imply any semantic consistency verification, the requirement for a consistent model requires delivery of relevant consistency feedback to the designer committing changes.

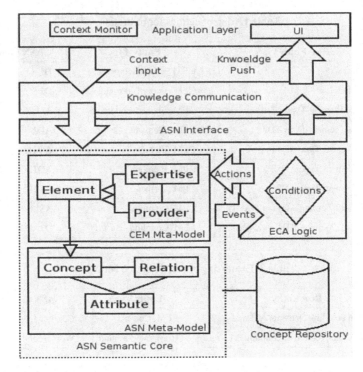

Fig. 4. Expertise distribution using ASN knowledge communication

The ECA feature of ASN is exploited for this requirement by utilization of conditioned triggers hooked to the change of concepts related to CEM_Element, CEM_ExpertiseProvider, CEM_Expertise. The result of a commit action is an on-time update of the context information of the designer modeling tool.

The actual retrieval of the semantical data from the ASN is performed by the developed knowledge communication layer [9] mediating user input and results of the acquired knowledge from the semantic network. Its active elements are embeddable in the user-interface and allow interception of the user-input which is then translated into ASN queries to extract semantically near elements or features.

5   Conclusions

The discussed approach strongly supports cooperative work of designers in distributed environments, working on the same prototype/model, by giving them relevant expertise information in the process of concurrent development. It integrates easily with currently developed methods for knowledge representation as we have shown by introducing and using the active semantic network in this context.

Machine-understandable semantics allow for meaningful query-searches and proactive knowledge propagation to locations and situations where it is needed.

The expertise is not only model-element-related (specific), but is supported also through communication and social relations between designers and provides for more efficient work flows.

References

1. Belkada, S., Cristea, A.I., Okamoto, T.: DiscoverNet: Adaptive Simulation-Based Learning Environment. In: Proc. of Artificial Neural Networks in Engineering (ANNIE'00), Missouri, USA (2000)
2. Kemp, J.L.C., Albiez, A., Wagner, F., Roth, N.: A Knowledge Management Solution for Improving Corporate Product Development. In: Proc. of the International Conference on Concurrent Enterprising (ICE'01), Bremen, Germany, pp. 277–280 (2001)
3. Luo, Y., Galli, R., Sánchez, D., Bennasar, A., Fornés, J., Serra, J.C., Huéscar, J.M., Gayà, J.: A Remote Cooperative Design System Using Interactive 3D Graphics. Int. J. Image Graphics 1(1), 153–167 (2001)
4. Mešina, M., Roller, D., Lampasona, C., Opletal, S.: Ontology-based element-selection in CAD Models, in: Applications of Digital Techniques in Industrial Design Engineering. In: Pan, Y., Vergeest, J., Lin, Z., Wang, C., Sun, S., Hu, Z., Tang, Y., Zhou, L. (eds.) Proceedings of the 6th International Conference on Computer-Aided Industrial Design & Conceptual Design, pp. 413–418. International Academic Publishers, Beijing World Publishing Corporation, Beijing (2005)
5. Sriram, D., Logcher, R.D., Groleau, N., Cherneff, J.: DICE: An Object Oriented Programming Environment For Cooperative Engineering Design. In: Artificial intelligence in engineering design. knowledge acquisition, commercial systems, and integrated environments, vol. III, pp. 303–366. ACM, New York (1992)
6. Opletal, S., Roller, D.: Semantics and Validation of Large Inter-Company Product Models. In: Samuel, A., Lewis, W. (eds.) Engineering Design and the Global Economy, pp. 91–92. Institution of Engineers, Australia (2005)
7. Roller, D., Eck, O., Dalakakis, S.: Knowledge based support of Rapid Product Development. Journal of Engineering Design 15(4), 367–388 (2004)
8. Shapiro, M., Ferreira, P., Richer, N.: Experience with the PerDiS Large-Scale Data-Sharing Middleware. In: Kirby, G.N.C., Dearle, A., Sjøberg, D.I.K. (eds.) Persistent Object Systems. LNCS, vol. 2135, pp. 55–70. Springer, Heidelberg (2001)
9. Dalakakis, S., Stoyanov, E., Roller, D.: A Retrieval Agent Architecture for Rapid Product Development. In: Yan, X.-T., Jiang, C.-Y., Juster, N.P. (eds.) Perspectives from Europe and Asia on Engineering Design and Manufacture, pp. 41–58. Kluwer Academic Publishers, Dordrecht (2004)

A Speech-Controlled User Interface for a CAFM-Based Disaster Management System

Rüdiger Schütz, G. Glanzer, A.P. Merkel, T. Wießflecker, and U. Walder

Graz University of Technology, Institute for Building Informatics,
Lessingstraße 25/I, 8010 Graz, Austria
{ruediger.schuetz,gerald.glanzer,adrian.merkel,
thomas.wiessflecker,ulrich.walder}@tugraz.at
http://bauinformatik.tugraz.at

Abstract. Due to the numerous important decisions with major consequences which have to be taken within a short period of time in case of disasters like fire, terror attacks or floods up-to-date information about the site affected as well as positions and activities of the deployed rescue teams should be available in real-time. This information can firstly be gathered from Computer Aided Facilities Management-systems (CAFM-systems), which are based on the graphical and alphanumerical base data of the building, and are used to manage large real estates and infrastructural installations in developed countries nowadays and secondly by real-time data from master control systems and security installations of the building. Thirdly data from an "inertio-tracker" based on accelerometers and gyroscopes and used for tracking rescue teams within buildings or underground constructions can be implemented to superimpose the building data with actual position information.

The Institute for Building Informatics at Graz University of Technology in cooperation with the security industry is currently researching and developing such a CAFM-based Disaster Management System (DMS). The main challenges are locating and tracking persons, the local information management and the communication between the on-site staff and the command center. This paper gives a brief introduction and description of the whole system with a main focus of outlining the special aspects of an efficient and easy-to-use user interface.

Keywords: user interfaces for CV, CAFM, indoor positioning, interactive visualization, voice user interface, HMD.

1 Introduction

1.1 Necessary Information During Extraordinary Situation

The necessary information during extraordinary situations differs greatly from those needed for the normal management of buildings and installations. Regular CAFM-Data focuses primarily on the efficient and cost-effective management of buildings and only in special areas like energy consumption real-time data is

Y. Luo (Ed.): CDVE 2007, LNCS 4674, pp. 80–87, 2007.

gathered. In emergency situations on the other hand, numerous important decisions have to be taken on the spot which are influenced greatly by the current circumstances. Further, the information has to be made available to people who generally are not familiar with the building in question (such as fire brigades, police force, ambulance crews) and have no or very limited knowledge of using a CAFM-system. Such systems should further be extended to allow for the integration of sensor data (from smoke detectors, location data of emergency crews) and for processing and displaying those data in real-time. Operating the system has to be very easy so that the squad leaders and the emergency crews on-site can be trained within a very short time, and the efficient and safe functioning of the system is guaranteed. These requirements lead among other things to some special aspects to consider when developing a user interaction for emergency units.

1.2   Goals of the CADMS-Project

In the following, some special aspects of the research project 'Computer Aided Disaster Management System' (CADMS) carried out by the Institute for Building Informatics at Graz University of Technology will be outlined. The objective is to develop an easy to use, safe tracking system which allows the permanent real-time representation of information within a CADM-system, with emphasis on the position of rescuers in buildings and underground structures. Such a CADM-system will be based on a widely used, commercial CAFM-system together with integrated sensor data. One major focus is on the development of an efficient and easy to use user interface for the command system – not even the GUI but also the speech enabled interaction – used in emergency situations by the showcase of real-time positioning of people by a multi-sensor system.

2   Graphical and Alphanumerical CAFM Base Data

State-of-the-art CAFM-systems into which a CADMS can be integrated use two different types of base data to describe and evaluate the buildings. By base data the underlying data about the real-estate is meant which is vital to the processes within the building and is therefore absolutely necessary for an efficient CAFM-system to function (Fig. 1). The first type of data is the graphical data and the second one is the alphanumerical data. Graphical data is concerned with the visual representation of the real-estate and its contents. This type of data is particularly important for the CADMS as the process of locating emergency crews within the building is to be based on the existing floor plans of the real-estate in question.

The second type of base data utilised by CAFM-systems is the alphanumerical data. Alphanumerical data mainly describes the 'contents' of a real-estate and is therefore of great importance for the CADMS. The on-site emergency crews need to know for example which hazardous substances are kept on the site and where those are located. Further it is vital to know how many people are in the

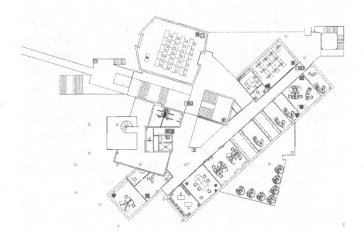

Fig. 1. CAFM Representation of graphical and alphanumerical data [Source: speedikon® FM]

entire building and which offices they utilise so that they can be rescued if needs be. All these information can instantly be extracted from the CAFM-system and then superimposed on the plans used by the emergency crews.

3 Realtime Indoor Positioning

A number of different technologies are available for positioning. Only methods that calculate the position relative to a known environment can be used for indoor positioning. This is due to the technical limitations of systems that use either an absolute position (GNSS) or one relative to the location of external transmitters (GSM, UMTS). Generally, one can distinguish between two different solutions.

3.1 Inertial Tracking

The exact location of an individual is traced from a point of origin using a 3-axis gyroscope and 3 accelerometers so that the position can be displayed in a geometric reference model. This model may be a map, a 3D building model or a $2\frac{1}{2}$D model made up of superimposed floor plans. For the positioning the angles of all 3 axes are constantly measured and from the acceleration the covered distance is calculated using double integration. The precision of the results depends on a number of factors, especially measurement errors by the sensors, the mechanical inaccuracy of the setup of the sensors and the accuracy of the measurements themselves [1]. Further sources of errors are temperature changes and noise. Most of these errors are inconsistent but occur stochastically. Own experiments proved that the goniometry of small, low-cost gyroscopes is only precise enough to allow for the orientation inside a room for a very short period of time under extreme conditions. Therefore, tracking the covered distance fails due to the drift within the inertial system. To overcome these difficulties, the test system which could be used in terms of size and weight uses a novel inertial tracking algorithm based on the movement recognition of the individual. The accuracy of the measurements can be improved by using a Kalman-Filter and periodically repositioning the moving system using known fix-points.

3.2 Additional Sensor Systems

The moving individual continuously positions itself in relation to a point of origin using different sensors. The point of origin is repositioned periodically through measurements and user interaction relative to known points and walls within the building [4].

The choice of the most adequate solution depends on the circumstances under which the system will be applied. It has to be assumed that in extraordinary situations the local infrastructure does not exist anymore and there is no time to set up a new or additional infrastructure. Therefore both solutions could be used for a CADMS. Though, the second solution has some uncertainties as well. Up-to-date floor plans are required, in order to perform constant adjustments of the origin (new fixed points) and calculations of the positions based on the measurements. Problems could arise as these floor plans may have become obsolete because of destructions.

Further means of measurement, such as the laser distance measurements, may be influenced by thick smoke, water from sprinklers or new obstacles (debris for example). Moreover, for the positioning it is necessary that the path can be tracked without interruptions, as the overall position within a building cannot only be determined from the position within a room. The first solution allows less user interaction than the second but relies on periodical repositioning. The need for repositioning is caused by the relatively poor performance of the gyroscopes (heading drift). One possible solution for repositioning may be the use of further sensors (e.g. magnetometers).

4   User Interaction

The possible application of an electronic device in a real-life scenario such as a fire will ultimately be determined by its accuracy and user friendliness. The latter mainly depends on the user interaction. The required information has to be recallable and displayed in real-time. The system to be created not only has to ensure that there is a significant advantage in comparison to the orientation with plans and maps used today but also has to enable the orientation in a situation of no sight due to smoke or concrete dust.

4.1 Graphical User Interface

Even though the development of the graphical interface is still at its early stages several major ideas can already be outlined.

Today it is not necessary to discuss whether or not a virtual 3D building model should be used. Firstly the necessary data is simply not available and secondly in the event of emergency situations information outside the current field of vision is needed. In those situations 2D floor plans provide the best possible orientation. They can easily be adapted to the constantly changing circumstances and needs and may be extended by superimposing additional data.

The main activity at the command centre is controlling, commanding and guiding the rescue teams. The most important information therefore is a 'bird's eye' view over all the events happening on-site. Therefore all the graphical information is displayed using a layer technique. The basic floor plan will be displayed on one layer and is used as a kind of frame for all other information. Further layers containing additional information can then be superimposed on top of the base layer. These superimposed layers could contain crucial information such as the locations of technical installations, hazardous materials and furniture within rooms. In addition to already existing data from the data base can be displayed using shadings, symbols and highlighted texts. Furthermore vital information from the document management system can be visualised. Since the emergency crews and the control room will need a lot of information all the layers mentioned above can be displayed at the same time. This guarantees that the largest possible amount of information can be visualised and therefore be taken into account by the staff in charge. In order to allow for effective communications and of course the safety of the on-site staff the current positions of the rescue teams are constantly updated. Several positions of teams can be displayed simultaneously (Fig. 2).

Displaying the sensor information in real-time is one of the major challenges. In addition to the inertial data the environment will be scanned using a laser rage metre and the results of the measurements will be displayed on the floor

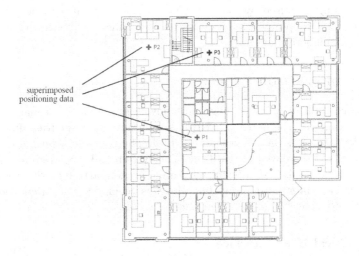

Fig. 2. Superimposed ground plan and positioning information

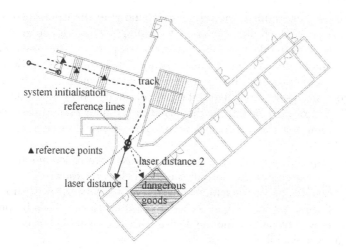

Fig. 3. Track and position representation of an emergency crew

plan. The measurement results of the current position as well as the reference points will be represented in the floor plan using colours and symbols (Fig. 3).

In order to avoid an 'information overload' meaning too much information to handle at any given moment in time, only data crucial for the current situation and tasks on hand is to be displayed.

4.2 Voice-Controlled Interaction

The user interface of the mobile devices will have to adhere to certain boundary conditions. First of all the interaction can only be in form of voice entry. It has to be assumed that the emergency crews will wear gloves and of course need their hands for the rescue-related tasks. Therefore the user-interaction will have to take the form of speech recognition for the rescue crews to use the system.

In case of an extraordinary situation, the emergency crews using the CADMS will have to make numerous other very important decisions. Therefore the user-interaction by voice control has to be as simple as possible in order not to distract the staff from their main tasks. It has to be ensured that commands which are very likely to be used in the situation have to be on a high level in the control hierarchy. A two-layer command structure for controlling the CADM-system could be a possibility with commands like *"reposition – column"* to reinitialise the tracking system, *"display – next exit"* to highlight special aspects in the GUI or *"pan – up"* to move the ground plan and furthermore all vital commands such as zoom, displaying and hiding layers should be accessible that simple.

The user interface and users' interaction with a CADMS have to be optimised for the different users of the system. This is particularly important as for example the squad leader in the control room will most certainly require different information and possibilities for interventions than the on-site rescue team. Therefore it is reasonable to implement shortcuts to the "top-ten" of the most important commands used. For example the rescue unit who is in the front line could just obtain commands enabled like *"persons"* to highlight other rescue units or *"water"* for the next available water supply to be displayed. The research of the actually amount of information required in an extraordinary situation will be carried out in cooperation with the project partners from the security industry.

Any important observations like collapsed columns or broken fire doors made by the rescue teams also have to be displayed in the floor plan almost instantly. In order to allow for this, a voice-controlled red-lining function needs to be implemented.

The most auspicious technology to realize a speech-controlled mobile system is VoiceXML. It is a standardized format based on the well known XML-standard to specify interactive human-machine voice dialogues. VoiceXML is supposed to gain an easy format for building speech-based applications. It has be proven to be an adequate way to build a mobile device with voice-enabled user-interaction in a technical context [3].

4.3   Hardware

In terms of the hardware, the current aim is to use a so called Head Mounted Display (HMD) (Fig. 4) for displaying the graphical user interface. In addition the HMD is to be equipped with a microphone to allow for the voice control as well as all other crucial verbal communications. Again, a number of crucial factors arise and have to be taken account of.

To ensure the usability of the system it has to be created in such a way that it is like any other existing piece of equipment the emergency crews already have in use. In the end the CADMS is there to help and must not interfere with any of the tasks on hand.

The HMD has to be suitable to the extreme circumstances under which it will be used. Any malfunctions of the system or even complete failures can lead to potentially life-threatening situations for the on-site emergency crews.

Fig. 4. Head Mounted Display in combination with a helmet [©Liteye Systems, Inc.]

Another problem that ties in with the suitability is the microphone. It has to effectively filter all the background noises in order to minimise the possibility of system malfunctions and to ensure that the verbal commands can be recognised by the system.

5 Expected Results

Rescue organisations in future shall take advantage of an integrated CADM-system, which supports the management of disasters based on commonly used CAFM-data and data gained through active sensors. A prototype which allows the tracking of people in buildings and the graphical representation of all necessary information in an ad-hoc network of static and mobile equipment will be developed. Special attention is given to developing a simple user interface for the mobile components based on a HMD and speech recognition. Such a multimodal user interface could be applicable not only in special emergency situations but even in daily routine work in the AEC-business by the showcase of an inspection engineer who needs access to the reinforcement plans on a construction site. The main goal of the project still is the reduction of injuries and damage in case of extraordinary events.

References

1. Barbour, N.M., Elwell, J.M., Setterlund, R.H.: Inertial Systems: Where to Now. The Charles Stark Draper Laboratory, Inc., Cambridge, Massachusetts 02139, USA, AIAA-92-4414-CP, pp. 566-574
2. Glanzer, G.: An Indoor Positioning System Based on MEMS Inertial Sensor Technology. In: Proceedings of Sensor + Test 2007, Nürnberg, Germany (2007)
3. Kondratova, I.: Speech-Enabled Mobile Field Applications. In: Proceedings of the International Association of Science and Technology (IASTED) International Conference on Internet an Multimedia Systems (IMSA), Hawaii, USA (2004)
4. Retscher, G., Thienelt, M.: NAVIO - A Navigation and Guidance Service for Pedestrians. Journal of Global Positioning Systems 3(1-2), 208–217 (2004)
5. Walder, U.: Integration of Computer Aided Facility Management Data and Real-Time Information in Disaster Management. In: Proceedings of ECPPM2006, Valencia, Spain (2006)

Private Data Management in Collaborative Environments*

Larry Korba, Ronggong Song, George Yee, Andrew S. Patrick,
Scott Buffett, Yunli Wang, and Liqiang Geng

Institute for Information Technology, National Research Council of Canada
Building M-50, Montreal Road, Ottawa, Ontario K1A 0R6
{Larry.Korba,Ronggong.Song,
George.Yee,Andrew.Patrick,Scott.Buffett,Yunli.Wang,
Liqiang.Geng}@nrc-cnrc.gc.ca
http://iit-iti.nrc-cnrc.gc.ca

Abstract. Organizations are under increasing pressures to manage all of the personal data concerning their customers and employees in a responsible manner. With the advancement of information and communication technologies, improved collaboration, and the pressures of marketing, it is very difficult to locate personal data is, let alone manage its use. In this paper, we outline the challenges of managing personally identifiable information in a collaborative environment, and describe a software prototype we call SNAP (Social Networking Applied to Privacy). SNAP uses automated workflow discovery and analysis, in combination with various text mining techniques, to support automated enterprise management of personally identifiable information.

Keywords: Privacy, compliance, workflow, social network analysis.

1 Introduction

The quantity of personal data that organizations must manage is increasing at a phenomenal rate. The main reason is the dramatic increase in the exploitation of communication and network technologies for collaboration, marketing, and sales. Other contributing factors include competitive pressures, as well as inexpensive computers and mass storage. While the amount of personal data is increasing, the prevalence of computer and network-based collaborations has made it very difficult for organizations to know where all the private data is stored and exactly how it is being used. This can occur despite attempts at controlling access to the data through centralization.

In the reality of the collaborative environments of today, the prospect of assuring privacy compliance, as may be required by legislation, regulations, or best practices, has become almost impossible. Our approach towards a solution is to combine several technologies in a manner that would allow organizations to understand and manage the life cycle of private data. The different technologies include: private data

---

* National Research Council Paper Number 49356.

Y. Luo (Ed.): CDVE 2007, LNCS 4674, pp. 88–96, 2007.

discovery, social network (workflow) analysis, knowledge visualization, and effective human-computer interaction operating within a policy enforcement framework. Private data discovery involves text and data mining techniques to determine the location and use of personally identifiable information (PII) in different contexts across an organization. Social network analysis produces an understanding of workflow activities related to PII, providing measures for assessment of compliance with privacy policies, and a means for performing forensics analyses on the activities related to private data. In this paper we detail the challenges organizations have with privacy compliance, describe our progress in the development of a prototype for an automated privacy compliance system, outline early results, and detail the further challenges we are exploring.

2 Problem Description

The challenges for businesses today in the handling private data can be understood by referring to Figure 1. Key factors that put pressures on increasing the amount of private data collected include:

- Cheap Storage. Storage costs continue to drop so there are few impediments to collecting growing amounts of data of all sorts.
- Expanded Services. As new services are put in place, often more PII in different forms is collected and stored in order to assess product or service quality, and to facilitate follow-on sales.
- Marketing and Competition. Marketing pressures stemming from the desire to improve existing products and services or from competitive market conditions often lead to the collection and retention of more PII, e.g. e-service personalization where the consumer's contextual product selections are tracked for service improvement.
- Increasing Client Numbers. As an organization provides more products and services, and they become popular, more clients are garnered, leading to the collection and retention of larger amounts of PII.
- Computers Everywhere. Within organizations, desktop, portable, and handheld computers are being deployed at a high rate, due to their convenience and decreasing costs. The computers enable staff to share the work of creating and delivering services and products, which can lead to distributed, local storage of PII.

The pressures to decrease the amount of PII stored and managed within an organization include the following:

- Risk Management. Loss of customer PII is injurious not only to the customer but also to the organization. Data breaches can lead to lost sales due to a decrease in client trust. These risks can be reduced by minimizing PII collection and retention.
- Regulations and Policies. An organization may operate in a regulated sector (healthcare, banking, legal services, gaming, etc.) where there are specific, mandatory requirements for PII handling. In addition, an organization may have its own policies to manage its business and to evoke a stronger level of client trust.
- Legislation Enforcement. Beyond regulatory requirements, some jurisdictions, such as the European Union, may have legislation in place specifying how different types of PII must be handled.

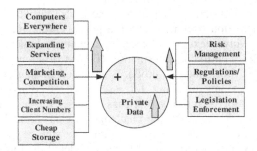

Fig. 1. This is a schematic representation of the pressures on organizations concerning their collection and handling of personal data. The magnitude of the pressures to increase the collection of data (left side) is currently greater than pressures to control access and use (right side).

While the analysis depicted in Figure 1 illustrates the pressures that are leading to increases in the amounts and type of personal data collected and retained, another consequence has to do with how technologies are used. With the widespread availability of computers, networks, and collaboration tools, there is a dramatic increase in the numbers of work artifacts that may be shared amongst different staff. This may be by design (dictated by the organizational workflow), or by necessity (for instance, deferring to the shared experience of others or spreading the work among different geographic locations). The result is that PII may be readily shared amongst many different users, leading to challenges for the organization to understand fully where private data is stored, whether it is accurate, and how it has been used. It is within this context that we are developing technology to make it easier for organizations to manage personally identifiable information.

3   Our Approach

In our approach, which we call Social Network Applied to Privacy (SNAP), we have combined data mining techniques to discover PII, social network analysis to reveal workflows, automated analysis for decision making on PII usage, and data visualization techniques to improve understanding within in the organization, all mediated by electronically-readable policies. The system architecture is agent-based, with the SNAP agent, as described in [1], installed on every computer within the enterprise.

3.1   Overall Design

Figure 2 provides a high-level view of the SNAP system. The system consists of separate parts or modules that perform different functions:

- Machine-readable rules express privacy and security policies, and the prescribed workflow for the organization. This information is interpreted to control the operation of the SNAP system.
- Data collection is performed by a SNAP monitor agent that collects data from the host computer system by searching the file systems and monitoring system activities.
- Analysis involves the discovery and affirmation of personally identifiable information, examining any relationships among the personal data, and the

determination of PII work flows based upon comparisons of local activities with the activities of others in the organization. Outputs from the analyses processes are displayed to the system operators and, depending upon the appropriate policies, can lead to automatic actions.

- The display functions present different aspects of the collected and analyzed data to the system operators. The displays include tables of raw data and graphical images of social networks based on the correlated operations by multiple users.
- Actions performed by the system are determined by policies. They can be prescriptive or reflexive. Prescriptive actions are, for example, warnings to an end user or a system operator about a policy breach involving some from of personal data. Reflexive actions include taking security and access control measures to prevent a breach of a privacy policy before it occurs.

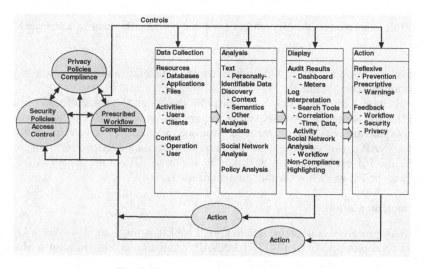

Fig. 2. The overall framework for SNAP

Figure 3 provides more details on the data collection and analysis portions of the system. At the lowest level, data is collected from two main sources: the file system and system hooks. When the SNAP agent is first installed, the file system is searched for PII. This allows for existing (historical) private data to be discovered, and for the data discovery to be updated should additional data be added to the system or the privacy policies changed.

Anytime that SNAP is running, system hooks are used to interrogate user activities (including current file activity) for the presence of PII. In order to lower the processing load and to limit the data collected, we restrict the data collection to certain privacy-sensitive contexts, such as when the user is using an email application or a web-based email account. In these cases, keystrokes and other information is passed onto the SNAP system for PII discovery. Discovery is currently done through regular expression matching and semantic analysis. The current prototype supports discovery of postal addresses, email addresses, titles, dates, dollar amounts, religion, and race. Strings of characters that appear to be credit card or social insurance numbers are also assessed further using Luhn's algorithm [2]. Due to the potentially large and varied

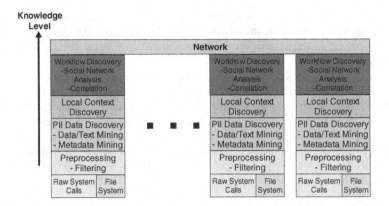

Fig. 3. This figure presents the data collection and analysis hierarchy amongst a series of SNAP agents

search scope, we have attempted to optimize the efficiency and order of the regular expression matching routines.

Local context discovery involves measuring the distance between locally discovered PII. This is done to assess whether disparate discovered PII should be grouped together (potentially as part of one record for one individual). For correlation discovery, the SNAP agents communicate with one another, on a peer-to-peer basis, to determine the PII events that are common among users. This information is used to determine the PII workflows within an organization.

3.2 Implementation

Our SNAP prototype is implemented in C++, Java [3] and uses the Java Agent Development Environment (JADE) [4]. Each SNAP installation is comprised of a Monitor Agent, and an Interface Agent, and these agents are described in [1].

The discovery of PII, through file system searches or system monitoring, is captured in detailed event logs that are stored locally for later analysis and display. The event information is analyzed to build a model of local interactions with PII. These events can be checked against policies for permissible or prohibited authorizations, actions, types of data, or retention periods on a user by user basis. Additionally, in order to discover the workflow patterns, each SNAP agent communicates with the other agents operating on other computers in the enterprise eliciting requests for matches between with their locally discovered PII. If and when other agents find a match, it is reported back to the requesting agent.

A SNAP user can display reports about interactions on all local PII, or on all the interactions within the organization. The displays may be modified based upon time, type of data, agreement/disagreement with policy information, etc., or filtered to search for interactions of special interest.

4   Results

The SNAP prototype features a multi-pane display, shown in Figure 4. A user can select from different display modes, filtering the data as required. Figure 4 shows the

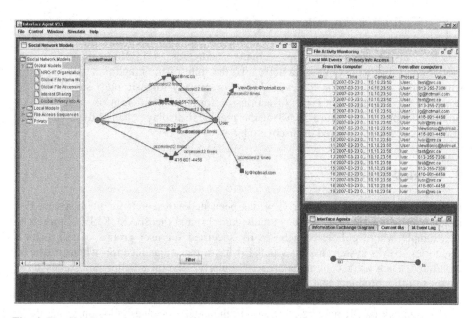

Fig. 4. The SNAP interface when two individuals ("luor" and "User") access multiple forms of PII

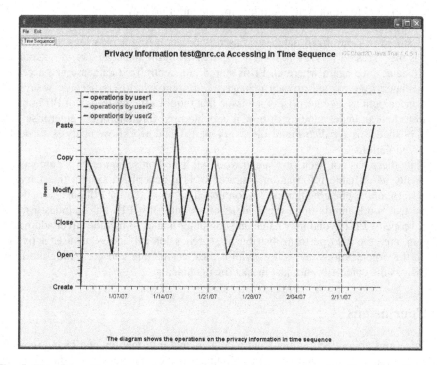

Fig. 5. This figure illustrates a time sequence of operations on email address "test@nrc.ca" (private data in this case) over time, amongst three users

display of several different PII accessed by two users. In this example the users "luor" and "User" both accessed two email addresses and two telephone numbers, while "User" also accessed the email addresses "lg@hotmail.com" and "viewSonic@hotmail.com" separately.   To the right of the graph is a table showing some of the data from the PII event logs. For privacy forensic purposes, it may be useful to see the different types of actions performed by different users at different times, as depicted in Figure 5. All of the graphical displays change dynamically as new PII is accessed, entered or discovered.

5 Related Work

Policy-based management of privacy has been under research for many years. For instance, IBM's Enterprise Privacy architecture [5] and the SPARCKLE [6] project is an example where policies can be easily specified for user groups or information categories. IBM's system assumes that PII has a particular location where it can be monitored, such as a central database. Similarly, several smaller companies have begun to offer products that focus on various policy-based management approaches towards limiting insider threats (e.g., Vontu, Oakley Networks, and others) [7]. Our work assumes that PII may be anywhere in the enterprise, but builds on some of the techniques for insider threat detection, and focuses on the discovery of PII and social network analysis to discover privacy-related workflows to understand the context of work on PII and to support the overall enforcement of privacy policies.

In the academic research domain, systems like PRIVDAM [8] focus on protection of PII stored in centralized databases based upon analyzing access logs. Other work such as the "Trusted Privacy Manager" [9] deals with the management of outsourced private data, once again where all PII is stored in a centralized database and accesses are mediated by a trusted privacy manager. Our approach differs because we regard PII management as an enterprise-wide issue that requires the discovery of PII in many locations and an understanding of how it is being used throughout the enterprise. We accomplished this by distributed discovery of PII and workflow analysis to detect privacy violations.

While there has not been very much work published on scanning of documents for personally identifiable information, Aura et al. [10] describe a system that harvests text strings and applies regular expression matching to search for PII leakage in documents. Our work builds upon those ideas of scanning for PII, but includes a much wider scope of PII beyond user name and computer names to include street addresses, religion, etc. We also perform distributed searches for PII across all user activities within the organizations, as well as within files, correlating and presenting the findings across the enterprise, not just in specific documents.

6 Conclusions

Organizations are collecting more and more personal information, and facing increasing pressure to manage and to protect it. In this paper we have described the pressures on organizations regarding personally identifiable information and have introduced and described the development of our SNAP system, which can automate the management of personally identifiable information within an organization.

One of the technical challenges we face is to reduce the false positives and false negatives when discovering PII. We currently use regular expression matching and Luhn's algorithm to discover potential PII, and we measure the similarity between the discovered PII (time of occurrence, or location in files) to group disparate data that may be attached to the same user. We are currently assessing other means for discovering PII, including semantic feature analysis (looking for features around groupings of text that may indicate PII, even though it is not found with regular expression matching), and rule-based PII discovery (analysis employing dictionaries, domain ontologies, and rule-based matching). Additionally, we are expanding our use of context and workflow analysis to substantiate the discovery of PII.

Other technical challenges include PII contained within images. For instance, screen snapshots of PII records, or photographs of individuals, may represent sensitive information for individuals or organizations. It is a considerable technical challenge to search all image data in all file types within an organization for what might be personally identifiable information. A first step to this challenge is to use the location and creation time of picture objects to determine the possible links with PII being processed concurrently. Through our workflow analysis we can also use the context of linked files (images and text) but there is still a chance that images of significance may be missed.

Another challenge is presented by links or indirect references to PII. The information pointed to by links (e.g., hyperlinks or database references) may contain very sensitive information, yet without following and analyzing all of those links, their significance may be missed. With respect to metadata, data used to describe other data, there is a challenge in being able to accommodate all of the possible varieties of metadata, including both machine-readable and human-readable metadata types. The metadata problem is complicated because people working alone, or in collaboration, often use a variety of different tools, often in ways not originally envisioned by the developers. This leads to rather complicated metadata for analysis.

Appropriate visualization of any discovered knowledge and representing the relationships between workflows and PII handling is another area where there are interesting challenges. It is not sufficient (or even possible, in some cases) to display the multitude of instances of PII found within an organization. Analyzing workflow and comparing it against prescribed workflow or authorizations to highlight problem areas and risks is one approach we are exploring. Other approaches include display and navigation through multidimensional data spaces.

Other research underway in our team includes developing techniques to recommend corrections in privacy and security policies or workflow models based upon the measured workflow patterns. We are also exploring improved techniques for extracting workflows (represented as colored Petri nets), security techniques to protect SNAP agents, their datasets, and communications, and instilling trust in the system operators and employees within an enterprise [11].

A clear social challenge is the fact that our technology has the potential to monitor and analyze many different user activities and behaviors as people work individually or in collaboration. We have attempted to address this by layering the functionalities within our system so it only tracks events that relate to PII processing in the context of particular operations. It is our intention to work with potential end users from different industries of this type of automated privacy management technology (e.g., the banking industry) in order to set functionality targets and research goals that will address the real challenges for managing private data in those domains.

Acknowledgements

The authors acknowledge the programming support of Luc Belliveau and the development contributions of Arlen Gallant and Rougu Lou.

References

1. Korba, L., Song, R., Yee, G., Patrick, A.: Automated social network analysis for collaborative work. In: Luo, Y. (ed.) CDVE 2006. LNCS, vol. 4101, Springer, Heidelberg (2006)
2. Luhn's Algorithm on Wikipedia (last accessed March 20 2007), http://en.wikipedia.org/wiki/Luhn_algorithm
3. Java programming language. Available at: http://java.sun.com/ (March 2007)
4. Jade Platform available at: http://sharon.cselt.it/projects/jade/ (March 2007)
5. Ashley, P., Powers, C., Schunter, M.: From privacy promises to privacy management: a new approach for enforcing privacy throughout an enterprise. In: Proc. of the, New Security Paradigms Workshop, Virginia Beach, Virgina, pp. 43–50 (2002)
6. SPARCKLE (Server Privacy ARchitecture and CapabiLity Enablement) policy Workbench, IBM Watson Labs available at: http://domino.watson.ibm.com/comm/research.nsf/pages/r.security.innovation2.html (March 2007)
7. Heck, M.: Guard your data against insider threats, Oakley, Reconnex, Tablus and Vontu prevent costly data leaks, available at: http://www.infoworld.com/article/06/01/13/73680_03TCdataleak_1.html (March 2007)
8. Bhattacharya, J., Dass, R.: Kapoor, Vishal, Chakraborti, D., Gupta, S.K.: PRIVDAM: privacy violation detection and monitoring using data mining, available at: http://ideas.repec.org/p/iim/iimawp/2005-07-01.html (March 2007)
9. Carminati, B., Ferrari, E.: Trusted privacy manager: a system for privacy enforcement of outsourced data. In: Proc. of the 21st workshop on Data Engineering, April 5-8, 2005, pp. 1195–1203 (2005)
10. Aura, T., Kuhn, T.A., Roe, M.: Scanning Electronic Documents for Personally Identifiable Information. In: Proc. of the 5th ACM Workshop on Privacy in Electronic Society, Alexandria, Virgina, pp. 41–50 (2006)
11. Patrick, A.S., Briggs, P., Marsh, S.: Designing systems that people will trust. In: Cranor, L., Garfinkel, S. (eds.) Security and Usability: Designing Secure Systems That People Can Use, O'Reilly & Associates (2005)

A Scalable Method for Efficient Grid Resource Discovery

Yan Zhang[1], Yan Jia[1], Xiaobin Huang[2], Bin Zhou[1], and Jian Gu[1]

[1] School of Computer Science, National University of Defense Technology,
Changsha,410073 China
Jane325@tom.com
[2] Department of Information Engineering, Air Force Radar Academy,
Wuhan, 430019 ,China
Hxbtougao@gmail.com

Abstract. How to discover resource rapidly and exactly in distributed and heterogeneous grid environment is a key problem that affects grid computing performance. In this paper, the P2P method is used to improve scalability of resource discovery mechanism, and a decentralized resource discovery method with well scalability is presented, this method uses binary tree to manage data, each node in grid is responsible for managing a part of resource information. Experimental result shows that the method presented in this paper can resolve many problems that exist in centralized mechanism, such as poor scalability, heavy load on resource information server and single point failure.

Keywords: Grid Computing, Resource Discovery, P2P, Binary Tree.

1 Introduction

The grid [1] is a large scale distributed computing environment supporting scientific applications that require high throughput computation. The computing resources in the grid are workstations and supercomputers distributed across the Internet. Resources are contributed to the system by a number of different autonomous entities. Applications have different requirements for the number and capabilities of the resources to complete their execution. So, how to look up resources rapidly and exactly in grid environment is important to the grid performance.

The early grid resource discovery methods are mainly based on centralized mechanism. As grid size grows rapidly, we should decentralize resource discovery methods to avoid performance bottlenecks. P2P [2] systems have been proven to be highly scalable and highly available which are indicated by the popularity of file sharing applications among users. So using P2P principle to design a well scalable grid resource discovery method will be a good idea.

In this paper, we use binary tree to manage resource information. Each node in the grid manages a part of resource information and maintains a routing table in order to dispatch queries to neighbor nodes. Resource providers publish their resource information to corresponding node based on some rules. Therefore, each node in the grid can acts as resource information server, which not only avoids putting too much load on one resource information server, but also resolves the problem of poor scalability existing in centralized discovery methods.

Y. Luo (Ed.): CDVE 2007, LNCS 4674, pp. 97–103, 2007.

The rest of this paper is organized as follows. Section 2 presents the related work. Section 3 introduces how to allocate, manage and publish resource information. Section 4 discusses how to process resource query and gives the resource search algorithm. Section 5 gives our grid prototype and presents experimental results. Finally, section 6 presents the conclusion.

2 Related Work

A lot of work has been done on the grid resource discovery mechanism. Early grid resource discovery is based on centralized mechanism, Globus Toolkit [3], Condor [4] and Legion [5] are the excellent examples. The MDS-4 (Monitoring and Discovery Services) of Globus Toolkit provides a Web Service Resource Framework (WSRF) [6] compliant implementation of the Index Service, as well as novel mechanisms for delivering notifications in the presence of events that match a set of specified rules (Trigger Service). Matchmaker in Condor uses a centre server to match the attributes in the user's specification and those in the service providers' declaration. Such approach has a single point of failure and scales poorly. In Legion, Collections, the information database, are populated with resource description. The scheduler queries the Collection and finds proper resource for applications. A few global Collections will prohibit the scalability of the system.

Much work has been done to improve the scalability of resource discovery methods. A typical solution is offered by P2P models. In [7], information nodes are organized into a flat unstructured network and various request-forwarding policies are studied. This approach suffers from higher numbers of required hops to resolve a query compared to our approach and provides no lookup guarantees, i.e., an unsuccessful lookup does not necessarily mean that no resource meeting the requirements because a suitable peer was simply not reached. A DHT based service discovery approach is studied in [8]. Another study [9] organizes information nodes into hierarchical topologies to reduce redundant messages. An information node grouping technique is also studied in [10], in which information nodes are randomly grouped together. In [11], Talia et al. propose a P2P architecture for resource discovery in OGSA-compliant Grids, within each VO (Virtual Organization), a hierarchy of Index Services provides information about local resources. Discovery messages are routed across Peer Services using a modified Gnutella protocol. In this method, the centralized mechanism is used when searching resources within one VO. All these methods are not totally decentralized, and some of them also adopt centralized mechanism, whereas our method is a fully distributed one by making each node in the grid as information server.

3 Management and Publication of Resource Information

3.1 Management of Resource Information

The resources provided by nodes have feature of diversity, they can be data, service or computation resources. The resources described in this paper are computation resources. This kind of resource commonly has the following attributes: CPU_GHz and Memory_MB. The attribute CPU_GHz describes the frequency of CPU, and the attribute Memory_MB describes the capacity of memory. For example, a resource can be described as CPU_GHz=1.6 and Memory_MB=1024.

In this paper, we use the data structure of binary tree to manage grid resource information. Taking resources with two attributes as our examples, the root node of the binary tree is responsible for the total research space. Below the root node, We partition the resource attribute in each layer alternately, in other words, the first attribute is dimidiate in the first layer, and the second attribute is dimidiate in the next layer, this process is done recursively. One attribute after n partitions is divided into 2^n parts. Resources with more than two attributes can be done similarly. The number of layers is determined by concrete applications. An example for processing resources with two attributes, namely CPU_GHz and Memory_MB, is described as follows.

If the upper bound of CPU is T, then the attribute range of CPU_GHz is $[0,T]$. After one partition, this range is divided into $[0,T/2)$ and $[T/2,T]$; if the upper bound of Memory is H, then after one partition, the attribute range of Memory_MB is divided into $[0,H/2)$ and $[H/2,H]$. In order to avoid overlap of attribute range, we assume that the left range is close, and the right range is open. In the above example, if we let T=5, H=1024, then after one partition of attribute CPU_GHz and Memory_MB, the corresponding binary tree is shown as figure 1.

Each leaf node in the binary tree has a corresponding path. We append "0" to each "left-turn" or "1" otherwise. Then, the path of a leaf node is a binary string which is composed of bits from the root node to this leaf node. For example, the path of node 1 is "00", and the path of node 4 is "11".

In the binary tree, the data stored by each leaf node has its path as prefix. For instance, the path of node 1 in figure 1 is "00", so it stores all data whose prefix is "00".

Initially, all nodes are responsible for the whole search space, i.e. all search keys. At that stage, when two nodes meet initially, they decide to split the search space into two parts and take over responsibility for one half each. They also stored the reference to the other node in order to cover the other part of the search space. The same happens whenever two nodes meeting. We call this operation "meet-exchange". With the meeting and exchanging between nodes, all nodes in a grid are mapping to the leaf nodes in a binary tree. Of course, there may be many grid nodes mapping to the same node in the binary tree (here these nodes are called duplicate nodes). When this occasion happens, it is good for avoiding single point failure.

In this paper, the binary tree is a virtual tree. In order to guarantee that the search can start at any node, all nodes maintain a routing table. For each bit in its path, a node stores a reference to at least one other peer that is responsible for the other side of the binary tree at that level, shown as figure 2.

3.2 Publication of Resource Information

When a node decides to publish its resource information, it firstly checks whether the resource information is in the range maintained by itself or not. If the resource information is in the range that it maintains, then the resource information would be published on this node, otherwise, it would be published on other node which is

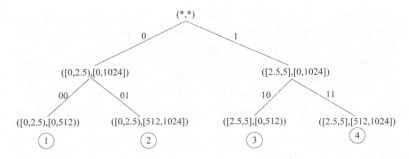

Fig. 1. The corresponding resource attribute binary tree after one partition

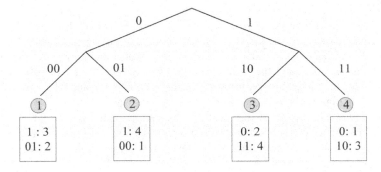

Fig. 2. The information of the routing table. The item of routing table $i{:}p$ denotes sending the resource request to node p when the prefix is i.

responsible for this resource information. Therefore, all nodes in the grid can act as information server, which avoid putting too heavy load in one node.

For example, the information of a resource that described as CPU_GHz=1.6, Memory_MB=512 should be published on node 2, because from figure 1, we know that node 2 is responsible for resources whose CPU frequency is between 0G and 2.5G, and Memory capacity is between 512M and 1024M.

4 Handling of Resource Query

In actual applications, the requested resources are specified in terms of range predicates, e.g., CPU_GHz≥1.6 and Memory_MB≥512, which means that all the resources with CPU frequency higher than 1.6G and less than 5G, and Memory capacity greater than 512M and less than 1024M are satisfied user's request. Therefore, the resource request is actually a range query. A resource query can be processed as follows. First, we decide the lower and higher bounds for the current request, then find the two corresponding nodes in the binary tree that are responsible for the lower and higher bounds, finally the query range is composed by two paths of the found nodes. For example, if the required resource is described as CPU_GHz≥1.6 and Memory_MB≥512, then the corresponding query range is [01, 11].

In our method, a range query algorithm is presented. When query arrives at a node, this node will first check whether its responsible search space is in this query, if so, it returns immediately, otherwise, it would forward this query to other node according its routing table. The process is recursive. The range query algorithm is shown as follows:

```
Query(R, l_current , p)
    If path(p) ⊆ R then
        Return (d ∈ δ(p)| key(d) ∈ R )
    End if
    l_l = length of commonPrefix(Lower(R), path(p))
    l_h = length of commonPrifix(Upper(R), path(p))
    mLevel= min(max(l_l , l_h ), length of path(p)-1)
    For (int i= mLevel; l ≥ l_current ; l-- )
        r = randomly selected element from REFS_l
        If path(r) ⊆ R then
            Query(R, l+1,r)
        End if
    End for
```

Comment: 1. $path(p) = p_1 p_2 \dots p_n$: The path of node p ;

2. $\delta(p)$ denotes the data that stored by node p , For any $d \in \delta(p)$, the binary key $key(d)$ is calculated using a hash function.

3. commonPrefix($p_1 \cdots p_k \; p_{k+1} \cdots p_n$, $p_1 \cdots p_k \; q_{k+1} \cdots q_l$)$= p_1 \cdots p_k$

4. Lower(R) means the lower bound of range R

5. Upper(R) means the upper bound of range R.

5   Experiment

We design and implement a grid prototype called StarGrid which based on the method presented in this paper. The StarGrid uses some components in P-Grid[12], which have been modified to adapt to our system.

As the scalability of discovery methods is the main topic of this paper, we did some experiments in order to answer the following question: how does the performance of our method scale when the size of the grid increasing?

Throughput and response time are the primary metrics in our study. We define throughput as the average number of requests (or queries) processed by a service component per second. The response time denotes the average amount of time (in seconds) required for a service component to handle a request from a user.

We did experiments about four methods, i.e., Globus Toolkit MDS-4, the methods presented in paper [3] and paper [8] and our method. The number of nodes in the grid increased from 500 to 1500. The results of our experiments are shown as follows.

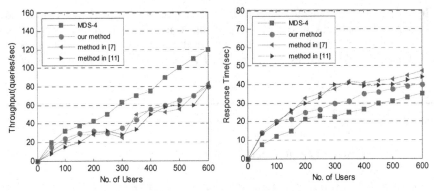

Fig. 3. Throughput vs. No of Concurrent Users. (The number of nodes in grid=500).

Fig. 4. Response Time vs. No of Concurrent Users.(The number of nodes in grid=500).

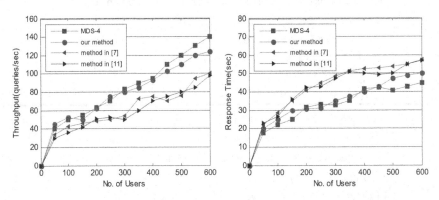

Fig. 5. Throughput vs. No of Concurrent Users. (The number of nodes in grid=1000).

Fig. 6. Response Time vs. No of Concurrent Users.(The number of nodes in grid=1000).

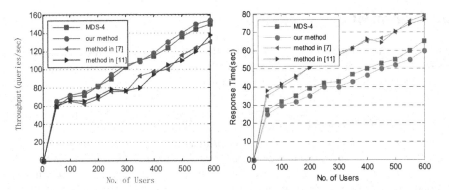

Fig. 7. Throughput vs. No of Concurrent Users. (The number of nodes in grid=1500).

Fig. 8. Response Time vs. No of Concurrent Users.(The number of nodes in grid=1500).

From figure 3 to figure 8, we can see that when the number of the node in the grid is small, the Globus Toolkit MDS-4 has better performance than ours. As the grid size growing, our method has better performance than Globus Toolkit MDS-4 and the methods in [7] and [11].

The experimental results proved the feasibility and scalability of the method presented in this paper. This method can not only resolve the problem of single-point failure, but also can improve the scalability of the grid resource discovery mechanism.

6 Conclusion

In this paper, a new method for resource discovery in grid environment is proposed. The P2P technology is applied to deal with poor scalability of centralized resource discovery mechanism. This method uses binary tree to manage resource information, each node in grid is responsible for managing a part of resource information. Experimental result shows that the method presented in this paper can resolve many problems that exist in centralized method, such as poor scalability, heavy load on resource information server and single point failure.

Acknowledgments. This work is supported by 973 project (No. 2005CB321800) of China.

References

1. Foster, I., Kesselman, C., Tuecke, S.: The Anatomy of the Grid: Enabling Scalable Virtual Organization. The International Journal of Supercomputer Applications 15(3), 200–222 (2001)
2. Dejanm, S.M., Vana, K., Rajan, L.: Peer-to-Peer Computing. http://www.hpl.hp.com/techreports/2002/HPL-2002-57R1.pdf
3. Globus project: http://www.globus.org
4. Raman, R., Livny, M., Solomon, M.: Matchmaking: Distributed Resource Management for High Throughput Computing. In: Proc of the 7th IEEE HPDC, pp. 140–146. IEEE Computer Society Press, Washington, DC (1998)
5. Chapin, S.J., Katramatos, D., Karpovich, J., Grimshaw, A.: Resource Management in Legion. Future Generation Computer System 15(5), 583–594 (1999)
6. Czajkowski, K., Ferguson, D., Foster, I., Frey, J., Graham, S.: The WS-Resource Framework Version 1.0, http://www-106.ibm.com/developerworks/library/ws-resource/ws-wsrf.pdf
7. Iamnitchi, A., Foster, I.: On Fully Decentralized Resource Discovery in Grid Environments. In: Proceedings of 2nd IEEE/ACM International Workshop on Grid Computing 2001, pp. 51–62 (2001)
8. Andrzejak, A., Xu, Z.: Scalable, Efficient Range Queries for Grid Information Services. In: Proceedings of IEEE P2P 2002, pp. 33–40 (2002)
9. Huang, L., Wu, Z., Pan, Y.: A Scalable and Effective Architecture for Grid services' Discovery. In:Proceedings of SemPGRID 2003, pp. 103–115 (2003)
10. Chander, A., Dawson, S., Lincoln, P., et al.: NEVRLATE: Scalable Resource Discovery. In: Proceedings of IEEE/ACM CCGrid 2002, pp. 382–388 (2002)
11. Domenico, T., Paolo, T.: Web Services for Peer-to-Peer Resource Discovery on the Grid. In: DELOS Workshop: Digital Library Architecture, pp. 73–84 (2004)
12. Karl, A., Philippe, C., Anwitaman, D.: P-Grid: A Self-organizing Structured P2P System. ACM SIGMOD Record 32, 29–33 (2003)

Modeling and Analysis for Grid Service Cooperative Scheduling Based on Petri Nets*

Yaojun Han[1,2], Changjun Jiang[1], and Xuemei Luo[2]

[1] Department of Computer Science & Engineering, Tongji University,
Shanghai, 200092, China
[2] College of International Business Administration,
Shanghai International Studies University, Shanghai 200083, China
yjhan@shisu.edu.cn

Abstract. As the complexity of application system for enterprises, an important challenge is to dynamically schedule and integrate the heterogeneous and distributed services or activities to work cooperatively and efficiently. An effective technology to resolve the problem is grid service. A grid service built on both grid computing and web services technologies is an extended Web service. An application system for enterprises is a grid service composition that consists of a collection of grid services related by data and control flow. Therefore, there is a need for modeling and analyzing techniques and tools for reliable and effective grid service composition. The Petri net based method is an idea approach. In this paper, we use a colored dynamic timed Petri net (CDTPN) to model the grid service composition. The definition of CDTPN for grid service and an algorithm to construct a composite service are proposed. We give a definition of reachable service graph and an algorithm for constructing the reachable service graph of CDTPN. Finally, we discuss the correctness and effectiveness of the grid service composition by analyzing the reachable service graph.

Keywords: grid service, composition, dynamic timed Petri net, performance analysis

1 Introduction

As the development of Internet and World Wide Web, many organizations are rushing to put their core business competencies on the Internet to survive the massive competition created by new online economy [1]. An important challenge is to dynamically schedule and integrate the heterogeneous and distributed services or activities to work cooperatively and efficiently. An effective technology to resolve the problem is grid service. A grid service built on both grid computing and web services technologies is an extended Web service [2]. Grid computing is becoming a mainstream technology

* This work is support partially by projects of National Basic Research Program of China(973 Program)(2003CB316902, 2004CB318001-03), National Natural Science Fund (90612006, 90412013, 60473094), Humanities and Social Sciences Foundation of Ministry of Education (06JA870006), and Science Research Funds of Shanghai International Study University.

Y. Luo (Ed.): CDVE 2007, LNCS 4674, pp. 104–112, 2007.

for large-scale distributed resource sharing and system integration [3]. Grid applications for service-based systems are usually not based on a single service, but are rather composed of several services working together in an application specific manner. As the complexity of application system for enterprises, an important challenge is to dynamically schedule and integrate the heterogeneous and distributed services to work cooperatively and efficiently. Therefore, there is a need for modeling and analyzing techniques and tools for reliable grid service composition because of dynamic and complex service composition process.

Petri nets are promising tools for modeling and analysis information processing systems that are characterized as being concurrent, parallel and distributed [9,10,11]. Many researchers model and analyze Web service using Petri Nets, since they are well suited for capturing flows in web services, for modeling the distributed nature of web services, for representing methods in a web service and for reasoning about the correctness of the flows [1,4-7]. The existing approaches have difficulties in modeling and analyzing dynamic and complex grid service composition process, so we propose a colored dynamic timed Petri Net (CDTPN) model for grid service composition, which is an extended timed Petri-net model. In CDTPN, the time delay of transition is a function of execution time of a service instead of time constant, which is convenient for modeling and analyzing dynamic performance of grid service composition.

The rest of this paper is organized as follows. The concepts of Petri nets related to this paper are reviewed in section 2. In section 3, we present CDTPN model of grid service and give the algorithm for four basic structures of grid service composition workflow. In section 4, we propose a definition of reachable service graph, give algorithms for constructing the reachable service graph of CDTPN and discuss the correctness and performance of the grid service composition by analyzing the reachable service graph. Section 5 presents a case study of public services in a city. We conclude the paper in section 6.

2 Concepts of Petri Nets Related to the Paper

In this section, we simply review some concepts of Petri nets related to this paper. For the details of the definitions, the reader can see references [8,9,10].

Definition 1[8]. A Petri Net is a bipartite directed graph represented by a three-tuple $PN = (P,T;F,M_0)$, where,

$P=\{p_1,p_2...p_n,\}$ is a finite set of place nodes;
$T=\{t_1,t_2,...t_m\}$ is a finite set of transition nodes;
$P \cap T = \varphi$, $P \cup T \neq \varphi$;
$F= P \times T \cup T \times P$ is a finite set of directed arcs from P to T and T to P, where directed arcs from P to T are called input arcs, directed arcs from T to P are called output arcs;
$M_0 : P \rightarrow N$ is called an initial marking.
Let $PN = ((P,T;F,M_0)$ be a Petri net. For $x \in P \cup T$,
$x \bullet = \{y \in P \cup T | (y,x) \in F \}$ and
$\bullet x = \{y \in P \cup T | (x,y) \in F\}$

are called the pre-set and post-set of x respectively.

A transition $t \in T$ is enabled in M iff $M(p) \geq 1$ for any $p \in$ pre-set of t. A transition t enabled in M can fire and yield a new marking $M'(p)=M(p)-1$ for any $p \in$ pre-set of t and $M'(p)=M(p)+1$ for any $p \in$ post-set of t.

Definition 2[9]. A colored Petri net (CPN) is a eight-tuple $CPN=(\Omega,P,T,F,C,G,E, M_0)$, where,

$(P,T; F,)$ is a Petri net;
Ω is a set of colors;
C is a color function, $C: P \rightarrow \Omega$;
G is a guard function, $G: T \rightarrow$ Boolexpression, $\forall t \in T$: Type$(G(t))=$Boolean$\wedge$ Type$(\text{var}(G(t))) \subseteq \Omega$;
E is an arc expression function, $E: F \rightarrow$ expression, $\forall f \in F$: Type$(E(f))=C(p)_{MS}$ $\wedge$ Type$(\text{var}(E(f))) \subseteq \Omega$, where $C(p)_{MS}$ is the set of all multi-sets over $C(p)$;
M_0 is an initial marking function, $M_0:P \rightarrow$ expression, $\forall p \in P$: Type$(M_0\ (p))$ $=C(p)_{MS}$.

Definition 3[10]. A timed Petri net (TPN) is a five-tuple $TPN=(P,T;F,M_0,D)$, where,

$(P,T;F,M_0)$ is a Petri net;
$D: T \rightarrow R$ is a firing time delay, where R is the set of nonnegative rational numbers. For $t \in T$, $D(t)=a$ represents the firing time delay of t is a.

3   Petri Net Model for Grid Service

Definition 4. The Petri net model for a grid service is a colored dynamic timed Petri net (CDTPN, shown in Fig. 1). CDTPN = $(\Omega,P,T,F,C,E, G, M_0, D)$, where,

$\Omega=$ Ip$\cup$Op$\cup$QoS, where Ip and Op represent the input and output parameters of service respectively, QoS is the user's QoS requirements;
Variable: x: Ip$\cup$QoS; y: Op$\cup$QoS;
$P=\{si,so\}$, where, si and so represent input and output of the service S;
$T_=\{s\}$, where s represents the service S;
$F_=\{(si, s), (s,so)\}$;
$C=\{C(si)=$ Ip$\cup$QoS, $C(so)=$Op$\cup$QoS$\}$;
$E=\{E(si, s)=x, E(s, so)=y\}$;
$G=G(s)$. It is a function of x;
$M_0(si)=1'x$, $M_0(so)=0$;
$D=D(s)$. It is a function of x.

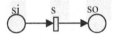

Fig. 1. CDTPN model for a grid service

A grid service has a specific task to perform and may depend on other grid services. The grid services cooperative scheduling is grid services composition. The composition of two or more services generates a new service providing both the original individual behavioral logic and a new collaborative behavior for carrying out a new composite task. A composite service consists of a collection of grid services related by data and control flow. Sequence, alternative, parallel and iteration are typical structures specified in the workflow.

Algorithm 1. Construction of CDTPN model for a grid application composed of some grid services:

(1) Input all grid services with input parameters as well as user's QoS requirements.

(2) Input the dependent relation (Sequence, alternative, parallel and iteration) of all grid services,

(3) Construct the CDTPN model for every grid service using definition 4.

(4) For all services, according to dependent relation of all grid services, construct the CDTPN model for composition of all grid services as following.

(4.1) If grid services S1 and S2 are sequential, i.e., a composite service (denoted by S1→S2) that performs the service S1 followed by the service S2, the S1→S2 is a CDTPN(Fig. 2), where $C(in)=QoS$, $C(out)=Op \cup QoS$, $E(in,t_1)=E(t_1,si_1)=QoS$, $E(so_1,t_{12})=E(t_{12},si_2)=x$, $E(so_2,t_2)=E(t_2,out)=y$, $G(t_1)=G(t_2)=G(t_{12})=Null$, $M_0(in)=QoS$, $M_0(out)=0$, $D(t_1)=D(t_2)=D(t_{12})=0$;

(4.2) If grid services S1 and S2 are alternative, i.e., a composite service (denoted by S1⊕S2) that behaves as either service S1 or service S2 (Once one of them executes its first operation the second service is discarded), the S1⊕S2 is a CDTPN(Fig.3), where $C(in)=C(p_1)=QoS$, $C(out)=C(p_2)=Op \cup QoS$, $E(in,t_1)=E(t_1,p_1)=E(p_1,t_{11})=E(p_1,t_{21})=E(t_{11},si_1)=$ $E(t_{21},si_2)=QoS$, $E(so_1,t_{12})=$ $E(so_2,t_{22})=E(t_{12},p_2)=E(t_{22},p_2)=E(p_2,t_2)=E(t_2,out)=y$, $G(t_{11})=(S1 \in QoS)$, $G(t_{12})=(S2 \in QoS)$, $G(t_1)=G(t_2)=G(t_{12})=G(t_{22})=Null$, $M_0(in)=QoS$, $M_0(out)=M_0(p_1)=M_0(p_2)=0$, $D(t_1)=D(t_2)=D(t_{11})=D(t_{12})=D(t_{21})=D(t_{22})=0$,

(4.3) If grid services S1 and S2 are parallel, i.e., a composite service (denoted by S1∥S2) that performs service S1 and S2 independently from each other, the S1∥S2 is a CDTPN(Fig. 4), where $C(in)=QoS$, $C(out)=Op \cup QoS$, $E(in,t_1)=E(t_1,si_1)=E(t_1,si_2)=QoS$, $E(so_1,t_2)=E(so_2,t_2)=E(t_2,out)=y$, $M_0(in)=QoS$, $M_0(out)=0$, $D(t1)=D(t2)=0$, $G(t_1)=G(t_2)=Null$.

(4.4) If grid services S1 is iterative, i.e., a composite service (denoted by nS1) that performs service S1 for n times, the nS1 is a CDTPN(Fig. 5), where $C(in)=QoS$, $C(out)=Op \cup QoS$, $E(in,t_1)=E(t_1,si_1)=QoS$, $E(so_1,t_2)=E(so_1,t_{11})=$ $E(t_2,out)=y$, $E(s_1,so_1)$ is a function including calculation of n-1, $G(t_2)=(n==0)$, $G(t_{11})=(n>0)$, $G(t_1)=Null$, $M_0(in)=QoS$, $M_0(out)=0$, $D(t1)=D(t2)=0$.

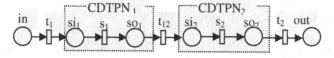

Fig. 2. CDTPN for the sequential composition of grid services S1 and S2

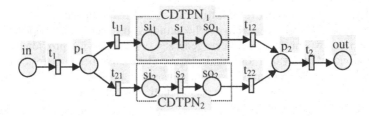

Fig. 3. CDTPN for the alternative composition of grid services S1 and S2

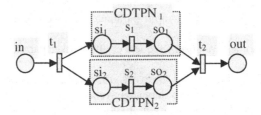

Fig. 4. CDTPN for the parallel composition of grid services S1 and S2

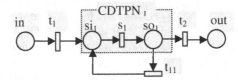

Fig. 5. CDTPN model for *n* times iteration of grid service S1

4   Analysis of a Grid Application Composed of Some Grid Services

A major strength of Petri nets is their support for analysis of many properties and problems associated with concurrent systems. After modeling the grid service with Petri nets, we will analyze the correctness and performance of the grid application in order to ensure the correctness and effectiveness of the grid service composition. A fundamental and most widely applied method for analyzing behavioral properties of Petri net models is coverability tree[10]. In this paper, we use the reachable service graph of the model instead of coverability tree to analyze the correctness and effectiveness of the grid service composition.

Definition 5. Let CDTPN be a colored dynamic timed Petri net model for a grid application composed of some grid services. The reachable service graph (RSG) of CDTPN is defined as a directed graph with labeled directed edges and labeled nodes.

RSG(CDTPN)=(V,E,FT, FM). Where,
$V=\{R(M_0)\}$,
$E=\{(M_i, M_j)| M_i, M_j \in R(M_0), \exists t_k \in T: M_i[t_k > M_j,$

$FT(M_i, M_j)= t_k/ct_k$, where ct_k is the current time of transition t_k firing.
$FM(M_j)=OP$, where OP is a set of output parameters of a service.

The reachable service graph of CDTPN is constructed by the following algorithm.

Algorithm 2. Construction of reachable service graph of CDTPN

(1) Let V={M_0}, E={φ}, tag M_0 "new".
(2) If there exists no "new" node in V, then the algorithm ends, otherwise go to (3).
(3) Select a "new" marking M and do the following:
   (3.1) If there no exist enabled transition t at M, then tag M with "end node".
   (3.2) While there exist t at M, do the following for each enabled transitions t at M:
    (3.21) Obtain M' that results from firing t at M.
    (3.22) If $M' \notin V$, then V=V+{M'} and tag M' with "new".
    (3.23) E=E+{M,M'}, tag {M,M'} with t_i/ct_i, where ct_i is the current time of transition t_i firing.
    (3.24) If $t=s_i$, then tag M' with a set of execution time and output parameters of service s_i.
    (3.25) Otherwise, tag M' with "[0,0]"(generally, [0,0] is omitted).
   (3.3) Remove "new" from M and go to (1).

The correctness of the algorithm 2 can be easily proven according to the definitions of CDTPN and RSG.

Proposition 1. Let CDTPN be a colored dynamic timed Petri net model for a grid application composed of some grid services.The CDTPN is deadlock-free iff for any end node $M \in RSG(M_0)$, $M(out) \neq 0$ and any $p \neq out \in P$, $M(p)=0$.

Definition 6. The grid service composition is correct iff CDTPN is deadlock-free.

Proposition 2. Let CDTPN be a colored dynamic timed Petri net model for a grid application composed of some grid services and deadlock-free. $RSG(M_0)$ is a reachable service graph of CDTPN.

(1) The total execution cost (EC) of a grid application is equal to $\sum c_i$, where $c_i \in M_i$ ($s_i \bullet$) is the execution cost of service s_i, $M_i \in RSG(M_0)$.
(2) The total execution time (ET) of a grid application is equal to $\max\{\sum e_i\}$, where $\sum e_i$ is the sum of tag with M_i. M_i is the node of path from M_0 to M. M_0, M_i, $M \in RSG(M_0)$ and M is the end-node. e_i is the execution time of service s_i.

Definition 7. A grid application composed of some grid services is feasible iff the turnover time is less than or equal to the deadline given by user, where the turnover time is the time interval between when a grid application is submitted and when it is completed. A grid application composed of grid services is economical iff the total transmission and execution cost is less than or equal to the budget given by user.

Proposition 3. Let CDTPN be deadlock-free. B and D are the budget and deadline given by user. The grid application is economical iff $EC \leq B$, where EC is the execution cost of the grid application. The grid application is feasible iff ct_e-$ct_1 \leq D$, where ct_1 is the tag t_1/ ct_1 of edge (M_0, M_1). ct_e is the tag t_e/ ct_e of edge (M_i, M), where t_e is pre-set of place *out*, M is the end-node.

5   A Case Study

We discuss public service system of a city as a case study. Suppose that a citizen want to see a doctor. , he will take taxi. Otherwise he will take bus. The public service system does the following. First, it looks up the weather forecast (service S1), meantime transfer money to hospital account from the user bank account (service S2). Second, it books taxi (service S3) for the user if it rains, otherwise tells the bus information (service S4) to the user according to the weather forecast. Last, it makes an appointment with doctor for the user (service S5). Obviously, S1 and S2 are parallel; S3 and S4 are alternative. We select the execution times and costs of services as the input and output parameters of services. Suppose that the execution times and costs of services S1, S2, S3, S4 and S5 are (10,30), (20,50), (40,70), (15,30) and (48,90) respectively. The user's deadline and budget are 100 and 220 units respectively.

(1) Construct CDTPN according to the definitions 4 and algorithm 1. The graphic representation of CDTPN is shown in figure 6, where $G(t_{31})$=(rain==True), $G(t_{41})$=(rain==False).

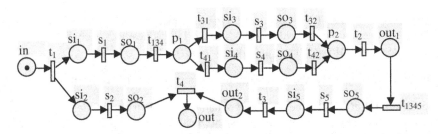

Fig. 6. Public service system S=((S1→ (S3⊕ S4) →S5)‖S2)

(2) According to algorithm 2, construct RSG of CDTPN and show in figure7 (Suppose that there is no delay for executing every grid service after the condition is content).

(3) Analyze the correctness of the grid application. From figure 7, we know CDTPN is deadlock-free according to proposition 1. So, the grid application is correct.

(4) Analyze the performance of the grid application. From figure 7, we know if it rains, the total execution time and cost of the grid application are 98 and 240, and the grid application is feasible but not economical because ct_e-ct_1=98<user's deadline140 and cost 240>user's budget 220. If it doesn't rain, the total execution time and cost of the grid application are 73 and 200 , and the grid application is feasible and economical because 73<140 and 200<220.

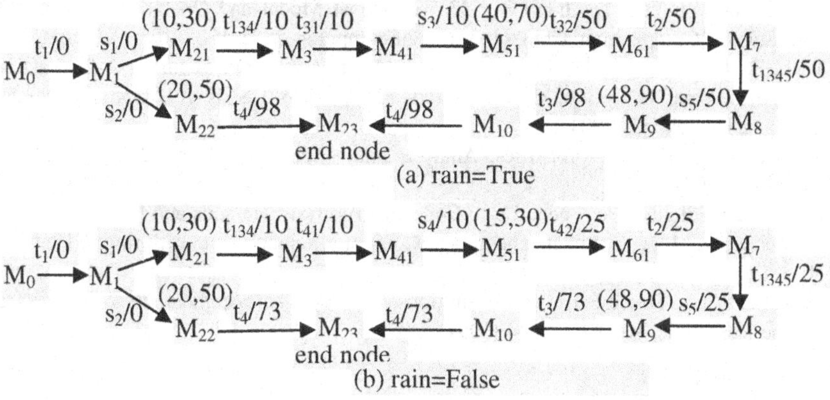

$$M_0 \xrightarrow{t_1/0} M_1 \xrightarrow{s_1/0} \overset{(10,30)}{M_{21}} \xrightarrow{t_{134}/10} M_3 \xrightarrow{t_{31}/10} M_{41} \xrightarrow{s_3/10} M_{51} \xrightarrow{(40,70)} M_{61} \xrightarrow{t_2/50} M_7$$

(a) rain=True

(b) rain=False

Fig. 7. RSG of Fig. 12

6 Conclusions

In this paper, we use a colored dynamic timed Petri net (CDTPN) to model the grid service composition (i.e. the grid services cooperative scheduling). The definition of CDTPN for grid service and an algorithm to construct a composite service are proposed. We give a definition of reachable service graph and an algorithm for constructing the reachable service graph of CDTPN. We get some conclusions about the correctness and effectiveness of the grid service composition by analyzing the reachable service graph. Finally, we discuss public service system of a city as a case study. From the example, we know that the CDTPN model given by us can represent the logical flow of grid service composition clearly and is very effective for analyzing the correctness and effectiveness of the grid service composition. In our future work, we will develop the software tools for composing the services automatically.

References

1. Hamadi, R., Benatallah, B.: A Petri Net-based Model for Web Service Composition. In: Proceedings of the Fourteenth Australasian database conference on Database technologies, Adelaide, Australia, pp. 191–200 (2003)
2. Tuecke, S., Czajkowski, K., Foster, I., Frey, J., Graham, S., Kesselman, C.: Grid service specification (2002)
3. Foster, I., Kesselman, C., Tuecke, S.: The anatomy of the grid: Enabling scalable virtual organizations. Int'l Journal of Supercomputing Applications 15(3), 200–222 (2002)
4. Tan, Z., Li, C., et al.: Approximate Performance Analysis of Web Services Flow Using Stochastic Petri Net. In: Jin, H., Pan, Y., Xiao, N., Sun, J. (eds.) GCC 2004. LNCS, vol. 3251, pp. 193–200. Springer, Heidelberg (2004)
5. Tang, Y., Chen, L., He, K.-T., Jing, N.: SRN: An Extended Petri-Net-Based Workflow Model for Web Service Composition. In: Proceedings of IEEE International Conference on Web Services (ICWS'04) , pp. 591–599. IEEE Computer Society Press, Los Alamitos (2004)

6. Yu-Bin, G., Yu-Yue, D., Jian-Qing, X.: A CP-Net Model and Operation Properties for Web Service Composition. Chinese Journal of computer 29(7), 1067–1075 (2006)
7. Tang, F., Li, M., et al.: Petri-Net-Based Coordination Algorithms for Grid Transactions. In: Cao, J., Yang, L.T., Guo, M., Lau, F. (eds.) ISPA 2004. LNCS, vol. 3358, pp. 499–508. Springer, Heidelberg (2004)
8. Murata, T.: Petri Nets: Properties, Analysis and Application. Proceedings of IEEE 77, 541–584 (1999)
9. Jensen, K.: Coloured Petri nets: Basic Concepts, Analysis Methods and Practical Use, Basic Concepts. Mono-graphs in Theoretical Computer Science. vol. 1, Springer, Heideberg (1997)
10. Zuberek, W.M.: Timed Petri nets: Definitions, Properties and Applications. Microelectronics and Reliability 31(4), 627–644 (1991)

Capturing Designers' Knowledge Demands in Collaborative Team

Zhen Lu, Jiang Zuhua, Liu Chao, and Liang Jun

School of Mechanical Engineering, Shanghai Jiao Tong University, Shanghai, P.R.C.
{lzhen,zhjiang,chliu,jliang}@sjtu.edu.cn

Abstract. Collaborative team members usually come from diverse disciplines; their demands for knowledge are also different from each other. This paper is mainly concerned with how to capturing designers' knowledge demands in collaborative team. With the view from workflow, designers' knowledge demand is modeled from three aspects, members, roles, and tasks' requirements for knowledge. Based on the model of knowledge demand, some intelligent mining methods are proposed so that designers' knowledge demand could be derived automatically. With the knowledge demand model, a knowledge supply system could be developed to realize: knowledge within an appropriate domain could be delivered to the proper user among the collaborative team.

Keywords: Knowledge Management, Knowledge demand, Collaborative design, Workflow.

1 Introduction

Team members among a collaborative design team usually come from diverse disciplines, each with particular expertise and contribution from their relevant areas. So, their demands for knowledge are also different from each other. Collaborative team requires a mechanism to efficiently distribute knowledge such as news, seminar announcements, patents, technique documents, software services, etc. The knowledge has to be delivered in the right context to the right person, in the right time for the right purpose [1], which is called knowledge supply, knowledge logistics, or knowledge distribution. As to above target, the fundamental issue lies in how to accurately capture the characteristics of user profiles and find each user's demand for knowledge. Based on those knowledge demand descriptions, a proper volume of knowledge within a proper domain could be delivered to the proper user among the collaborative team.

"Demand" is the premise for "supply", all of those demands for knowledge buildup the basis for the knowledge supply. Our goal is to develop a new approach for mining the knowledge demands of each designer among collaborative team from their backgrounds, roles' description, tasks' requirement, query\browser history, email records, and work schedules.

The crucial technologies related to capturing users' demands for knowledge include representation and modification of user profile, the representation of resource, the recommendation technology, and the architecture of personalization. Some famous

Y. Luo (Ed.): CDVE 2007, LNCS 4674, pp. 113–121, 2007.

personalized systems have been developed among both academia and industry: e.g. IBM's WebSphere, BroadVision, ILOG, ant etc. Citeseer [2], Webpersonalizer [3] and etc. filter web information according to the similarities between the web resources and users' interests. In addition, GroupLens[4], SiteSeer [5] and etc. are collaborative method which filtering web information according to users' similarities among them. However, those systems mainly concern personalized recommendations of web information. They have not considered specific applications of knowledge recommendation in among a collaborative team about some specific business or research processes.

Our approach is workflow-centric because we view knowledge distribution as an organizational process and investigate process-oriented solution for it. It helps us design efficient and utilizable solution for routing process among enterprises or institutes, rather than pure algorithm research about information filtering, or just web pages recommendation among internet.

2   The Model of Knowledge Demand

Members are the core factor in knowledge management in enterprises; all the knowledge is produced and also used by members during their design tasks. Each member in a collaborative team may have one or more roles in a collaborative team, e.g. product manager, system engineer, mechanical engineer, electrical engineer, and etc. Moreover, there are up-low relationships between those various roles, all of which constitute a role hierarchy, named role tree. The role tree reflects the organization architecture of an enterprise or a team.

The above reference model RM is defined as: RM=<T,R,M>;

Here, T is the total set of tasks, $T=\{t_i|i=1,\cdots,t_{num}\}$, t_{num} is the number of tasks;

R is the total set of roles, $R=\{r_i|i=1,\cdots,r_{num}\}$, r_{num} is the number of roles;

M is the total set of members, $M=\{m_i|i=1,\cdots,m_{num}\}$, m_{num} is the number of members;

- ✧ **Member list:** each unit in member list is corresponding to a real member in a collaborative team. Their member ID and interests are stored in it. Those interests reflect the member's knowledge background, specialty, research interests, strong points and etc.

- ✧ **Role tree:** different from member list, role is a virtual concept; and each role reflects a position and rank in collaborative team. Different positions are corresponding to different qualification of capabilities and skills, which are also described by some keywords.

- ✧ **Task model:** task in a workflow reflects an activity among some project. Each task (or activity) needs distinct requirement for fulfilling it. Similarly, those task requirements are described by some keywords about the task's domain, technical requirements and etc.

The above three parts concern three demand sources for knowledge: demands for knowledge according to (1) one member's interests, (2) qualification of capabilities about roles that are correlative with some members, (3) requirements of workflow's tasks that are also correlative with some members.

The **task knowledge demand** model is defined as: $KD_T=<t_i, V>$; Here, t_i denotes a task, $t_i \in T$; V denotes knowledge demand description for the task, and is a set of tuples: $V = \{(c_i, w_i) \mid c_i \in C, w_i \in W\}$; C is a set of pre-defined knowledge categories, and W is the set of weights for rating the categories.

Similarly, the **role knowledge demand** and **member knowledge demand** models are defined as above: $KD_R=<r_i, V>$; $KD_M=<m_i, V>$, Here, r_i denotes a role, $r_i \in R$; m_i denotes a member, $m_i \in M$.

The above reference model concerns three sorts of knowledge demands as to one member. Based on those demands, knowledge could be retrieved from knowledge source, and delivered to the members who may need the knowledge. Fig.1 illustrates the process of knowledge supply (or called knowledge distribution) based on knowledge demand model.

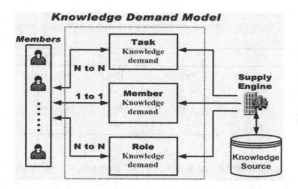

Fig. 1. Knowledge supply based on model of knowledge demand

3 Dynamic Mining Knowledge Demand

Typical application environments of a collaborative design team have many dynamic aspects: members' preferences, tasks and roles change. How to make the recommended knowledge adapt to changing demands automatically and intelligently is the key issue for developing a knowledge supply system. Intelligent mining collaborative designers' knowledge demands could find members' interests or preferences from understanding the commonalities among documents they have read or queried in the past. The members' interests in member knowledge demand model will be updated dynamically and automatically rather than maintained by themselves. Then, the knowledge that have high degree to whatever the member's preferences would be recommended. It also could find the knowledge that is potentially useful or interesting for them. Sometimes, members are not very sure about their knowledge demands very clearly, and they are often limited to being recommended items that are similar to those already read. Our system could overcome the overspecialization problem and supply them with some knowledge that is different to their domains or preferences but may be potentially useful for them.

(1) Content-based filtering from documents read or queried in the past

The Members will be recommended knowledge document which is similar to the ones they preferred in the past. The characteristics of members' preference are represented by "member knowledge demand model" which is defined in section 3.2:

$$KD_M = <m_i, V>, \quad V = \{(c_i, w_i) \mid c_i \in C, w_i \in W\}.$$

So, how to determine the category c_i and its weight w_i for the target member is the key issue. Before the content-based filtering, a keyword thesaurus corresponding to the application domain should be established by the domain experts or knowledge engineers in advance. Based on a set of training documents with pre-assigned classification categories, the keyword set can be automatically extracted from specified domain documents. Furthermore, after deriving the frequency of each keyword in the domain documents, the correlation between the keywords and categories can be summarized as Table 1.

Table 1. Correlation between keywords and categories

	C_1	...	C_j	...	C_{Cnum}
KW_1	$R_{1,1}$	...	$R_{1,j}$	...	$R_{1,Cnum}$
...	...	...	...	...	
KW_i	$R_{i,1}$	...	$R_{i,j}$	...	$R_{i,Cnum}$
...	...	...	...	...	...

The second step is computing the keyword frequencies of documents the target member has read, or queried in the past. In this paper, we used a general method of document keywords extraction for mining the member preferences from documents they have read, or queried in the past. One of the best-known measures for specifying keywords weights in information retrieval is the *term frequency/inverse document frequency (TF-IDF)* measures. It is employed to calculate terms' weights for each document. Each document D_j is represented as a weighted term vector $D_j = \{w_{1j}, w_{2j}, w_{3j}, \cdots, w_{i,j}, \cdots\}$ by standard *TF-IDF* function:

$$w_{i,j} = \frac{f_{i,j}}{\max_z f_{z,j}} \times \log \frac{N}{n_i}$$

Where: $f_{i,j}$ is the number of times keyword t_i appears in the document D_j. The maximum is computed over the frequencies $f_{z,j}$ of all keywords that appear in the document D_j. N is the total number of documents, and keyword t_i appears in n_i of them.

Then, based on the analysis of all documents that were read by the member in the past, some keyword terms' weights could be calculated as follow. As to a certain term t_i:

$$w_i = \sum_j dw_j \times w_{i,j} = \sum_j 2^{-age(D_j)/hl} \times w_{i,j}$$

Where: dw_j is the weight of document D_j. It is computed mainly according to that the relevant of a document with the member decay with time. So a time factor $2^{-age(Dj)/hl}$ is introduced to adjust the contribution of the relevant document for the member knowledge interest model according to its age $age(D_j)$. The algebraic difference between the current date and the date when the document D_j was read is given by $age(D_j)$. The half-life span hl is set at 30 on the assumption that the effect of relevant documents in a topic reduce by 1/2 in one month [6].

Based on above method, as to each member, a set of keywords with weights could be derived as following table 2.

Table 2. Keywords' weights for each member

	M_1	$\cdots$	M_k	$\cdots$	M_{Mnum}
KW_1	$w_{1,1}$	$\cdots$	$w_{1,k}$	$\cdots$	$w_{1,Mnum}$
$\cdots$	$\cdots$	$\cdots$	$\cdots$	$\cdots$	
KW_i	$w_{i,1}$	$\cdots$	$w_{i,k}$	$\cdots$	$w_{i,Mnum}$
$\cdots$	$\cdots$	$\cdots$	$\cdots$	$\cdots$	$\cdots$

The third step is deriving the relationship between the members and categories. Based on keyword-category relationship (Table 1) and keywords' weights for each member (Table 2), the correlation between the kth member and the jth category (denoted by $Rmc_{k,j}$) can be determined by following formula:

$$Rmc_{k,j} = \sum_i R_{i,j} \times w_{i,k}$$

Above correlation can be normalized by following formula:

$$Rmc_{k,j}' = \frac{Rmc_{k,j}}{\sum_j Rmc_{k,j}}$$

The Table 3 illustrates the correlation between members and categories, which is also member knowledge demand model. Based on above mining algorithm, members' interests or knowledge demand categories can be determined and knowledge supply system can automatically deliver appropriate knowledge documents that meet the member characteristics and requirements.

Table 3. Correlation between members and categories

	C_1	$\cdots$	C_j	$\cdots$	C_{Cnum}
M_1	$Rmc_{1,1}$	$\cdots$	$Rmc_{1,j}$	$\cdots$	$Rmc_{1,Cnum}$
$\cdots$	$\cdots$	$\cdots$	$\cdots$	$\cdots$	
M_k	$Rmc_{k,1}$	$\cdots$	$Rmc_{k,j}$	$\cdots$	$Rmc_{i,Cnum}$
$\cdots$	$\cdots$	$\cdots$	$\cdots$	$\cdots$	$\cdots$
M_{Mnum}	$Rmc_{Mnum,1}$	$\cdots$	$Rmc_{Mnum,j}$	$\cdots$	$Rmc_{Mnum,Cnum}$

(2) Collaborative filtering from role or task knowledge demand model
Unlike content-based recommendation methods, collaborative methods try to predict a member's preferences based on other members. More formally, the weight of a category c for member m is estimated based on the weights assigned to category c by those members who are "similar" to member m.

Various approaches have been used to compute the similarity between members, such as Pearson correlation coefficient, Cosine-based approach, and etc. In this paper, we make use of the information of task and role, and make an assumption: members in the same task or role could be regarded as "similar" members. In this way, we could avoid calculation for members' similarities, and the process for determining the "similar" members based on task or role could be much faster and more rational.

As to the member knowledge demand model, the weight of category c_i for member m, denoted by $w_{m,i}$, is calculated as follow:

$$w_{m,i} = \overline{w_m} + k \sum_{m' \in \hat{M}} w(m') \times (w_{m',i} - \overline{w_{m'}})$$

Where: $\hat{M}$ denotes the set of N members that belong to the same task or role. $w(m')$ is the weight of the member m' in the task or role. In this paper, it is measured by the year difference between the current year and the year the member joined into the task or role. So the veteran members will have more influence for others' knowledge demand trends than novice members. Assuming that a member with hl years experience will have a half influence of expert who may have the highest influence value. The weight of the member is defined as:

$$w(m') = \frac{2}{\pi} \arctan(\ Year\ (m')\ /\ hl\ )$$

$$k = 1 / \sum_{m' \in \hat{M}} w(m') \ , \ \overline{w_m} = (1/|S_c|) \times \sum_{c \in S_c} w_{m,c} \ , \text{ where } S_c = \{c \in C \mid w_{c,m} \neq \phi\}$$

(3) Collaborative filtering from email records among team members
Members usually highly interact with others of similar characteristics. Therefore, the email frequency (including email sending, email forwarding, email reply and etc.) of the target member with other members in the email record can be used as an index to determine the correlation between two members. Based on the member correlation, the target member's knowledge demand could be derived from members who are "similar" to him (or her).

The first step is to derive the correlation. In this paper, the correlation between members is measured by the frequencies that target member receive, send or forward emails to the other members. That is, the frequencies that the target member M_t receive, send, or forward emails to the ith member M_i' can be multiply with the corresponding weighting values to derive the correlation:

$$Correlation(M_t, M_i') = Wr \times N_r(M_t, M_i') + Wf \times N_f(M_t, M_i') + Ws \times N_s(M_t, M_i')$$

Where, Wr, Wf, Ws denote the weight coefficients for receive, forward, send emails. In this paper, they are assigned by 0.25, 0.35, 0.4 respectively. The $N_r(M_t, M_i')$, $N_f(M_t,$

M_i'), $N_s(M_t, M_i$'),denote the number of emails that are received, forwarded, or sent from the target member M_t to the ith member M_i' respectively.

After sorting the email correlation, representative contact members can be determined. If the top S contact members are selected as representative members, each one could be assigned a weighting value a_i ($i=1,2, \cdots, S$) based on the email correlations. In this paper, S is 5, and $a_1=1$, $a_2=0.8$, $a_3=0.6$, $a_4=0.4$, $a_5=0.2$.

Then, as to the member knowledge demand model, the weight of term t_j for member m, denoted by $w_{m,j}$, is calculated as follow:

$$w_{m,j} = \frac{\overline{w_m} + \sum_{i=1}^{S} a_i \times (w_{i,j} - \overline{w_i})}{1 + \sum_{i=1}^{S} a_i} \quad \text{where } 1 \geq a_1 \geq a_2 \geq \cdots \geq a_S \geq 0$$

$\overline{w_m}$ and $\overline{w_i}$ denote average weight of all keyword terms as to the target member or the ith other member respectively.

4 A Working Scenario

This section will present a working scenario of the knowledge supply in collaborative design team based on knowledge demand model. The demonstration case is in a scenario about product design process. As product design becomes increasingly knowledge-intensive and collaborative, the need for knowledge to support the enterprises or teamwork's innovative design processes becomes more critical. The knowledge supply system just aims at that target: globally distributed knowledge resources could be delivered to the potential users, which could make best of enterprises' knowledge. We have implemented a prototype system for knowledge supply. The methodology proposed in this paper can be used for the knowledge supply to deliver customized knowledge services to the members. As to members, their knowledge demand models can be built automatically. According to their knowledge demand models, our system could supply them with an appropriate volume of knowledge documents which may give them some hints or inspiration and be potentially useful for their innovative design work.

When a member logins the system, and system verify his (or her) Member ID. According to the ID, knowledge demand information about this member is loaded during login process. The demand information includes three aspects: (1) member's interests, (2) Roles' capabilities, (3) Activities' requirements. Every aspect is described by some knowledge categories. In the example shown in Fig.2, the member has two roles: Product manager for fuel pump, and Design engineer for fuel pump. As to the later role, Design engineer for fuel pump, two knowledge documents are supplied to the member. If selecting one item, the right portion of interface would illustrate the detail information: title, knowledge sort, domain keywords, and UKL. By clicking the yellow button, the system will connect to the knowledge source for the knowledge service. While, by clicking the blue button, the system will add this knowledge item to the member's own document for favorite knowledge for the later uses.

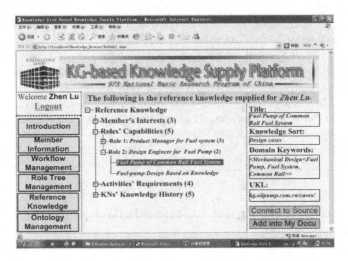

Fig. 2. An interface in the prototype system for knowledge supply

5 Summary

Team members among a collaborative design team usually come from diverse disciplines, each with particular expertise and contribution from their relevant areas. So, their demands for knowledge are also different from each other. This research proposed the knowledge demand models and a series of mining algorithms to build the knowledge demand model automatically. Furthermore, according to the member knowledge demand models, knowledge server could intelligently provide an appropriate volume of potentially useful knowledge which meets members' demands.

The knowledge has to be delivered in the right context to the right person, in the right time for the right purpose, which is the final target of knowledge supply. The mechanism of knowledge supply involves two key issues: (1) demand side: building knowledge demand model to describe users' need; (2) supply side: organizing knowledge items in knowledge source. This paper focuses on the first one. As to the second issue, our ongoing work mainly concerns two aspects: (1) Investigating the mechanism for packing, publishing and invoking diverse types of knowledge services, so as to enrich the repositories in knowledge source; (2) Using knowledge grid to organize globally distributed knowledge resources more effectively, so as to make the extension of knowledge supply much wider, rather than just inside a collaborative work team or an enterprise.

Acknowledgement

The authors are most grateful to 973 / National Basic Research Program of China (2003CB317005) and Shuguang Program of Shanghai Educational Committee (No. 05SG15), for financial supports that made this research possible.

References

[1] Smirnov, A., Pashkin, M., Chilov, N., Levashova, T.: Knowledge logistics in information grid environment. Future Generation Computer Systems 20, 61–79 (2004)

[2] Bollacker, K.D., Lawrence, S., Giles, C.L.: Discovering relevant scientific literature on the Web. IEEE Intelligent Systems 15(2), 42–47 (2000)

[3] Mobasher, B., Cooley, R., Srivastava, J.: Automatic personalization based on web usage mining. Communications of the ACM 43(8), 142–151 (2000)

[4] Konstan, J., Miller, B., Maltz, D.: GroupLens: applying collaborative filtering to usenet news. Communications of the ACM 40(3), 77–87 (1997)

[5] Rucker, J., Siteseer, M.J.: Personalized navigation for the web. Communications of the ACM 40(3), 73–75 (1997)

[6] Sugiyama, K., Hatano, K., Yashikawa, M.: Adaptive web search based on user profile constructed without any effort from users. In: Proceeding of the 13th Conference on World Wide Web (AAMAS 2004), pp. 675–684. IEEE Computer Society Press, Los Alamitos, CA (2004)

"Integrare", a Collaborative Environment for Behavior-Oriented Design

Lian Wen[1], Robert Colvin[2], Kai Lin[1], John Seagrott[1],
Nisansala Yatapanage[1], and Geoff Dromey[1]

[1] Griffith University, Brisbane, Qld, Australia
[2] University of Queensland, Brisbane, Qld, Ausralia
{l.wen,j.seagrott,g.dromey}@griffith.edu.au,
{robert,nisansala}@itee.uq.edu.au,
kai.lin@student.griffith.edu.au

Abstract. In this paper, we introduce a new cooperative design and visualization environment, called "Integrare", which supports designers and developers in building dependable, component-based systems using a new behavior-oriented design method. This method has advantages in terms of its abilities to manage complexity, find defects and make checks of dependability. The environment integrates and unifies several tools that support multiple phases of the design process, allowing them to interact and exchange information, as well as providing efficient editing capabilities. It can help formalize individual natural language functional requirements as Behavior Trees. These trees can be composed to create an integrated tree-like view of all the formalized requirements. The environment manages complexity by allowing multiple users to work independently on requirements translation and tree editing in a collaborative mode. Once a design is constructed from the requirements, it can be visually simulated with respect to an underlying operational semantics, and formally verified by way of a model checker.

Keywords: behavior-oriented design, behavior tree, software environment.

1 Introduction

Software tools, from editors and compilers to software engineering environments, which are integrated collections of different tools, have been developed and used from the very early days of software engineering [4]. As software systems are becoming larger and more complex, selecting the right tools and environments is critical to the quality and speed of developing these systems [6]. In this paper, we introduce a new collaborative environment "Integrare", which can be used throughout multiple phases in the software design cycle, such as requirement engineering, simulation, formal specification, and model checking.

Integrare is built to support the Behavior Tree (BT) design method [1], which is a process that constructs a component-based software design from the system's functional requirements. This process is a systematic method for translating informal natural language functional requirements into a formal BT representation, in a

Y. Luo (Ed.): CDVE 2007, LNCS 4674, pp. 122–131, 2007.

straightforward and traceable manner. Validation of the system model is one of the most important tasks in developing software that meets the client's needs, and Integrare supports this in a rigorous manner by including simulation and model checking facilities, in contrast to many commercially available modeling tools based on UML [24]- [27] and requirement engineering tools [28]-[30]. The first version, which has been released for internal testing, includes the following functions:

- Visio-styled user interface.
- A collaborative (multi-user) working mode.
- A Requirement Translation Assistant (RTA).
- Simulation.
- Translation of BT to SAL for model checking.

Integrare was developed using C++, employing Visual Studio [21] and Microsoft Foundation Classes [22]. It uses XD++ [23] as the library to support graphical editing. The architecture is a hybrid of model-view [33] and event-driven [32] architectures.

The paper is organized as follows: in section 2 we briefly introduce the BT design process and notations. The architecture and GUI are described in section 3, and from section 4 to section 7, we present four major features of the tool, which are its collaborative working mode, the requirement translation assistant, simulation, and SAL translation. Related work is discussed in section 8.

2 The Behavior Tree Design Approach

The Behavior Tree (BT) approach is a software design process that constructs a component-based software design from the system's functional requirements. This process is a systematic method for translating informal natural language functional requirements into a formal BT representation, in a straightforward and traceable way [1] [7]. The constructed BT can be used to support different stages and different aspects of software engineering such as requirements engineering [11], architecture and component design, software change [3], architecture normalization [2], model checking [9] safety [14], reliability issues [10], verification [15] and simulation.

Compared with UML, independent researchers find that the lack of precise [40], formal [36] and unambiguous [37] semantic models is one of the major difficulties in checking the consistency between different UML diagrams [38], translating UML into formal languages [39], and simulating UML models [40]. In contrast, the formal semantics of the BT notation has been stressed from the beginning; a formal semantic language Behavior Tree Specific Language (BTSL) has been developed [11], and a BT can be automatically translated into formal languages such as CSP [9] and SAL [10], and described by a metamodel [8]. Even though a BT is a formal specification, unlike formal languages such as CSP, SAL or B notation [41], the flowchart-styled graphic notation of BT can be easily understood by non-experts. Therefore, the BT notation has both advantages as a formal language with precise semantics so it can be mechanically checked, analyzed and simulated, as well as a soft and casual modeling [5] that non-technical stakeholders find appealing.

The BT approach also provides a systematic way to transform the natural language described user requirements into component-based designs, in contrast to approaches based on UML use case diagrams, PLUSS [42], or interdependency graphs (SIG) [43]. The transformation process follows three steps [1]. Firstly, each individual functional requirement is translated into one or more corresponding Requirement Behavior Tree(s) (RBT). This process, aided by tools such as the RTA (see section 5), is focused on traceability and preserving the intention of the natural language requirements. Secondly, the RBTs are integrated into a Design Behavior Tree (DBT). The DBT may be validated by the client, both by-hand and with the aid of a visual simulation tool. The DBT may also be model-checked to formally verify that it fulfills safety or performance requirements. Finally design diagrams are projected out from the DBT. Details of the BT approach can be found from [16].

3   Architecture and the GUI

The architecture of Integrare, shown in Fig. 1, can be described from two different aspects. One is the static aspect that focuses on the composition and structure of the architecture, where the architecture is similar to a model-view architecture [24]. The other aspect is dynamic, describing the runtime working flows of the system, from which the architecture is like an event-driven architecture [32].

The model-view architecture includes two major parts: the data model and the views. The data model holds the application data and provides interfaces to query and modify the data, while the views are collections of ways to present the data stored in the data model. In the event-driven architecture, all the runtime operations should be consequences of events.

In Integrare, the center component, called data manager, includes 6 sub components: "event handler", "data query", "data operation", "action recorder",

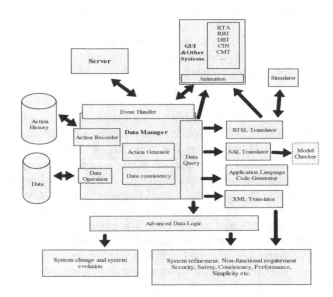

Fig. 1. The architecture of Integrare

"action generator" and "data consistency". The "data operation" is the only component that can directly access the raw data; the "data query" is the public interface for other components to query the data of the system. The only way to modify the data is to post events to the "event handler". An event can be triggered from the GUI, other systems or the server, which support cooperative design. When the "event handler" receives an event, it will pass the event to the "action generator"; with the help of the "data consistency", the "action generator" may generate a sequence of actions; these actions will be recorded by the "action recorder" into the action history and also executed by the "data operation" to modify the data. The component "action history" records the completed sequence of the executed actions. This information can be used to reproduce the data images of a system in the different stages, and it may be helpful to study the evolution of a system.

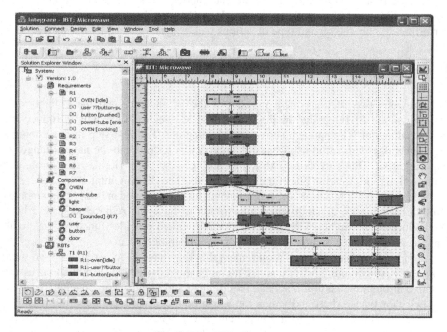

Fig. 2. The GUI of Integrare.

Visualization is an essential part of Integrare, which uses a graph editing library XD++ [23] to power the GUI. Fig. 2 is a screenshot of Integrare. It supports many standardized GUI functions such as zooming, cut/paste, layout arrange and redo/undo. People who have experience with other graph editing tools such as Visio or Smartdraw [31] will find it is easy to use Integrare.

4   Collaborative Mode

The Collaborative mode is important for designing large systems, which usually require a team of people to work simultaneously.

To meet the requirement of high responsiveness in the slow network environment, replicated architecture is adopted in Integrare. Shared documents are replicated at the local storage of each collaborating site, so that operations can be performed at local sites immediately and then propagated to remote sites. However, concurrent editing in the replicated architecture may cause three kinds of inconsistency problems [35]: (1) causality violation: operations may arrive and be executed out of their natural cause-effect order; (2) divergence: operations may arrive and be executed at different sites in different orders; and (3) intention violation: the actual execution effect of an operation may be different from the intention of this operation. Moreover, in collaborative Integrare, many constraints must be maintained automatically.

It is obvious that if operations are executed in the same order at each collaborating site, convergence is guaranteed. In Integrare, we separate two different types of actions; the first type will not change the data model of BT approach, and the second type of actions will change the data model related to BT approach. To improve the performance, only the second type of actions will be synchronized by the server.

5   Requirement Translation Assistant (RTA)

The previous two sections have introduced the architecture and the collaborative working mode of Integrare. In this and following sections we will introduce the functionalities of BT approach supported by Integrare. The first step in developing a requirements specification using the BT approach is to translate the natural language requirements. This involves extracting all of the behavioral, structural and compositional information out of the requirements. The RTA facilitates this task.

In carrying out translation, the requirements for the system can be split up amongst multiple developers. An individual only needs to have the requirements that have been allocated to him/her. The cooperative environment provides functions ensure all team members use a common vocabulary when integration occurs.

An individual can take each requirement that they have been given and read them thoroughly, so obtaining a full understanding of the requirement. It is then necessary to move through the natural language requirement and identify components, behavior and behavior types. These individual items can be identified separately, but it is then necessary to link behavior to a component and a behavior type. This provides the information necessary to create a BT node. This process results in one or more BT nodes for each natural language requirement. Once we have a set of BT nodes for a given natural language requirement, we can export them to the main BT editing tool, where they can be joined together to form BTs.

6   BTSL and Simulation

One of the key capabilities for developing a behavioral model of a system is the ability to rapidly validate that the system being designed behaves in the intended manner. As such Integrare includes an interface to a BT simulator, BTsim. The user can observe each step the system takes (each step typically corresponds to the "execution" of one node), with the most recently executed node highlighted. The user can also observe the values of the components after each step, and can provide safety properties for the simulator to check.

The simulator is written in the logic programming language Mercury [44], and encodes the rules of an operational semantics for BTs [11]. The simulator takes as input a BT, initial values of the components, and an optional list of safety properties to check. The simulator operates in two main modes: it can generate a random trace (sequence of nodes) of the system, either interactively or automatically; and it can exhaustively generate all traces. In addition, at each step it checks that the properties it was given on initialization still hold.

To interact with the simulator, Integrare first translates the BT into the simulator syntax. This syntax is a logic programming term, based on a recursive, tree data structure. The translation process walks down the tree from the root node recursively building up the term. Each node is augmented with its internal node label within Integrare; this provides the mechanism by which BTsim communicates to Integrare which node is executed at each simulation step. Once the translated tree has been sent to BTsim, it immediately executes an atomic step, according to the operational semantics, and returns the identifier of the executed node. On reading this output, Integrare highlights the appropriate node, and displays the new value of the components. If a property has been violated, the simulation halts, and the violated property is shown to the user. The process is repeated until the tree finishes execution, or the user stops the simulation. The user can step through the execution one step at a time, or can set a time interval for steps to be executed (and can mix the two approaches).

Simulation not only provides a way for the modeler to concretely observe dynamic behavior, but also to quickly check that the model maintains certain properties, for instance, that a component never reaches some erroneous state, or that eventually a component reaches a healthy state.

7 SAL Translation and Model Checking

Recent approaches for the verification of system designs have involved formal methods, including model checking. Model checking is a process in which a model of the system is verified against specified properties, such as safety requirements [45]. The model checker either proves that each property holds for the model, or provides a counterexample, which describes the steps which lead to the violation of the property.

Model checking usually requires expert knowledge of the input language, making it difficult to use for those without experience in formal methods. For this reason, a translator was created for automatic translation from BTs to the input language of the SAL framework [46]. SAL is a suite of tools which provide various capabilities for the analysis of concurrent systems, including symbolic and bounded model checkers.

A set of syntax rules for BTs have been devised, along with a translation scheme from BTs to the SAL language corresponding to each rule. BT nodes are translated into transitions in the SAL language, with variables representing components and messages. State-realizations are translated into updates to the variables, while BT guards and selections are translated into tests on the state of variables. Program counters provide the flow of control and enable branching and other BT concepts, such as thread kill and reversion, to be represented.

These rules form the basis of the translator, which first parses the BT according to the syntax rules to ensure that the BT is syntactically correct. The sequence of syntax rules is then used for the translation phase. The translation rule corresponding to each syntax rule in the sequence is applied, producing the SAL model.

8   Related Work

Many commercial tools and environments currently exist for modeling in UML (eg, [26] [27]). Such tools typically focus on the presentation of the models and generating code from them. The BT method covers a larger range of the software development process, and hence Integrare, to support the method, contains features not found in UML-based tools. In particular, BTs aid in the construction of models in a systematic, traceable way from natural language [1]. This is covered in Integrare by the Requirements Translation Assistant. As part of the validation process, models can be dynamically simulated within Integrare as they are developed, giving immediate feedback on how different requirements interact. The BTs may also be model checked against safety properties of the system. These two features crucial to validation, simulation and model checking, are missing from all commercial environments we surveyed. The other distinguishing feature of Integrare is that it allows multiple users to edit the same BT in real-time.

In the research community, the SOFL method [47] is supported by a range of tools. Integrare combines a similar range of tools into one environment, allowing for quick and easy exchange of information. Integrare is also different in that it uses a single notation, BT, across all facets of software design.

Compared with existing BT environments such as BTE [17], CoGSE [18] and GSET [20], Integrare covers more aspects of the development process and aim for real applications (a few companies has shown interest in using Integrare in their large-scale software projects). The other environments are generally for research purpose and usually focus on one or a few particular phases of the design process, for example, BTE is generally for model checking, the CoGSE is used for testing the collaborative working mode, and the GSET is for modeling software change.

9   Conclusions

In this paper we have described a prototype tool that supports the BT program development framework. It incorporates several tools, starting from a RTA that begins the process of formalizing a natural language specification, through to tools for simulating and model checking designs. They have been unified under a common, easy-to-use graphical interface and, crucially, the interface supports real-time cooperative design and visualization. This increases productivity by allowing concurrent development without the need to separately merge individual work. The unified tool provides a sound base for future research and industrial applications.

Integrare was from the outset designed to progressively accommodate new functionality as it is developed. In addition to a versioning system, there are two key areas in which Integrare will be extended: support for Composition Trees (CT) and source code generation. CT works as a supporting platform, on which the BTs will be more precisely defined. Just as BTs can be automatically translated to formal languages such as SAL, it is also possible to translate them into implementation languages such as Java or C++. Some unpublished research has been done on this subject already and the results will be integrated into Integrare in the future.

Acknowledgments. The authors would like to thank Ankur Choudhary, Diana Kirk, Maria Aneiros, Saad Zafar and Lars Grunske for their contribution on this environment. This work is supported by ACCS (ARC Center for Complex Systems).

References

1. Dromey, R.G.: From Requirements to Design: Formalising the Key Steps. In: IEEE International Conference on Software Engineering and Formal Methods, pp. 2–11 (2003)
2. Wen, L., Dromey, R.G.: Architecture Normalization for Component-based Systems. Electronic Notes in Theoretical Computer Science 160, 335–348 (2006)
3. Wen, L., Dromey, R.G.: From Requirements Change to Design Change: A Formal Path. In: SEFM 2004, pp. 104–113.
4. Harrison, W., Ossher, H., Tarr, P.: Software engineering tools and environments: a roadmap. In: The Conference on The Future of Software Engineering, pp. 261–277 (2000)
5. Nuseibeh, B., Easterbrook, S.: Requirement Engineering: a Roadmap. The Future of Software Engineering, ACM press (2000)
6. Bruckhaus, T.: The impact of inserting a tool into a software process. In: The conference of the Centre for Advanced Studies on Collaborative research, vol. SE - 1 (1993)
7. Glass, R.L.: Practical Programmer: Is This a Revolutionary Idea, or Not? Communications of the ACM 47(11), 23–25 (2004)
8. Gonzalez-Perez, C., Henderson-Sellers, B., Dromey, G.: A Metamodel for the Behavior Trees Modelling Technique. In: ICITA 05, pp. 35–39 (2005)
9. Winter, K.: Formalising Behavior Trees with CSP. In: Boiten, E.A., Derrick, J., Smith, G.P. (eds.) IFM 2004. LNCS, vol. 2999, pp. 148–167. Springer, Heidelberg (2004)
10. Grunske, L., Lindsay, P., Yatapanage, N., Winter, K.: An Automated Failure Mode and Effect Analysis Based on High-Level Design Specification with Behavior Trees. In: Romijn, J.M.T., Smith, G.P., van de Pol, J. (eds.) IFM 2005. LNCS, vol. 3771, pp. 129–149. Springer, Heidelberg (2005)
11. Colvin, R., Hayes, I.J.: "A Semantics for Behavior Trees, ACCS Technical Report, No. ACCS-TR-07-01, ARC Centre for Complex Systems (April 2007)
12. Dromey, R.G., Powell, D.: Early Requirements Defects Detection, TickIT International, 4Q05, pp. 3–13 (2005)
13. Dromey, R.G.: Scaleable Formalization of Imperfect Knowledge. In: 1st Asian Working Conference on Verified Software (AWCVS'06), Macau (2006)
14. Zafar, S., Dromey, R.G.: Integrating Safety and Security Requirements into Design of an Emedded System. In: Asia-Pacific Software Engineering Conference, pp. 629–636 (2005)
15. Zafar, S., Winter, K., Colvin, R., Dromey, R.G.: Verification of an Integrated Role-Based Access Control Model. In: 1st Asian Working Conderence on Verified Software (2006)

16. Behavior Engineering (2007), http://www.behaviorengineering.org/index.php
17. Smith, C., Winter, K., Hayes, I., Dromey, R.G., Lindsay, P., Carrington, D.: An Environment for Building a System Out of its Requirements. In: ASE 2004, pp. 398–399 (2004)
18. Lin, K., Chen, D., Sun, C., Dromey, R.G.: Maintaining constraints in collaborative graphic systems: the CoGSE approach. In: 9th European Conference on CSCW(2005)
19. Lin, K., et al.: Maintaining multi-way dataflow constraints in collaborative systems. In: Int. Conference in Collaborative Computing: Networking, Applications and Worksharing (2005)
20. Wen, L.: What is GSET and what it can do, http://www.sqi.gu.edu.au/gse/tools/gset.html
21. Visual Studio 2005, (2007) http://msdn.microsoft.com/vstudio/
22. MFC (2007), http://www.visionx.com/mfcpro/
23. XD++ (2007), http://www.ucancode.net/
24. Poseidon (2007), http://www.gentleware.com/
25. Altova UModel (2007), http://www.altova.com
26. MagicDraw (2007), http://www.magicdraw.com/
27. IBM-Rational Rose, http://www-306.ibm.com/software/awdtools/developer/rose/
28. Analyst Pro (2007), http://www.analysttool.com/
29. Borland Caliber, http://www.borland.com/us/products/caliber/
30. Telelogic DOORS (2007), http://www.telelogic.com/products/doors/doors/index.cfm
31. SmartDraw, http://www.smartdraw.com/
32. Gerndt, R., Ernst, R.: An Event-Driven Multi-Threading Architecture for Embedded Systems. In: 5th Int. Workshop on Hardware/Software Co-Design, pp. 29–33 (1997)
33. Krasner, G.E., Pope, S.T.: A cookbook for using the model-view controller user interface paradigm in Smalltalk-80. J. Object Oriented Program, 26–49 (1, 3, August, 1988)
34. Sun, C., Chen, D.: Consistency maintenance in real-time collaborative graphics editing systems. ACM Transactions on Computer-Human Interaction 9(1), 1–41 (2002)
35. Sun, C., et al.: Achieving convergence, causality-preservation, and intention-preservation in real-time cooperative editing systems. ACM Transactions on Computer-human Interaction 5(1), 63–108 (1998)
36. Simmonds, J., Bastarrica, M.C.: A tool for automatic UML model consistency checking. In: The 20th IEEE/ACM international Conference on Automated software engineering, ACM Press, New York (2005)
37. Malgouyres, H., Motet, G.: A UML model consistency verification approach based on meta-modeling formalization. In: ACM symposium on Applied computing (2006)
38. Vidal, J.S., Malgouyres, H., Motet, G.: UML2.0 consistency rules identification. In: The International Conference on Software Engineering Research and Practice, SERP (2005)
39. McUmber, M.E., Cheng, B.H.C.: A General Framework for Formalizing UML with Formal Language. In: The 23rd International Conference on Software Engineering (2001)
40. Cavarra, A., Riccobene, E., et al.: A Framework to Simulate UML Models: Moving from a Semi-formal to Formal Environment. ACM symposium on Applied computing (2004)
41. Bouquet, E., Legeard, B., Peureux, F., Torreborre, E.: Mastering Test Generation from Smart Card Software Formal Models. In: Barthe, G., Burdy, L., Huisman, M., Lanet, J.-L., Muntean, T. (eds.) CASSIS 2004. LNCS, vol. 3362, pp. 70–85. Springer, Heidelberg (2005)
42. Eriksson, M., Morast, H., Börstler, J.: The PLUSS toolkit – extending telelogic DOORS and IBM-rational rose to support product line use case modelling. In: Proceedings of the 20th IEEE/ACM international Conference on Automated software engineering, pp. 300–304 (2005)

43. Cooper, L., Chung, L.: Managing Change in OTS-Aware Requirements Engineering Approach. In: The 2nd international workshop on Models and processes for the evaluation of off-the-shelf components, pp. 1–4 (2005)
44. Somogyi, Z., Henderson, F.J., et al.: Mercury, an efficient purely declarative logic programming language. In: The 8th Australasian Computer Science Conference, pp. 499–512
45. Clarke, E.M., Wing, J.M.: Formal Methods: State of the Art and Future Directions. ACM Computing Surveys 28(4), 626–643 (1996)
46. Bensalem, S., Ganesh, V., Lakhnech, Y., Muñoz, C., Owre, et al.: An Overview of SAL. In: Fifth NASA Langley Formal Methods Workshop (LFM 2000), pp. 187–196 (2000)
47. Liu, S.: Formal Engineering for Industrial Software Development using the SOFL Method. Springer, Heidelberg (2004)

Differential Conversion: DWG – SVG Case Study

Martin Ota and Ivan Jelínek

Czech Technical University in Prague, Department of Computer Science and Engineering,
Praha 2, 131 25 Karlovo nám. 13, Czech Republic
{otam,jelinek}@fel.cvut.cz

Abstract. This paper is focused on differential conversion, which is a new approach to data transformation between different software systems. The strategy of differential conversion, which is built on a log of changes and identifier mapping, was introduced in CDVE 2006 in a purely theoretical paper entitled *Data Exchange in CAD during Iterative Work with Heterogeneous Systems*. A specific case study of differential conversion in use is elaborated in this text. It is about an intelligent bi-directional transformation between DWG and SVG. DWG is a proprietary CAD-format of the AutoCAD system, whereas SVG is an open, generic graphics format, based on XML. The implemented transformation allows usage of a model created in a CAD-system within a cooperative design intended for non-CAD users. It is useful not only for reading, but even for writing into the model and modifying it. Any changes made are returned back to the original model. The following case exemplifies the previously discussed strategy. For example, a project submitter, or another party in the review process, can use a normal, generic SVG editor for writing comments and proposals into the model. A solver can transform them back into the CAD-model, without other entities in the model being damaged. This case study describes differential export and import tools and takes note of the particular solutions of the log of changes and identifier mapping problems. It also describes the relationship to the original differential conversion proposal, discusses the particular implementation, and again generalizes into some *design pattern* for differential conversion implementation projects in the conclusion.

Keywords: CAD, cooperative design, cooperative engineering, data exchange, differential conversion, SVG.

1 Introduction

Differential conversion (DC) was introduced in CDVE 2006 [1] as a way of exchanging data during cooperative engineering and design between heterogeneous systems, which minimizes data distortion during its conversion. Utilization of DC is meaningful when the data is converted for modification in another system and then converted back to the original format. The main idea of DC is to transfer only new and changed objects and the objects without any changes are kept from the original data representation. The generic proposal of DC uses identifier mapping and the log of changes to reach it. The identifier mapping controls the preservation of information, which object was transformed into what (it cannot be simply a 1:1 relation), and the log of changes,

Y. Luo (Ed.): CDVE 2007, LNCS 4674, pp. 132–139, 2007.
© Springer-Verlag Berlin Heidelberg 2007

which must be supported by the system when data is modified after the conversion and is used for identifying changes in objects in the temporary data format. *New, modified* and *deleted* states are distinguished. The state of the object that is not in the log is *no change*.

Since our research is focused on CAD, we therefore deal with DC in this area as well. The following text describes a specific implementation of DC between two considerably different graphic formats – DWG and SVG. The domain of the case study is the design of the interior of an office building.

2 Case Description

The requirements are the following: The output of the office building design is, among others, the interior plan with a unified draft of the offices. Department managers should fill in comments and can eventually reconfigure the furniture, change the number of chairs and tables or change how the cubicle installations are divided. In this draft, they should fill in the names of employees on the single chairs. Managers modify only that part of the interior where their department is going to be placed. Merged modifications should be incorporated into the final model, which should be published for the employees on the intranet in two stages. First, the anonymous draft, and afterwards should come the modified final model with the employee names.

The building model is in DWG format of AutoCAD 2007. The managers do not have this system and thus is economically required to use a freeware editor based on SVG [2]. SVG is planned to be used for the intranet presentation of the model.

The SVG model is equipped with instructions on how to edit it. For example, an employee name is connected to a chair as a prepared text element EMPLOYEE_NAME, which correspond with a block attribute in DWG, and should be modified by filling in the name. The next example is that adding furniture must be done as object copying, etc. The exact rules are not important for this description of the case study.

3 Case Solution

A solution of the case uses DC, but it is not possible to follow the basic form because the selected SVG editor does not allow adding the functionality for on-line log of changes creating. The SVG editor used has two qualities that subsequently helps deduce the log of changes. The first quality is that the SVG editor respects identifiers stored in the 'id' objects attributes. The second quality is that the representation of unchanged objects is kept identical, even after saving the SVG representation, which is changed in the other positions. Thus, the objects' changes can be deduced from the comparison of the XML trees of the SVG representations before and after editing.

3.1 Process Model

Figure 1 depicts a conceptual process model of the case solution. The model does not contain a requirement solution for publishing on intranet, because it can be reached anytime by the conversion from DWG to SVG, without the utilization of helper out-puts of DC. So, from the process description perspective, it is not an important issue and the diagram would only be less clear. The process model is modelled in UML 2 [3], which is not so popular for business process modelling; however, it is closer to the readers who implement the supporting software for business processes (for a proof of the qualitative equality of UML and often preferred BPMN [4] see [5] and [6]).

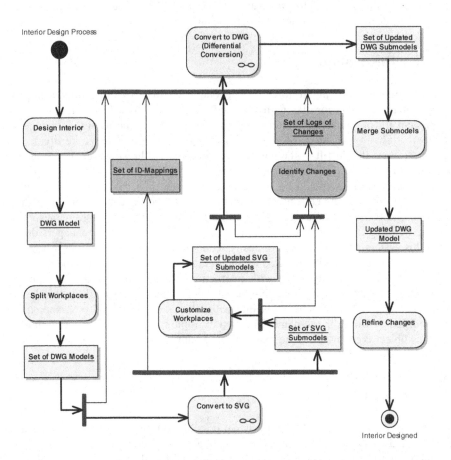

Fig. 1. Process Model of Whole Case Study

The thicker line marks how *normal* conversion would flow. The shaded-grey clas-sifiers concern exclusively DC and 'Identify Changes' represents the change of basic DC.

3.2 DWG to SVG Conversion Details

The conversion from DWG to SVG can be done in several ways. The most frequently used way – an analysis of source and target formats and the creation of a transforming application – was not used. The DWG format is neither public, nor does it guarantee compatibility with future versions (a possible reuse reduction). It was more suitable to develop an application nested into AutoCAD for the discussed solution.

As AutoCAD 2007 is a very open system, a lot of languages and interfaces can be used [7]. The language-dependent interfaces offer AutoLISP/VisualLISP, C or C++ with ADS, C++ with ObjectARX, and VBA. The interfaces which are less language-dependent are based on ActiveX and COM and finally on the ObjectARX Managed Wrapper Classes for .Net. From many reasons, we chose C# language with ObjectARX Managed Wrapper Classes for .Net.

The transfer of graphical information from the AutoCAD database/model to SVG can be done in two ways. One is analyzing the entity types and programming the transformation into SVG for each of them. An alternative is creating a context for drawing (as when drawing on the screen or to the preview picture of a file) – a

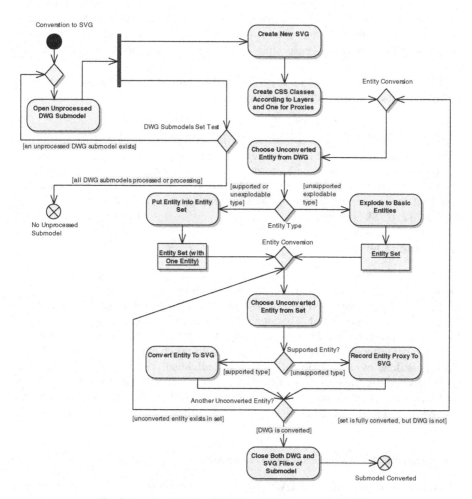

Fig. 2. Process Model of DWG to SVG Conversion Details

specialization of Autodesk.AutoCAD.GraphicsInterface.Context class – and calling the WorldDraw methods of entities during conversion. Benefits of the context are limited and fixed in the number of graphic elements. A disadvantage is that some entity types are only approximated, in spite of the fact that SVG supports them directly (e.g. an ellipse is approximated by an enormous number of straight lines). A drawback of the first way is that the number of entity types is high and not limited (the AutoCAD allows for creating user entity types). The advantage is a more reasonable transformation of entity types to SVG elements. The solution is based on a compromise, in a way that uses the direct transformation of entity types, but only types that are 'primitives'—that the AutoCAD's entities are exploded as a result of the Explode method invocation. The unsupported types are exploded just by this method. The conversion process is depicted in Fig. 2.

The AutoCAD's system of layers is transformed into the CSS styles used in SVG. In addition to that, a style for proxy objects (see [1], paragraph 4.1) is added, which is set to invisible. The DWG objects that are not possible to represent in SVG are converted into invisible SVG text objects (with necessary data). Those are 3D objects (not used in the discussed case study) and, for example, non-graphical database objects.

Each SVG file is enriched by a new XML file with identifier mapping. A simple algorithm is used for generating the target identifiers:

$$id=handle + `\text{-}' + x [+ `\text{-}' className];$$

where the *handle* is a persistent AutoCAD identifier in hexadecimal form, x is the decimal serial number of an SVG element of conversion of one entity (one entity can be converted into one or more elements), and the optional postfix with *className* describes the name of the class of original entity type (e.g. AcDbLine for lines). The design of the converting algorithm does not enable a conversion of more than one entity into each SVG element.

3.3 Identify Changes

The *Identify Changes* activity is a main difference from the basic proposal of DC – the log of changes is not generated on-line, but after editing the SVG model. SVG files are the input. Always, a pair of SVG files – the state before and after editing – for a sub-model is processed. The identifier-mapping file is not needed, because the SVG editor preserves the identifiers of objects that were with the model before its processing (i.e. modified objects and objects with no change). The identification of changes is done by the simple comparison of individual graphic objects in the XML tree of SVG. From this, the log of changes can be deduced– the XML file of attributed identifiers is an output for each SVG pair. The attributes are *modified*, *new* and *deleted*. The objects with no change (*no change* attribute) are not contained in the log of changes.

3.4 SVG to DWG Differential Conversion Details

The transformation of SVG to DWG follows the normal rules of DC. The input for each sub-model is a foursome: the original DWG model, updated SVG model, identifier mapping, and log of changes. The process of DC is depicted in Fig. 3.

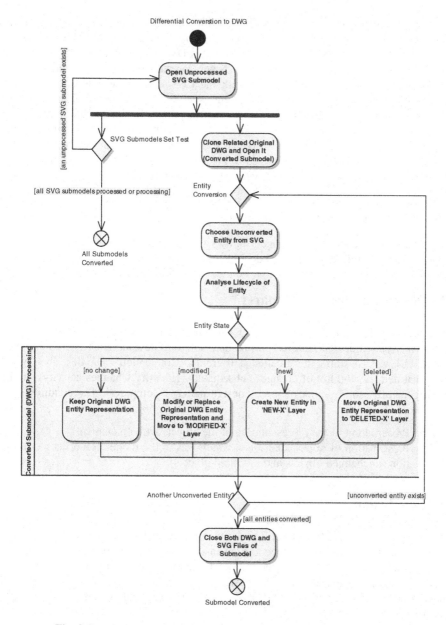

Fig. 3. Process Model of SVG to DWG Differential Conversion Details

The implementation of the transformation of SVG elements into DWG database objects is similar to the transformation of DWG into SVG. Again, it is the C# and ObjectARX managed classes for .Net module. For newly created objects, there is a transformation of each SVG element into DWG object(s). The element types that are not possible to convert exactly (e.g. fillings with colour gradients) are not transformed into proxy objects, but the closest approximation by AutoCAD's objects is performed. The reason is simple – the primary data format is DWG representation and the model must be fully controlled by AutoCAD. Newly created objects are inserted into a NEW-X layer, where X corresponds with the CSS-style name, and are eventually inserted into a NEW layer, if an unambiguous style is not assigned. The analogous rules are used for the other layers. A similar transformation of modification is provided for modified objects. If the unsupported modification is found, then the original object is deleted and a new one is created following the rules for newly created objects. The modified objects are moved to layer with MODIFIED- prefix. Finally, the deleted objects are moved to a layer with a DELETED- prefix.

Note #1: The layer prefixes (NEW-, MODIFIED-, and DELETED-) can be configured, and the possible conflicts with the original model layer names are controlled.

Note #2: The conversion component allows for keeping the objects in the original layers (without prefixes) and direct deletion of deleted objects.

4   Design Pattern – 'Comparer'

The best practices are beginning to be formed in patterns [6], [8], [9], [10], and [11], frequently called design patterns, in practical software development. At the moment, we see DC as a design pattern called 'Differential Conversion'. The described mutation that deduces the log of changes subsequently (Identify Changes activity) can be used generally, so we think of it as a design pattern 'Comparer'. The conditions for use are:

- Preservation of the representation of the objects with no change;
- Preservation of object identifiers, which was in the model before its modification (unchanged objects and modified objects).

5   Conclusion

The described case study has verified the viability of differential conversion, including combination with proxy objects, even in the case of incomparable graphics formats, which are dedicated for different uses. Differential conversion was declared as a design pattern and enriched by the design pattern 'Comparer', which can be used under the specified conditions when creating an on-line log of changes is not possible or effective.

Acknowledgements

This research has been supported by MSMT under research program No. 6840770014. The research has been supported by the grant of the Czech Grant Agency No. 201/06/0648.

References

1. Ota, M., Jelínek, I.: Data Exchange in CAD During Iterative Work with Heterogenous. In: Luo, Y. (ed.) CDVE 2006. LNCS, vol. 4101, pp. 25–32. Springer, Heidelberg (2006)
2. W3C: Scalable Vector Graphics (SVG) 1.1 Specification, W3C Recommendation 14 (January 2003), http://www.w3.org/TR/SVG11/
3. OMG: UML 2.1.1, (April 2007), http://www.omg.org/technology/documents/formal/uml.htm
4. White, S.A.: Introduction to BPMN, IBM Corporation, USA (April 2007), http://www.bpmn.org/Documents/Introduction%20to%20BPMN.pdf
5. White, S. A: Process Modeling Notations and Workflow Patterns, IBM Corporation, USA (December 2006), http://www.bpmn.org/Documents/Notations%20and%20Workflow%20Patterns.pdf
6. Col.: Patterns, (December 2006), http://is.tm.tue.nl/research/patterns/patterns.htm
7. Autodesk: AutoCAD 2007 on-line developers quides (2006)
8. Gamma, E., Helm, R., Johnson, R., Vlissides, J.: Design Patterns: Elements of Reusable Object-Oriented Software, 1st edn. Addison-Wesley Professional, Reading (1995)
9. Hohpe, G., Woolf, B.: Enterprise Integration Patterns: Designing, Building, and Deploying. Addison-Wesley Professional, Reading (2003)
10. Fowler, M.: Patterns of Enterprise Application Architecture, 1st edn. Addison-Wesley Professional, Reading (2002)
11. Fowler, M.: Analysis Patterns: Reusable Object Models, 1st edn. Addison-Wesley Professional, Reading (1996)

A Study of Version Control for Collaborative CAD

Zhiyong Chang, Jie Zhao, and Rong Mo

The Key Laboratory of Contemporary Design and Integrated Manufacturing Technology,
Ministry of Education, China at Northwestern Polytechnical University, Xi`an
changzy@nwpu.edu.cn

Abstract. Version control is the prerequisite of collaborative product development environment, which, in its turn, has attracted increasing attention of CAD/CAM engineers. We aim to present our research results on a strategy of supporting evolution of versions in a collaborative environment. The strategy we provide is consists of a functional model which make application developing more easier, a deployment model in which a Version Management Unit is the deploying cell and a communication agent is included to exchange version information, a storage model which support that version information is saved in space of personal, group or global respectively. The topics discussed also in this paper are definition of version status, the transform of version status, the storage location of version and corresponding version operations.

Keywords: collaboration, version control, model.

1 Introduction

In a general way, the development process of product is consisting of a serial of sub-process in which some local result, such as drawing, 3D model, CAE analyze, is formed. Because of the non-linearity attribution of those sub-processes in whole process of product development, so development process is a complicated one which can be identified by attempt and reiteration[1]. The results mentioned above, which express a certain state belonging to whole lifecycle of product development, can be formalized and managed by means of version.

There are researches which show that engineer spends lots of time to search relative information in which version information is an important part. Although configure management and version management are the important and necessary function of PDM system, but the most of commercial PDM has only a simple version module which is very difficult of supporting development process of complicated product which is familiar in fields of aero-engine, airplane and in which engineer is trying, modifying, negating and re-trying. It is hard to image that engineer can work effectively without the support of a nice method and tool of version management.

There are more complicated problems involved in collaborative product development than in traditional product development. So in this paper, we present architecture of version management which aims at supporting collaborative product development. The remainder of the paper is organized as follows. In section 2 we briefly review the related works. In section 3 we detail the architecture from three aspects. In section 4 version operations is given. Section 5 is conclusion.

Y. Luo (Ed.): CDVE 2007, LNCS 4674, pp. 140–148, 2007.

2 Related Works

The successful applying of CAD system makes a huge industry from 1980, then researchers realize that CAD system has non-regular requirement for data storage and regular DBMS(such as relational DBMS) is not suit for managing CAD model any more. So version management is presented as a available solution for the requirement of storage of historical development data, description of multi-view and multi-domain of product , hiberarchy of product data and so on, and it become a important research field recently.

Haskin and Lorie[4] from IBM present an extended relative model which has the ability of complicated object combination and supporting to long-term transaction to save and manage engineering data. Although their research is not associated directly with version management, but many later research of version is based on their works because of their large contribution for presenting combined object in relational DBMS.

Mcleod[5] develop a semantic based data model framework, which use a serial of relative table to express semantic model, to support version management. Landis[6] focuses on version management for such complicated system as CAD by means of ontology method. The method based on four conceptions: non-linear version history, version reference, change spread and restriction of spread. Chou and Kim[7] give a new model extended from model of Batory and Kim[8], the new model emphasize the notifying of change spread. They present a message based notifying policy and a sign based notifying policy in which message about change is sent either immediately or later and product designer can be notified the change which might affect their own model only when they re-inquire for the design object. Vines[9] presents a version model for change control in which four conceptions are engaged to control change spread. Firstly, Timestamp instead of version number is used as ID of version to connect event with succedent version clearly. Secondly, relationships among objects, which can be marked as change-sensitive or change-insensitive, are created distinctly to define the spread range of change. Thirdly, such change management objects as change query object, change notify objects are used to manage change. Finally, the changes are grouped by means of configure object.

Wang[9][10] discuss and realize a system which can manage version of engine database on a collaborative environment. His method makes a structure by using version dictionary, which include system dictionary and designer dictionary, to organize and save version. The operations to version include setting up current version, recovering version, merging version and deleting version. Zhang[11] gives a version management model which is based on such conceptions as card file and file serial. Also a dictionary is used to manage structure and restriction of file card. The storage of model is based on a relative DBMS.

Although there are large numbers researches about version management which aims at constructing a frameworks and give corresponding arithmetic of version operation, but the most of works is based on or aim at version control about software development. The version management aimed at managing CAD data on a collaborative environment of product development is less researched and reported.

3 Version Manage Model on Collaborative Environment

In this section, we introduce a new version manage model and try to explain it from three aspects including function model, deploying model and storage model.

3.1 Function Model

Fig.1 shows a function model which includes four layers that rely on each other. Based on consideration of scalability and flexibility, Physics Storage Layer provides a storage policy which separate up layer (Object Manage Layer) from storage item. Because of uniform functions provided by Physics Storage Layer, the version-relative information is saved on RDBMS and product development-relative data, such as CAD model, CAM instruction and CAE analyze, are saved on operation system in form of disk file.

For the purpose of management and organization of version objects, Object Manage Layer provides a nonobjective presentation of version data. A method of E-R modeling is used to define target data and their relationship which can present complicated and various engine data which involves such simple data as design specification, NC code and such combined data as assembly tree

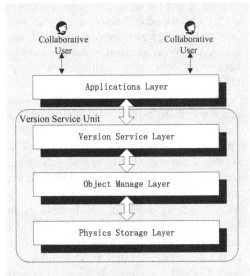

Fig. 1. Function Model

of product and version historic information. Object Manage Layer call functions from Physics Storage Layer and provide functions to up layer (Version Service Layer).

The base services from Object Manage Layer are assembled and restricted on Version Service Layer to provide a version operation service for its up layer (Applications Layer).

A VSU (Version Service Unit) is constructed by integrating these three layers mentioned above and serve as the core of version service.

The applications, which are used to create, access, manage product data on product collaborative development, such as CAD tools, office tools and PDM system, should be reopen in order to use version service provided by Version Service Layer.

3.2 Deploying Model

As the distributed feature of product collaborative development, Version management has same distributed feature shown as fig.2.

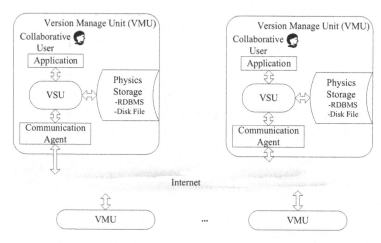

Fig. 2. Distributed Deploying Model

Participators who are distributed on working time and working place are connected by Internet. A VMU (Version Management Unit) is constructed, which include USV, application, and policy of physics storage, communication agent and collaborative users, to support every single working place. The policy of physics storage in charge of storage of version data. It can be a relational DBMS or a disk file of operation system and encapsulated by VSU. Communication agent in charge of connecting each VMU distributed on Internet by means of message which is formulized by a set of Meta-Language designed for version management.

3.3 Storage Model

On the process of product collaborative development, work-along and work-collaboration is two inherent features for participators. Work-along needs independent data storage space and work-collaboration means exchange and share of product data between participators. Collaboration can include big one, in which collaborative period is more longer and collaborative range is more extend and management is more rigorous, and small one, which means short-time collaboration and small correlative data and loose management. So we present a storage model as shown in Fig.3.

Local Storage is corresponding to host (a network node) one by one. A host is a single cell which provides storage service with the support of physics Storage Layer and Object Manage Layer on VSU and independent with other host.

Personal Storage Space is corresponding to participator one by one and based on Local Storage. One Personal Storage Space can include one or more Local Storages as while as one Local Storage can provide support of data saving for one or more Personal Storage Space, which means that participator can transfer work space from one to another but not be limited to specific work space. Unlike Local Storage is a physics conception, Personal Work Space is a logic conception which consists of set of product object belonging one participator, relative restrict and access limits. The product objects in Personal Work Space are private and can not be access or referred by other participator.

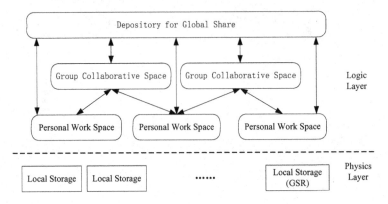

Fig. 3. Storage Model

Like Personal Work Space, Group Collaborative Space is also a logic conception which consists of group number and version data submitted by participator. It is a loose organization because any participator can create a group for any reason and then invite other participator who can join or reject freewill. The creator becomes administrator of group by default and in charge of management of numbers and access control. The number can share steady product model from Personal Work Space to Group Collaborative Space and other numbers can access these shared product model.

Depository for Global Share is Global Share Space for all participators conceptually and it is a inherent storage in perpetuity but not a temporary one and there are more restrict rules, which ensure that version object in it is valid and verified, of access and modifying in it. Product object can be submitted from Personal Work Space by number or from Global Work Space by administrator. Depository for Global Share marked with Global Shared Repository (GSR) shown as Fig.3 monopolizes one certain Local Storage which is not accessible for participator or group.

4   Version Operations

In this section, we define the state of version and give a serial of operations to change the status and storage location of version object.

4.1   Version Status

The product object existing in Personal Work Space must belong to one of four statuses as below.

(a) Validated
Validated version has the features of: (1) All attributes of object are not allowed to be modified, (2)If object is a assembly, All of its components must belong to validated status, (3)Deriving new version from this object is allowed, (4)It can be referred by other object.

(b) Stable
Stable version has the features of (1) All version- correlative attributes of object are not allowed to be modified, (2) If object is a assembly, All of its components must belong to validated status or stable status, (3) Deriving new version from this object is allowed, (4) It can be referred by other object.

(c) Transient
Transient version has the features of (1) version new created must belong to transient status, (2) All attributes that maintained by participator are allowed to be modified, (3) Deriving new version from this object is not allowed, (4) It can not be referred by other object.

4.2   Operations of Change Version Status

We define four operations to change the status of version as follows.

(a) Create Object
The creation operation is the start point of all version operation. It consists of two major steps:

STEP 1: After participator give some define of attributes such as attribute name and data type, system creates an abstract representation Base of Version Histories.

STEP 2: After participator give corresponding values of attributes, system creates a real representation object.

(b) Promote Version Status
Promote operation can be applied on transient object and stable object and change version status to stable and validated respectively. It will not create new object.

(c) Derive Version
Derive operation can be applied on stable object and validated object. It will create a new representation object and consists of five steps as follows:

STEP 1: The system creates a new representation object in depository of representation objects.

STEP 2: This new representation object has a version number which is minimum of non-repeated.

STEP 3: This object has status of transient.

STEP 4: All values of version-relative attributes of original version are inherited by this object and all values of version-independent attributes of original are confirmed by participator.

STEP 5: The deriving relationship from original version to new version is recorded by system.

(d) Delete Version
When delete operation is applied on transient object, the object will disappear forever. When it is applied on stable object or validated object, system will inspect if there is relative object of deleted object. A delete operation to relative object will be executed according to result of inspection.

Fig.4 shows status change of version when version operation is applied.

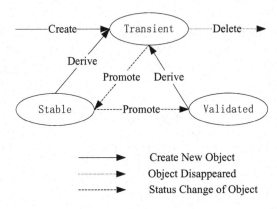

Fig. 4. Status Change of Version

4.3 Change of Storage Location

As described in sub-section 3.3, Product Object can be saved in Personal Work Space, Group Collaborative Space and Depository for Global Share from logic viewpoint as can be saved in Local Storage of various network node. System set up a Local Storage of certain network node as Global Share Repository. We define a serial of operations to change storage location of product object.

(a) Share Object
Share operation make private object accessible for other number in group by sharing product object from Personal Work Space to Group Collaborative Space. Only the validated object and stable object can be shared while transient object can not. Share operation change the attribute of object but not create a new object.

(b) Release Object
The representation object saved in Personal Work Space or in Group Collaborative Space can be released to Depository for Global Share by its owner. Only the validated object can be release while stable object and transient object can not. Unlike share operation, release operation creates a new copy of original object in Depository for Global Share and original one is deleted from Personal Work Space or Group Collaborative Space. Before released to Depository for Global Share, the object should be approved by administrator by means of a collaborative meeting or an approval workflow. The object saved in Depository for Global Share can be referred by all participator but can not be modified.

(c) Check Out Object
The representation Object saved in Depository for Global Share can be check out to Personal Work Space by participator. This operation is equal to performing a derive operation from Depository for Global Share to Personal Work Space and new object has status of transient.

(d) Check In Object
The Object Checked out from Depository for Global Share can be check back in it when status of object is validated. The storage location of object shifts from Personal

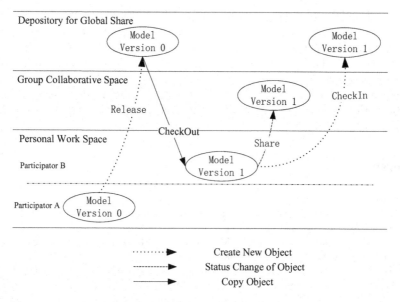

Fig. 5. Change of Storage Location

Work Space to Depository for Global Share. Like the release operation, an approval is necessary before checking object in.

Fig.5 shows a sample about change of storage location. A version 0 of model in Personal Work Space of participator A is released to Depository for Global Share, and then participator B checks it out to himself Personal Work Space. Some modification are make to model and a new version 1 of model is come into being, then participator B share version 1 of model to Group Collaborative Space for the purpose of emendation from other participators. If Status of version 1 become stable, participator B can check it in to Depository for Global Share.

5 Validation

Based on the models and operations mentioned above, we have built a prototype system to validate the completeness and correctness of model. We design and implement a serial of classes to support layered function, distributed deploying and grouped storage, the prototype has also include a simple interface in which user can create, promote, derive and delete version as while as share, release, check out and check in object. Because version management is the essential part of PDM system, the credible validation should be carried out by means of integrating the model with PDM system. This is our future works also.

6 Conclusion

Version management is more complicated in collaborative product development than in traditional mode. The researches to these items can provide work-mode and applications to manage evolution history of product data for a collaborative team. The architecture of version management we present in this paper has the features of: (1) A layered function model makes clear definition of functions of each layer, (2) Distributed deploying is suit for collaborative product development. (3) A layered storage model provides an information sharing tools for numbers among groups. (4) The architecture can support various CAD tools on a uniform way. Our future works will be carried out among management of version configure and spread restriction of change.

References

1. Youshu, Q., Yongsheng, Y., Huagong, C.: Categorizing of Versions in Engineering Design and a Data Model for Management of Product Versions. Journal of Huazhong University of Science and Technology 26(8) (1998)
2. Meilin, S.: Computer Supported Collaborative Work- Theory and Practice (12), 277 (2000) ISBN 7-5053-6293-3 TP 3398
3. Jian, C., Youliang, Z., Haiyang, Z.: Version Management for Collaborative Design. Computer Integrated Manufacturing Systems, CIMS (6), 16–20 (1998)
4. Haskin, R.L., Lorie, R.A.: On extending the functions of a relational database system. In: Proceedings of the ACM SIGMOD Conference, May 1982, pp. 207–212. ACM, New York (1982)
5. Mcleod, D., Narayanaswamy, K., Bapa Rao, K.: An approach to information management for CAD/VLST applications. In: Proceedings of the SIGMOD conference on Databases for Engineering Applications, San Jose,Calif., May 1983, pp. 39–50. ACM, New York (1983)
6. Laddis, G.S.: Design evolution and history in an object-oriented CAD/CAM database. In: proceedings of the 31st COMPCON Conference, San Francisco, Calif., March 1986, pp. 297–305 (1986)
7. Chou, H., Kim, W.: A unifying framework for version control in a CAD environment. In: proceedings of the 12th VLDB Conference, Kyoto, Japan, August 1986, pp. 336–346 (1986)
8. Vines, P., Vines, D., King, T.: Configuration and change control in GAIA, September 1988. ACM, New York (1988)
9. Qianping, W., Zongkai, L., Yuchai, G.: Version Control OF EDBMS for Computer Supported Cooperative Design. Journal of Software 7(11) (1996)
10. Qianping, W.: Path Based Version Management and Implementation for EDBMS. Journal of Computer Aided Design & Computer Graphics 9(2) (March 1997)
11. Pengcheng, Z., Renhou, L., Ming, Q., Xinhua, G.: Strategy of the Document Management in Computer Supported Cooperative Design. Computer Engineering and Applications 4, 201–203 (2003)

Semantic Web Services Discovery System with QoS for Enhanced Web Services Quality

Okkyung Choi[1], Heejai Choi[1], Zoonky Lee[1], and Sangyong Han[2]

[1] Yonsei Graduate School of Information, New Millennium hall, 134
Shinchon-dong, Seodaemun-gu, Seoul, 120-749, Korea
[2] Department of Computer Science & Engineering, Chungang University, 221,
Huksuk-dong, Dongjak-ku, Seoul, 156-756, Korea
okchoi20@gmail.com, {yena9419,zlee}@yonsei.ac.kr,
hansy@cau.ac.kr

Abstract. Semantic Web Services are the key technology providing services for the users' convenience in the semantic web environment. Many companies in various fields are researching and developing languages for constructing Semantic Web Services such as DAML-S, WSDL, X-LANG and BPEL4WS. DAML-S is a method that accesses the existing Web Service method from a semantic web environment. However, the current Semantic Web Services Discovery System does not provide sufficient processing of quality factors (performance, accessibility, availability, reliability and transaction) nor reliable and accurate service results desired by the user through a UDDI search method. The present study analyzes the disadvantages of the current web services and suggests a Semantic Web Services Discovery System based on QoS applying semantic web technologies as a solution to the problems. The suggested system provides a UDDI and DAML-S based discovery engine to allow efficient web service discovery and composition.

Keywords: Semantic Web Services, QoS(Quality of Services), Information Retrieval, DAML-S(DAML+OIL Services), UDDI(Universal Description, Discovery, and Integration).

1 Introduction

Semantic Web Services enable discovery, execution and composition of automated web services by combining web services based on standards, such as SOAP, WSDL and UDDI, with semantic web technologies, such as RDF, DAML+OIL and OWL. The weak points of former methods have been improved to enable effective Web Services registration, search, organization, execution and composition [7].

However, DAML-S does not support automated web services yet. First, the system does not use the appropriate method for expressing the information with restrictions of conditions and it does not response to user's requests. Second, quality of service (performance, transaction and reliability) is insufficient.

For such reasons, this paper suggests the Semantic Web Services Discovery System to solve the problems. Suggested system is capable of searching for general web documents, UDDI and semantic web documents.

Y. Luo (Ed.): CDVE 2007, LNCS 4674, pp. 149–156, 2007.

2 Methodologies for Web Services Quality Evaluation

2.1 Web Services Requirements for Quality Evaluation (Evaluation Factors)

The requirements for web service quality evaluation can be categorized as suggested in Table 1 below.

Table 1. Web Services Requirements for Quality Evaluation

Factor	Definition
Performance	Performance is a qualitative aspect that can be measured by execution time etc. The quantity that is processed during a certain period of time and the waiting time between the point of service request and reply.
Reliability	Reliability refers to the processed rate of the data transmitted during a certain period of time. The web service's reliability is determined by the number of success and failure.
Transaction	The transaction technology plays a very important role in web service automation and is a prerequisite for realizing faultless web services. Transaction refers to the state of having every processed unit satisfy "ACID," atomicity, consistency, isolation and durability

2.2 Problem Analysis of Former Research and Studies

Based on web services related quality evaluation factors, this section will deal with the problems with the current web services framework in the semantic web environment. The problems can be described largely in four aspects as outlined below.

Table 2. Problem Analysis of Web Services by Quality Evaluation Factors

Factor	Problem Analysis
Performance	Bottlenecks can occur due to limits of transmission protocols and messaging systems such as HTTP and SOAP. Also, other web services methods currently used do not process reliable messages and the waiting time, message processing and transferring time is too long resulting in poor performance.
Reliability	The current methods are not equipped with the base technologies for processing in the message sending and receiving ends, which is required for reliable messaging. Furthermore, they do not support standardization and interoperability.
Transaction	Lacks in monitoring functions for efficient web service support and fault preventing functions for preventing faults from occurring during execution.

The most important factor of the semantic web service is how much the user can trust and rely on the service provided. However, other web services methods currently used do not process reliable messages and the waiting time, message processing and transferring time is too long resulting in poor performance.

3 QoS Measurement Algorithm

For more accurate and reliable web service results, the provided matching method must reflect QoS factors such as time, price, reliability and performance. The current systems such as Larks[2] or Infosleuth[1] do not apply these factors in their match-making methods. Though METEROS[3] developed by the University of Georgia does reflect QoS factors in matchmaking, no adjustments are made in regard to each individual QoS factor. Instead, the overall QoS similarity is determined by only one of the factors. Thus, considerably relevant and meaningful web services could be evaluated lower than their actual ranking.

For such reasons, this study classifies quality evaluation factors and suggests separate algorithms for each factor. After applying algorithms to each QoS measurement factor value, the adjusted value and standard value are calculated. Then, the QoS score is calculated by multiplying all the QoS measurement factors. The QoS measurement procedures are as shown in Figure 1 below.

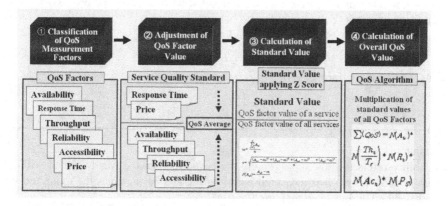

Fig. 1. QoS Measurement Process

3.1 QoS Measurement Algorithm

QoS measurement algorithm suggested in this study is classified into availability, responding time, maximum processing amount, reliability, accessibility and price. These factors are calculated and applied in matchmaking. Here, service quality is better the lower the value of response time, price and higher the value of availability, maximum processing amount, reliability and accessibility. As so, for accurate and efficient QoS measurement, it is important to calculate the adjusted and standard values of QoS factors and apply them all in calculating the overall QoS score.

* Availability
Availability refers to whether the web service currently exists or not and if the service is usable. It is calculated by how much of a certain unit time (min.) the user can request for the service.

▪ Definition 1

When the unit time is T_u and service failure time T_d, the average time the service is usable during the unit time, in other words, Availability (A_u) is as indicated below.

$$A_u = 1 - \frac{T_d}{T_u}$$

* Performance
Performance refers to how fast and stably the web service is provided. It is evaluated based on the time it requires to respond to the user's requests and the maximum number of services that can be processed during the unit time.

▪ Definition 2

When the system complete response time is T_{sr} and user request time is T_{ur}, the response time (T_r) is as indicated below.

$$T_r = T_{sr} - T_{ur}$$

If unit time is T_u and the maximum number of services that can be processed is S_{MR}, then the throughput (Th_s) is as indicated below.

$$Th_s = \frac{S_{MR}}{T_u}$$

Thus the overall performance (P_s) is as indicated below.

$$P_s = \frac{Th_s}{T_r}$$

* Reliability
Reliability refers to how appropriately the requested service was executed within a given period of time. It is measured based on the number of times the requested service has failed during a certain period of time.

▪ Definition 3

When unit time is T_u, and the average time error occurred in the system is S_{MF}, then the Reliability (R_s) is as indicated below.

$$R_s = 1 - \frac{T_{MF}}{T_u}$$

*Accessibility
Accessibility refers to whether the service is usable when requested. It depends on how easily the desired information can be attained. For measurement, the current service is regularly checked to see whether it is available.

■ Definition 4

When the number of messages the service responds to is S_{SRM} and the number of messages sent by the user is S_{URM}, Accessibility (Ac_s) is as indicated below.

$$Ac_s = \frac{S_{SRM}}{S_{URM}}$$

*Price

Price refers to the cost required for executing the web service. From the user's view, preference for the web service is higher the lower the price is.

■ Definition 5

When the price requested by the user is P_u and the price suggested by the service is P_r, the QoS factor Price (P_s) is as indicated below.

$$P_s = P_u - P_r$$

*Calculation of Standard Value

Calculation of the standard value of each QoS factor based on the adjusted QoS value is as follows. Standard value refers to the how much the QoS factor value of a service accounts for among the QoS factor value of all services.

In other words, the standard value is measured to prevent a single factor from determining the overall similarity after adjustment of QoS factor value. Generally, the standard value is indicated by the Z score or the T score. The Z score is based on the average of 0 and variation of 1 while the T score is based on an average of 50 and a variation of 10 to improve the inconvenience of Z scores that are usually negative numbers or have decimals [8]. The present study applies the Z score in order to regularize score matching with other coinciding factors.

■ Definition 6

When the availability (A_u), which is an average time of the service during a unit time is $N(A_u)$, the total number of services is n, the average of services is m and a certain service is k, then the average of $N(A_u)$ is calculated as shown below.

$$m = \frac{\sum_{i=1}^{n} A_{ui}}{n}$$

$$s = \sqrt{\frac{\left(A_{u1} - m\right)^2 + \left(A_{u2} - m\right)^2 + \left(A_{u3} - m\right)^2 \ldots \ldots + \left(A_{un} - m\right)^2}{n}}$$

$$N(A_{uk}) = \frac{A_{uk} - m}{s}$$

*QoS Measurement Algorithm

The QoS measurement algorithm based on the sum of standard values (Definition 6) of each QoS factor (Definition 1-5) is as indicated below.

■Definition 7

The QoS measurement algorithm, the multiplication of the standard values of each QoS factor including Availability (A_u), Response Time (T_r), Throughput (Th_s), Reliability (R_s), Accessibility(R_s) and price (P..) is as indicated below.

$$\sum(Qos) = N(A_u) * N(\frac{Th_s}{T_r}) * N(R_s) * N(Ac_s) * N(P_s)$$

3.2 Comparison and Evaluation

Currently the University of Georgia's METEOR-S[3] is the only system reflecting QoS factors in matchmaking. METEOR-S' QoS measurement algorithm based on time, price and reliability calculates the difference between the query and service based on the minimum, average and maximum values between QoS factors. But even when QoS factors time and reliability are low, the overall QoS score could still be high if the price is excessively high and thus be ranked high in matching. In other words, a particular factor alone could determine the overall similarity value.

In order to modify the problem above, the present study classifies the QoS measurement factors into availability, responding time, maximum processing amount, reliability, accessibility and price and calculates each factor individually. Furthermore, the standard values were also calculated after adjusting QoS factors' values to consider how much a service's QoS accounts for among the overall QoS factors.

Table 3. Comparison and Evaluation of QoS Measurement Algorithms

Condition	METEOR-S	Proposed System
QoS Factors	Time, price, reliability	Availability, responding time, max. processing amount, accessibility, price
Measuring Method	Uses min., average and max. values of QoS factors.	Adjusts QoS factor values and then calculates standard value.
Weak Point	-Problems from ranking based on difference between query and service -A single factor could determine the overall similarity.	-May require long searching time due to more various QoS factors.

4 Semantic Web Services Discovery System with QoS

As a solution to the problems of the current web services system observed in chapter 2 based on quality evaluation, the present study suggests the QoS based Semantic Web Services Discovery System. Chapter 4 will describe the overall structure of the suggested system and the functions of each module.

4.1 Architecture

Figure 2 illustrates how the service advertisement requested by the service requester is searched for using the Extended DAML-S/UDDI and the Web Services QoS Checker.

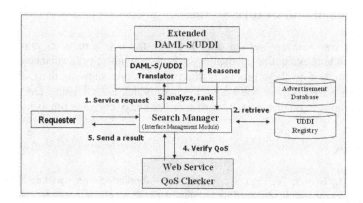

Fig. 2. Architecture

Step1: Requester submits a request to the Search Manager.
Step2: Search Manager retrieves all the advertisements from the Advertisement Database and UDDI Registry.
Step3: Search Manager sends it to DAML-S/UDDI Translator that constructs a UDDI service description. Then Reasoner computes the level of match and ranks the results.
Step4: Search Manager sends results to the Web Service QoS checker using QoS measurement algorithm if it is verified or not.
Step5: Search Manager sends final results to the requester.

4.2 Function of Each Module

(1) Search Manager
The Search Manager is located in the center surrounded by the Requester, Extended DAML-S/UDDI and Web Service QoS Checker and functions as a mediator to allow the service requester to receive more accurate and verified results. The Service Manager retrieves the requester's service request from the UDDI Registry and Advertisement Database and requests to the Extended DAML-S/UDDI and Web Services QoS Checker for accurate analysis and verification of the returned results.

(2) Extended DAML-S/UDDI
The basic web services methods including UDDI are simple search methods such as syntax analysis that do not apply semantic factors. As a result, it is difficult to verify and confirm the user's requests. Problems with the simple searching method can be solved by the *Extended DAML-S/UDDI. Extended DAML-S/UDDI* analyzes and ranks the results returned from the UDDI Registry using DAML-S/UDDI Translator and Reasoner, and sends the results to the Search Manager.

(3) Web Services QoS Checker
The Web Services QoS Checker does not exist in the original UDDI model. It evaluates the quality of the results analyzed by the Extended DAML-S/UDDI and sends the final results to the Search Manager.

5 Conclusion and Future Studies

The current web services system does not take the user's requests into account or provide sufficient evaluation of quality such as reliability, performance and transaction. As a solution to these problems, the present study suggests the QoS based Semantic Web Services Discovery System. It provides a UDDI and DAML-S based discovery engine to enable efficient web services discovery and composition.

References

1. Nodine, M., Bohrer, W., Ngu, A.: Semantic multibrokering over dynamic heterogeneous data sources in InfoSleuth. In: Proceedings of the Fifteenth International Conference on Data Engineering, Sydney, pp. 358–365. IEEE Computer Society Press, Los Alamitos (1999)
2. Sycara, K., Widoff, S., Klusch, M., Lu, J.: LARKS: Dynamic Matchmaking Among Heterogeneous Software Agents in cyberspace. Autonomous Agents and Multi-Agent Systems 05, 173–203 (2002)
3. Cardoso, J., Sheth, A.: Semantic e-Workflow Composition. Journal of Intelligent Information Systems (JIIS), 191–225 (2003)
4. Sycara, K., Paolucci, M., Soudry, J., Srinivasan, N.: Dynamic Discovery and Coordination of Agent-Based Semantic Web Services. IEEE Internet Computing 08(3), 66–73 (2004)
5. Paolucci, M., Kawamura, T., Payne, T., Sycara, K.: Semantic matching of web services capabilities. In: Proc. of the 1st International Semantic Web Conference (ISWC) (2002)
6. Greenwood, D., Buhler, P., Reitbauer, A.: Web Service Discovery and Composition using the Web Service Integration Gateway. In: Proceedings of the 2005 IEEE International Conference on e-Technology, e-Commerce and e-Service, IEEE Computer Society Press, Los Alamitos (2005)
7. Choi, O., Han, S., Abraham, A.: Semantic Matchmaking Services Model for the intelligent Web Services. In: International Conference on Computational Science and Applications, UK, pp. 146–148. IEE Press, UK (2006)
8. So-Yeon: Algorithms for Intelligent Web Service Discovery considering Process Information and Qos. Chungnam National University, Korea (February 2005)

Intelligent Library and Tutoring System for Brita in the PuBs Project

Arturas Kaklauskas, Edmundas Zavadskas, Edmundas Babenskas, Marko Seniut, Andrejus Vlasenko, and Vytautas Plakys

Vilnius Gediminas Technical University
Sauletekio al. 11, LT-10223 Vilnius, Lithuania
artka@st.vgtu.lt

Abstract. As digital libraries become more popular, information and knowledge overload has become a pressing yet required literature searching problem. Problems with searching in digital libraries will become more complex as the amount of information/knowledge increases. Traditional digital libraries often index words and documents while learners think in terms of topics and subjects. As a result, learners cannot determine how well a particular topic and/or subject is covered, or what types of search methods will provide the required information and knowledge without problems. In order to increase the efficiency and quality of the Brita in PuBs project's activities, an Intelligent Library and Tutoring System for the Brita in PuBs project (ILTS-BP) was developed. ILTS-BP has the ability to personalize, maximize reuse, index, analyse and integrate valuable information and knowledge from a wide selection of existing sources. Also, the authors have integrated ILTS-BP with a Voice Stress Analyser Subsystem. ILTS-BP is briefly analysed in this paper.

Keywords: real-time system, knowledge management, multiple user, intelligent library and tutoring system, Brita in PuBs Project, voice stress analysis.

1 Introduction

Most advanced e-libraries select, organize, retrieve, and transmit tacit and explicit knowledge. Different reports contain explicit criticisms of the libraries' focus on their specific collections and recommendations to focus more on the user's needs. There is a need to overpass key limitations in the development of traditional libraries, i.e. libraries which have been developed for particular content and a specific group of learners. We believe that future libraries will become a practical knowledge storehouse and will offer intelligent opportunities for users.

Search engine rankings have been adopted in most advanced intelligent libraries (Alexandrov et al., 2003, Gutwin et al., 1999, Hsinchun et al., 1998, Kaklauskas et al., 2006, Ruch et al., 2007, Trnkoczy et al., 2006, J. Wang, 2003) and tutoring systems (Armani et al., 2000, Brusilovsky, 2000, Day et al., 2007, Lucence, 2005, and Pouliquen et al., 2005). As part of the ongoing Illinois Digital Library Initiative project, research proposes an intelligent personal spider (agent) approach to Internet searching, which is grounded on automatic textual analysis, general-purpose searches

Y. Luo (Ed.): CDVE 2007, LNCS 4674, pp. 157–166, 2007.

and genetic algorithms (Hsinchun *et al.*, 1998). Pouliquen *et al.* (2005) that uses parsing techniques to extract information from texts, and provide a proper semantic indexation that is used by a medical-specific search engine. Day *et al.* (2007) use the Jakarta Lucene full-text indexer to index full-texts of textbooks. Jakarta Lucene is a high-performance, fully-featured text search engine library written entirely in Java. Its technology is suitable for nearly all applications that require full-text searches. ITA (Pouliquen *et al.*, 2005) index chapters, sections, and subsections of textbooks. Highlighters are used to highlight the index context. Finally, the ITA provides reading recommendations for students via a chapter similarity function. However, intelligent libraries (Alexandrov *et al.*, 2003, Gutwin *et al.*, 1999, Hsinchun *et al.*, 1998, Kaklauskas *et al.*, 2006, Ruch *et al.*, 2007, Trnkoczy *et al.*, 2006, J. Wang, 2003) and intelligent tutoring systems (Armani *et al.*, 2000, Brusilovsky, 2000, Day *et al.*, 2007, Lucence, 2005, and Pouliquen *et al.*, 2005) with search engine rankings cannot select chapters (sections, paragraphs) of specific texts, which are the most relevant to a student, cannot integrate the chapters (sections, paragraphs) of specific texts into learner-specific alternatives of teaching material and cannot select the most rational alternative, i.e. cannot develop alternatives of training materials, perform multiple criteria analysis and automatically select the most effective variant. However, an Intelligent Library and Tutoring System for the Brita in PuBs project (ILTS-BP) can perform the afore-mentioned functions. To the best of our knowledge the above function has not been implemented before, and so this attempt is the first time someone has done so. The proposed approach helps students to obtain suitably tailored material for any e-learning course. The above-mentioned and other improvements are possible when using the ILTS-BP.

The Brita in PuBs (Bringing Retrofit Innovation to Application in Public Buildings) project is being carried out with the financial assistance of the Framework 6 Programme. The BRITA in PuBs proposal on Eco-buildings aims to increase the market penetration of innovative and effective retrofit solutions so as to improve energy efficiency and implement renewables, with moderate cost additions. In order to increase the efficiency and quality of the delivery of training, teaching and research activities: an Intelligent Library and Tutoring System for Brita in PuBs project (ILTS-BP) have been developed. The developed System is also practically used in three distance MSc study programmes of Vilnius Gediminas Technical University (Real Estate Management; Construction Economics and Business; Internet Technologies and Real Estate Management). Currently, 236 students attend these two-year study programmes. All of them can use ILTS-BP. The main obstacle to wide application of the System in practice is the rather small Domain Model, which is small due to the problems related to copyright: learning material can be included in the Domain Model only with the consent of its authors. Therefore, considerably high financial expenditures are needed.

This paper is structured as follows: after this introduction, Section 2 describes the Intelligent Library and Tutoring System for Brita in PuBs Project; Section 3 depicts the Voice Stress Analyser Subsystem; Section 4 analyses ILTS-BP with Special Emphasis on the Multivariant Optional Module Design and Multiple Criteria Analysis and finally, concluding remarks and future works are presented in Section 5.

2   Intelligent Library and Tutoring System for Brita in PuBs Project

The Intelligent Library and Tutoring System for the Brita in PuBs project (ILTS-BP) consists of six subsystems: Domain Model, Student Model, Tutor and Testing Model, Voice Stress Analyser Subsystem, Subsystem of Multivariant Optional Module Design and Multiple Criteria Analysis, Database of Computer Learning Systems, Decision Support Subsystem and Graphic Interface. The Domain Model, Student Model, Tutor and Testing Model, Database of Computer Learning Systems and Graphic Interface are similar to the existing Intelligent Tutoring Systems. The Voice Stress Analyser (VSA) Subsystem and Multivariant Optional Module Design and Multiple Criteria Analysis (MOMD-MCA) Subsystem are innovative Intelligent Tutoring Systems solutions. Therefore VSA and MOMD-MCA Subsystems are only briefly analysed.

3   The Voice Stress Analyser Subsystem

The muscles of a human throat vibrate in a range of 8-12 Hz and this range is called a micro-tremor. When a person is emotional or stressed the vibration shifts from 8-9 Hz to 11-12 Hz and the more intensive the stress the higher the frequency of such vibrations. The Voice Stress Analyser Subsystem (VSA) measures stress in a human voice.

The research's aim was to compare data received during an examination with ILTS-BP (information on correct and incorrect answers, time periods for each question, and the number of times a student changed an answer to each question of a test) with similar data received from the Voice Stress Analyser (VSA) Subsystem, to make practical conclusions and to plan future research. This research helped to determine changes of a student's psychophysical condition during examinations. During an e-test, students were asked to select one correct answer from the provided alternatives and to say the answer aloud. The sounds of each answer that were recorded were then saved into a PC memory with an identification code for further analysis. Records were analysed by using the VSA Subsystem and the frequency range of micro-tremors for each specific answer to an e-test question was determined. A higher frequency of voice vibrations was determined when analysing voice answers to "unknown/difficult" questions. Also, it was found that the student's emotional stress was greater when answering "unknown/difficult" questions.

Reliability of the results was assessed by making a correlation analysis of emotional stress and of the evaluations of correct/incorrect answers to test questions. The analysis showed that a correlation exists between emotional stress and the correctness of an answer. During the experiment, a total of 4,000 voice records of four student groups (total 200 students in total) were examined and analysed. Only volunteering students participated in the e-examination by voice. The first group of students was offered to have 1.5 points added to the points they score (in a ten-point system) as a reward for the participation in the experiment. All students agreed. In further experiments, the students were offered to have one point added to the points they score. About 80% of students agreed. We did not try several recordings (exams) within the same group of students. Besides, we did not analyse the differences of the examination by voice according to gender. These research points are planned for the nearest examinations session.

The research helped in determining whether questions can be classified (in respect to students) as "known/simple", "unknown/difficult" and remaining questions in-between these two groups. The "unknown/difficult" experienced higher than average emotional stress, and zero or minor emotional stress when answering "known/simple" questions. On analysis of the whole set of answers, a direct relationship was noticed between emotional stress and correct/incorrect answers to an e-test, i.e. answers to "unknown/difficult" questions scored less than answers to "known/simple" questions (see Fig. 1). During the research, the average microtremor was calculated for each question. Part of the results is shown in Figure 1.

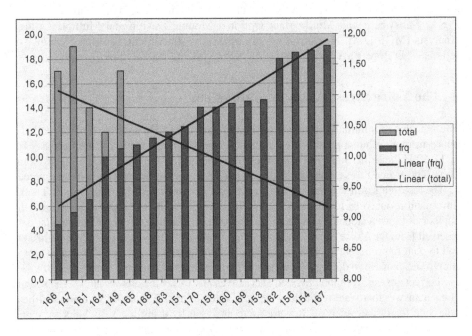

Fig. 1. Correlation of relationships between emotional stress and correct/incorrect answers to an e-test

Figure 1 also shows the relation between a student's grade and the average mi-crotremor frequency of the answers to test questions. The x-axis shows ID numbers of students who were sitting for the examination. During the examination students had to mark and to say aloud the right answers to 20 questions within 10 minutes. The left side of the y-axis shows the scale of points received by each student. A student who correctly answered all questions could get a maximum of 20 points. The right side of the y-axis shows the average microtremor frequency of each student during the ex-amination. In addition, Figure 1 shows two correlating curves obtained during the re-search; the curves show the direct relationship between the grade and the average microtremor frequency. For instance, the higher the average microtremor frequency is, the worse the grade and vice versa.

As seen from the data in Fig. 1, a student can be assessed according to the regres-sion relationship between emotional stress and correct/incorrect answers to e-tests.

With the development of a more exhaustive database of voice analysis such evaluations will become more precise. For example: when a teacher gives a student such questions before an examination as "Are you well-prepared for the exam? What mark would you give to your knowledge?, and Have you learned everything?", the VSA Subsystem determines the average micro-tremor of the answers, and the student can be assessed precisely by being given a mark.

In the future there will be a possibility to assess students' knowledge automatically by using VSA Subsystem on the basis of accumulated historic data and determined regression equation. For example, the VSA Subsystem will automatically assess a student's knowledge during an examination according to the student's spoken/oral answers, i.e. the VSA Subsystem will convert student's answers into Hz and the IITS will show a mark according to the amount of Hz. solutions.

4   ILTS-BP: Special Emphasis on the Multivariant Optional Module Design and Multiple Criteria Analysis

Indexing is often used to refer to the automatic selection and compilation of 'meaningful' keywords from e-textbooks into a list that can be used by a search system to retrieve texts. This list is more properly called a *concordance*. As this procedure involves no intellectual effort, indexers distinguish their own work by calling it intellectual indexing, manual indexing, human indexing or back-of-book-style indexing. Indexing also means the intellectual analysis of the e-textbooks to identify the concepts represented in the document and the allocation of descriptors so as to allow these concepts to be retrieved. During indexing, the Multiple Criteria Analysis (MOMD-MCA) Subsystem visits definite Brita in PuBs project modules and collects required information/keywords. Intelligent copy and paste from many modules with retention of a link/reference to the module can be performed. Development of a new module is performed by using a combination of knowledge that is found with the possibility of easy editing and integrating. Learners can use MOMD-MCA Subsystem for computer-assisted extraction of data from text for their own purposes, making their work more efficient. Equally important, is that this data can then be reused and made useful for a large learners community: the obtained data can be incorporated (connected, interlinked) into a large distributed knowledge base.

Table 1 shows the frequency of each specific keyword in the analysed text. Keyword ranking in modules seeks to determine the level of relevance of chapters and sections for student's needs. The level of relevance to student's needs can be defined by the term "Keyword density and significance" as described by indicators provided in the Table 1: weight (shows the significance of one keyword over another from a student's perspective in a search for specific learning material), difficulty of a text (the level of difficulty is determined on the basis of previous examination results related to a specific topic) and other indicators (number of pages, words and sentences in the analysed text) which help to determine the keyword's density. Information describing the usefulness of the analysed text for a learner's needs is summarised in Table 1. Also, the relevance of a text to a student's learning needs is described by the presence of different keywords within one sentence. The occurrence of several different keywords that are specified by a student in the same sentence shows higher relevance of the text to the learner's needs.

Table 1. Density of specific keywords in analysed text

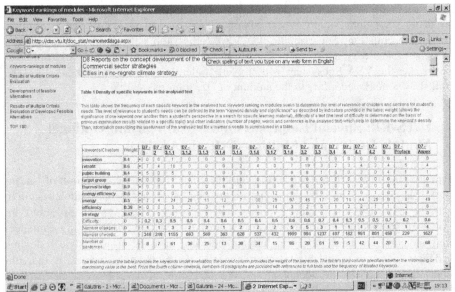

Legend - The first column of the table provides keywords under evaluation; the second column provides the weight of the keywords. The table's third column specifies whether the minimising or maximising value is best. From the fourth column onwards: numbers of paragraphs are provided with references to full texts and the frequency of iterated keywords.

The significance/efficiency (Q_j) of alternatives of the teaching material is determined on the basis of keyword density characteristics (i.e. frequency of each specific keyword, weight, difficulty of text, number of pages, and words and sentences in the analysed text). Significance Q_j of the learning material a_j indicates the satisfaction degree of requirements and goals pursued by students, e.g. the greater the Q_j the higher the efficiency of the learning material.

The degree of utility N_j of the teaching material a_j indicates the level of satisfying the needs of the actual student. The more learning goals that are achieved and the more important the goals are, the higher the degree of the teaching material's utility. The degree of the teaching material's utility reflects the extent to which the goals pursued by the student are attained. The greater the Q_j is, the higher the priority of the teaching material.

The significance/efficiency (Q_j) of alternatives of the teaching material is determined on the basis of keyword density characteristics (i.e. frequency of each specific keyword, weight, difficulty of text, number of pages, and words and sentences in the analysed text). Significance Q_j of the learning material a_j indicates the satisfaction degree of requirements and goals pursued by students, e.g. the greater the Q_j is, the higher the efficiency of the learning material.

Table 2. Fragment of development of feasible alternatives (combinations of best selected paragraphs) of module (*left*)

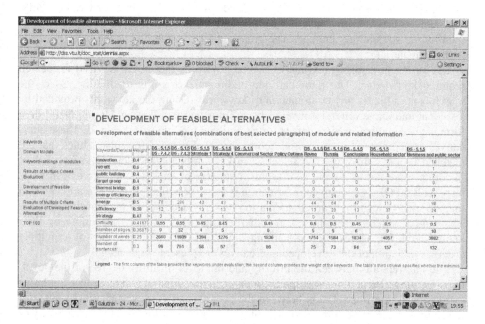

Table 3. Fragment of results of multiple criteria evaluation of developed feasible alternatives (*right*)

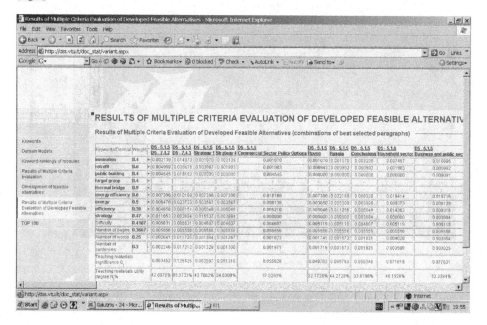

The degree of utility N_j of the teaching material a_j indicates the level of satisfying the needs of the actual student. The more learning goals that are achieved and the more important the goals are, the higher the degree of the teaching material's utility. The degree of the teaching material's utility reflects the extent to which the goals pursued by the student are attained. The greater the Q_j is, the higher the priority of the teaching material.

ILTS-BP can display previously covered keywords that might be used for search required knowledge. The tutor can add additional keywords to this list. Also, the search is possible by any combination of keywords. Using the keywords provided by a student and some criteria delivered by a Tutor and the Testing Model, the system formulates a number of alternatives for an optional module (see Table 2). These alternatives are composed of sections or components of many different modules that are matched in a certain way. The selection of keywords and the determination of their importance are not as simple as it seems. Numbers of feasible alternatives can be as large as 100,000. The received information is used for action plans, i.e. *mini curricula* that are used to lead the learner/student to rationally accomplish the learning process. The *Mini Curricula* are adapted to individual learner's needs - depending on their knowledge level, age, study and learning styles and difficulties. Results of a multiple criteria evaluation of the developed alternatives are presented in Table 3.

The interrelation between the priority and the level of utility degree of the developed learning alternatives is graphically expressed in Figure 2. It is in fact a graphic expression of the interrelation between the priority and the level of utility degree of the learning alternatives provided in Table 3. The axis x in Fig. 2 shows the priority of alternatives, and the axis y shows the level of utility degree of the learning alternatives (in percent).

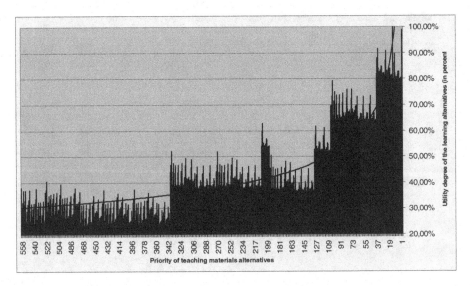

Fig. 2. Graphical interrelation between the priority and the level of utility degree of the developed learning alternatives

As constantly increasing amounts of information and knowledge in the library of e-learning modules become available to an increasing number of learners, it becomes very difficult for students to find the information and knowledge they need. Moreover, different students with different educational backgrounds, objectives, requirements and priorities can expect particular and individualized ILTS-BP behaviour. What distinguishes the personalized ILTS-BP from traditional e-libraries' systems is the existence of the Student Model that stores data that is specific to each individual learner. These learner profiles allow the ILTS-BP adapt its behaviour to the education objectives, requirements and priorities of individual learners.

In general, ILTS-BP performance may be adapted, i.e., personalized at different levels, e.g. at the content's selection, content's presentation (electronic format of textbooks, video, audio, computer-software, computer learning systems), and services (life-long learning, master degree studies, and PhD degree studies, etc.), content volume (i.e. 50, 100 or 250 pages of a textbook) or interaction level, by taking into account a learner's objectives, requirements and priorities. For example, various learners are provided with diverse content according to their requirements and priorities. The same content can be offered to different learners in a summarized or extended format or in a variety of multimedia formats. Various learners can have access to different services, which can be customized according to learner's requirements and priorities.

Permanent streams of statistical information (information based on voice analysis of a student's answers, information on correct and incorrect answer, time distribution on every question, and the number of times a student changed an answer to each question of a test, history of the interaction between students and tutors) is integrated into the Tutor and Testing Model. The Tutor and Testing Model provides the function to process and integrate permanent data streams and provides access to this data to different learners. ILTS-BP provides appropriate mechanisms for online processing of the aggregated stream data. Statistical aggregated stream data are particularly important in a library of e-learning modules for all stakeholders and for later improvement and development of the e-library. For example, on the basis of available statistical information, it is possible to determine which topics are the most relevant to learners and what their presentation form should be (e-books, audio, video, etc.). Further, strengths and weaknesses of existing modules could be determined, and then this information could be used as a basis to provide specific recommendations on how to improve the modules.

5 Conclusions

During Brita in PuBs project the Intelligent Library and Tutoring System for the Brita in PuBs project (ILTS-BP) was developed by the authors. ILTS-BP is able to search and find useful material, carry out a multivariant optional module design, multiple criteria analysis and select the most rational study material alternatives according to individual students' demands. The authors have also integrated ILTS-BP with a Voice Stress Analyser Subsystem. The research presented in the paper shows not only the general talk in this field but also contains sufficiently new idea related to e-development of alternatives of learning materials, to multiple criteria analysis and to automatic selection of the most effective variant.

References

Alexandrov, V.N., Dimov, I.T., Karaivanova, A., Tan, C.J.K.: Parallel Monte Carlo algorithms for Information Retrieval. Mathematics and Computers in Simulation 62(3-6), 289–295 (2003)

Armani, B., Bertino, E., Catania, B., Laradi, D., Marin, B., Zarri, G.P.: Repository Management in an Intelligent Indexing Approach for Multimedia Digital Libraries. In: Ohsuga, S., Raś, Z.W. (eds.) ISMIS 2000. LNCS (LNAI), vol. 1932, Springer, Heidelberg (2000)

Brusilovsky, P.: Course Sequencing for Static Courses? Applying ITS Techniques in Large-Scale Web-Based Education. In: Gauthier, G., VanLehn, K., Frasson, C. (eds.) ITS 2000. LNCS, vol. 1839, pp. 19–23. Springer, Heidelberg (2000)

Day, M., Lu, C., Yang, J., Chiou, G., Ong, C., Hsu, W.: Designing an Ontology-Based Intelligent Tutoring Agent with Instant Messaging (Accessed January 28, 2007), http://iasl.iis.sinica.edu.tw/webpdf/paper-2005-Designing_an_Ontology-based_Intelligent_Tutoring_Agent_with_Instant_Messaging.pdf

Gutwin, C., Paynter, G., Witten, I., Neville, M.C., Frank, E.: Improving Browsing in Digital Libraries with Key-phrase Indexes. Decision Support Systems 27(1-2), 81–104 (1999)

Hsinchun, C., Yi-Ming, C., Ramsey, M., Yang, C.C.: An Intelligent Personal Spider (Agent) for Dynamic Internet/Intranet Searching. Decision Support Systems 23(1), 41–58 (1998)

Kaklauskas, A., Zavadskas, E., Ditkevicius, R.: An Intelligent Tutoring System for Construction and Real Estate. In: Luo, Y. (ed.) CDVE 2006. LNCS, vol. 4101, pp. 174–181. Springer, Heidelberg (2006)

Lucence, J.: Jakarta Lucene Text Search Engine in Java (Accessed February 23, 2005), http://jakarta.apache.org/lucene/docs/index.html

Pouliquen, B., Le Duff, F., Delamarre, D., Cuggia, M., Mougin, F., Le Beux, P.: Managing Educational Resource in Medicine: System Design and Integration. International Journal of Medical Informatics 74(2-4), 201–207 (2005)

Ruch, P., Boyer, C., Chichester, C., Tbahriti, I., Geissbühler, A., Fabry, P., Gobeill, J., Pillet, V., Rebholz-Schuhmann, D., Ovis, C.: Using Argumentation to Extract Key Sentences from Biomedical Abstracts. International Journal of Medical Informatics 76(2-3), 195–200 (2007)

Trnkoczy, J., Turk, Z., Stankovski, V.: A Grid-Based Architecture for Personalized Federation of Digital Libraries. Library Collections, Acquisitions, and Technical Services 30(3-4), 139–153 (2006)

Wang, J.: A Knowledge Network Constructed by Integrating Classification, Thesaurus, and Metadata in Digital Library. The International Information & Library Review 35(2-4), 383–397 (2003)

Quality Information Management System Under Collaborative Environment

Junjie Yang[1], Rongqiao Wang[1], Jiang Fan[1], Xinmin Du[2], and Zebang Zhang[2]

[1] School of Jet Propulsion, BeiHang University, Beijing, 10083, China
[2] System Engineering Research Institute, Beijing, 10036, China
junjiey@buaa.edu.cn, wrq@sina.com.cn, fanjiang@buaa.edu.cn,
duxm@263.net, zhangzebang@163.com

Abstract. Under collaborative environment based on PDM, the coupling of information between PDM and QIMS makes the development of QIMS complicated. During constructing cooperative circumstance, the development of QIMS can be simplified through fusing rules of quality control into the processes managed by PDM. On the other hand, since the joint model of processes managed by PDM is equivalent to the virtual product model in the collaborative environment, QIMS can also reach quality objectives of enterprise by controlling the quality view of joint model. On the basis of the quality view, an integration model between QIMS and PDM is designed to achieve the combination between quality management and process management by information integration and interface.

Keywords: collaborative environment, PDM, system integration, quality information management, distributed system.

1 Introduction

A Quality Information Management System (QIMS) cooperating in harmony with collaborative design environment, which supports share of information and task collaboration between different software tools used within enterprise, can ensure that quality objectives are able to be reached better. Contrasted with other general quality information management systems, which are major in studying the professional field of quality management and do not pay enough attention to the collaborative environment in enterprise, its development is more complicated because it is not a disintegrated system but the part of collaborative environment.

This paper focuses on the development of QIMS under the collaborative circumstance based on PDM (Product Data Management). First, a appropriate plan of developing QIMS is presented by analyzing the characteristics of PDM and QIMS, Second, a integration model is designed under the plan guidance, Finally, according to the plan and integration model, a Web-based distribute QIMS is developed in a ship enterprise.

2 Development of QIMS Under PDM Environment

In general, PDM is used for the fundamental platform of collaborative design environment in enterprise. Because PDM has the powerful capabilities of data

Y. Luo (Ed.): CDVE 2007, LNCS 4674, pp. 167–174, 2007.

management and process management, many simulation and design tools are integrated into it to describe all details on processes and technology of product design in enterprise, which is called virtual product model. It seems that it is possible to control quality of product through managing quality of virtual product model in enterprise, as also is the motivation of developing QIMS. In other word, the key to developing QIMS under cooperative circumstance is that how to extract the quality view from the virtual product model and then to control it.

As the two features of PDM, data management is the basic function, and process management is the core function. Especially, the virtual product model is described relying mainly on the process management. Besides, it is more important that the powerful ability of process management is very fit for one of primary principles of modern quality control— Process Method, which emphasizes that any kind of activities in the course of quality control including the management of quality information should be accomplished in some processes.

Today, actually, the combination of quality management and process management is not only a possibility but also a tendency. To accomplish this combination, a common way is to fuse rules of quality control into these processes managed by PDM. But since the implementation of this way demands coordination and cooperation of all departments and various professional groups in enterprise, it is often performed during constructing the collaborative environment through separating from the development of QIMS to minimize interferences between PDM and QIMS and.

On the other hand, PDM manages these processes by controlling their joints generally; therefore joint model of processes management can be seen as the equivalent of the virtual product model. Accordingly, the quality objective of virtual product model can be reached by controlling the quality view of joint model on processes. Thus, according to the characteristic of quality management of enterprise, the quality view extracted from the joint model becomes the foundation of the information model on the development of QIMS and the interface model on the integration between QIMS and PDM, and then on the basis of these models, an appropriate integration model can be designed by adopting some effective methods.

3   Integration Model of QIMS and PDM

The integration between PDM and QIMS is able to be achieved in two ways including application encapsulation and interface, which are adopted in different situations. When users operate other application systems under collaborative environment, they only want to query and browse some quality information sometimes. In such case, encapsulating the application of QIMS in PDM platform is very convenient because the QIMS can be activated directly according to user's request; but, for the second case, they have to submit some problems on quality to loop them sometimes, and then it is inevitable to communications between PDM and QIMS which include two courses, one is that information is transferred to the database of QIMS from the database of PDM, and another is inversed. In this condition, the interface is very effectual because it can be performed automatically in the background. In fact, the integration also can be accomplished by the addition way—compact integration, but which is not fit here because of requesting the same structure of database besides it is very hard in technology.

Since encapsulation needs not the exchange of information between QIMS and PDM, it can be performed easily. But as for the interface, it is very important to choose an appropriate format of file to exchange data. Extensive Markup Language (XML), which is very flexible and convenient and compatible and cross-platform, has become the preferred file format for data exchange.

Thus, an integration model between QIMS and PDM is designed, as shown in figure 1. First, the quality management of all processes of PDM is standardized by these rules of quality management during building the collaborative environment. Meanwhile, according to these characteristics of quality management in enterprise, the entire data model on the quality view in XML is released to the PDM firstly, and then the data exchange interfaces between PDM and QIMS are designed according to the model. Finally, PDM encapsulates the application of QIMS in these right places.

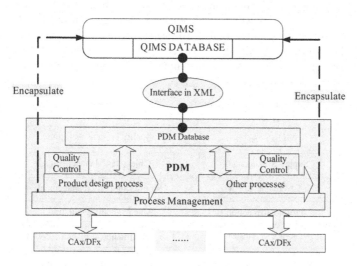

Fig. 1. The integration model of QIMS and PDM platform

4   Quality Management in a Ship Enterprise

Stimulated by the dual pressure of market competitions and military requirements, the design of product in ship enterprise is changing the traditional serial mode into the concurrent collaborative mode. Although more and more information systems are built, the transformation of ship enterprise is still in the initial stage. Under this status, however, the ship enterprise can learn more advanced management ideas and the latest research results and can learn from the experiences of transformation of other enterprise during constructing the collaborative design circumstance. In fact, it is of advantage to developing QIMS in the primary phrase of constructing cooperative circumstance because rules of quality control can easier fuse synchronously into these processes to be managed by PDM platform. Therefore, to develop the QIMS in the enterprise, only some features of quality management in collaborative design environment need to be considered in particular.

A ship enterprise provides mainly some equipment for the warship, which has some characteristics of dynamic enterprise and virtual enterprise. First, the core equipment are designed by the enterprise itself, and then all components of equipment are machined by entrusting to suppliers or purchased directly on the market, afterward, these components are assembled according to the design of product, finally, the integrated products are delivered to clients after testing. Therefore, the quality control of the ship enterprise through whole life-cycle of products focuses on four processes including product design, quality control of supply, testing and inspecting, and sale & service. Among them, the quality control of supply is achieved by such means as auditing qualification of suppliers, monitoring process of manufacture, and inspecting products.

Besides the quality control through the whole life-cycle of product, the entire quality management of enterprise also includes other processes related quality of management such as quality objectives management, performance management, monitoring daily and management evaluation, which aim at ensuring the long-time quality of product,. In one word, quality management involves all aspects of the operation of quality in the enterprise. Therefore, the QIMS should cover all processes mentioned above to collect and manage all quality information in the enterprise, as shown in figure 2.

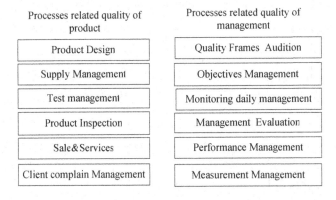

Fig. 2. The function model of QIMS

5   Analysis of Data Structure of QIMS

To ensure the consistency of information, all databases in the collaborative environment including the database of QIMS and the database of PDM should form a single data source in logic. As the fundamental platform of collaborative design, PDM organizes all information by the structure of product of enterprise in order to form the complete representation of virtual product model through the whole life-cycle of product. On the other hand, because QIMS is seen as the concentrated expression of quality perspectives on the virtual model, therefore, the database of QIMS can keep consistent with the database of PDM in theory. In other words, the data model of QIMS is able to be established on a basis of the structure of product.

The figure 3 is a simple object diagram to indicate generally the relationship of objects and only shows some main objects in QIMS, but it can still illustrate clearly the main logic structure of data model of QIMS. Despite the data of QIMS are very complicated, it is very optimistic surely that the anticipative model can be established successfully by analyzing these relations among objects in the figure 3.

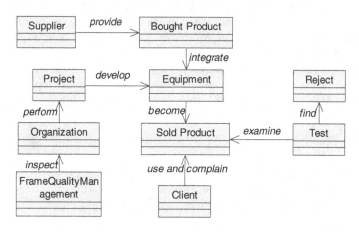

Fig. 3. The logic relationship of some main objects of QIMS

As shown in figure 3, the aim of project is to design and carry out equipment, which is assembled by integrating some components bought on the market and provided by the supplier. And the equipment needs to be examined by the means of testing and inspecting before delivery, in this process, some rejects may be found. Once the equipment is delivered to the clients, it is called the sold-product. Moreover, the client may complain about the sold-products during using them, in fact it is inevitable usually. Obviously, all information on such processes related product as product design, quality control of supply, product test, client complain management can be organized easily by the clue of product.

On the one hand, each project must be executed by some organization of enterprise. Therefore, the structure of organizations of enterprise is consistent with the structure of products of project in some sense; on the other hand, the aim of the quality management frame is to inspect that whether every organization complies with these quality management rules of enterprise. Therefore, the structure of product is able to not only relate all information on product quality, but also string all information arising from these processes related systematic quality management. As a result, the data model of QIMS is established by the structure of product as the core foundation and the structure of organization as the assistant clue.

6 Design and Realization of QIMS

Under the collaborative design environment, users always locate different sites in enterprise. To be convenient, the QIMS ought to be able to cover every corner of enterprise where the quality information may be inquired or submitted at any moment. But, the management of quality information should be centralized to economize resources. Therefore, the QIMS in the cooperative circumstance must be adapted to this conflict between geographical decentralization and centralized management.

The distributed system based on the Browser/Server (B/S) mode can handle the conflict availably. The database is managed in some place, and these users are able to operate the QIMS expediently at any place by the browser. Besides, the B/S mode can also reduce the burden of the Client. Moreover, since the QIMS adopts this mode, the platform of PDM can encapsulate these pages of client easily.

Furthermore, component technology and hierarchical framework are adopted in the QIMS. As shown in Figure 4, there are four layers from bottom to top including data layer, application service layer, web layer and client layer, each layer is composed of different components to achieve different functions.

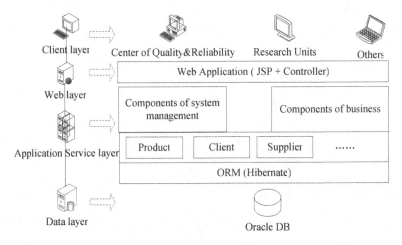

Fig. 4. The structure of QIMS

(1) Data layer: the data layer is main the Oracle as the database management tool to store all quality information and system information.

(2) Application service layer: the application service layer is the core component of system; it can be partition three layers in detail, which are data mapping layer, object layer and business logic layer from bottom to top. Among them, the data mapping layer communicates with the database by the Hibernate which is a kind of open source data mapping tools based on java; the object layer includes all persistent objects of the system, such as product, client and supplier; the business logic layer performs specific missions on quality management of enterprise by invoking some objects of the object layer.

(3) Web layer: The web layer provides mainly two services, one is the JSP (Java Server Page) application to generate all pages of the client layer; another is the

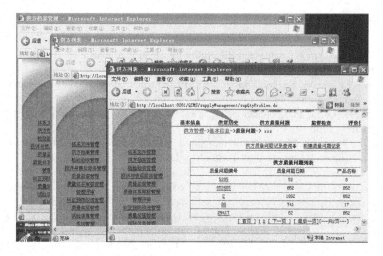

Fig. 5. Some instances of client pages of QIMS

controller of page to handle all requests from the client layer. These controllers transmit requests to different services relevant to business according to these types of requests, and then return results to the client layer.

(4) Client layer: The client layer is composed of many JSP pages, which provide various functions to users. Users can deal with all requests on business by the browser, as shown in figure 5.

7 Conclusion

The focus of this paper is on developing the QIMS that can control the quality view of virtual product model in the collaborative environment based on the platform of PDM. There are two main contributions on this work, the first contribution is the presentation of the plan of developing QIMS, which can not only decrease the complicacy of development but also accomplish the combination of quality management and process management; Another contribution is the building of integration model according to this plan, which supports share of quality information and quality management collaboration on processes in enterprise.

In addition, on the basis of the plan and integrated model, the web-based distributed QIMS has achieved successfully in a ship enterprise. It shows that the plan and integration model are feasible not only in theory but also in engineering, it is possible that the research can provide some references for similar question in other enterprise.

Acknowledgements. We wish to thank the center of quality and reliability of the System Engineering Research Institute who funds this research, our gratitude also goes to the chief of the center, Madam Yi Jin, and the engineer of center, Madam Yuanfan Xu, for their supports on research. In addition, we want to thank the reviewers for their advices.

References

1. Yang, J.: Research on Quality and Reliability Information Management System for Ship (in Chinese). Master degree of BeiHang University (2006)
2. Fan, W., Li, T., Xiong, G.: Principle and Implementation of PDM (in Chinese). China machine press, Beijing (2004)
3. Schottner, J., Qi, G.: Productdatenmanagement in der Fertigungsindustrie: Prinzip-Konzepte-Strategien (in Chinese). China Machine Press, Beijing (2000)
4. Yang, X., Wang, D., Ma, Y.: Study on Quality Management Information System Based on CIMS (in Chinese). Chinese High Technology Letters 75, 70–72 (2000)
5. Chen, X., Liao, W., Shen, J.: The Model Collaborative Design of Virtual Products in Agile Manufacturing (in Chinese). Manufacturing Technology & Machine Tool 38, 30–32 (2006)
6. Lu, Q., Tang, X.: Quality Management Information System for Cooperative Manufacturing (in Chinese). Journal of Beijing University of Aeronautics and Astronautics, 316–320 (2004)
7. Li, M., Cheng, Y., Zhao, B.: Collaborative Application Platform for Small and Medium-sized Enterprise (in Chinese). Computer Integrated Manufacturing Systems , 762–764 (2002)
8. Rebolj, D.: Virtual Product Model, http://itc.scix.net

A Service-Oriented, Scalable Approach to Grid-Enabling of Manufacturing Resources

Lei Wu, Xiangxu Meng, and Shijun Liu

School of computer science and technology, Shandong University,
Jinan, 250100, P.R. China
i_lily8002@hotmail.com, {mxx,lsj}@sdu.edu.cn

Abstract. To meet the challenges of geographically and logically distributed development processes. Manufacturing resources have to be encapsulated into services. The paper presents an extensible resource encapsulation framework and provides an approach to grid-enable manufacturing resources following Web Service Resource Framework (WSRF) specification which can make them offer their services and functionality in grid environment. The framework includes a Resource Container Factory Service and many Resource Container Instance Services. The same kinds of resources are deployed in one resource container instance. The encapsulation framework has many advantages such as extensible, plug-and-play deployment, automatic encapsulating and manageable. The paper presents the design principle of the resource encapsulation framework. One kind of resource container-resource container for legacy binary codes is introduced as an example in this paper, which can cast legacy binary codes into web services. At last, we give a use case to validate our method and put forward the future work.

Keywords: grid, service-oriented, manufacturing resource, Web Service Resource Framework (WSRF), encapsulation.

1 Introduction

Development of industrial and large-scale products and services poses complex problems. The processes used to develop these products and services typically involve a large number of independent organizational entities at different locations grouped in partnerships and supply chains. They need cooperate with each other, and all engineers want to work on the same set of data, share the same processes and can drive the whole development process in an integrated environment. To meet the challenges of geographically and logically distributed development processes, many resources, such as industrial simulation codes, data resources and equipment resources have to be integrated into the uniform problem solving environment. We want to share these resources based on union and open standards. Grid technologies are the viable alternative to fulfill these requirements. The major challenge is to develop strategies how to cast various manufacturing resources into services for use in service-oriented problem solving environments.

Y. Luo (Ed.): CDVE 2007, LNCS 4674, pp. 175–183, 2007.

We want to encapsulate manufacturing resources into services based on union and open standards and provide an extensible encapsulation framework, which can encapsulation various resources and manage these resources deployed in it. Encapsulated resources can be deployed without restart service container and users have not to know much knowledge on grid and web service. The paper focuses on solving these problems.

The rest of the paper is organized as follows: Section 2 introduces some related works and the different characteristic of our approach. Section 3 presents the extensible encapsulation framework of manufacturing resources and introduces the Resource Container Factory Service and Resource Container Instance Services in detail. Section 4 introduces an example of resource container: resource container for legacy binary codes. The prototype is presented in section 5. At last, the conclusion and further work are presented.

2 Related Work

Many efforts have been made towards the integration of manufacturing resources. There are also some methods to transform legacy application into services. [1] puts forward tactics of CAD (Computer Aided Design) encapsulation and realize the encapsulation and invocation using Web Service technologies. It mainly solved the problem of the data exchange between CAD, PDM (Product Data Management) and CAM (Computer Aided Manufacturing) systems. [2] presents an approach to virtualize an AGV(Automated Guided Vehicle) following WSRF. The process of virtualization is very complex and user have to program for different resources. It's difficult to use for enterprise users. SIMDAT project team [3] develops strategies how to cast industrial simulation codes into grid enabled analysis services. The project put the focus on the analysis services. In-VIGO [4] presents two solutions to virtual legacy command-lined application: Generic Application Service (GAP) [5] and Virtual Application Service (VAS). The two solutions are fit for virtualizing command-oriented scientific applications.

The solutions mentioned above have some limitation and poor expansibility. They can only solve certain kind of resource encapsulation problem. The paper presents an extensible resource encapsulation framework. We can extend the resource encapsulation framework by developing new resource container instance service, which can be seen as component and added to the framework easily.

3 Framework of Resource Encapsulation

The paper presents an extensible framework of resource encapsulation [Shown in Fig.1]. Manufacturing resources are encapsulated into WS-Resource. The framework includes a Resource Container Factory Service and some Resource Container Instance Services. They are web services following Web Service Resource Framework (WSRF) [6] specification. A Resource Container Instance Service can cast one kind of resource into web services. The Resource Container Instance Service can be generated according to the profile by Factory Service, which make the framework can be extended easily to support various manufacturing resources. The Resource

Container Factory Service can manage these resource container instances deployed in it, such as deploying, undeploying, gain the information of resource container. The interface of all the Resource Container Instance Services are same, otherwise the implementations are different, which makes the invoking of all kinds of resources easy and uniform.

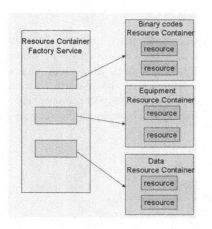

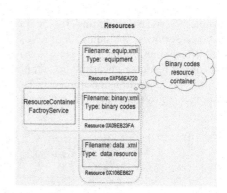

Fig. 1. Resource encapsulation Framework   **Fig. 2.** Design Principle of Resource Container

3.1 Design Principle

Web services and service-oriented architecture were chosen because they are [7,8]:

. Technology Neutral: Service endpoints are platform-independent. .

. Standards-Based: Protocols are standard-based and hence allow interoperation of different implementations.

. Abstracted: Service interface are independent from, and hide details of, service implementations.

. Publishable and consumable: A service interface, in the form of WSDL and service endpoint (for the "generic" application service to be described), can be published in, and discovered from, a UDDI directory.

. Stateful: Applications allowing parameter sweeps or workflows have inherent states. By encapsulating those following with WSRF, it is possible to maintain and interact with state in a standard way.

Web Service Resource Framework, currently under standardization by OASIS[9], provides the means to express state as stateful resources and codifies the relationship. In WSRF, a WS-Resource is the combination of a Web service and a stateful resource on which it acts. A WS-Resource has various properties. The values of these properties define the state of the resource. To change a property value can change the state of resource.

The Resource Container Factory Service is service following WSRF specification. The configuration file of resource container is the resource of Resource Container Factory Service.[shown in Fig. 2] Factory Service can generate Resource Container

Instance according to the configure file. Resource Container Instance Services are WSRF-based services too. Manufacturing resources are encapsulated into WS-Resource. The end user can access these resources by the Resource Container Factory Service or relative Resource Container Instance Service. These services are following WSRF specification, so they can be integrated into grid environment.

3.2 Resource Container Factory Service

The Resource Container Factory Service can generate many Resource Container Instance Services according to the profile. It also provides interface to manage instance services, including deployResourceContainer, undeployResourceContainer, getAllResourceContainers, getResourceContainerInfo. It is the uniform accessing port of the resource encapsulation framework. Some public support services such as security and data transmission service are on this layer. They ensure the security of resource deployed in resource container.

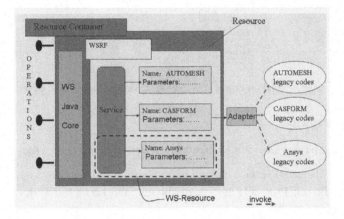

Fig. 3. Architecture of Resource Container

3.3 Resource Container Instance Service

The resource container is actually a WSRF service. It can be deployed in GT service container conveniently. Resource description files are resources of the WSRF service, which combined with the service form the WS-Resource (shown in Fig. 3.).One resource container can cast certain category of resources into WS-Resource, which make them can offer their services and functionality in a standard web service environment. The resource container instance service can manage and invoke these resources deployed in it. The interfaces of all the resource containers are same. Table1 describes the interface of resource container instance service.

The encapsulation template is developed, used in resource container instance service. It includes adaptor and resource description schema. The adaptor gains the information of resource by reading the resource description file and invokes the resource. Different kinds of resources have the different adaptor and resource description schema. Encapsulating resource requires only the provision of necessary configuration information that will be used dynamically when the resource is consumed.

Table 1. Resource Container Instance Service Interface

Interface	function
deployResource()	Deploy new resource in the resource container
undeployResource()	Undeploy some resource in the resource container
getAllResources()	Get all resource deployed in the resource container
getResourceInfo()	Get the information of certain resource deployed in the resource container
getTaskInputParameters()	Get the input parameters of the resource
syncExecuteTask()	Execute Task synchronously
asyncExecuteTask()	Execute task asynchronously
getTaskStatus()	Get the status of the task

4 Resource Container of Legacy Binary Applications

There are many legacy code applications in industry. Legacy applications are broadly defined as codes developed with technologies that precede in time the introduction of Grid computing, Web-services and other recent computing approaches and programming best practices. Many such legacy applications are widely used, but are impractical to redevelop. Some of them may only be distributed in binaries, i.e., the source code is not available. Other applications have source code available, but a lack of proper documentation can make redevelopment difficult. Also, some legacy applications are quite complex and laborious to redevelop [10]. The legacy code is provided as a black box with specified input and output parameters and environmental requirements. Only the executable is available, and required, in this case, together with a user-level understanding of the application. In order to reuse these codes, they should be encapsulated as web service. We deploy binary codes resource container, which can cast binary codes into web services easily. Furthermore, by providing a service-based job execution interface for legacy program, it can be invoked or composed into a workflow as an activity.

4.1 Application Model and Profile

The resource container for binary application gets the information of the resource deployed in it by an application description. This description contains all the necessary application-specific information for Grid-enabling, but does not contain any Grid-specific information, and thus, does not require the application enabler to have the technical knowledge of the underlying Grid middleware. The application description is categorized into three categories: General Information, Parameters and Execution Environment-related information. The general information includes application name, description, version etc. The parameters describe the input/output parameters of the application. The execution environment information describes the requirement on the execution environment.

4.2 The Adaptor of Resource

One resource container has an adaptor. The main function of adaptor is to get resource config information and invoke the resource. All resources deployed in the resource container have the same service interface, which make it easier to invoke and compose these services. The adaptor for binary application will implement the interface as follows:

public void initResource(IResourceRefrence ref);   //Initialize the resource, such as set the status of resource
public HashMap executeTask(HashMap input); //execute the task, invoke the legacy application
public HashMap getTaskInputParameters(); /get the input parameters of the task
public String getResDescription(); /get the resource description

application Name	AUTOMESH		
Description	generate mesh for any quadrangle		
	parameters (* is required)		
para Name	value		type
number of mesh		*	(int)
material		*	(String)
input file		浏览...	PreProcessor
	invoke		

Fig. 4. The user interface of AUTOMESN

4.3 Portlets-Based Dynamic Interface

Portlet technology is used to automatically and dynamically generate user interfaces for legacy code applications. Portlets are Java-based web components, managed by a Portlet container that process requests and generate dynamic content. Portlets are used by portals as pluggable user interface components that provide a presentation layer to information systems [11]. The choice of Portlet technology for this project is influenced by many factors. Portlet specification is an open standard supported by most of the portal server vendors. Portal API attempts to create a well defined interface and hence ensures interoperability between different portal servers. Portlets also provide better support for multiple devices. One can define different JSP pages for different devices for the same Portlet and hence support multiple devices while reusing the logic programmed in the Portlets. Portlets provide a modular structure. A web page is created by aggregating Portlets. Users have their choice of what Portlets to aggregate and what layout to use. This enables users to have personalized user interfaces. Also, administrators have the liberty of organizing permission on per Portlet basis which gives them finer access control granularity. The GridSphere [12] portal server is used in this project.

The novel aspect of the user interface design is that the structure of the user interface is dynamic and automatic. The structure is determined by analyzing the description of the arguments in the application description. Then widgets like text boxes, combo boxes, labels, etc. are rendered accordingly.

Fig. 4. shows a dynamically created interface for AUTOMESH legacy code application[13], a mesh generation tool.

5 Prototype

We have developed resource encapsulation tool (shown in Fig.5). It is provided to users, they can encapsulate their legacy codes through fill out some information of the application. It is very convenient. We encapsulated the AUTOMESH [13] and CASFORM [14] software using our encapsulation template and deployed in our integration platform. Figure 4 shows the use interface of the application. In order to encapsulate AUTOMESH into web service using our encapsulation tool, the end user needs to take the following steps:

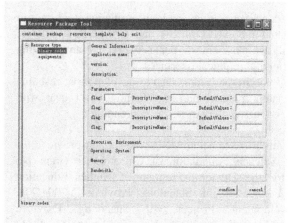

Fig. 5. Encapsulation Tool

1) Install the application in a machine: it is necessary to successfully install the application in a machine with the application's native environment. The user should make sure that the application can successfully run in an execution environment that is typically hosted in single administrative domain.
2) Fill out the application configuration information: select the appropriate resource and then fill out the form (shown in Fig.5.). The configuration file will be generated automatically.
3) Deploy resource: deploy the resource into the resource container.
4) Publish the service: publish the web service and provide accessible tool through a user interface such as a web-based portal.

6 Conclusions and Future Work

This paper presents out the extensible resource encapsulation framework. They have the following capabilities:

1) Extensible: The framework can be extended through deploy new resource container instance service, so it can support a broad range of manufacturing resources;
2) Automatic generation and integration: Based on the resource description, the framework provides means to automatically generate or modify all the middleware

components as needed for resource integration. It also automatically generates the resource-specific user interface to use the resource through a web portal. No Web programming or middleware development needs to be done

3) Plug-and-play deployment: Encapsulating new resource in this framework does not require the interruption (i.e., stopping and restarting) of an existing running resource container.

4) Manageable: Resources deployed in the resource containers can be managed easily through the manage interface of the Resource Container Instance Service.

We have developed resource container service and encapsulation tool in our prototype platform. We encapsulated the AUTOMESH and CASFORM software using our encapsulation tool and deploy them in our networked manufacturing platform. Our approach provides friendly graphical interfaces.

There are some works we need to do in the future, such as develop more resource container instance services to sustain more resources. We now can't deal with complex application such as that need many alternations during running.

Acknowledgments. The authors would like to acknowledge the support provided for the project by National Natural Science Foundation of China under Grant No 90612021, the Research Fund for the Doctoral Program of Higher Education 20050422019, Natural Science Foundation of Shandong Province Y2004G08, Science & Technology Development Projects of Shandong Province (2004GG1104011, 2004GG1104017) and National Key Technologies R&D Program(2006BAF01A24).

References

1. Donghua, L., Dekun, C.: Collaborative design basde on CAD encapsulation in manufacuring grid. Manufacturing Automation 27(5), 48–50 (2005)
2. Kumar, R.S., Yang, Z., Zhang, J.B., Zhuang, L.: Virtualization for Manufacturing Web Services: a WS-RF approach. International journal of information technology 11 (2005)
3. http://www.scai.fraunhofer.de/simdat.html
4. Adabala, S., et al.: From Virtualized Resources to Virtual Computing Grids: the In-VIGO System. Future Generation Computer Systems (to appear)
5. Sanjeepan, V., Matsunaga, A., Zhu, L., Lam, H., Fortes, J.A.B.: A Service-Oriented, Scalable Approach to Grid-Enabling of Legacy Scientific Applications. In: Proceeding of International Conference on Web Services (ICWS), July 2005, Industry Track (2005)
6. Oasis web services resource framework (wsrf) tc. Web Page
7. Neat, D.G.: Embracing SOA for the legacy world (June 2006), http://www-128.ibm.com/developerworks/library/ar-embsoa/ ?S_TACT=105AGX52&S_CMP=cn-a-ws
8. Understanding Service-oriented Architecture (2004), http://msdn.microsoft.com/library/default.asp?url=/library/enus/dnmaj/html/aj1soa.asp
9. Oasis.: Home-Page: http://www.oasis-open.org/

10. Zhu, L., Matsunaga, A., Sanjeepan, V., Lam, H., José, A., Fortes, J.A.B.: Application Modeling and Representation for Automatic Grid-enabling of Legacy Applications. In: Proceedings of the First International Conference on e-Science and Grid Computing (2005)
11. Java Portlet Specification Version 1 (2003)
12. Novotny, J., Russell, M., Wehrens, O.: GridSphere: An advanced portal framework, EUROMICRO (2004)
13. Automesh, http://www.cmse.sdu.edu.cn/mjzx/yjka-automesh.htm
14. CASFORM, http://www.cmse.sdu.edu.cn/mjzx/yjka-casform.htm

A Collaboration Environment for R&D Project

August Liao[1], Li-Dien Fu[2], and An-Pin Chen[3]

[1,3] Dept. of IIM, National Chiao Tung University, Management Building 2,
1001 Ta Hsueh Road, Hsinchu, 300, Taiwan
[2] Rm. 232, Bldg. 2, 195, Sec. $, Chung-Hsing Rd. Chutung, Hsinchu, 310, Taiwan
csliao@tsmc.com, apc@iim.nctu.edu.tw, ldfu@itri.org.tw

Abstract. The research question here is "how to effectively integrate the R&D experts and software developers to realize an effective R&D project collaboration software?" This research conducted a case study on the deployment of an integrated development methodology in a world-class semiconductor manufacture company. From the case study, the integrated methodology, Development Collaboration Diamond Model (DCDM), was designed, implemented and obtained the dramatic performance.

Keywords: Development Environment, Concurrent Engineering (CE).

1 Introduction

Concurrent Engineering (CE) is one of the remedies used to shorten the TTM. However, the proper implementation of this CE software architecture is relatively rare. The evidence shows that there are great barriers, potential pitfalls and difficulties for the successful implementation of CE [Sprague et al., 91; Gary, 93; Shinna, 92.] Moreover, the implementation of CE usually demands much investment. Consequently, how to properly introduce CE principles, technology and methods to the product and software has been a central concern to the industry and research community.

Our research question is "what's" the effective model to add quality while the software architecture realization, especially in the dynamic and complex R&D project management? This research presented and applied an engineering discipline development methodology, Development Collaboration Diamond Model (DCDM), to add the quality of the software architecture for the R&D project management. It successfully fulfills the major issues while the constructing a brand new R&D project collaboration architecture in the aspects of how to develop and implement the effective environment to the team and the project? Which of development or business processes need to be selected and improved? How to design an effective collaboration capability of the selected process?

2 Methodology and Implementation

This research utilizes the methodologies and concepts from the concurrent engineering, software engineering and total quality management disciplines to

Y. Luo (Ed.): CDVE 2007, LNCS 4674, pp. 184–186, 2007.

propose the model, Development Collaboration Diamond Model (DCDM) aims to integrate the major 4 dimensions of the collaboration architecture realization process in an integrated environments. The company X, a largest company in the global semiconductor foundry, was chosen as the case subject. In the case study, the Integrated Development Environment (eDevelopemnt, IDE) was designed. In order to allow easier access, the Integrated Development Environment (eDevelopemnt, IDE) was designed as a web-based application.

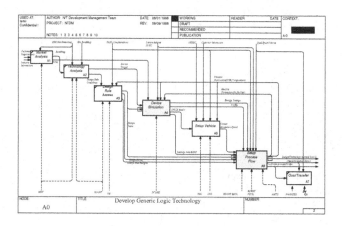

Fig. 1. IDEF chart of development process- An example on level 1

The phase 1 is to analyze the development as the business process perspective. The IDEF0 has successfully introduced to model the complex development process. From Figure 1, the development team can have a clear view to define the ICOMs for each activity. The hierarchy decomposition function of IDEF, provides the information linkage among different levels. It enables the top management considerations and policies could be executed by the bottom level activities. The "agreement form" was defined and used to define the development activity, information, responsibility. While the phase 2, the research utilized the visualized processes derived to evaluate the targets and performances, assess collaboration capability. With the multi-functional team discussion, this phase identifies the improvement opportunities and determines the priority. In the phase 3, the detailed solutions were design and tested to meet the precise design and specification for the system development. In the last phase, the actual implementation of collaboration functions were developed to a web environment, eDevelopment

3 Results and Conclusion

Adapting the results confirmation of total quality management, the possible improvement areas in the gap analysis phase were completely refined with the new released collaboration functions. It shows that cycle time of Development Information

Integration Process had been improved from 133 Hr to 25 Hr with the target achievement 102%.

With the support of the IDE, engineers simply update the agreement form report for the development target setting, and then the updated development information is automatically linked to the failure mode knowledge base, and a new version of the FMEA table is generated. Tangibly, the development efficiency of the following development process had been improvement 80 % in average, in the key realized collaboration capability-Development Information Integration, Project management It tells that the Development Collaboration Diamond Model (DCDM) successfully developed the Integrated Development Environment and the Integrated Development Environment achieved our research questions and significantly got the performance of R&D. As the conclusion, Development Collaboration Diamond Model (DCDM) is a proven effective methodology to be a reference process for both the concurrent environment deployment and new technology development process reengineering while the quality realization.

References

Shinna, S.G.: Concurrent Engineering and Design for Manufacture of Electronics Products, Van Nostrand Reinhold (1991)

Sprague, R.A., Singh, K.J., Wood, R.T.: Concurrent Engineering in Product Development. IEEE Design & Test of Computers, 6–13 (1991)

Haque, B., Pawar, K.S.: Improving the management of concurrent new product development using process modelling and analysis. R&D Management 31, 27–24 (2001)

A Bumpless Switching Scheme for Dynamic Reconfiguration

Limin Liu and Ping Yan

Institute of Embedded Systems
IT School , Huzhou University
Huzhou, Zhejiang, 313000, China
liulimin@hutc.zj.cn, yanipng@hutc.zj.cn

Abstract. The bumpless switching is a concept from cybernetics. It refers to the smooth switching condition when a new system replaces the old one in operation. We implemented the dynamic reconfiguration of SoC based on delta MPU architecture to reach a bumpless switching. The dynamic reconfiguration of SoC with bumpless switching depends on a co-design of some bumpless switching algorithm and a SoC hardware with delta core structure. Since bumpless is a desired condition in system switching, the scheme is significant for the dynamic reconfiguration of SoC.

Keywords: bumpless switching, SoC, dynamic reconfiguration.

1 Bumpless Switching and Dynamic Reconfiguration of SoC

The bumpless switching is a concept in cybernetics [1]. It refers to a smooth condition of a new system replacing the old one in operation. A bumpless switching means the switching is smooth. The concept is introduced here.

The transfer matrices of a system in the state space are as follows [2].

$$\dot{x}(t) = Ax(t) + Bu(t)$$

$$y(t) = Cx(t) + Du(t)$$

Where, y(t) is the output; u(t) is the input; and x(t) is the state variable; A, B,C and D are gain matrices.

$$A = \begin{bmatrix} A_{11} & ... & A_{n1} \\ ... & ... & ... \\ A_{1n} & ... & A_{nn} \end{bmatrix}$$

$$B = \begin{bmatrix} B_{11} & ... & B_{n1} \\ ... & ... & ... \\ B_{1n} & ... & B_{nn} \end{bmatrix}$$

Y. Luo (Ed.): CDVE 2007, LNCS 4674, pp. 187–190, 2007.
© Springer-Verlag Berlin Heidelberg 2007

The matrices C and D are similar to A and B. If A, B switch value and C, D remain fixed (i.e. C and D are constant matrices), the system is said to be bumpless.

Actually, we can call a switching system bumpless if its output $y(t)$ remains a continuous function of time, even during a change of transfer matrices, provided that its input $u(t)$ is continuous. Otherwise, the system switching is called bumpy.

For most SoC, System on a Chip, applications, the function of the state space is zero order. And the C and D are fixed constant matrices. Assuming a SoC system with zero order, for example its state space can be described as

$$y(t) = Cx(t) + Du(t)$$

$$C = \begin{bmatrix} 1 & 0 & 0 \\ 0 & 1 & 0 \\ 0 & 0 & 1 \end{bmatrix}, \quad D = \begin{bmatrix} 0 & 0 & 0 \\ 0 & 0 & 0 \\ 0 & 0 & 1 \end{bmatrix}.$$

When C and D are constant matrices, the system switching is bumpless. The switching result for a DRSoC, Dynamic Reconfiguration SoC, depends on the input parameters of SoC and some adjustment algorithm [3]. Normally a SoC in operation is a steady and controllable system with zero order description of state space [4]. Therefore, as a controlled system, SoC is simpler, and its algorithm of bumpless switching is easier fetched.

2   A Scheme of Bumpless Switching for SoC with Delta Core

The dynamic reconfiguration of SoC with bumpless switching depends on a co-design [5], the combination of some bumpless switching algorithm and a SoC hardware with delta core structure.

There are three MPUs embedded in the SoC with delta core. They are monitor MPU, operating MPU and backup MPU respectively. The structure of operating and backup MPU is similar. They may be considered as twin cores.

The algorithm of bumpless switching is embedded monitor MPU. In most cases, the backup MPU with similar algorithm to operating MPU, the monitor MPU detects the output status of backup MPU [6]. When the running state of backup MPU is statically closed to operating MPU. The monitor MPU realizes some instructions to transfer the backup MPU as a new operating MPU. The original operating MPU would become a backup MPU. When the inputs/outputs of the MPU cores are consistent and the timing control is available, the switching procedure may be bumpless. If the original operating MPU is replaced by the new operating MPU, the SoC is reconfigured or repaired.

In order to take a solution for SoC dynamic reconfiguration with bumpless switching, so far, we have designed and simulated some switching circuit based on FPGA with VHDL. A basic output cell of the circuit is shown as Fig.1. The MPU1 and MPU2 in Fig.1 are two cores in the SoC. One is operating core. Another is backup core. The out1 in Fig.1 means output1 of a MPU. May there be n outputs for a MPU. They are out1 to outn.

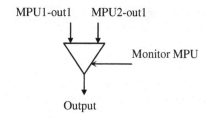

MPU1-out1   MPU2-out1

Monitor MPU

Output

Fig. 1. A basic cell of switching circuit for dynamic reconfiguration

The circuit is embedded into the same chip with MPU cores and controls the input/output of backup MPU to switch on the relevant pins of the SoC system. At the same time, its operation may be managed by the monitor MPU.

The circuit is a physical support for bumpless switching of dynamic reconfiguration. It is an essential hardware for the solution. A result of simulation for the circuit is satisfied.

In software side, a bumpless switching algorithm has been designed for dynamic reconfiguration of the SoC in steady operation. The algorithm is based on parameter feedback and fast switching scheme. For a system as

$$y(t) = Cx(t) + Du(t) .$$

The condition of bumpless switching is to guarantee that C and D are constant matrices. Actually, if the y(t) is not any bump in a switching procedure, the system switching is bumpless. Since SoC is a discrete system normally, its state space can be described as

$$y(k) = Cx(k) + Du(k) .$$

The next state may be

$$y(k + 1) = Cx(k + 1) + Du(k + 1) .$$

Since the output of SoC is controlled by the operating MPU core, at some time point, the algorithm can let the y(k)=y(k+1). At this point, the switching algorithm lets the output of backup MPU same as the output of operating MPU and switches the output of backup MPU to the output of SoC. Then, the switching is bumpless.

The bumpless switching scheme is useful to improve the dynamic feature of SoC reconfiguration. Further research is focus of cooperation of multi-core in a SoC, dynamic analysis of reconfiguration, more algorithm modeling and simulation.

References

1. Arehart, A.B., Wolovich, W.A.: Bumpless switching controllers. In: Proceedings of the 35th IEEE International Conference on Decision and Control, Kobe, Japan, vol. 11, pp. 1654–1655 (1996)
2. Zheng, K., Lee, A.H., Bentsman, J., Taft, C.W.: Steady-state bumpless transfer under controller uncertainty using the state/output feedback topology. IEEE Transactions on Control Systems Technology 14(1), 3–17 (2006)

3. Wallner, S.: A configurable system-on-chip architecture for embedded and real-time applications: concepts, design and realization. Elsevier Journal of Systems Architecture 51, 350–367 (2005)
4. Saleh, R., Wilton, S., et al.: System-on-chip: reuse and integration. Proceedings of the IEEE 94(6), 1050–1069 (2006)
5. Vikram, K.N., Vasudevan, V.: Hardware–software co-simulation of bus-based reconfigurable systems. Elsevier Journal of Microprocessors and Microsystems 29, 133–144 (2005)
6. Claasen, T.M.: An industry perspective on current and future state of the art in system-on-chip (SoC) technology. Proceedings of the IEEE 94(6), 1121–1137 (2006)

Real Estate's Market Value and a Pollution and Health Effects Analysis Decision Support System

E. Zavadskas, A. Kaklauskas, E. Maciunas, P. Vainiunas, and A. Marsalka

Vilnius Gediminas Technical University
Sauletekio al. 11, LT-10223 Vilnius, Lithuania
property@st.vtu.lt

Abstract. The authors of this paper participated in the project Framework 6 *Intelligent Cities* and the Lincoln Institute of Land Policy Fellowship. One of the above project's goals was to develop and improve a Real Estate's Market Value, and the Pollution and Health Effects Analysis Decision Support System (RE-MVPHE-DSS). RE-MVPHE-DSS consists of a market value analysis, air and noise pollution, premises microclimate, health effects, voice stress analysis, complex determination of the weights of the criteria, cooperative decision making and multiple user subsystems. RE-MVPHE-DSS is briefly analysed in this paper.

Keywords: cooperative decision making, multiple-user, market value, air pollution, premises microclimate, health effects, voice stress analysis.

1 Introduction

Certain groups of patients included in this study are those such as asthmatics, atopic patients, patients with emphysema and bronchitis, heart and stroke patients, people with diabetes, pregnant women, and the elderly and children who are especially sensitive to the health effects of outdoor air toxicants [1]. It is estimated that about 20% of the USA's population suffers from asthma, emphysema, bronchitis, diabetes or cardiovascular diseases and are thus especially susceptible to outdoor air pollution (American Lung Association, 2005). Outdoor air quality plays an important role in maintaining good human health. Air pollution causes large increases in medical expenses, morbidity and is estimated to cause about 800,000 annual premature deaths worldwide [5]. Much research [2, 3, 7, etc], digital maps and standards [6, 8, 12] on the health effects (respiratory effects, cardiovascular effects, cancer, reproductive and developmental effects, neurological effects, mortality, infection and other health effects) of outdoor air pollution, a premise's microclimate, and real estate valuation, has been published in the last decade.

The above-mentioned and other problems are related to a built environment's air pollution, the premise's microclimate, health effects, and real estate market value, etc. However, a Real Estate's Market Value, Pollution and Health Effects Analysis Decision Support System (RE-MVPHE-DSS) can analyse the above factors in an integrated way. Other positive characteristics of our System are compared with other systems and described in Section 2-5. No-one thought of the above integration function before, and

Y. Luo (Ed.): CDVE 2007, LNCS 4674, pp. 191–200, 2007.

so our attempt is the first time someone has done so. The authors of this paper participated in the project Framework 6 *Intelligent Cities* (INTELCITIES) and the Lincoln Institute of Land Policy Fellowship *Development of Market-Based Land Mass Appraisal Online System for Land Taxation*. One of the above project's goals (on the Lithuanian side) was to develop and improve the RE-MVPHE-DSS.

This paper is structured as follows: after the introduction, Section 2 describes a Model of RE-MVPHE-DSS. Section 3 analyses air and noise pollution, health effects, multiple user and cooperative decision making subsystems. Section 4 describes a voice stress analyser, premises microclimate and market value analysis subsystems. Finally, some concluding remarks, testing the developed System and future research are provided in Section 5.

2 The Model of RE-MVPHE-DSS

Real Estate's Market Value, Pollution and Health Effects Analysis Decision Support System (RE-MVPHE-DSS) consists of the following subsystems: market value analysis, air and noise pollution, premise's microclimate, health effects, voice stress analysis, complex determination of the weights of the criteria, cooperative decision making and multiple user. The complete technical description of all the subsystems and how they are connected to serve the general purpose – cooperative decision-making – will follow. The Model of RE-MVPHE-DSS and of relations between its subsystems is shown in Figure 1.

In order to make a comprehensive analysis by RE-MVPHE-DSS of built and human environment, the built and human environment must be described in digital quantitative and qualitative forms.

All stakeholders of a real estate market can use the created system. Stakeholders are recommended to use as much of their knowledge as possible before making final decisions. For example, in order to perform the multiple criteria analysis of a real estate, buyers, sellers, brokers, financial institutions, neighbours and other stakeholders' requirements should be estimated and submitted in a quantitative form.

Several sources of quantitative information are used. The Lithuanian State Enterprise Centre of Registers is the main source of data about real estate transactions. The Environmental Protection Agency provides information about air and noise pollution. Data about indoor microclimates and allergens is obtained by measuring the related parameters in typical apartments. Data about health effects is derivative and it is obtained by transforming data on air and noise pollution by using the Air Quality Index. The obtained data is used to prepare digital maps of real estate transactions, air and noise pollution, indoor microclimates, and allergens, etc. Other data, e.g. floor area of apartments, room height, the floor in which an apartment is located, the year of construction, availability of parking, etc for quantitative descriptions of built and human environments is obtain from the Lithuanian State Enterprise Centre of Registers. This obtained data is used to develop a quantitative decision making matrix (DMM) of values of the criteria.

Qualitative (subjective) information, which provides comprehensive descriptions of built and human environments, can be classified as conditionally stable and as changing. Conditionally stable indicators describe the opinions of stakeholder groups

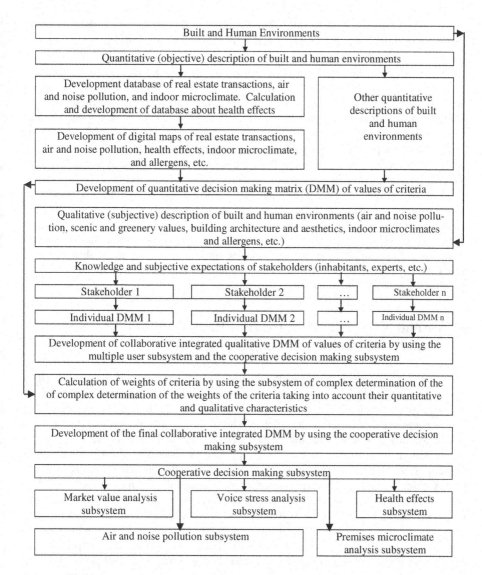

Fig. 1. Model of RE-MVPHE-DSS and of relations between its subsystems

in areas such as scenic and greenery values, building architecture and aesthetics, etc
and on built and human environments where such opinion change insignificantly over
time.

Conditionally unstable indicators (air and noise pollution, indoor microclimates
and allergens, etc.) depend on the knowledge possessed by stakeholder groups. Residents who do not know about the harmful effects of air pollution on their health do
not pay much attention to it. They live quietly in their houses close to busy streets and
when buying an apartment they do not intend to pay more for unpolluted air. The
situation changes when residents are better informed about the negative effects of air

and noise pollution on their health. Higher subjective knowledge about the harm of air and noise pollution on inhabitant's health reduces the value of apartments significantly. Currently most residents in Vilnius are not fully informed about the effect of air and noise pollution on their health. Also, many stakeholder groups (inhabitants, experts, etc.) have different levels of knowledge and subjective expectations about built and human environments. In order to express the opinions of stakeholder groups digitally, a quantitative decision making matrix (DMM) has been developed for each of stakeholder groups. In order to make a more objective decision which satisfies all stakeholder groups in a better way, the prepared matrixes are transformed into a collaborative integrated qualitative DMM of the values of the criteria by using the multiple user subsystem and the cooperative decision making subsystem.

Then, the weight of criteria is established by using the subsystem of complex determination of the weights of the criteria by taking into account their quantitative and qualitative characteristics.

Having calculated the values and weights of quantitative and qualitative criteria and by using the cooperative decision making subsystem, the final collaborative integrated DMM is developed. The database of built and human environments was developed on the basis of the above digital quantitative and qualitative information.

3 Air and Noise Pollution, Health Effects, Multiple User and Cooperative Decision Making Subsystems

The air and noise pollution subsystem accumulates information and digital maps from the Environmental Protection Agency and Vilnius Gediminas Technical University on pollution (carbon monoxide, noise, particle pollution (see Fig. 2 (*left*)), volatile organic compounds, nitrogen dioxide, etc.). The obtained information and digital maps can be used by different interested parties (inhabitants, real estate developers, Vilnius municipality, etc.) for completing a multiple criteria analysis of different pollution preventing alternatives. For example, with regard to pollution maps rational measures of city planning and development could be proposed in the form of rational design of street networks, bypasses, constant traffic highways, priority development of public transport, rational arrangement of buildings in development territories, application of houses – screens, and application of noise isolating windows, which could influence the reduction of pollution. Public transport passengers and drivers of private cars could choose less polluted routes, which can reduce traffic jams and pollution in the most polluted city streets.

The health effects subsystem accumulates information and pollution digital maps on carbon monoxide, noise, particle pollution, volatile organic compounds, nitrogen dioxide, etc from the air and noise pollution subsystem. Digital maps on the health effects (see Fig. 2 (*right*)) are developed according to the above data. Inhabitants may establish different housing purchase alternatives and choose a rational dwelling place according to the established pollution maps and their current health status as a way to reducing the negative impacts of pollution on their health. In parallel, other interested groups (real estate developers, Vilnius Municipality, etc) can establish different real estate and urban development alternative decisions and choose the most appropriated.

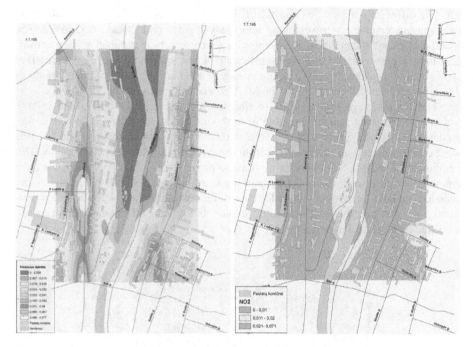

Fig. 2. Concentration levels of particle pollution (*left*) and zones of concentration of NO_2 (*right*) pollutions dangerous to people with respiratory disorders and asthma

This can help to implement the main goal of the System, i.e. to create conditions for inhabitants to live in a healthy environment.

Several initial digital maps of respiratory disorders and asthma have been prepared on the basis of data from the above air pollution digital maps and Air Quality Index. These Digital maps show clear zones of pollutant concentrations that are dangerous to people with respiratory disorders and asthma. Digital maps also show the zones with a dangerous concentration of NO_2 (marked in red). Such concentrations of pollutants can cause respiratory disorders and asthma (see Fig. 2 (*right*)).

The multiple user subsystem (MUS) stores data that is specific to each individual client. The MUS is used to accumulate information about the requirements, preferences and needs of a client for a real estate and his/her financial capabilities, etc. Therefore, the MUS accumulates information about the aggregate client's requirements for a real estate. The MUS starts by collecting data on the client's needs and his/her knowledge of the required real estate as well as data on what the client already wants and knows. Sometimes, clients do not know or do not know fully understand the importance of some information that characterizes the real estate, e.g. the surrounding's pollution and noise levels, and/or the interior's microclimate. The MUS uses the above data to create a representation of the client's requirements and knowledge by representing the client's knowledge in terms of deviations from an expert and/or a typical real estate seeker's knowledge. On the basis of these deviations it is possible to decide what criteria, or criteria weights and values should be added to the client's decision making matrix. During the e-negotiation process, brokers and client/s can take different perspectives but must reach an agreement in that they should share the same understanding in searching and analysing for real estate alternatives. The found real estate alternatives, according to a set of searching parameters, are considered to be a part of the MUS. The significance of the analysed real estate alternatives for a client is measured by priority, utility degree and market values of the alternatives that are under consideration. Also, the MUS research focuses on the Statistical Model that is statistically generated so as to find the average criteria system and criteria weights. In particular, clients are able to study and utilize a typical real estate seeker model, i.e. a typical criteria system and criteria weights, by allowing clients to see what can be inferred about the client from the typical real estate seeker's model. Development of the MUS involves a systematic process for continually improving the typical real estate seeker's model by learning from different client's navigational and decision making activities. The addition of incorporating new knowledge is performed so that credible statistical information is gained and client's activities are modified by historical experience.

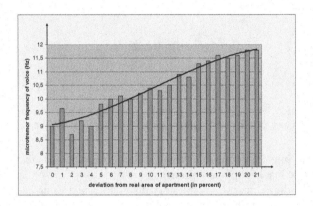

Fig. 3. Relationship between deviation from real area of apartment and microtremor frequency of voices

Over the past three years the Statistical Model has accumulated information about client navigational activities and his/her decision making. Concrete statistics about clients' navigational activities - number of concrete real estate alternative visitors, time period of analysing this alternative and decision making -selection of criteria system, criteria values and weights, was collected in the Statistical Model. The statistical information can be used to determine the most marketable real estate, and the most important criteria and their weights. The received statistical information reflects the navigational purposes of clients. The ability to statistically measure the clients' navigational activities allows one to statistically generate the average criteria system and criteria weights for a typical real estate seeker. This solution improves the accuracy of the development of the criteria system and criteria weights for the client. The above statistical information can also be applied to supplement the MUS so as to better adapt the searching process to the client's needs.

Cooperative decision making systems are gaining in importance globally. Cinderby and Forrester [4] report on a novel empirical approach to capturing and analysing the public's non-professional understanding of spatially related environmental issues and representations of people's local knowledge about air pollution and related problems. Public participation is an essential part of democratic and legitimate political decision-making, since the awareness of environmental problems on the side of potential investors and that of the public can have a significant effect on environmental protection in the area [10]. Environmental impacts of air pollutants have an impact on public health, vegetation, and material deterioration etc [11].

Currently, intelligent systems for real estate have been mostly looked at from a single-buyer's perspective, where only the purposes of a single client are taken into account. The cooperative decision making subsystem considers the circumstances where a group of interested parties are planning a common real estate development (with special emphasis on pollution and health effect), purchase and other activities, and therefore can include many potentially conflicting objectives that have to be analysed and dealt with. The cooperative decision making subsystem allows different stakeholders to solve common tasks in collaborative ways, e.g. the development of a joint criteria system, the estimation of criteria weight and qualitative criteria values. For example, RE-MVPHE-DSS can help interested parties to achieve a cooperative decision on Web-based real estate's search, analysis, negotiation and in decision making. This is done by transforming individual client models (individual decision making matrix) to the collaborative (medium) client model (collaborative integrated decision making matrix) and by using the collaborative client model to mediate, a group discussion aiming at arriving at a compromise that is acceptable to all the group's members. The cooperative decision making subsystem also allows stakeholders by using expert's methods to develop collaborative integrated decision making matrix. The developed integrated collaborative decision making matrix helps to decrease mistrust problems between stakeholders and to select most appropriate solution to satisfy all interested parties.

4 Voice Stress Analyser, Premise's Microclimates and Market Value Analysis Subsystems

The voice stress analyser (VSA) subsystem measures stress in a human voice. The VSA subsystem can be used for analysis and a better understanding of different situations in built and human environments, e.g. work of brokers, analysis of stakeholders' subjective opinions about pollution and health effects, etc. However, it is necessary to develop exhaustive statistical information database in order to efficiently use the VSA subsystem in practice.

As an example, the practical application of the VSA subsystem in the sales of real estate is briefly analysed as follows: A typical situation of a first visit to an apartment was selected. The discussion between the seller and the broker inspecting an apartment for sale was recorded (with consent from both parties). Standard questions were asked during the conversation. Advantages and disadvantages of the apartment were detected, and the sales price was established, as well as the size of the broker's commission and the negotiations of the conclusion of a mediation agreement were included. The VSA subsystem analysis records show the vibration curve of a sound document, which indicates the sound frequency in real-time. If a sound frequency is high, the oscillation of the sound curve is denser. Such density of oscillations of a sound curve shows that a person is not sure of the correctness of his/her statement or could be concealing something. For example, it was noticed that a sound vibration curve is typically very dense when a client speaks about the brokering contract. Evidence provided by the VSA subsystem can show whether a client's statement is false or doubtful.

Research conducted by the authors with the VSA subsystem determined that people are usually unsure or conceal part of the truth when speaking about a brokering contract, the exact floor area of an apartment, furniture for sale with the apartment, sale's price of the apartment, and remuneration to a broker etc. All these criteria are essential in the activities of a broker. False information can leave a broker without remuneration for his/her work. Knowledge that a client is lying when he/she speaks about the above-mentioned aspects can also protect a broker against fraud. Currently, while sufficient statistical information is not yet available, it would be wrong to rely on evidence provided only by the VSA subsystem. However, historical statistical data can help to avoid a number of misunderstandings and other problems.

As an example: A relationship between the deviation from the real area of an apartment deliberately increased by the seller (in percentages, see x-axis) and the microtremor frequency of the voice (see y-axis) when claiming a bigger floor area is presented in Fig. 3. The x-axis shows the deviation (in %) of the increased area of the apartment (compared to the real area of the apartment) as was specified by the seller during the conversation. The y-axis shows the scale of the average microtremor frequency noticed in the seller's voice during the conversation. Besides, Fig. 3 clearly shows the relationship between the level of untruth told by the seller and the average microtremor's frequency. The higher the microtremor frequency the more *dummy* area is added to the real area of an apartment by a seller during the conversation with a buyer.

In the future there will be a possibility to assess the accuracy of provided information (in %) automatically by using the VSA subsystem on the basis of accumulated historic statistical data and as determined by the regression equation. For example, according to a seller's answer about the floor area of an apartment, the VSA subsystem will automatically converts the answer into frequency and specifies the actual floor area of an apartment and the percentage of deviation from the floor area of the apartment as specified by a buyer.

Premises microclimate subsystem accumulates information about internal microclimate parameters - illumination, volume flow, air velocity, air temperature, relative humidity, dew point temperature, vibration impulse amplitudes and house allergens. The database of a premises microclimate was developed and passed on to the Cooperative decision making subsystem.

On the basis of the developed final collaborative integrated DMM, the real estate market value is calculated by using the market value analysis subsystem. The degree of real estate utility is directly associated with quantitative and conceptual information that is related to it. If one real estate is characterized by the best comfort, aesthetics and price indices, while the other shows better maintenance and facilities management characteristics, both having obtained the same significance values as a result of multiple criteria evaluation, then this means that their utility degree is also the same. With the increase or decrease of the significance of a real estate having been analysed, then its degree of utility also increases or decreases. Solving the problem of determining the market value of a real estate that is being valuated, to find what would make it equally competitive on the market as compared with a real estate that has been already sold, a particular method [14] of defining the utility degree and market value of a real estate was developed by authors.

In this case, the market value analysis subsystem creates conditions for clients to choose rational housing in a clean and healthy environment in respect to cost-benefits; and contributes to the implementation of the goals of the System.

5   Testing the Developed System, Conclusions and Future Research

The authors of the research presented in this article have suggested the idea of integrating knowledge-based, devices-based, environment friendly and decision support systems. In order to demonstrate the integration of the above systems in the real estate sector, a Real Estate's Market Value, Pollution and a Health Effects Analysis Decision Support System (RE-MVPHE-DSS) have been developed during a project in Framework 6 *Intelligent Cities* and the Lincoln Institute of Land Policy Fellowship as examples of such research. During the implementation of these two project contracts, separate subsystems of RE-MVPHE-DSS were used for practical purposes in Vilnius by several organisations (Lithuanian State Enterprise Centre of Registers, etc.). In order to check the correctness of the developed System, the whole of its solution process has been gone through manually. The results of manual and computer calculations matched. Besides, all separate working stages of the System as well as all subsystems have been coordinated with experts in this field - i.e. the essence of the calculations has been found to be in conformity with the expert's logical reasoning. Owing to suggestions from these experts, some useful changes have been introduced into the System. The check-up by the experts is bound with the fact that universal decision making methods are not always suitable for specific tasks and can lead to gross errors or to bad results.

The results of the developed System were introduced to the Ministry of Environment and the Ministry of Health of the Republic of Lithuania. These ministries certified further development of the System and provided assistance for the preparation of a feasibility study. After the preparation of the feasibility study it will be aimed to receive financing from structural funds for future System development. A completely established system is planned to be applied in three of the largest cities of Lithuania (Vilnius, Kaunas, and Klaipėda).

During the creation of RE-MVPHE-DSS a particular input in the development of cooperative decision making methods in general was performed by the integrating cooperative decision making methods with multiple criteria analysis methods, proposed by authors [15, 16]: a method of complex determination of the weights of the criteria taking into account their quantitative and qualitative characteristics; a method of multiple criteria complex proportional evaluation of the projects; a method of defining the utility and market value of a project.

However, during the development and application of RE-MVPHE-DSS and integration of its subsystems certain technical problems appeared: the interchange of electronic data and information among the subsystems of the System is not completely arranged; System is not integrated with Lithuanian e-Health system, intelligent decision support is not insufficient, etc.

References

[1] American Lung Association. American Lung Association, State of the Air 2005(2005)
[2] Atkinson, R.W., Anderson, H.R., Sunyer, J.: Acute effects of particulate air pollution on respiratory admissions: results from the APHEA2 study. Am. J. Respir. Crit. Care. Med. 164, 1860–1866 (2001)
[3] Brook, R.D., Franklin, B., Cascio, W., Hong, Y., Howard, G., Lipsett, M., et al.: Air pollution and cardiovascular disease: a statement for healthcare professionals from the expert panel on population and prevention science of the American Heart Association, Circulation, vol. 109, pp. 2655–2671 (2004)
[4] Cinderby, S., Forrester, J.: Facilitating the local governance of air pollution using GIS for participation. Applied Geography 25(2), 143–158 (2005)
[5] Cohen, A.J., Ross Alexander, H., Ostro, B., Pandey, K.D., Kryzanowski, M., Kunzail, N., et al.: The global burden of disease due to outdoor air pollution. J. Toxicol Environ. Health A 68, 1–7 (2005)
[6] Environmental Management Centre, 2006. Environmental Management Centre, A comparison of ambient air quality standards applied worldwide (2006)
[7] Grossman, C.M., Nussbaum, R.H., Nussbaum, F.D.: Cancers among residents downwind of the Hanford, Washington, plutonium production site. Arch. Environ. Health 58, 267–274 (2003)
[8] Hubbell, B.J., Hallberg, A., McCubbin, D.R., Post, E.: Health-related benefits of attaining the 8-hr ozone standard. Environ. Health Perspect. 113, 73–82 (2005)
[9] Kaklauskas, A., Zavadskas, E., Ditkevičius, R.: An Intelligent Tutoring System for Construction and Real Estate. In: Luo, Y. (ed.) CDVE 2006. LNCS, vol. 4101, pp. 174–181. Springer, Heidelberg (2006)
[10] Peterlin, M., Kontic, B., Kross, B.C.: Public perception of environmental pressures within the Slovene coastal zone. Ocean & Coastal Management 48(2), 189–204 (2005)
[11] Pummakarnchana, O., Tripathi, N., Dutta, J.: Air pollution monitoring and GIS modeling: a new use of nanotechnology based solid state gas sensors. Science and Technology of Advanced Materials 6(3-4), 251–255 (2005)
[12] US Environmental Protection Agency (EPA), US Environmental Protection Agency (EPA), Revisions to the National Air Ambient Air Quality Standards for particulate matter, Fed. Regist. 52, pp. 24634–24669 (1987)
[13] Zavadskas, E.K., Kaklauskas, A., Vainiunas, P., Saparauskas, J.: A model of sustainable urban development formation. International Journal of Strategic Property Management 8(4), 219–229 (2004)
[14] Kaklauskas, A., Zavadskas, E.K., Raslanas, S.: Multivariant design and multiple criteria analysis of building refurbishments. Energy and Buildings 37(4), 361–372 (2005)
[15] Zavadskas, E.K., Kaklauskas, A., Lepkova, N.: Multiple Criteria Analysis of Facilities Management Alternatives. International Journal of Strategic Property Management 6(1), 31–39 (2002)
[16] Zavadskas, E.K., Kaklauskas, A.: Efficiency Increase in Research and Studies While Applying up-to-date Information Technologies. Journal of Civil Engineering and Management 6(6), 397–414 (2000)

Cooperative Decision-Making with Scheduler Agents

İnci Sarıçiçek and Nihat Yüzügüllü

Eskişehir Osmangazi University, Department of Industrial Engineering
26030 Eskişehir, Turkey
{incid,nyuzugul}@ogu.edu.tr

Abstract. In this study, an Agent-Based Collaborative Scheduling System is represented as a model of scheduling among shops. Agent-based system describes the behaviors of distributed decision maker agents in manufacturing systems. Agents in the system are Production Planning Agent and Shop-Floor Agents. Shop-Floor Agents are semi-autonomous agents so that the degree of autonomy is determined by the Production Planning Agent. The distributed system forming heterogeneous units was designed by hybrid control architecture. The study focuses on constructing an Agent-Based Collaborative Scheduling System that is capable of conducting scheduling negotiations among shop-floor agents. The designed system is capable of scheduling by considering heterogeneous objectives of the shop-floor agents within a collaborative manufacturing environment. Negotiation is co-operative not competitive. Shop-Floor Agents generates collaboratively their schedules. The schedule for the best interest of the system as a whole is selected by the Production Planning Agent.

Keywords: Agent-Based Production Systems, Collaborative Scheduling, Cooperative Decision-Making.

1 Introduction

Manufacturing system control entails the coordination of a large number of physical activities and information processing activities related to the entities on the shop-floor to achieve desired production goals. In the last decade manufacturing research started to study potential applications of agent theory to production systems. According to this theory decision making process is distributed among intelligent and autonomous agents. The overall objective, in fact, is split into many local one. And agents act to reach local objectives. The approach allows overcoming the problems of complexity such as large volume data, production capacity distributed among resources [1].

Advances in Computer and Communication Technologies now make it possible to provide manufacturing system entities with intelligence and communication capabilities. So the studies on using agent technology in shop-floor control have been increased. This shop-floor control system can be characterized as a collection of intelligent autonomous entities capable of individual decision making on the basis of local information and information obtained through communication with other entities. This alternative control system is gaining increasing levels of attention and acceptance in academia and industry [1].

Y. Luo (Ed.): CDVE 2007, LNCS 4674, pp. 201–208, 2007.

A Multi-Agent System (MAS) is an artificial intelligence system composed of a population of autonomous agents that cooperate with each other to reach common goals, while simultaneously pursuing individual objectives [2]. The increasing interest in MAS research is due to the significant characteristics inherent in such systems [3]. According to the writers, these characteristics are as follows:

- Taking initiative to reach certain objectives
- Independent decision-making by individual agent based on its domain knowledge, local and global conditions.
- Perceiving changes in their environment and acting as a consequence.
- Interacting with other agents and humans for effective negotiation, cooperation and coordination.

Most MAS designed for shop-floor control are actually designed for homogeneous systems and apply the assigning rules involving only market-based mechanisms. Studies on heterarchical pattern are more limited and the interest in this subject has increased over the last decade. Agent technology is considered to be a significant approach towards developing industrially distributed systems. Many researchers have applied agent technology to supply chain management systems, manufacturing scheduling and control systems, and material transportation systems. Some of them:

Kadar et al. (1998), surveyed agent-based structures to distributed manufacturing architectures[4]. Maturana et al. (1999), presented an adaptive multi-agent manufacturing system architecture called MetaMorph [5]. Fox and et al. (2000), investigates issues and presents solutions for the construction of such an agent-oriented software architecture [6]. Ottaway and Burns (2000), presented Adaptive Production Control System (APCS) that it has dynamically changing control architecture [7]. Huang and Nof (2000), describes a modelling approach developed to design a manufacturing system as a society of autonomous agents called Autonomous Agent Network [8]. In the paper of Gjerdrum et al. (2001), multi-agent modeling techniques are applied to simulate and control a simple demand-driven supply chain network system, with the manufacturing component being optimized [9]. Maione and Naso (2001), propose an approach to job flow adaptive operational control in advanced manufacturing systems [10]. Agents are implicitly coordinated by a nature-analogous adaptation mechanism. (Lu and Yih, 2001), presented an agent-based collaborative production control framework. It is capable of conducting scheduling and dispatching functions among production entities [11].

Multi-agent systems are designed to decentralize the control of the manufacturing systems, so as to reduce the complexity and to increase the flexibility [12]. This study focused on an Agent-Based Collaborative Scheduling System (ABCSS). The system makes the realization of the scheduling possible by balancing the heterogeneous aims of three shops following each other. The collaborative scheduling system recalls the patterns of pull and push systems. The control architecture is hybrid control which is designed without taking over the central control of production planning unit.

The paper is organized as followed. In section 1, there is an introduction and literature review of paper. Section 2 presents Agent-Based Collaborative Scheduling

System. In section 3 cooperative decision-making process in the system is given. Conclusion of the study is given in last section.

2 Agent-Based Collaborative Scheduling System

Shop-floor is a dynamic environment where unexpected events and changes on planned activities are possible. In dealing with problems associated with these uncertainties, the shop-floor control system plays a very important role. The developments in communication and computer technology have made it possible to form smart independent units about distributed artificial intelligence. The strategy has been developing distributed collaborative control architectures promoting the cooperation of independent, distributed agents. For planning the communication between the production planning unit and shops, and the communication among the shops themselves in an organization, Agent-based system has been designed to realize an active shop-floor management and coordination of units, which are inherently distributed in terms of time and space.

This study focuses on establishing an agent-based collaborative shop-floor control framework in a manufacturing environment susceptible of loading and scheduling functions among production units. All the agents perform in active and collaborative ways to help each other in decision-making. The relevant collaborative control framework is capable of searching and realizing the balance among heterogeneous objectives of production units in a collaborative manufacturing system.

2.1 System Behavior

The most studies related to control architectures for production systems structurally focus on extremes as hierarchical and heterarchical control. By focusing on opposite ends of the continuum, researchers ignore the myriad of control architectures that lie between these extremes [7]. By synthesizing the desired qualities of hierarchical and heterarchical control architectures, it will be possible to develop a smart control architecture which uses the superior aspects of both control architectures.

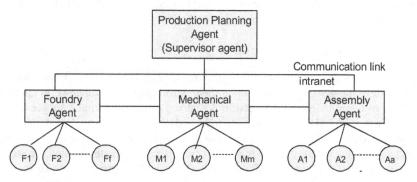

Fig. 1. Hybrid control architecture of agent-based collaborative scheduling system

In the designed system, there is heterarchical control on shop-floor basis, and hierarchical control between shop-floor and production planning unit. Hybrid control architecture will make it possible to utilize the positive qualities of both control architectures (Fig. 1).

The system makes the communication of shops with each other possible. The communication among shops themselves and the communication between shop-floor and Production Planning unit can be realized via intranet.

Data-level concepts

The basis component of the system is the agent. Shop-Floor Agents, Foundry, Mechanical, and Assembly Agents and Production Planning Agent collaborate on generating the schedules. Each agent in the system consists of

- the local database where the production data necessary to achieve main production functions is stored,
- the module necessary for internal resource management,
- the communication module needed for the communication between the other agents and the environment.

Production data involves the ability and capacity information about the production system. The data recorded in database about the related machine for each part is used during the scheduling stage. Besides, the data about machines and routes is also stored in local database.

Symbolic-Level Concepts

There are four agents within Agent-Based Collaborative Scheduling System as supervisor agent Production Planning Agent (PPA) and Shop-Floor Agents (Foundry, Mechanical, and Assembly). The aim is to develop symbolic-level concepts to code data-level within the agent architecture using the corresponding agents.

When an order reaches PPA as the supervisor agent decides to accept the order or not by considering the environment data. PPA might make decisions through communication with Shop-Floor Agents if it needs. PPA contacts appropriate agents to provide and schedule necessary resources. Shop-Floor Agents make the final schedule collaborating on scheduling the parts to be manufactured. On each request by PPA for scheduling, collaboration is performed to generate the new schedule. Supervisor agent behaves like a manager over the shop-floor.

2.2   The Architecture of the System

The basis component of the system is the agent. The data and the information are stored in local databases. The data about the environment about other agents is gained by means of communication. Deduction is realized through internal resource module. The interfaces include the agent interface and the environment interface. In the system, each shop is an independent unit that owns objectives and limitations to produce its own schedule. The extent of this independence is determined through the supervisor role of Production Planning unit. The general formation of the system is shown in Fig. 2. Shop-Floor agents are in contact with each other through a communication network.

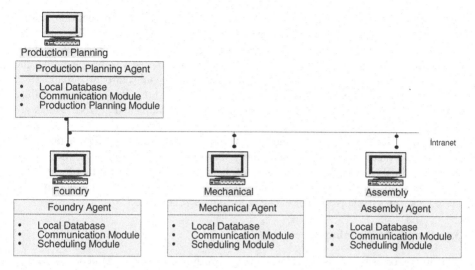

Fig. 2. The formation of Agent-Based Collaborative Scheduling System

3 Collaborative Scheduling in the System

In this study, in which shop-floor are classified as the foundry, the mechanical and assembly, each shop has the opportunity to generate its own scheduling that fits into its aims and limitations most. The system allows formation of schedules suitable for any type of production. In traditional systems, however, a global solution is searched for certain objectives under certain limitations to scheduling problem, which is considered as a whole. The difference between the performed and planned scheduling increases problems within shop-floor. The differences that increase due to the lack of communication among shops decrease the performance of the system.

The scheduling in the system is performed through using scheduling modules of Shop-Floor Agents and Production Planning Agent (PPA). PPA prepares part-order list with BOM database for the orders. It accepts and communicates them to shop-floor agents. Shop-Floor Agents are able to form their schedules through negotiations with each other. The schedule which each shop will form for corresponding parts is meant to perfect the performance of its own shop. However the possibility that shops' schedules contain different orders is quite high and it is intended to obtain the schedule that considers the system's performance as a whole. The scheduling system has been designed in which schedules are gained by replacing the priorities of shops which are in constant contact with each other and in which schedules concerning shops are determined through evaluating their performances. Therefore, it has been achieved that, instead of overcoming conflicts, shops generate their schedules by helping each other.

It is clear that a schedule which is meant to perfect the performance of the entire system for the orders which manufacturing processes are realized in sequential shops can be performed through the collaboration of related production units with each other and an active information exchange brought about by agent technology. The system contains heterogeneous resources (shops) and there's no competition among them. What is aimed here is that each shop utilizes the schedule that fits into their limitations and objectives. Because there might be conflicts about the sequence of the tasks, we have found it applicable to get different alternatives by changing the priorities of shops. It is intended that shops form their schedules through collaboration and any case that a potential delay or alteration by a cause like machinery failure occurs in shops is immediately communicated to other shops and new schedules are formed together.

In this study, it has been assumed that there are three different shops, namely the foundry, the mechanical, and the assembly. Parts are processed in sequential shops. The parts finished with the foundry and mechanical shops get the product form in the assembly shop. In the system, schedules towards back and forward are obtained by giving priorities to shops so that they can form their schedules.

3.1 Forward Scheduling

Scheduling priority of shops is presented according to process sequence. Product-orders are transformed into part-orders by PPA and communicated to shops. Units of shop-floor generate their schedules considering their own objectives and limitations according to their priorities. The generated schedule is a data resource for the next shop that contains the arrival times of part-orders to the relevant shop.

In the forward scheduling, at first, PPA sends part-orders to Shop-Floor Agents through assigning them part-delivery times on product delivery times basis. Using local databases, FSFA (Foundry Shop-Floor Agent) schedules part-orders according to its aims and limitations. It sends forward-1 schedule to MESFA (Mechanical Shop-Floor Agent). Assuming that the completion data of part-orders in Foundry Shop-Floor is the arrival time of them to Mechanical shop, MESFA generates forward-2 schedule. The completion times of part-orders in MESFA schedule are taken as arrival times of the part-orders to the Assembly shop. Assembly Shop-Floor Agent (ASFA) determines the earliest times to start assembly concerning the relevant product and produces forward-3 schedule.

The requested delivery time concerning product-order is known. However, a part is used in more than one product. Because there are order-related parts in shops, data about part delivery time is needed. The data about product-orders delivery time needs transforming into the data about part-order delivery time for the shops performing scheduling for part-orders. PPA assigns delivery times on part basis for orders by means of the assigning part delivery time process. In this process, the delivery time of the product with the earliest delivery time among the products for whose assemblies a part is used has been assigned as part-order delivery time for each part.

3.2 Backward Scheduling

The first schedule is generated by ASFA. Depending on the product-assembly starting times, ASFA performs the delivery time assigning process concerning part-orders. Here, delivery time assigning process is performed in accordance with assembly starting times in assembly shop. However, the time referred as part-delivery time in backward scheduling refers to the delivery time to assembly shop. Considering their objectives and limitations according to their priorities, shops generate schedules using part delivery time data. The schedule produced contains the information on the latest completion time of the part-orders in the relevant shop for the preceding shop. For practical reasons, the priorities of foundry and mechanical shops have been exchanged in backward scheduling and the second priority after the assembly has been taken from mechanical shop and given to foundry shop.

In the backward scheduling, at first, ASFA produces backward-3 schedule and sends them to FSFA by assigning part-delivery times on the basis of products' assembly starting times. Then, FSFA schedules part-orders by using local databases. It sends the backward-1 schedule to MESFA. Assuming that the completion data of part-orders in Foundry Shop is the arrival time of them to Mechanical shop, MESFA generates its own schedule, backward-2, by considering assembly starting times. The completion times of tasks in MESFA schedule are taken as arrival times of the part-orders to the assembly shop. ASFA determines the earliest times to start assembly. It makes necessary changes, if there are deviations from backward-3 schedule.

In backward scheduling, delivery times gain importance beginning from assembly shop. For the manufacturing environment mentioned in this study, matching time is another important performance indicator. Matching time is defined as the elapsed time between the arrivals of the first and the last part for a product's assembly. Because a longer time means an increase in the stock of the parts waiting for the assembly, matching time is supposed to be short.

After forward and backward schedules generated, one of the schedules is chosen by PPA through paying attention to criteria such as matching times, completion times concerning orders for the entire system.

4 Conclusions

An appropriate controlling system responsible for the coordination and control of material flow and data flow should be adopted in shops, where unexpected events take place and planned activities are subject to changes constantly. In this study, an Agent-Based Collaborative Scheduling System has been designed. The superiorities of both central and distributed controlling have been considered to be employed in the system designed with hybrid control architecture.

Having enough collected knowledge about own manufacturing process, each shop possesses the potential to create its own schedule. In this study, the agent-based system which suggests collaborative scheduling among shops has been presented. In the system, shops form their schedules according to their objectives and limitations depending on the priority given by Production Planning unit. Besides, the communication network among the designated agents makes it possible for shops to form their new schedules depending upon the changes in other shops. Therefore, the problems caused by the difference between planned and realized schedules in traditional systems are reduced and shops are controlled efficiently. The formation in scheduling negotiations is collaborative rather than competitive. Production schedule is generated by the cooperative decision-making process. After shops generate their forward and backward schedules and one of the schedules is chosen by Production

Planning Agent through paying attention to criteria such as the matching times concerning orders for the entire system, completion times and flow times of tasks.

The innovations in Communication Technology have greatly expanded the dimensions of the issue concerning supply chain in production. Geographical distances among manufacturing units have lost their significance with modern production technologies. It has turned out to be possible to share the common resources and collaborate in technology with another company in the far end of the world. This study is about the dimension within the company that could be an example of the corresponding supply chain and ensures the scheduling of production schedule through the collaboration of shops.

References

1. Veeramani, D., Wang, K-J.: Performance Analysis of Auction-Based Distributed Shop-Floor Control Schemes from the Perspective of the Communication Systems. International Journal of Flexible Manufacturing Systems 9, 121–143 (1997)
2. O'Hare, G.M.P., Jennings, N.R. (eds.): Foundations of Distributed Artificial Intelligence. Wiley, New York (1996)
3. Li, J-H., Liu, W-J.: Development of an Agent-Based System for Collaborative Multi-Project Planning and Scheduling. In: Proceedings of the Fourth International Conference on Machine Learning and Cybernetics, August 2005, Guangzhou (2005)
4. Kadar, B., Monostori, L., Szelke, E.: An Object-Oriented Framework for Developing Distributed Manufacturing Architectures. Journal of Intelligent Manufacturing 9, 173–179 (1998)
5. Maturana, F., Shen, W., Norrie, D.H.: MetaMorph: An Adaptive Agent-Based Architecture for Intelligent Manufacturing. International Journal of Production Research 37(10), 2159–2173 (1999)
6. Fox, M., Barbuceanu, M., Teigen, R.: Agent-Oriented Supply-Chain Management. The International Journal of Flexible Manufacturing Systems 12, 165–188 (2000)
7. Ottaway, T.A., Burns, J.R.: An Adaptive Production Control System Utilizing Agent Technology. International Journal of Production Research 38(4), 721–737 (2000)
8. Huang, C-Y., Nof, S.Y.: Formation of Autonomous Agent Networks for Manufacturing Systems. International Journal of Production Research 38(3), 607–624 (2000)
9. Gjerdrum, J., Shah, N., Papageorgiou, L.G.: A Combined Optimization and Agent-Based Approach to Supply Chain Modeling and Performance Assessment. Production Planning & Control 12(1), 81–88 (2001)
10. Maione, B., Naso, D.: Evolutionary Adaptation of Dispatching Agents in Heterarchical Manufacturing Systems. International Journal of Production Research 39(7), 1481–1503 (2001)
11. Lu, T-P., Yih, Y.: An Agent-Based Production Control Framework for Multiple-line Collaborative Manufacturing. International Journal of Production Research 39(10), 2155–2176 (2001)
12. Tang, H.P., Wong, T.N.: Reactive Multi-Agent System for Assembly Cell Control. Robotics and Computer-Integrated Manufacturing 21, 87–98 (2005)

Classification of the Investment Risk in Construction

Leonas Ustinovichius[1], Galina Shevchenko[1], Dmitry Kochin[2],
and Ruta Simonaviciene[1]

[1] Vilnius Gediminas Technical University
Saulėtekio al. 11, LT-10223 Vilnius, Lithuania
[2] Institute of System Analysis,
Prosp. 60-letija Octjabrja 9, 117312, Moscow, Russia
leonasu@st.vtu.lt, galina@st.vtu.lt, dco@mail.ru

Abstract. The determination of the investment project risk is an important stage in cooperative decision-making and in choosing the most profitable project with the lowest risk level in engineering and construction. Risk management is a systematic process for integrating professional judgments about relevant risk factors, their relative significance and probable adverse conditions and/or events leading to identification of auditable activities. The paper aims to present a verbal method of determining investment risk in construction. The main problem considered is the assessment of investments, which depend on the risk level. This article presents a new way to solve the problem - the CLARA expert verbal method. Formally, the problem is stated as one of multicriteria classifications. A hierarchical approach to the considered effectiveness indicators is proposed. The proof of the method effectiveness is presented. The process of method's practical application is described.

Keywords: expert verbal method, engineering and construction, cooperative decision making.

1 Introduction

Risk management is a systematic process for integrating professional judgments about relevant risk factors, their relative significance and probable adverse conditions and/or events leading to identification of auditable activities [1, 10, 15].

Risk management at the construction stage of the project life cycle influences not only the economic effect of the investment [11], but also efficient functioning of the building in the future [5]. The lack of proper actions in construction can increase the probability of defects, failures, accidents or even catastrophes and eventually ruin the whole project.

In multicriteria environment it is hardly possible to achieve this without resorting to special techniques [12, 13, 14]. This article presents review of the verbal expert methods, because they very efficient in multicriteria environment.

In practice, the task of getting expert knowledge in many cases can be formulated like the task of classification because expert intelligence helps to sort objects (alternatives, states of object) through classes of decision. Elements that comprise the

Y. Luo (Ed.): CDVE 2007, LNCS 4674, pp. 209–216, 2007.

whole to be classified may have a different origin. They can be different physical objects, cases of choice or conditions of some object.

Describing the method of prescription of the object to a certain class of decision is complicated because of inverbality of the strategy expert uses. When the expert solves the task of classification in his sphere of knowledge, these inverbal skills are effectively and promptly used. One of the tasks preparing the base for classification is the setting of numerous criteria (attributes), which can be used to describe any object [3]. The scale of all criteria is formed by setting a finite set of possible values. If in a certain task the scale of values of one or more criteria is infinite, it can be modified to finite by cutting it to a finite set of intervals. Finally, a classification of definite intervals and its components must be organized, i.e. the rules, according to which any object can be prescribed to one of the predefined classes, based on the expert knowledge, must be formulated. Classified projects are described by assessing various efficiency criteria that could be both qualitatively and quantitatively expressed.

The purpose of this article is to demonstrate how multiple criteria can be used in analyzing the facility location problems.

The paper is structured as follows. The next section presents the formal problem statement and overview, where explains the most popular international multiple objective analysis methods, and demonstrates their application on real problems. Section 3 discusses the CLARA (verbal expert method) framework architecture, the system components, and how single-user application can be extended by CLARA. In section 4 the consistency model that is applied in the default implementation of the CLARA is briefly discussed. In section few requirements, limitations and future work is discussed and in the last section research findings and contributions in this paper are summarized.

2 Formal Problem Statement

Very often investment decision-making and research planning are referred to non-structured problems. Since the essential characteristics of such problems are qualitative, they can hardly be used in the analysis. On the other hand, the quantitative models are not sufficiently reliable. Non-structured problems have the following common characteristics. They are unique decision-making problems, i.e. every time a decision-maker is faced with an unknown problem or the one having new features compared with the previously considered case. These problems are associated with the uncertainty of the alternatives to be evaluated, caused by the lack of information for making a decision. The evaluation of the alternatives is of qualitative nature, being usually expressed verbally (in statements). Classification is a very important aspect in decision making [9]. Classes in decision making are determined by the particular parameters, i.e. the efficiency of technical and technological decisions concerning the subject individuality. Formalizing the considered problem step by step, the analysis was performed.

Given [5, 6, 9]:

1. G is a feature, corresponding to the target criterion (e.g. treatment effectiveness).
2. $K = \{K_1, K_2, ..., K_N\}$ is a set of criteria, used to assess each alternative (course of treatment).

3. $S_q = \left\{ k_1^q,..., k_{w_q}^q \right\}$ for $q=1,..., N$ is a set of verbal estimates on the scale of criterion K^q, w_q is a number of estimates for criterion K^q; estimates in S_q are ordered based on increasing intensity of the feature G;

4. $Y = S_1 \times ... \times S_N$ is a space of the alternative features to be classified. Each alternative is described by a set of estimates obtained by using criteria $K_1,..., K_N$ and can be presented as a vector $y \in Y$, where $y = (y_1, y_2,..., y_N)$, y_q is an index of estimate from set S_q.

5. $C = \{C_1,..., C_M\}$ is a set of decision classes, ordered based on the increasing intensity of feature G.

6. A binary relation of strict dominance was introduced. The relation is anti-reflexive and anti-symmetric and transitive. It may be also useful to consider a reflexive, anti-symmetric, transitive binary relation of weak dominance Q. The goal of decision making preferences is to create the imaginary $F: Y \to \{Y_i\}, i = 1,..., M$, where Y_i is a set of vector estimates belonging to class C_i, satisfying the condition of consistency: $\forall x, y \in Y : x \in Y_i, y \in Y_j, (x, y) \in P \Rightarrow i \geq j$.

Many different methods for solving multicriteria classification problems are widely known [2, 4, 6, 7, 8, 9]. ORCLASS [6], as an ordinary classification, was one of the first methods designed to solve these kinds of problems. More recent methods, such as DIFCLASS, CLARA and CYCLE have been applied for multicriteria expert analysis [7, 8, 9].

The essential principles of verbal analysis used to assess the profitability of investment in construction project may be briefly described in the following way:

- Problem description used by decision-maker and his environment should not be altered at any stage of analysis.

- According to psychological research findings, methods of obtaining the information from people should comply with the human data processing system.

- Logical operations on verbal variables (i.e. alternative evaluation based on various criteria) should be mathematically correct.

- The information obtained from decision maker should not contain conflicting data.

Verbal analysis helps to reduce the gap between the demand for effective decision-making methods and the capacity of human data processing system.

3 CLARA (Classification of Real Alternatives)

A classification problem, composed of risk evaluation criteria and final class decisions, is compiled for determining the investment project risks [4]. Constructional investment project risk evaluation criteria are provided for the first and second criteria levels.

Very often experts cannot measure qualitative variables on an absolute scale. The first hierarchic level is the main one. Constructional investment project risk can be evaluated according to the criteria of this level. Each first hierarchy level criterion is evaluated as low, medium, high or very high.

When the estimates are introduced, the result is obtained, i. e. risk levels are determined. These criteria (1st level) are not always sufficient for establishing the construction investment project risk level. Therefore, each criterion of the first hierarchic level is subdivided into lower level criteria. The second hierarchic level is composed in this way. The criteria of the second hierarchic level are required for performing an accurate analysis (each of the risk types is analysed) [4].

Such risk evaluation work course is obtained from the drawn scheme in Fig 1.

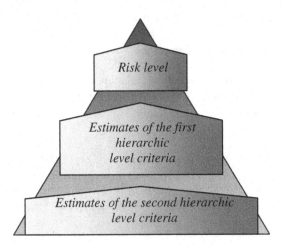

Fig. 1. Determining the values of the investment project risk

A general block-diagram of the algorithm CLARA is presented in Fig 2. Let us consider the main steps of the classification algorithm CLARA:

1. When classification proceeds, dichotomy coefficient d_i for searching for the boundary between classes C_i and C_{i+1} is assumed to be equal to ½.

2. The directed graph of the alternative domination $G(Y, E)$ may have several connectivity components. Therefore, all the available alternatives from the set Y^* which have not been classified yet are examined one by one. The chosen alternative x_S is referred to as the *initial* alternative.

3. In a certain connectivity component (including x_S) of the directed graph $G(Y, E)$, a chain w_{max} of the longest alternatives, going through the initial alternative x_S and containing the maximum value of non-classified alternatives from Y^* is built.

4. Since classes $\{C_n\}$ are ordered according to quality, the boundaries between classes are constructed in consecutive order by separating the class of higher quality C_n from the lower quality class C_{n+1}.

5. An expert is given the element x_d of the chain w_{max}, where $d = d_n \cdot L(w_{max})$. In this case, if the alternative x_d proved to be unsuitable or already classified, a suitable non-classified element of the chain with the closest index is taken as another x_d.

6. An expert is presented with an allowable alternative x_d of the chain w_{max} and his/her decision is extended to include the maximum number of suitable elements, whose membership of the classes C_n and C_{n+1} is still not determined.

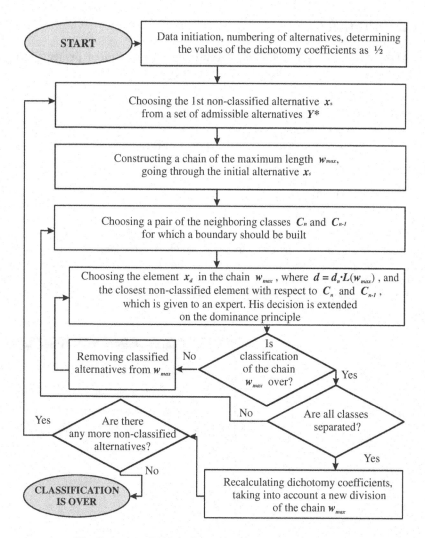

Fig. 2. A general block-diagram of the algorithm CLARA

7. If w_{max} still contains admissible non-classified elements, the dichotomizing of the chain w_{max} is continued until all suitable alternatives are directly or indirectly classified with respect to classes C_n and C_{n+1}. Otherwise, another boundary between classes is sought in the chain (by returning to step 4). If the chain is classified with respect to all classes, index k is found for each class in the chain w_{max}, where class C_{n+1} is substituted for C_n. It is assumed that $d_{nw}=k/L(w_{max})$. At any subsequent step d_n there is an arithmetical mean of all previously calculated d_{nw}.

8. The cycle is continued until all admissible alternatives from the admissible set Y^* are classified with respect to this pair of classes.

4 Classification Course

1 STAGE. Evaluation of technical – technological investment project (IP) risk (Fig 3). For second hierarchy level evaluation criteria are introduced:

- Criterion 1 – qualified labour force;
- Criterion 2 – supply of construction materials;
- Criterion 3 – designing mistakes;
- Criterion 4 – course of the constructional works.

Criteria evaluation classes:

- Class A – high;
- Class B – average;

Class C – low.

Criteria 1 – 4 are chosen for evaluation of technical – technological IP risk. When analysing the project the expert determines whether the chosen labour force is qualified enough, whether permanent continuous supply of materials will be ensured during the construction and what the estimated course of jobs is. After the project is analysed, it is checked for mistakes.

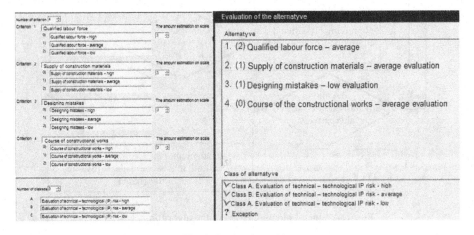

Fig. 3. Evaluation tables

The input of other (financial, ecological and any) data of evaluation of investment project risks into the program is analogous to the first stage. Classification is performed after verbal risk evaluation scheme data are inserted in the program.

Classification implementation into the program. After the introduction of all the criteria that will be taken into consideration to classify all available investment projects, the process of classification can be started. The classification (Fig 4) is made in the following way: the program composes a combination of the criteria evaluations.

The expert assigns the evaluations combination to the respective class. When the assignment is finished, we proceed to the next stage (by pushing the button "NEXT").

During the work the expert might make a mistake or change his opinion, therefore, contradictions might appear in his answers. In such case, the program shows a warning that contradictions have occurred and it will ask to confirm the new answer or to change it. If program CLARA is used, all the contradictions are eliminated during the work.

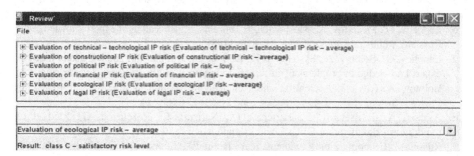

Fig 4. Evaluation of the alternative

After the work is finished, the program saves all the data, performs analysis and shows the number of the given DM questions, the number of classified combinations and the number of eliminated combinations. It also shows how many of the evaluated combinations were assigned to classes A, B or C. Evaluations of all second hierarchy level criteria are established in an analogous way.

5 Conclusions

In project development, it is hardly possible to get exhaustive and accurate information. As a result, the consequences of some situations can be very damaging to the project. Due to close cooperation of the participants of the project, the risk occurring at one stage of the project can be transferred to other stages and one type of risk can be changed by another. This means that chain reaction is characteristic of the risk and the efficiency as well as safety of any project is decreased.

In the present paper, a novel algorithm CLARA is offered for ordering multicriteria alternatives. It differs from the existing similar methods in a wider range of application allowing it to be used with various scales of criteria evaluation, a random number of the solution classes, incomplete order of the criteria scales as well as in the considerably rarefied space of the alternatives. The suggested algorithm is more effective in terms of the time spent by an expert.

References

1. Ustinovichius, L., Zavadskas, E.K.: Assessment of investment profitability in construction from technological perspectives (in Lithuanian). Publishing house Technika, VGTU, Vilnius (2004)
2. Ashihmin, I.V., Furems, E.M.: UNICOMBOS - Intellectual Decision Support System For Multicriteria Comparison (in Russian). In: Artificial Intelligence (Iskustvenij intelekt) Proceedings of the Ukrainian Academy of sciences, Kiev, vol. 2, pp. 243–247 (2004)

3. Korhonen, P., Larichev, O., Moshkovich, H., Mechitov, A., Wallenius, J.: Choice behavior in a Computer-Aided Multiattribute Decision Task. J. Multicriteria Decision Analysis 2(2), 43–55 (1997)
4. Larichev, O., Kochin, D., Kortnev, A.: Decision support system for classification of a finite set of multicriteria alternatives. Decision Support Systems 33(1), 13–21 (2002)
5. Ustinovichius, L., Kochin, D.: Verbal analysis of the investment risk in construction. Journal of Business Economics and Management 4(4), 228–234 (2003)
6. Larichev, O., Mechitov, A., Moshovich, E., Furems, E.: Revealing of expert knowledge (in Russian). Publishing house Nauka, Moscow (1989)
7. Larichev, O., Bolotov, A.: System DIFKLASS: construction of full and consistent bases of expert knowledge in problems of differential classification (in Russian). In: Larichev, O., Bolotov, A. (eds.) The scientific and technical information, a series 2, Informacionie Procesi i Sistemi. Information processes and systems, (9) (1996)
8. Asanov, A., Borisenkov, P., Larichev, O., Nariznij, E., Rozejnzon, G.: Method of multicriteria classification CYCLE and its application for the analysis of the credit risk (in Russian). Economy and mathematical methods (Ekonomika i Matematicheskije metodi) 37(2), 14–21 (2001)
9. Ustinovichius, L., Sevenko, G., Kochin, D.: Classification of Real Alternatives and its Application to the Investment Risk in Construction. In: Trzaskalik, T., Katowice (eds.) Book: Multiple criteria decision making '05, pp. 299–318 (2006)
10. Slowinski, R., Zopounidis, C.: Application of the rough set approach to evaluation of bankruptcy risk. International Journal of Intelligent Systems in Accounting Finance and Management 4(1), 27–41 (1995)
11. Nowak, M.: Investment projects evaluation by simulation and multiple criteria decision aiding procedure. Journal of civil engineering and management 11(3), 193–202 (2005)
12. Baccarini, D., Archer, R.: The risk ranking of projects: a methodology. International Journal of Project Management 19(3), 139–146 (2001)
13. Nedzveckas, J., Rasimavichius, G.: Investment currency risk and ways of its decrease. Economy. Publishing house of VU, Vilnius, vol. 51(2), pp. 63–74 (2000)
14. Greco, S., Matarazzo, B., Slowinski, R.: A new rough set approach to evaluation of bankruptcy risk. In: Zopounidis, C. (ed.) Operational Tools in the Management of Financial Risks, pp. 121–136. Kluwer Academic Publishers, Dordrecht (1998)
15. Ustinovichius, L.: Determination of Efficiency of Investments In Construction. International Journal of Strategic Property Management 8(1), 25–44 (2004)

A Composite-Service Authorization Prediction Platform for Grid Environment*

Chuanjiang Yi, Hai Jin, and Sheng Di

Services Computing Technology and System Lab
Cluster and Grid Computing Lab
School of Computer Science and Technology
Huazhong University of Science and Technology, Wuhan, 430074, China
hjin@hust.edu.cn

Abstract. In workflow and grid environment, the security challenges with the appearance of composite service increasingly become more severe than before especially to the traditional static access control model and dynamic authorization model. To solve these challenges, we presented a Dynamic Access Control Prediction mechanism for service workflow on the basis of Markov Chain. In fact, this prediction mechanism is only one part of the larger system, *Composite-Service Authorization Prediction* platform (CAP), which is totally composed of three key modules---- composite-service pre-processing, result feedback, and authorization prediction. In this paper, we present the design of its architecture as a whole.

1 Introduction

With the Internet and business globalization substituting the separation which used to be a typical role in the traditional business paradigm [1], some problems to the traditional static and dynamic access control model occurred, especially in the workflow [1][2] and grid environment [3]. According to the background knowledge of workflow and grid, we can find a common range in which subjects and objects belong to different organizations and finally condense them into a composite service model. So, it is probable that the sub-elements of composite service belong to completely different organizations, or limited by various policies.

The appearance of composite service causes three challenges to static access control model:

- The relations between subjects and objects cannot maintain a fixed connection, in that they are constrained by their respective security rules and can be added or deleted anytime.
- The previous simple static access control policy on objects is not able to distinguish diverse access requests from various organizations submitted by one and the same subject.

---

* This paper is supported by National Science Foundation under grant 90412010 and China CNGI project under grant CNGI-04-15-7A.

Y. Luo (Ed.): CDVE 2007, LNCS 4674, pp. 217–225, 2007.
© Springer-Verlag Berlin Heidelberg 2007

- When a subject belongs to varied real organizations, an object will be put into different VOs in different jobs. If the rules to control the access of the object are all static, it is probable that a static access control policy would be used in different VOs. This will cause confusion in managing VO.

In addition, it also causes another two challenges to dynamic access control model:

- Different dynamic authorization policies on different services may conflict each other. Thus it may cause failures of executing jobs.
- The authorization policy may be changed temporarily and dynamically just before the service is called, and this unexpected state will cause the job failure either.

To solve all the challenges mentioned above, we focus on the dynamic creation of access control policy for grid environment based on the CGSP project [4] and present a Dynamic Authorization Prediction mechanism for service workflow on the basis of Markov Chain. Consequently, we develop *Composite-Service Authorization Prediction* platform (CAP) to help achieve flexible and reliable access control.

The remainder of this paper is organized as follows. Section 2 describes our motivating scenario. We review related authorization research in section 3. Section 4 presents the architecture of CAP and the modules function. In section 5, we introduce key methods used in CAP. Conclusions and our future work are given in Section 6.

2 Scenario

The underlying common grid computing platform in ChinaGrid project is called *ChinaGrid Supporting Platform* (CGSP) [4]. One important characteristic of CGSP 2.0 is that the Job Manager module can parse, schedule, execute and monitor composite services. After modeling a composite service as an Ordered Service Sequence, we develop a new approach to calculate the conditional probability of one service execution in a set of service sequence in Markov Chain. We create access control rules dynamically according to these calculated values.

Imagine such a scenario: the CGSP environment has deployed a composite service , *CS* for short, which is composed of 4 atomic services named *a, b, c* and *d*. Assume that a legal user of CGSP, called Alice, wants to access *a*. Not only has the *CS* job been successfully submitted, but its first three services, *a, b* and *c*, have also been finished. Unfortunately, the job may still fail just because Alice does not own the access to the last atomic service, *d*.

Consider another scenario: Alice, via role *r*, calls service *a* for a computational fluid dynamics job, *J1*, at 9:00, and at 14:00, she calls *a* again to finish an image-processing job, *J2*, through the same role *r*. These two requests are plausibly the same (just the original data are different), but in fact they are submitted for two different jobs. This situation will cause two potential security problems. One is that the static access control policy can not distinguish the difference between these two service calls. The other is that the same static access control policy will be used in different VOs. This situation will cause confusion on the management of VO. Therefore, when the two jobs belong to two different organizations, the service *a* will be put into different VOs in different jobs. The situation in which one static access control policy would appear in different VOs at the same time is filled with security-problem risks.

If we use dynamic access control model to check the access control policy before executing Alice's job, confirming it can be finished, both time and space will be saved a lot. But it is still possible that someone, say the administrator, changes the service d's access control during Alice running this job and this will still cause the job failures. This situation is caused by the second challenge of dynamical access control mentioned above. How should we design a mechanism to stop this situation happening? One candidate way is that we should make the access control dynamic and flexible, the other one is ensuring the dynamicity do not impact the running legal job. On the basis of two ways, we developed CAP, a kind of approach of authorization prediction for grid platform.

3 Related Work

The two well-known static access control models in the field of computer security are HRU [5] and RBAC (*Role-Based Access Control*) [6, 7]. Following them DAC (*Discretionary Access Control*) and MAC (*Mandatory Access Control*) appear. These two access control models are almost designed for a static and centrally administering security system. Their basic principle is: if subjects want to access objects, the subjects must get the privilege on target objects first. This static access control has not reached the demand of Internet and business globalization.

One dynamic access control mechanism introduced in [8-10] is called TBAC (*task-based access control*) which is a task-oriented model for access control and authorization. It can not only model the tasks in workflow, but dynamically manage the permissions through these tasks and their status. It is an active security model well suited for distributed computing and dynamic information processing activities, such as workflow management and agent-based distributed computing. In this paradigm, permissions are checked-in and checked-out in a just-in-time fashion based on activities or tasks.

Based on the idea of context information in TABC, we introduce a new access control prediction mechanism on the basis of Markov Chain and use the init probability and the transition probability to predict the authorization result of service sequence.

Community Authorization Service (CAS) is built on the Globus Toolkit middleware for grid computing [11,12], not only allowing a virtual organization to publish policies regarding resources distributed across a number of sites, but also itself to express and enforce expressive, consistent policies across resources spanning multiple independent policy domains [13]. CAS focuses on distributed security polices and assigns a set of appropriate rights on the requester temporarily when he/she wants to access a resource in a VO. However, it is through a central server that the CAS manages the VO's access control policy. It just considers the single service or resource but not the cooperation of multi-services or multi-resource. Comparatively, our work will focus on a composite service and introduce a method to solve authorization problem for the service sequence.

4 Architecture of CAP

In this section, we will describe the architecture of CAP before introducing the definitions and functions of the modules in CAP. Figure 1 shows the architecture of CAP. CAP includes 5 components: user client, job scheduler, composite service pre-processor, *Authorization Prediction and Dynamic Authorization Policy Creator* (DAPC).

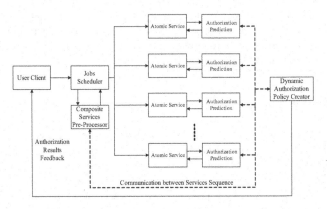

Fig. 1. The Architecture of CAP

User client: The functions of this module include defining composite service, submitting composite service, adding user's information and receiving authorization feedback. User client can change the security condition according to the feedback.

Jobs scheduler: This module takes charge of orchestrating composite service. In CGSP2, this module is implemented by *Business Process Execution Language* (BPEL) [14]. CGSP2 refers to ActiveBPEL engine [15] as the core of service-flow and extends it to support the CGSP composite service, defined in a *.bpel* file.

Composite service pre-processor: This module is parallel to the jobs scheduler. It gets the composite service *.bpel* file from the job scheduler and analyzes it before the job being executed. Based on this analytical result, *composite service pre-processor* will rearrange this composite service to build an *Ordered Service Sequence* (OSS) [16] logically. More details about this module will be described in section 5.

Authorization prediction: This module is implemented as a plug-in and deployed with every atomic service. The module receives the OSS created by *composite service pre-processor* and creates an *atomic access policy* (aap) by using Markov Chain. More details about the theory of *Authorization Prediction* can be found in [16].

Dynamic authorization policy creator: This module will collect all the atomic access policies from the *Authorization Prediction* and create a dynamic access policy set. After that, a temporary access control file in XML format will be created to record all atomic services before them practically being executed. And then, it will lock or create a copy for every atomic access policy avoiding the policy being changed by someone. Once all these operation done, *dynamic authorization policy creator* will return this authorization to user client and the user can modify or request a new privilege to fit the authorization policy. As soon as an atomic service is finished and its result has been sent to the next one, the temporary file will be deleted.

5 Key Methods of CAP

Once a user submits a composite service, the job manager will parse this composite service. Then, dynamic prediction in CGSP will obtain a file describing this composite service and rearrange to an *Ordered Service Sequence* (OSS) logically. Because OSS and *Atomic Service* (AS) have a very close relationship, we give the AS and OSS definition as follows:

Definition 1. *An Atomic Service* is the minimum service element, has the minimum function and can never be divided. We use *AS* to denote a set of *Atomic Service* and its element is expressed as_i: $AS=\{as_1, as_2,\ldots, as_i,\ldots, as_n\}$, $i\in N$

Definition 2. *Ordered Service Sequence* is a service sequence where each element is an *Atomic Service* and sorted by the order of execution. We use *OSS* to denote the set of *Order Service Sequence*: $OSS=\{as_1,\ldots, as_i,\ldots, as_j,\ldots\}$, $i, j\in N$, $i<j$, $as\in AS$.

Obviously, $OSS\subseteq AS$.

To get an OSS from a composite service, we must analyze the *bpel* file of the composite service and rearrange the atomic services set. The composite service pre-processing is responsible for this job. There are 5 service relationship types in CGSP environment, including sequential, parallel, loop, recursion, and selection. We use the composite service pre-processing technology to deal with every relationship and transfer them to OSS.

For sequential, this is the simplest relation and it is OSS itself. For parallel, the services with parallel relationship can be executed disorderly. To get an OSS from this relationship, we can just set the parallel services as any order and the transition probability is 1. For loop and recursion, these two relationships are referred to as executing the same service many times. From the security point of view, the authorization condition will not be changed no matter how many times it is executed. Hence we just consider this service one element in OSS. For selection/conditional, this is the most complex relationship, for this situation we must create many OSS for every condition.

Figure 2 illustrates how to transfer parallel relation to sequential relation with a practical example. (a) presents a task that contains five atomic services: as_1, as_2, as_3, as_4, and as_5. Among these atomic services, as_1 and as_2 are parallel to each other. But in the dynamic prediction point of view, the task can be rearranged to an ordered service sequence shown in (b) or (c). For as_2 parallels to as_3, (b) is considered equal to (c).

The transition probability is a definition in Markov theory. It is very difficult to calculate the transition probability from one atomic service to another, because different atomic services may exist in different domains. That the administrators of different domains can set their own access policy to atomic services makes the situation very complex. To simplify the process and make calculation easier, we abstract some common characteristics, say access time, from different atomic services.

Thus for every service, we just consider these common characteristics as a constrain condition. For two atomic services, as_i and as_k, we have their common access policy ap_i and ap_k: $ap_i \longleftrightarrow sp_{i1}(\vee/\wedge)sp_{i2}(\vee/\wedge)\ldots\ldots(\vee/\wedge)sp_{im}$, and $ap_k \longleftrightarrow sp_{k1}(\vee/\wedge)sp_{k2}(\vee/\wedge)\ldots\ldots(\vee/\wedge)sp_{km}$.

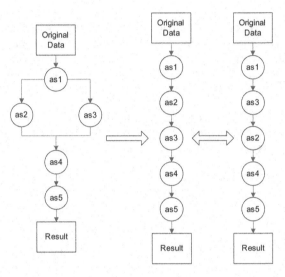

Fig. 2. Rearrange a composite service to an ordered service sequence in logical

In the situation of as_i that has been executed successfully, it is only when task condition satisfy the ap_i and ap_k at the same time that the as_k can be executed. The transition probability $p(ik)$ can be calculated by this way:

$$p(ik)=p(\frac{sp_{i1}\bigcap sp_{k1}}{sp_{i1}})\times p(\frac{sp_{i2}\bigcap sp_{k2}}{sp_{i2}})\times\ldots p(\frac{sp_{im}\bigcap sp_{km}}{sp_{im}})$$

Once we get the executable probability of an atomic service, we can confirm whether the system can run the service for some users or not. But in most situations, such a *yes* and *no* delineation is too coarse. So we import the Conditional Authorization to make the dynamic access policy more reliable. In [16], we have defined that the access policy of an atomic service may contain several sub-policies described as: $ap_i \longleftrightarrow sp_{i1}(\vee/\wedge)sp_{i2}(\vee/\wedge)\ldots\ldots(\vee/\wedge)sp_{im}$.

The relationship among these sub-policies may be *AND* or *OR*. We define four types of access control strategies: Unconditional Permit, Conditional Permit, Unconditional Deny, and Conditional Deny. Each strategy corresponds to an appropriate threshold which can be set by the administrator statically after deploying service. The relationships are presented in Table 1.

Table 1. An access control description for every atomic service ($T1<T2<T3<T4$)

Cur-task	Pre-task	Threshold	State
As_i	As_k	$T1$	Unconditional deny
As_i	As_k	$T2$	Conditional deny
As_i	As_k	$T3$	Conditional permit
As_i	As_k	$T4$	Unconditional Permit

We put corresponding weight on each sub-policy to denote the importance of sub-policy. We import a Conditional Authorization table shown as Table 2 to make the authorization result more clear.

Table 2. Conditional authorization table

Conditional Authorization
None sub-policys are met
Certain sub-policys can not be satisfied
Certain sub-policys are met
All sub-policys are met

From Table 1 and 2, we get the Conditional Authorization relationship shown in Figure 3. According to the minimum threshold and the maximum threshold, we can create a deny policy or a permit policy directly. We can also evaluate the weight of access strategy over the intermediate values.

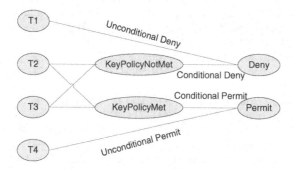

Fig. 3. Conditional authorization relationship

6 Conclusions and Future Work

In this paper, we describe an authorization prediction system, CAP, used for composite service in grid environment. We give the overview of CAP architecture and describe its module functions. We list some key technologies used in CAP to show the system's characteristics. CAP can rearrange the service sequence to predicate the executable probability of some steps of a task sequence and make an access control policy dynamically according to the prediction result. Thus we do not need set the access control statically before the system starts, so as to enhance the flexibility of access control, and we can import the conditional authorization to enhance the accuracy of our forecasts, to make reliable access control policy.

However, the work described in this paper is just a beginning and there are still lots of work to do. In the future, our work will focus on the following points:

1. How to analyze the BPEL file effectively and give the most reasonable OSS?
2. How to get a precise transition probability? In this paper, we just introduce an intuitive method to get the probability. In our future work, we will add the historical information of job manager and the service sensitive information to the judgment condition.
3. How to organize all the atomic access control policies to compose a whole authorization policy for composite service, or eliminate redundant atomic policies?
4. How to deal with complex service relationship exactly and cover all the control flow patterns?

References

[1] Kang, M.H., Park, J.S., Froscher, J.N.: Access Control Mechanisms for Inter-Organizational Workflow. In: Proceedings of 6th ACM Symposium on Access Control Models and Technologies, Chantilly, Virginia, USA, pp. 66–74. ACM Press, New York (2001)

[2] Workflow Management Coalition Terminology & Glossary (WFMC-TC-1011, v3.0), http://www.wfmc.org/standards/docs/TC-1011_term_glossary_v3.pdf

[3] Foster, I., Kesselman, C., Tuecke, S.: The Anatomy of the Grid: Enabling Scalable Virtual Organizations. International Journal of High Performance Computing Applications 15(3), 200–222 (2001)

[4] Jin, H.: ChinaGrid: Making Grid Computing a Reality. In: Chen, Z., Chen, H., Miao, Q., Fu, Y., Fox, E., Lim, E.-p. (eds.) ICADL 2004. LNCS, vol. 3334, pp. 13–24. Springer, Heidelberg (2004)

[5] Harrison, M.H., Ruzzo, W.L., Ullman, J.D.: Protection in operating systems. Communications of the ACM 19(8), 461–471 (1976)

[6] Ferraiolo, D., Kuhn, R.: Role-Based Access Controls. In: Proceedings of the 15th NIST-NCSC National Computer Security Conference, pp. 554–563 (1992)

[7] Sandhu, R., Conyne, E.J., Lfeinstein, H., Youman, C.E.: Role based access control models. IEEE Computer 29(2), 38–47 (1996)

[8] Thomas, R.K., Sandhu, R.S.: Towards a task-based paradigm for flexible and adaptable access control in distributed applications. In: Proceedings of the 1992-1993 ACM SIGSAC New Security Paradigms Workshops, pp. 138–142 (1993)

[9] Thomas, R.K., Sandhu, R.S.: Task-Based authorization: a research project in next-generation active security models for workflows. In: Proceedings of NSF Workshop on Workflow and Process Automation in Information Systems: State-of-the-Art and Future Directions (1996)

[10] Thomas, R.K., Sandhu, R.S.: Task-based authentication controls (TABC): A family of models for active and enterprise-oriented authentication management. In: Proc. of the IFIP WG11.3 Workshop on Database Security, pp. 166–181 (1997)

[11] Foster, I., Kesselman, C.: Globus: A Metacomputing Infrastructure Toolkit. International Journal of Supercomputer Applications 11(2), 115–129 (1998)

[12] GT 4.0: Security: Community Authorization Service, http://www.globus.org/toolkit/docs/4.0/security/cas/

[13] Pearlman, L., Kesselman, C., Welch, V., Foster, I., Tuecke, S.: The Community Authorization Service: Status and Future. In: Computing in High Energy and Nuclear Physics, La Jolla, California, pp. 24–28 (2003)

[14] Business Process Execution Language for Web Services Version 1.1, http://www-106.ibm.com/developerworks/webservices/library/ws-bpel/

[15] ActiveBPEL engine, http://www.activebpel.org/index.html

[16] Yi, C., Jin, H., Wang, C.: Dynamic Access Control Prediction for Ordered Service Sequence in Grid Environment. In: Proceedings of the 2006 IEEE/WIC/ACM International Conference on Web Intelligence, IEEE Computer Society, Hong Kong, China (2006)

[17] Web Services Business Process Execution Language Version 2.0, http://docs.oasis-open.org/wsbpel/2.0/wsbpel-specification-draft.pdf

A Document Recommendation System
Based on Clustering P2P Networks

Feng Guo[1] and Shaozi Li[2,*]

[1] Dept. of Computer Science, Xiamen University, Fujian,
China, 361005
betop@xmu.edu.cn
[2] Dept. of Computer Science, Xiamen University, Fujian,
China, 361005
szlig@xmu.edu.cn

Abstract. This paper presents a document recommendation system based on clustering peer-to-peer networks. It's an unstructured P2P system. In this system each agent-peer can learn user's interest, then it helps user share and recommend documents with the other users. Since each peer in our P2P networks is a node, in order to cluster them, we import the concept of Group. Each group is composed of peers. The types of documents, which belong to a same group, are uniform. This paper presents how these peers help users to share and to recommend documents, and how they cluster into groups. Our experiment results show the advantages of the document recommendation system.

Keywords: Recommendation System, Clustering P2P, Reputation Management.

1 Introduction

Nowadays information in the internet is quickly increasing, which promotes the development of text mining and information retrieval techniques such as file sharing systems based on P2P networks. These systems have gained wide popularity. Some reports [1] suggest that P2P traffic is the dominant consumer of bandwidth ahead of Web traffic. But these systems still have some problems in querying. The users can only query files by file-names, which is too simple to express their contents. This paper presents a document recommendation system based on clustering P2P networks, called hybrid filtering system, which uses document's content and user's opinions to decide the relationship between document and user. It has higher precision in querying than other file sharing systems.

Content-based information filtering can recommend documents effectively by users' interest which has been known before. While collaborative filtering can learn users' new interest from other similar users, but it suffers from cold start [2] problem. The core of filtering algorithm in our system is a hybrid document filtering algorithm, including content-based filtering and collaborative filtering.

---

* Corresponding author.

Y. Luo (Ed.): CDVE 2007, LNCS 4674, pp. 226–233, 2007.

In this paper we import the concept of Group, which is composed of peers. The types of documents, which belong to a same group, are uniform. Peers can calculate the similarity with each others. Then the similar peers can cluster automatically into a same group. But the "similar user" is very difficult to decide in an unstructured P2P networks without a central server [3]. So we develop a new reputation measurement in our system, which is called authority score and used to represent group's property. Moreover our system applies recommendation threshold instead of N-best in hybrid filtering.

This paper is organized as following. Section 2 provides the structure and advantage of our system. Section 3 describes the recommendation algorithm and the reason we use threshold instead of N-best. Section 4 describes the usage of authority score and the calculation algorithm. Section 5 presents the clustering algorithm of peer nodes. Section 6 is our experiment and conclusion.

2 Structure of the P2P Networks

Our system is an unstructured P2P networks based on JXTA, which is an open source P2P platform. Every peer in the system can join or leave the discussion group freely. They can not only share and search documents but also obtain recommendations of documents. Every peer can act as a rendezvous peer when necessary, typically when it is a gateway. The discussion group is a virtual community which allows users to join and share documents. The group information is spread and held by peers who have joined the group and have been the rendezvous peers in the group. The structure of our system is shown in Figure 1.

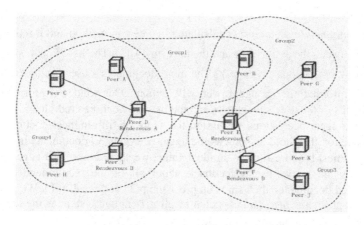

Fig. 1. Structure of the P2P networks

3 Recommendation Algorithm Based on Threshold

We use recommendation threshold in our system instead of the traditional N-best recommendation. The N-best recommendation algorithm works well in traditional systems, because in the C/S model the servers contain all the items and the number of items user may like is always far more big than "N". But in the unstructured P2P network, a new user knows few documents at first, and the number of known documents increases linearly as time going, so user won't be interested in the N highest recommendation documents.

The formula of our recommendation score is shown as follows:

$$reco(au, doc) = \alpha \times (1 + sim\_doc(pf, doc) / 2) \times \overline{R} + \beta \times reco\_rate(au, doc) \qquad (1)$$

In formula (1), au is the active user (the user our system recommend to), $sim\_doc(pf, doc)$ is the similarity between the active user's interest template (user's favorite keyword list) and the document computed by cosine vector formula. $Re\,co\_rate(au, doc)$ is the recommendation score of the document to the active user. This score is calculated by collaborative filtering algorithm according to evaluation information of the active user's nearest neighbors. $\overline{R}$ is the average evaluation made by the active user, it's used to normalize the recommendation scores of contend-based filtering and collaborative filtering. The detail formula of $reco\_rate(au, doc)$ is shown as follows:

$$reco\_rate(au, doc) = \overline{R} + \frac{\sum_i sim\_neighbor(au, p_i)(PR_{i,doc} - \overline{PR_i})}{\sum_i | sim\_neighbor(au, p_i)|} \qquad (2)$$

In this formula, p_i is a user in the discussion group, and it satisfies $p_i \in C_{auth} \cup C_{neighbor}$. The set C_{auth} represents the authoritative users in the discussion group, in other words, they are the highest 10% users in the order of reputation score. The set $C_{neighbor}$ is composed of the nearest neighbors of the active user. The $sim\_neighbor(au, p_i)$ is calculated by Pearson method and it represents the similarity between the active user and the user p_i [4][5]. The list of nearest neighbors is decided by $sim\_neighbor(au, p_i)$. The more documents a user evaluates, the more evaluation information the agent-peer will obtain. This kind of information will change the list of the user's neighbors and the list will be more credible.

When the agent-peer starts, we assign the score of fifth-highest document as the recommendation threshold as soon as the agent-peer gets 30 documents in the group. In order to adjust the threshold to an ideal value, we should modify it at runtime. The peer records the active user's feedback about all of the recommended and un-recommended documents, then sums up precision p(T) and recall r(T). We also define an expected precision $\mu(T)$ and expected recall $\varpi(T)$ in our system as the ideal effect; they are calculated by the following formulas:

$$\mu(T) = \mu(0) + (\mu(final) - \mu(0)) \times NOR(T) / \xi \qquad (3)$$

$$\varpi(T) = \varpi(0) + (\varpi(final) - \varpi(0)) \times NOR(T) / \xi \qquad (4)$$

Since the peer's performance is improved with recommendation and feedback, we set four expected values: $\mu(0) = 0.4$, $\mu(final) = 0.7$, $\varpi(0) = 0.2$, $\varpi(final) = 0.4$. In the formulas above, NOR(T) represents the number of recommended documents accepted by the active user. Algorithm 1 describes the auto-regulative algorithm of recommendation threshold.

Algorithm 1. Auto-regulative algorithm of recommendation threshold

```
Calculate p(T) and r(T) at time T.
if  p(T)≤μ(T) then
      TH(T+1)=TH(T)+ α (T+1)×(1-TH(T)).
else if  r(T)≤ϖ(T)then TH(T+1)=TH(T)×d
      else TH(T+1)=(1- β(T+1))×TH(T)
```

In a recommendation system, precision is far more important than recall, because users will discard a system when it recommends a wrong document. In our system, we take the precision as the most valuable standard, when it is lower than expected value the peer will increase the threshold (TH) by parameter α. Meanwhile α and β decrease linearly with the increase of NOR.

4   Recommendation with Reputation

Our system is an unstructured P2P system; peers in the system connect and communicate with each other directly without central servers. So the system is robust and easy to expand, but it's difficult to avoid cheating in the group and keep high quality of documents without checking. This paper presents a concept "Authority" in order to establish a standard of user's action. The authority extends from reputation, but it's more than reputation; the authoritative users have highest reputation score. A user's authority score will increase when his documents are widely accepted, and will decrease when his documents are denied. So the authority can protect good user and can avoid cheater and destroyer.

The update algorithm of authority is shown in Algorithm 2, where $nos(T)$ represents the number of documents the active user shares at Time T; $M(T)$ is the number of users in the discussion group at time T; $noa(T,i)$ is the accepted times of the no.i document shared by the active user at Time T, and the $NOAT(T,i)$ represents the refused times of the no.i document till time T.

Algorithm 2. The update algorithm of Authority score

```
1. Assume current time is T, then update the active
user's authority to a(T−1)
2. Define a temp authority variable aTemp.
3. aTemp=a(T-1)-2×nos(T), this formula calculates the
consumption of sharing documents. When a document is
shared, it will consume 2 authorities.
4. For each document d_i the active user shares,it will
be calculated as follows:
```

$$aTemp= aTemp + \frac{2\times noa(T,i)}{0.3\times M(T)}$$. With the increment

```
of accepting users, the active user's authority
increases. As long as there are 30% users accepting the
document, it will compensate the lost of sharing.
```

5. For each document d_i in the group, it will be computed as:

   a) If $(NOAT(T,i)+NORT(T,I))<0.6\times M(T)$ and $ch(T-1,i)=0$, continue to next circulation.

    b) $aTemp = aTemp - ch(T-1,i)$.

    c) $ch(T,i)=0$

    d) If the active user is interested in d_i

       If $NOAT(T,i)>0.6\times NORT(T,i)$, $ch(T,i)=0.05\times NOAT(T,i)-0.02\times NORT(T,i)$

       Else $ch(T,i)=0.03\times NOAT(T,i)-0.03\times NORT(T,i)$

    e) If the active user is not interested in d_i

       If $NOAT(T,i)>0.6\times NORT(T,i)$, $ch(T,i)=-0.05\times NOAT(T,i)+0.02\times NORT(T,i)$

       Else $ch(T,i)=-0.03\times NOAT(T,i)+0.03\times NORT(T,i)$

    f) $aTemp = aTemp + ch(T,i)$

6. a(T) = aTemp

5 Clustering Peer Nodes

Clustering peer nodes into different discussion groups makes routing algorithm have higher querying efficiency. We use BIRCH [6] to cluster peer nodes. This algorithm doesn't need the amount of category, which is unable to clear in a P2P networks.

Given n user data objects in a cluster, including user's favorite keyword eigenvector and evaluation information, xi, the BIRCH algorithm defines centroid x0, radius R, and diameter D of the cluster as follows:

$$Xo = \frac{\sum_{i=1}^{n} x_i}{n} \tag{5}$$

$$R = \sqrt{\frac{\sum_{i=1}^{n}(x_i - xo)^2}{n}} \tag{6}$$

$$D = \sqrt{\frac{\sum_{i=1}^{n}\sum_{k=1}^{n}(x_i - x_j)^2}{n(n-1)}} \tag{7}$$

Where R is the average distance from member objects to the centroid, and D is the average pairwise distance within a cluster. Both R and D reflect the tightness of the cluster around the centroid. A clustering feature (CF) is a three-dimensional vector summarizing information about clusters of objects. Then the CF of the cluster is defined as:

$$CF = <n, LS, SS> \tag{8}$$

Where n is the number of data in the cluster, LS is the linear sum of the n data (i.e., $\sum_{i=1}^{n} x_i$), and SS is the square sum of the data (i.e., $\sum_{i=1}^{n} x_i^2$).

Cluster features are additive. For example, suppose that we have two disjoint clusters, C1 and C2, having the clustering features, CF1 and CF2, respectively. The clustering feature for the cluster that is formed by merging C1 and C2 is simply CF1 + CF2.

A CF tree is a height-balanced tree that stores the clustering features for a hierarchical clustering. The nonleaf nodes store sums of the CFs of their children, and thus summarize clustering information about their children. A CF tree has two parameters: branching factor, B, and threshold, T. The branching factor specifies the maximum number of children per nonleaf node; we set it as 10. The threshold parameter specifies the maximum diameter of subclusters stored at the leaf nodes of the tree; we set it as 0.1. These two parameters influence the size of the resulting tree.

Every peer clusters all peer nodes that it knows once in a while. After clustering, every peer will find some closest groups it belongs to, and notifies the centroid peers of these groups. Usually these centroid peers are authoritative users. These discussion groups will regroup when most of their members are changed.

6 Experiments

6.1 Dataset

Since our system is a hybrid filtering system based on content filtering and collaborative filtering, we use Reuters-21578 as our dataset instead of the other evaluation datasets, such as MovieLens, MsWeb, Jester, and so on. We choose 4298 documents in the dataset whose text lengths are longer than 500 Bytes and whose categories are in the most 10 ordinary categories.

6.2 Evaluation Criterion

We use the ROC (Receiver Operating Characteristic) as our system's evaluation criterion. It represents the accepted percentage of recommendatory documents; and it represents the recommendation performance. The goal of our system is to make the recommendation performance higher. The expression of the ROC is:

$$ROC = \frac{NA}{NR} \tag{9}$$

Where NA is the number of documents that are recommended by system and accepted by users; NR represents the number of all the recommended items. Considering the influence of density of the evaluation information, we need another evaluation criterion, the Sparsity, which is shown as follows:

$$Sparsity = 1 - \frac{NNZ}{NI} \tag{10}$$

NNZ represents the number of non-zero items in the evaluation information matrix, and NI is the number of all the items in the matrix. When evaluation information is too sparse, recommendation systems based on collaborative filtering will be difficult to make right decision.

6.3 Results

In the experiments, we simulate 700 virtual users to share and read thousands of documents in the dataset. The interesting categories numbers of these simulated users vary from 1 to 5.

In order to simulate users' real action better, we also import some simulated actions, such as sharing probability, evaluation habit and preservation habit.

We run our system for several times. Each time we estimate the average ROC of all the users and the average sharing probability is set to different values. As soon as all the documents are shared, the system stops running and then calculates the ROC immediately. Figure 2 shows the ROC and Sparsity when average sharing rate is set to a special value.

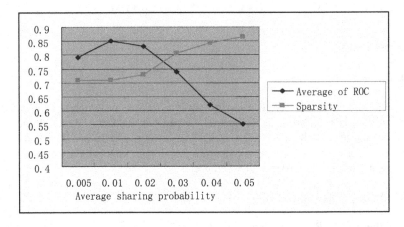

Fig. 2. The corresponding ROC and Sparsity when sharing probability is different

When the sharing probability is set to 0.01, the ROC reaches the best performance, 85%. Performance is influenced by the time of running. When the sharing probability is larger than 0.02, the system's performance declines quickly, because in this case running time is shorter than 350 minutes, and the peers share documents too fast for users to read and evaluate. So the authority is very hard to increase, which results in users joining and leaving discussion groups frequently. Peers are very difficult to cluster and groups are very difficult to build. On the contrary, when the sharing probability is set to 0.005, most of the users won't share documents, so the discussion groups are composed of a few users who are likely to share, and then most users' ROC declines.

7 Conclusion and Future Works

This paper presents a document recommendation system based on hybrid filtering that is built on an unstructured clustering P2P networks. We use recommendation threshold instead of N-best threshold to adapt to the condition of the unstructured P2P networks. In order to make the peers self-cluster into discussion groups easily, we import the authority measurement instead of pure reputation to represent users' action. Simulated experiments show the system has a better performance when using the authority score.

It is very difficult to assemble thousands of people to read thousands of documents time and time again, so we have to simulate experiments. In the future, we intend to perfect the user interface, and make the system to be a real application.

Acknowledgement

This project is supported by the Science & Technology Project of Fujian Province (Project Number: 2006H0037), the 985 Innovation Project on Information Technique of Xiamen University(2004-2007), and Academician Fund of Xiamen University, China.

References

1. Plonka, D.: Napster traffic measurement. Technical report, University of Wisconsin-Madison (2000)
2. Funakoshi, K., Ohguro, T.: A content-based collaborative recommender system with detailed use of evaluations. In: Fourth International Conference on knowledge-Based Intelligent Engineering Systems & Allied Technologies, pp. 253–256 (2000)
3. Kamahara, J., Asakawa, T.: A Community-based Recommendation System to Reveal Unexpected Interests. In: Proceedings of the 11th International Mutmedia Modeling Conference, pp. 433–438 (2005)
4. Sarwar, B., Karypis, G., Konstan, J., Riedl, J.: Analysis of Recommendation Algorithms for E-Commerce. In: Proceedings of the ACM EC'00 Conference, pp. 158–167 (2000)
5. Resnick, P., Iacovou, N., Suchak, M., Bergstrom, P., Riedl, J.: GroupLens: An Open Architecture for Collaborative Filtering of Netnews. In: Proceedings of ACM 1994 Conference on Computer Supported Cooperative Work, October 22-26, 1994, pp. 175–186 (1994)
6. Zhang, T., Ramakrishnan, R., Livny, M.: BIRCH: An Efficient Data Clustering Method for Very Large Databases. In: Proceedings of the 1996 ACM SIGMOD international conference, ACM Press, New York (1996)

SECGrid: Science and Engineering Computing Based Collaborative Problem Solving Environment

Xiaohong Chen, Bin Gong, Hui Liu, and Yi Hu

School of Computer Science and Technology, Shandong University, Jinan, P.R. China
cxh1983325@163.com, gb@sdu.edu.cn, amyliuhui@sdu.edu.cn,
huyi@sdu.edu.cn

Abstract. With the gradually extending of problem application scale, science and engineering computing becomes more and more complicated. Designing a collaborative problem solving environment aiming at specific fields is becoming more and more important. In order to integrate various heterogeneous resources and provide a flexible problem solving environment, we proposed a novel grid approach: SECGrid (Science and Engineering Computing Grid). SECGrid provides a dynamic grid application deploy environment. A grid portal is also adopted to present grid application from diverse sources in a unified way. We proposed a new scheduling algorithm (Application Demand Aware Algorithm) to make job scheduling more feasible. Moreover, SECGrid provides a lot of useful facilities, such as grid accounting, grid monitoring, etc. In the practical application, SECGrid encapsulates lots of computing modules from science and engineering, and provides an easy way for collaborative problem solving.

Keywords: PSE, grid computing, grid accounting, grid monitoring, scheduling.

1 Introduction

In recent years, the concept of grid computing has been investigated and developed to enlarge the concept of distributed computing environment. The grid infrastructure provides integrated services for resource scheduling, information sharing, data delivery, authentication, delegation and other related issues [1]. Due to the heterogeneity of resources, the complexity of computational applications increases. As continuous changes of applications as well as resources states, large amount of resources are involved. For the reasons above, the importance of problem solving environments has been more emphasized [2].However, problem solving environment (PSE) using open source software and widely available devices to support collaboration [3] has not been investigated extensively.

Based on forecited reasons, it makes sense to combine traditional problem solving environment with grid to build a collaborative PSE in Science and Engineering. SECGrid has the following characteristics: based on specific domains of grid; supporting sharing and cooperation; easily usable high performance PSE, which makes fully use of grid possibility in resource sharing and cooperation.

Y. Luo (Ed.): CDVE 2007, LNCS 4674, pp. 234–241, 2007.

There are some related projects already, such as the China National Grid (CNGrid) [4], which is a key project in the National High-Tech R&D Program (the 863 program); the European DataGrid (EDG)[5], commissioned by the European Union, with goals to develop the software to provide basic grid functionality and associated management tools for a large scale test-bed for demonstration projects in three specific areas of science; the Scientific Computing Grid (ScGrid)[6], and so on. Compared to these projects, this project focuses mainly on Science and Engineering aspects, with emphasis on providing a collaborative problem solving environment.

The rest of this paper is organized as follows. Section 2 introduces design issues and the system architecture which consists of four layers. Section 3 details the key technologies for building system as well as a job scheduling algorithm (Application Demand Aware Scheduling Algorithm). Section 4 presents an application case of SECGrid. Section 5 summarizes the SECGrid project and points out future directions.

2 Architecture

This system contains multi-layers and multi-management domains. From the job schedulers in the bottom layer to the specific application system in the top layer, there are various software and hardware, such as grid middleware, gird portal developing infrastructure, grid monitoring and grid accounting etc. They altogether emphasize the importance of system architecture design.

This system integrates and organizes different computation and storage resources in a heterogeneous environment. It shields bottom resource heterogeneity and multi-management domains via functions like application service access, data access and management services provided by system. It can exhibit users with incorporate file view and convenient, unified operating interfaces. The system is divided into four layers from bottom to top, namely Resources Layer, Core Layer, Portal Layer and Application Layer, as shown in Fig. 1.

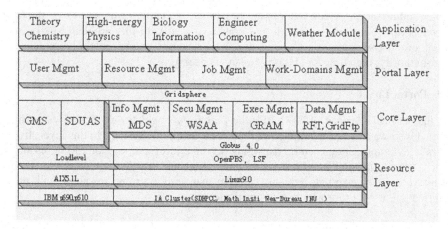

Fig. 1. SECGrid Layer Architecture

2.1 Resource Layer

High-performance computation and storage nodes are provided by this layer. Hardware resources are composed of machine resources distributed over different management domains and different locations. Software resources comprise Operating System (Linux or some other Unix-like operating systems), serial or parallel application software and various job schedulers.

2.2 Core Layer

Grid middleware, as the core layer, represents a series of instruments and protocol software. It conceals computation resources distribution, heterogeneity characteristic, and provides grid application layer with transparent and coherent interface. There are many kinds of grid middleware such as Globus[7,8] and Legion[7,9] of U.S.A, UNICORE[7,10] of Europe. Among them the most famous one is Globus which is lead by Ian Foster and is considered the most widely and suitably used grid middleware.

Globus Toolkit 4 adopts distributed computing modules and includes client and server ends deployment. Server and client ends are loosely coupled, interacting with each other by WSDL (Web Service Description Language) description file. The client end should get the WSDL description file created and passed from the server end to get corresponding resource services. Globus Toolkit 4 authenticates client resources by certificating the client end.

Server: The server is responsible for collecting resource information, receiving job requests, transferring data information and job requests from resource client and getting results from it.

Client: Mainly receiving job requests from upper server, transferring it to the machine resources for process, finally getting the results and re-transferring to the server.

Most existing systems adopt a single CA(Certification Authority) as the center to form a management domain. Any resources can join this system only through this CA center authorization, which reduces the flexibility of joining resources. Once the CA server is down, the whole system will crash. To deal with this problem, firstly, we adopt a robust server as our CA system server; secondly, we successfully implement inter-authority; then transfer authority to another server.

2.3 Portal Layer

As the service interface of SECGrid, the portal layer which provides services in a unified web way. It is the entrance of final users using this system. In this layer, from users' viewpoint, actions can be managing personal information, monitoring resource states, submitting and monitoring jobs, managing and transferring data, etc. From administrator's viewpoint, actions can be managing current resource and data information, user authorization, CA certificates, etc.

2.4 Application Layer

In the application layer, diversified computing programs are encapsulated as application services, providing user layer uniform entrance. The application layer receives requests information from portal layer when users call for application service, then it creates a job object and submits it to the next core service layer. In the process of job execution, this layer can call the core services layer to query job running state. When job finishes, users can get job execution results received by application layer from next layer.

3 Key Technologies

From the bottom grid middleware to the top specific applications, this system deals with many newly rising technologies such as grid monitoring and grid accounting, grid portal design, grid scheduling algorithm, etc. In order to make it clearly understood, this section describes these technologies briefly.

3.1 Grid Monitoring

System monitoring is very important for grid computing system. By monitoring we can discover and remove failures promptly, analyze monitored data to find out performance bottleneck, thereby offer reliable basis for system performance adjusting and job scheduling. This system adopts the monitoring system GMS [11] (Grid Monitoring Service) to implement such functions, as shown in Fig. 2.

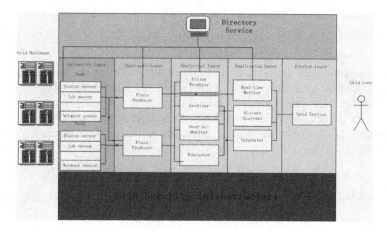

Fig. 2. GMS Architecture

GMS is a general purposed, scalable and distributed grid monitoring service based on GMA. It has a framework for grid monitoring system and introduces a pluggable module for performance information collection. Also, GMS implements a performance forecasting component which provides short time forecasting to help job scheduler work better. Meanwhile, it takes into account the security problems and ensures the safety of monitoring data.

3.2 Grid Accounting

The accounting system SDUAS (Shandong University Accounting System) [12], as shown in Fig. 3, is dedicated to deal with heterogeneous resources accounting and charging in grid environment, to provide users and administrators with grid services of high quality. The system improves grid resources usage efficiency by grid accounting. Our accounting system takes OGSA as design principle, fully takes into account extensibility and transplant ability under grid environment, lays emphasize on data description consistency and easy integrated installation.

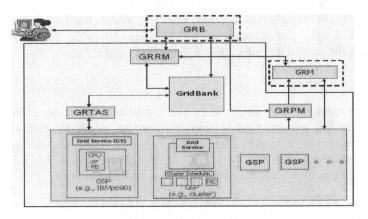

Fig. 3. SDUAS Components

It has characteristics as follows: (1) Extensibility: adopt open, standard protocols offered by OGSA to achieve good extensibility. (2) interference-free: need not to disturb work of each grid nodes and user system, achieving convenient deployment. (3) Data consistency: adopt uniform XML formats to collect data, record resource consumption. (4) Accurate accounting information: design with pertinency and test with rigidness. (5) Security: adopt client end authentication and authorization based on PKI.

3.3 Portal Design

This system adopts the rising grid portal [13] technology Gridsphere and Gridportlet to develop the application portal. It uses Tomcat Server to deploy Gridsphere as the portal middleware for obtaining basic functions like user and application groups management. Meanwhile, system deploys Gridportlets in Gridsphere based on changing its resource registry file Resource.xml, to realize Web operations on basic Globus middleware functions. It includes five parts: Registry, Credentials, Resources, Files, and Jobs. We install and deploy Gt4portlets as the private application service to support resource discovery and serving mechanism. For facilitating user job submission, we build file tag separately to realize transferring of data and execution file needed by jobs, downloading and checking resulting data. Users get authentication from My Proxy to use functions like resource browsing, file management and job submission.

3.4 Application Encapsulation

In order to integrate various computation and storage resources under heterogeneous environment and provide users with an incorporate file view in a convenient, standard accessing way, we must encapsulate application services. This system first encapsulates File Management function offered by Gridportlets as the public application, takes Ganglia monitoring and grid accounting as the system management application; then fills in corresponding parameters through re-using Job Submission Portlet and changes its core codes according to different URL for different computation module; consequently realizes the bardian display of application manipulation interface. This simplifies the manipulation because users need not to care about the concrete way, just pay attention to filling in a small quantity of parameters like executing directory, job description, etc.

3.5 Application Demand Aware Scheduling Algorithm

In this system, a new job scheduling algorithm-Application Demand Aware Scheduling Algorithm[14] is adopted. It accomplishes the function of making a feasible resources allocation for jobs in heterogeneous environment; meanwhile it guarantees most jobs to be completed ahead of their expected completion times (ECT) without losing good system performance.

In order to achieve the aim of feasible resources sharing for jobs in heterogeneous environment, this algorithm takes two steps in scheduling process.

The first step is determined by system performance and the second by application demand. In the first step, for each submitted job, select the most favorable node from available resources set, on which this job can be completed at the earliest time, then form a (<job, resource>) set which holds all the submitted jobs with their respectively most suitable nodes according to minimum completion time.

In the second step, this algorithm takes the effect of application into account. For users, they hope their jobs be dealt with as soon as possible, at least without exceeding expected completion times, then ECT_i (Expected Completion Time) of each job t_i should be considered. A comparison between ECT_i and Minimum Completion Time of each job t_i which asks for the same node, is made. According to the comparison results, the smaller the result value, the sooner this job will be executed.

4 Application

Based on the hardware and application software sources of Shandong High Performance Computing Center(SDHPCC), Shandong University, Jinan University and Shandong Weather Bureau, this system builds a collaborative PSE with a total 1.5T flops computing ability and 20TB storage capability. On this platform we deploy grid middleware, develop grid monitoring, grid accounting and grid portal. And finally the system realizes grid computing applications like High-energy Physics, Chemistry Theory, Biology Information, Numerical Weather Forecast and Engineer Computing, and provides users with an integrated, easily used collaborative PSE. As shown in Fig. 4 and Fig. 5.

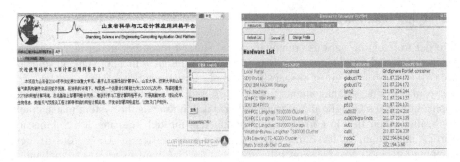

Fig. 4. SECGrid Homepage   **Fig. 5.** Hardware Resources

5   Conclusion and Future Prospects

In the process of designing this system, according to the application demanding of SECGrid, in the bottom layer, we adopt the Globus middleware to design and deploy a heterogeneous, easy-extending system to satisfy different users' needs. In the middle layer, we optimize and change the grid middleware supporting the application services, develop service uniform accessing interface. In the top layer, we use Gridsphere and Gridportlets to design platform portals and encapsulate different application modules.

The tasks that remain for the SECGrid project fall into the following categories:1) Although we have installed five kinds of applications (totally 10 computation modules), the number of applications supported in this PSE is relatively small. Large scale of application-supporting need to be added in future works. 2) As to the job scheduling problem, the new scheduling algorithms has improved the system efficiency greatly. But it is only aiming at independent tasks, in the future, scheduling algorithms about grid workflow need to be considered and designed.

Acknowledgments. This work was supported by a grant from the National High Technology Research and Development Program of China (863 Program, No. 2006AA01A113), Natural Science Foundation of Shandong Province (No.Y2004G08).

References

1. Foster, C.K.: The Grid: Blueprint for a New Computing Infrasteructure. Morgan-Kaufmann, San Francisco (1998)
2. Kadooka, Y.: Development of Problem Solving Environment for Grid and its Applications, Ph. D. Dissertation, Kanazawa University 2004, Kadooka, Y., Kobashi, H., Choi, J.W., Lee, Y.H., Tago, Y.: PIV Web Visualization System Toward PIV Visualization Grid, J.Visualization, vol. 6(3), pp. 283–291 (2004)
3. Maeda, T., Tago, Y.: Collaborative Problem Solving Environment 'Desk Side Laboratory. In: Proceedings of the First International Conference on e-Science and Grid Computing (e-Science05),0-7695-2448-6/05 2005 IEEE
4. http://www.cngrid.org/en_introduce.htm

5. http://eu-datagrid.web.cern.ch/eu-datagrid/
6. http://www.scgrid.cn/page/home.htm
7. Asadzadeh, P., Buyyal, R., Kei, C.L., et al.: Global grids and software toolkits: A study of four grid middleware technologies[EB/OL], http://arxiv.org/ftp/cs/papers/0407/0407001.pdf
8. Almond, J., Snelling, D.: UNICORE: Uniform access to supercomputing as an element of electronic commerce[J]. Future Generation Computer Systems, 613, 1–10 (1999)
9. Foster, I., Globus, K.S.: A metacomputing infrastructure toolkit[J]. International Journal of Supercomputer Applications 11(2), 115–128 (1997)
10. Grimshaw, A., Wulf, W.: The legion vision of a worldwide virtual computer[J]. Communications of the ACM 40(1), 39–45 (1997)
11. Shen, J., Gong, B., Hu, Y., Li, S.: The Design and Implementation of a GMA based Grid Monitoring Service. In: Proceedings of the 11th International Conference on Computer Supported Cooperative Work in Design 2007,CSCWD2007, pp. 588–593 (2007) IEEE Catalog Number:07EX1675,ISBN:1-4244-0962-4
12. Adu, J., Gong, B.: Grid Accounting System Based on OGSA, Computer Engineer, 32(19), pp. 270–272 (2006)
13. Ai-Ping, L., Yan, J., Quan-Yuan, W.: On Design of Agricultural Semantic Grid Portal and Implementation. In: International Conference on Hybrid Information Technology (ICHIT'06),0-7695-2674-8/06, IEEE Computer Society Press, Los Alamitos (2006)
14. Lin, J., Gong, B.: An Application Demand aware Scheduling Algorithm in Heterogeneous Environment? In: Proceedings of the 11th International Conference on Computer Supported Cooperative Work in Design 2007,CSCWD2007, pp. 599–604 (2007) IEEE Catalog Number:07EX1675,ISBN:1-4244-0962-4

Bandwidth-Aware Scheduling in Media Streaming Under Heterogeneous Bandwidth*

Jian Wang, Changyong Niu, and Ruimin Shen

Department of Computer Science and Engineering
Shanghai Jiaotong University, Shanghai, China, 200030
{jwang,cyniu,rmshen}@sjtu.edu.cn

Abstract. Data-driven media streaming has been deployed gradually over the Internet. In such systems, node periodically exchanges media block availability and fetches desirable blocks from neighbors. The issue on optimizing fetching blocks is called block scheduling and receives focus, especially in heterogeneous overlay. In this paper Bandwidth-Aware Scheduling (BAS) formulates such problem by incorporating bandwidth and block deadline, as well as node importance. Simulation results verify that BAS performs much better than existing ones.

Keywords: Peer-to-Peer, Media Streaming, Block Scheduling, BAS.

1 Introduction

Peer-to-peer (P2P) overlay populates in file-sharing, media streaming. The success originates from utilizing each peer's resource. Recently, media streaming applications called as data-driven approaches inspiring from BitTorrent [1] prevail on the Internet. Each peer chooses random node subset as neighbors so that an unstructured overlay is formed. Such gossip-style construction guarantees high system robustness and availability. Without explicitly building and maintaining block propagation path, these data-driven protocols determine block delivery direction based on block availability. The source node encodes media content into block sequence and pushes them to neighbors appropriately. Then, each peer exchanges block availability periodically. Upon such information each peer independently decides from which neighbor each desired block is fetched. And it requests blocks from respective neighbors. Both systematical studies [2] and realistic deployment [3] demonstrate that data-driven approach is better than other deterministic approaches such as tree-based ones, especially when churn is high or bandwidth varies greatly. As block scheduling is core of system, it is imperative to optimize scheduling to enhance system throughput further under heterogeneous network. In addition, steady playback rate requires that fetched blocks should arrive before deadline.

In media streaming application, the most valuable resource is bandwidth. However, existing measurements of overlay network reveal that peer usually exhibits

---

* This work is supported by the NFSC under Grant 60672066, China.

extreme heterogeneity on access bandwidth. Furthermore, the bandwidth between two peers is more diverse and tends to be exaggerating under network congestion. To accommodate bandwidth heterogeneity, the source node encodes media content into several layers through layered coding, where each layer is iteratively dependent on lower layers. That means a higher layer can only be decoded if all of lower layers are available. Each layer consists of a sequence of equal-size blocks. Node would adjust receiving number of layers based on available bandwidth. Further, each node has sliding window moving as playback rate. The front portion of the sliding window is called exchanging window. Blocks within exchanging window will be consumed one by one.

In this paper we consider bandwidth constraint and block deadline, as well as node importance, and propose Bandwidth-Aware Scheduling strategy to improve system throughput. The remainder is organized as follows. Section 2 discusses related work. Section 3 first presents potential ineffectiveness of most relevant work, DONLE [4], in an example, then several definitions and problem formulation are proposed. Section 4 evaluates BAS's performance in comparison and concludes in section 5.

2   Related Work

Achieving higher throughput is desirable in media streaming. There are several milestone works. The first is ESM [5] that aims to distribute media content to large population of peers through tree-based topology. It utilizes the peers' bandwidth and greatly increases system throughput. The next is RLM [6], which collects blocks from multiple senders instead of one and greatly stabilizes the receiving block rate. The third is PeerStreaming that [7] steps further, where each node notifies upper streaming nodes the interested partitions of content. By integrating multiple partitions, node recovers original content and adapts to bandwidth variation through regulating partition announcements. The last is CoolStreaming [8], inspiring from BitTorrent [1], and implements fine-grain block scheduling within finite sliding window. Several similar systems such as PPLive [3], GridMedia [9] emerge in the following years.

The techniques [12,13] constructing the overlay according to some specific QoS metrics are perpendicular to block scheduling problem studied in this paper. The common scheduling strategies include *random* strategy in Chainsaw [10], *local rarest first (LRF)* strategy in CoolStreaming [8], *round robin (RR)* strategy, and *DONLE* [4]. DONLE formulates block scheduling as an integer linear programming problem by imposing priority on each desirable block, which is also solved with min-cost network flow algorithm. By maximizing average priority sum of blocks that each node can receive under heterogeneous bandwidth constraints, DONLE strategy achieves better throughput than all others. Since no block deadline considered in DONLE, we are motivated to enhance system throughput further by incorporating block deadline as well as node importance.

Table 1. Notations

Notation	Description
N	Set of nodes except source
L	Number of encoded media layers
$r_i, i = 1, \cdots, L$	Cumulative rate from layer 1 to i
$I_i, O_i, i = 0, 1, \cdots, \|N\|$	Inbound and Outbound bandwidth of node i
$E_{ik}, i, k = 0, 1, \cdots, \|N\|, i \neq k$	The end-to-end bandwidth from node i to k
$h_{ij} \in \{0, 1\}$	$h_{ij} = 1$ reflects node i holds block j, 0 otherwise
NBR_i	Neighbor set of node i
τ	The request period
π_j^i	Priority of block j on node i
W_T	The exchanging window length scaled by time
T_i	The current time on node i
d_j^i	Playing deadline of block j on node i
D_i	Desirable block set for node i

3   BAS Formulation

First DONLE's ineffectiveness is shown in example. Then we propose new formulation of block scheduling incorporating deadline and node importance. Finally, distributed equivalent is also proposed as for realistic applications. For convenience, notations [4] used in the following are summarized in table 1.

3.1   Bandwidth-Aware Scheduling

By considering block deadline and bandwidth constraints, priority assignment function is imposed to guide block dissemination evenly and smoothly. The objective of BAS is to maximize the priority sum of all blocks received before deadline on each node in each request period. Usually, there are two types of bottlenecks, i.e. access one (inbound and outbound) and non-access one (end-to-end). Due to equal-size block concerned, we measured the bandwidth in terms of blocks per second. Further, many end-to-end pathes share same underlying link, which imposes aggregating bandwidth constraint on those pathes.

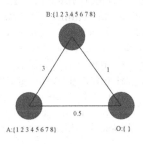

Fig. 1. An instance for bandwidth aware scheduling

In figure 1, potential design limitation in DONLE [4], that may cause block arrival after deadline, is illustrated. Node O has two neighbors A, B. The number near link denotes bandwidth in terms of blocks per second. Let request period $\tau = 4$, and playing rate is 2 blocks per second. At time t, node O has availability information as $\{1,2,3,4,5,6,7,8\}, \{1,2,3,4,5,6,7,8\}$ for neighbor A, B, respectively. Obviously, node O requests at most 2 block from A, as well as 4 from B in one request period. As DONLE maximizes averaged priority summarization, specific strategy shown in table 2 satisfies maximization. Assume node O plays block 1th at time t while request information message of O arrives neighbor nodes simultaneously, DONLE only guarantees block $\{5\}$th arrives before deadline, while BAS even makes $\{3,5,6,7\}$th blocks ahead of deadline. Thus BAS achieves higher delivery ratio than DONLE's where the upper bound is $\frac{1+0.5}{2} = \frac{6}{8}$ taking no deadline constraint into account.

3.2   Block Priority Definition

In file distribution such as BitTorrent, node only concerns minimum time to complete downloading file with no block arriving ordering. However, the media streaming requires successive order of block arrivals. By imposing appropriate priority on blocks, each node is able to maintain media content coherently. In layer coding, higher layer depends on lower ones. We should assure that blocks of lower layer have higher priority. The existing work [2] suggests that demanding block with rarest holders would improve diversity to the system, which consequently improves block dissemination. We adopt same rule in DONLE [4] as giving high priority for block of lower layer or approaching deadline.

$$\pi_j^i = \beta \prod_R \left(\sum_{k \in NBR_i} h_{kj} \right) + (1 - \beta) \theta \prod_L (\lambda_j) , \text{ where } \beta = \frac{d_j^i - T_i}{W_T} \quad (1)$$

Both $\prod_R$ and $\prod_L$ are monotonously decreasing functions. θ is relatively large while $\prod_L (\lambda_j) >> \prod_L (\lambda_k), \lambda_j < \lambda_k$.

3.3   Feasible Block Set

Given node i, neighbor $k \in NBR_i$. The duration for one block propagating between i and k is determined as $\alpha = \frac{1}{E_{ik}}$. Since block request arrives asynchronously on neighbor k, it often has delay γ before initializing delivery of requested block.

Table 2. Delivery ratio between different strategies

Strategy	Request	Received blocks vs. Time	Delivery ratio
DONLE	$A \leftarrow \{5,6\}$ $B \leftarrow \{1,2,3,4\}$	$\{1\}$:t+1 $\{5,2\}$:t+2 $\{3\}$:t+3 $\{6,4\}$:t+4	1/8
BAS	$A \leftarrow \{6\}$ $B \leftarrow \{3,5,7\}$	$\{3\}$:t+1 $\{5,6\}$:t+2 $\{7\}$:t+3	4/8

As requesting message is assumed to cost as same time as block propagating, the feasible block set A_k^i for node i with respect to neighbor k is defined as

$$A_k^i \subseteq \{x | d_x^i \geq T_i + \alpha + \gamma + \alpha, h_{kx} = 1, x \in D_i\}, \quad |A_k^i| \leq E_{ik} \quad (2)$$

$$d_y^i \geq T_i + \alpha + \gamma + |\{z | z < y, z \in A_k^i\}| * \alpha, \quad \forall y \in A_k^i \quad (3)$$

Such definition incorporates both bandwidth and block deadline constraints simultaneously. Equation (2) constrains the size of feasible block set and avoids requesting those obviously unnecessary blocks. And equation (3) imposes time delay between each successive blocks.

3.4   Node Importance

In Internet, one physical link is often shared by multiple overlay links. Consequently, the available bandwidth for each overlay link impacts with each other's. For specific node $i \in N$, node importance is defined as

$$weight\,(i) = \sum_{k \in NBR_i} E_{ik} \quad (4)$$

Upon importance weight, blocks preferentially flow to nodes with high aggregating end-to-end bandwidth. Obviously, such node would then contribute more on system throughput in next request period once receiving novel blocks. Importance weight is piggyback within block availability message and do not introduce additional control message.

3.5   BAS Formulation

We define decision variable x_{kj}^i where $i \in N, j \in D_i, k \in NBR_i$:

$$x_{kj}^i = \begin{cases} 1 & \text{node } i \text{ request block } j \text{ from node } k \\ 0 & \text{otherwise} \end{cases} \quad (5)$$

The goal is to maximize *priority-importance-product* sum of blocks received ahead of deadline under heterogeneous bandwidth constraints.

$$\text{maximize} \sum_{i \in N} \sum_{k \in NBR_i} \sum_{j \in D_i} \pi_j^i h_{kj} x_{kj}^i weight\,(i) \quad (6)$$

subject to

$$\sum_{i \in NBR_k} \sum_{j \in D_i} x_{kj}^i \leq \tau O_k, \forall k \in N \qquad \sum_{k \in NBR_i} \sum_{j \in D_i} x_{kj}^i \leq \tau I_i, \forall i \in N \quad (7)$$

$$\sum_{j \in D_i} x_{kj}^i \leq \tau E_{ki}, \forall i \in N, k \in NBR_i \qquad \sum_{k \in NBR_i} x_{kj}^i \leq 1, \forall i \in N, j \in D_i \quad (8)$$

$$\{j | x_{kj}^i = 1\} \text{ is a feasible set }, \forall i \in N, \forall k \in NBR_i \quad (9)$$

The BAS formulation is comprehensive integer linear programming, and looks similarly as BSP in [4]. Equation (7) declares the constraint with respect to outbound and inbound bandwidth, respectively. Equation (8) indicates blocks between two nodes do not overrun end-to-end available bandwidth. Further, it shows no duplicated blocks would be requested in one period. Equation (9) assures that set of blocks requested from a neighbor is a feasible block set. In addition, definition of x^i_{kj} in (5) reflects that the formulation is integer programming. Equation (4) gives weight and indicates node with high aggregating end-to-end bandwidth receives more weight than other nodes in this formulation objective.

3.6   Decentralized Implementation

The corresponding decentralized implementation of above formulation is similar to equivalent in [4]. The end-to-end bandwidth E_{ik} is estimated through moving average of bandwidth of last P time units. Let g^p_{ik} denote number of blocks received from neighbor k to node i in pth period. Thus, the estimate Q_{ik} for E_{ik} is defined as averaging previous P periods: $Q^{p+1}_{ik} = \xi * \left(\sum^p_{j=p-P+1} g^j_{ik} \right) / (P * \tau)$, where ξ is aggressive coefficient. Parameter $\xi(> 1)$ is chosen heuristically at beginning. In next period, ξ also increases 10% whenever g^p_{ik} is larger than previous one. Otherwise, $\xi = (\xi - 1) * 80\% + 1$. Such simple approach adapts ξ to E_{ik} continuously. In addition, γ used in feasible block set is also estimated similar as g^j_{ik}. Let μ^p denotes the duration between time pth block request message sent and time first block comes back. Base on Equation (2), $\mu^p \approx 2\alpha + \gamma$. Since $\alpha = \frac{1}{E_{ik}} \approx \frac{1}{g^p_{ik}}$, γ is derived consequently. Thus, $\gamma^{p+1}_{ik} = \sum^p_{j=p-P+1} \gamma^j_{ik}/P$.

4   Simulation

To determine the performance, useful blocks are defined as those arriving before playback deadline. Effective block is defined as those could be decoded properly since block dependency exists in layer coding. The delivery ratio is defined as count of effective blocks over number of blocks within one request period. For convenience, similar setting of DONLE [4] is adopted here. Media content is encoded into 10 layers, and each layer has rate of 50Kbps as well as 10Kbps for each block. To evaluate the quality of a specified layer, we average the delivery ratio of that layer over nodes in specified inbound bandwidth range. We simulate a network of size of 500 and set request period to 2 seconds. The node access bandwidth is asymmetric, the inbound bandwidth evenly distributes across 15Kbps to 1Mbps, while the outbound bandwidth of each node is randomly selected between half and one time of its inbound bandwidth. In addition, maximum end-to-end available bandwidth distribute across 10Kbps and 150Kbps. We set the outbound bandwidth of the source node to 2Mbps. Each node selects 14 random nodes as neighbors. Exchanging window is fixed as 10 seconds and the sliding window as 60 seconds. Each strategy runs on same unstructured overlay. Each curve represents average over 10 runs.

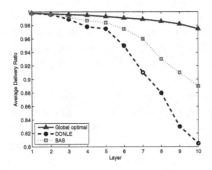

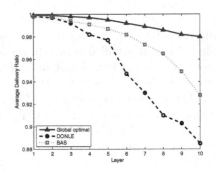

Fig. 2. Bottleneck on last mile for high bandwidth nodes [800K,1M]

Fig. 3. Bottleneck not only on last mile for high bandwidth nodes [800K,1M]

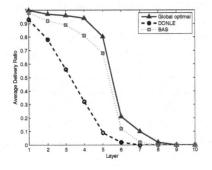

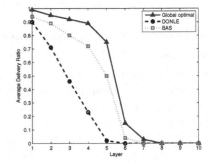

Fig. 4. Bottleneck on last mile for low inbound bandwidth nodes [200K,300K]

Fig. 5. Bottleneck not only on last mile for low inbound bandwidth nodes [200K,300K]

As shown in figure 2 and 3, we compare optimal, DONLE, BAS. As for nodes of high inbound bandwidth, three strategies could achieve high delivery ratio although DONLE is a little worse than others. This indicates that overlay formed has well bandwidth distribution, where high bandwidth nodes almost has multiple neighbors with sufficient outbound bandwidth. Such overlay is common under QoS-oriented construction. Those high bandwidth nodes always have opportunity to contribute resource. Of course, the bottleneck occurring on end-to-end path slightly impacts delivery ratio of all three strategies.

However, BAS performs much better than DONLE in figure 4 and 5. As low inbound bandwidth nodes are concerned, only fraction of original blocks could be fetched back. Since BAS pays more attention on block deadline and transmission time, it avoids requesting those unnecessary blocks that is illustrated in subsection 3.1. In figure 5, BAS achieves 50% delivery ratio on layer 5 while DONLE almost does nothing yet. That means end-to-end bandwidth and block deadline overwhelms DONLE on low inbound bandwidth nodes.

5   Conclusion

To enhance throughput of data-driven media streaming in heterogeneous network, we reformulate block scheduling by incorporating node importance and feasible block set. Evaluation confirms that Bandwidth Aware Scheduling performs much better than DONLE especially on low inbound bandwidth nodes. For future work, it is desirable to consider block loss and smart parameter estimator into consideration.

References

1. Cohen, B.: Bittorrent website: http://bitconjuer.com/
2. Silverston, T., Fourmaux, O.: Source vs data-driven approach for live p2p streaming. In: International Conference on Systems and International Conference on Mobile Communications and Learning Technologies (2006)
3. PPLive: website: http://www.pplive.com/
4. Zhang, M., Chen, C., Xiong, Y., Zhang, Q., Yang, S.: Optimizing the Throughput of Data-Driven based Streaming in Heterogeneous Overlay Network. In: The Proceedings of ACM Multimedia Modeling 2007, January 2007, vol. 4351, ACM Press, New York (2007)
5. Chu, Y.H., Rao, S.G., Zhang, H.: A Case for End Systems Multicast. ACM SIGMETRICS (2000)
6. McCanne, S., Jacobson, V., Vetterli, M.: Receiver-driven layered multicast. In: ACM SIGCOMM, New York, August 1996, vol. 26(4), pp. 117–130. ACM Press, New York (1996)
7. Li, J.: Peerstreaming: A practical receiver-driven peer-to-peer media streaming system. In: MSR-TR-2004-101 (September 2004)
8. Zhang, X., Liu, J., Li, B., Yum, T.-S.P.: CoolStreaming/DONet: A Data-driven Overlay Network for Live Media Streaming. In: IEEE INFOCOM 2005, Miami, FL, USA (2005)
9. Zhang, M., Zhao, L., Tang, Y., Luo, J.-G., Yang, S-Q.: Large scale live media streaming over peer-to-peer networks through global internet. In: Proceedings of the ACM workshop on Advances in peer-to-peer multimedia streaming 2005, New York, NY, USA, pp. 21–28. ACM Press, New York (2005)
10. Pai, V., Kumar, K., Tamilmani, K., Sambamurthy, V., Mohr, A.E.: Chainsaw: Eliminating Trees from Overlay Multicast. In: Proceedings of the Fourth International Workshop on Peer-to-Peer Systems (February 2005)
11. Bhrarmbe, A.R., Herley, C., Padmanabhan, V.N.: Analyzing and improving a bittorrent network's performance mechanisms. In: IEEE INFOCOM 2006, April 2006, Barcelona, Spain (2006)
12. Jiang, J., Nahrstedt, K.: Randpeer: Membership management for QoS sensitive peer-to-peer applications. In: IEEE INFOCOM 2006, April 2006, Barcelona, Spain (2006)
13. Venkataraman, V., Francis, P.: On heterogeneous overlay construction and random node selection in unstructured p2p networks. In: IEEE INFOCOM 2006, April 2006, Barcelona, Spain (2006)

"Virtual Real Communities" and Cooperative Visualization

Hans-Jürgen Frank

Dialogarchitect®
Lindenschmitstr. 30, 81371 München, Germany
frank@dialogarchitect.com

Abstract. In a global world we face the necessity for worldwide collaboration and long-term co-creation. We know different kinds of internet platforms and examples of successful remote team work within projects for a limited time but we do not have much experience about computer sustained communities working successfully beyond projects and generations with different cultures and conflicting interests. The challenge is to build and to maintain a very specific kind of virtual community realizing a successful mix of "real" (face-to-face) and "virtual" (remote) qualities creating a platform for successful dialogue between diverse points of view. The contribution describes key qualities for creating such communities. It is about how to build the bridge between technical potentials and human qualities for establishing cross-cultural and long-term processes beyond face-to-face work. The presented experiences are based on the creation of an open and frank dialogue culture consequently using cooperative visualization from the first step of the collaboration process.

Keywords: Community, network, networking, virtual, real, visual, cooperative visualization, intercultural, change, "Virtual Real Community".

1 Introduction

In a global world, decisions and actions of companies and organisations often have impacts beyond continents and beyond generations on a larger scale. This makes worldwide collaboration necessary as well as dialogue between stakeholders in different places around the globe. Building and maintaining virtual communities as a platform for dealing with conflicting interests is the basis for facing this situation.

The challenge is not only to establish long-term co-creation processes working beyond face-to face meetings (where people come together in a physical space). We also need the successful participation of a large number of people and groups located in different places all over the world, coming from very different cultures (i.e. not only different nationalities and languages, but also different social levels, professional fields, having different roles, opposite points of view and conflicting interests).

For facing this challenge we need a new form of communities. We know different kinds of web platforms. What we are talking about here are not internet structures for the distribution or the exchange of information or goods. We are dealing in this article with the transfer of ground-breaking and sense-making personal and group experiences created during workshops, events or projects which could first be small

Y. Luo (Ed.): CDVE 2007, LNCS 4674, pp. 250–256, 2007.
© Springer-Verlag Berlin Heidelberg 2007

seeds for new, long-term "cross-cultural" and "cross-interest" change processes. It is difficult to realize the transfer of such insights into reality and to assure their long-term further development, however, these experiences emerge more and more often from innovative project work groups and current corporate personal development programs.

We also are conscious of many examples of successful remote team work within projects for a limited time but we could not find many experiences about computer sustained communities working successfully beyond projects, beyond cultures and beyond generations dealing with conflicting interests. Very often projects of remote collaboration come from the technical side, driven by IT experts who sometimes concentrate on technicalities, but successful solutions first need the development of human collaboration processes which can be realized in a personal way even on a technical platform.

The author's processes focus on the following concerns:

- We have to build and to maintain a very specific kind of virtual community realizing a successful mix of "real" (face-to-face) and "virtual" (remote) qualities creating a platform for successful dialogue between people with very different points of view.
- The key for creating this kind of community is to find successful ways of building the bridge between technical potentials and human qualities for establishing cross-cultural and long-term processes beyond face-to-face work.
- Cooperative visualization has turned out to be an important tool for the creation of an open and frank dialogue culture in the collaboration with small groups as well as with a large number of people. It is important to use this means consistently from the first step of the collaboration process and in all different phases for establishing a visual dialogue culture.

2 "Virtual Real Communities"

Looking at the terms "real" and "virtual" is helpful for creating new forms of communities:

By "real" we understand being physically together in a face-to-face structure. Here we are able to touch each other, to look into each others' eyes, to use our different senses for communicating and for being present with each other. All interactions are based on natural perception and communication. This strongly involves human and personal experience. Soft factors, feelings, beliefs, values and emotional qualities are creating an atmosphere "between the lines".

In "virtual" settings participants are located in different places. They are part of a remote structure. For communicating they need technical tools for the exchange of information, experiences and feelings. This sometimes makes it difficult to share qualities which in "real" situations are "automatically" present.

At first, personal settings and "virtual" work seem to have contrasting, maybe even opposite aspects. They seem to represent very different fields of experience, organized and facilitated by different professional experts. Looking closer we see that

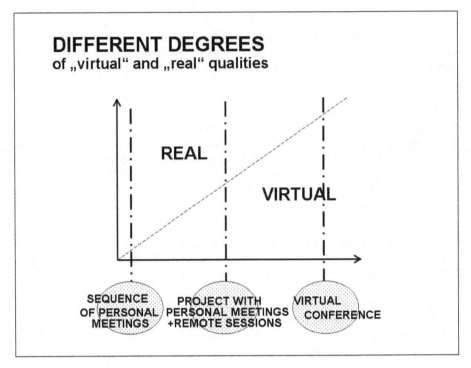

Fig. 1.

face-to-face meetings and "virtual" network activities are closely linked together. Every collaboration process is a mix of personal and remote qualities (Fig. 1).

2.1 Synergies Between "Virtual" and "Real" Qualities

We find different degrees of "virtual" and "real" aspects in all kinds of personal as well as "virtual" work. This observation shows possibilities for improving both "virtual" as well as "real" collaboration processes. This synergy potential can be used to develop new forms of communities.

On the one hand, in daily practice we observe that the success of "virtual" communities depends a lot on personal qualities like trust, personal involvement and group commitments to common aims and common values. For creating these qualities we can transfer a lot of learning and experiences from personal collaboration processes to the field of remote work (Fig. 2).

Unfortunately most of the current IT tools are unable to facilitate the maintenance or even the creation of such personal qualities. Developers of IT tools as well as managers of "virtual" networks are very often not aware that the most important factors which lead "virtual" collaboration tools to success are coming from the field of personal team work.

On the other hand we understand a lot about improving personal team work by studying "virtual" collaboration processes. Thus the success of personal face-to-face meetings depends a great deal on how the participants carry the outcomes of their "real" team work into a kind of "virtual" setting where they are not together any more

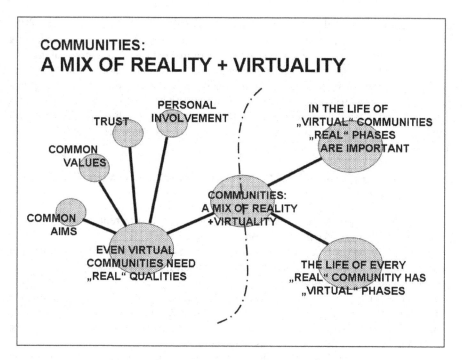

Fig. 2.

in the same physical space. After every face-to-face meeting in a "real" space we enter into a kind of remote situation. This "virtual" follow up is very often decisive for the transfer of ideas, insights and results from personal meetings, workshops and events into concrete actions. Here might be one of the reasons for the difficulty of implementing outcomes from face-to-face meetings into reality and to follow up on learning and experiences from "real" work sessions, seminars and personal development programmes.

2.2 Visual Dialogue in a Dramaturgy of "Real" and "Virtual" Cooperation Phases

For the creation of new forms of communities we can link "virtual" and "real" work phases in a common dramaturgy using common tools on a common surface.

- In the "virtual" steps we maintain personal qualities which we cultivate in "real" meetings.
- In "real" meetings we create "virtual" rituals for following up on team work with the support of other participants who will be far away from our own location later.
For creating a successful mix of "virtual" and "real" qualities we use different tools:
- On the level of the physical "real" side we apply manual visualization.
- On the level of the remote and "virtual" side computer aided means are used.
Both tools work together hand in hand using the same visual content basis and symbols, the same methodology and language consistently and continuously. Thus we

create a common visual culture continuously practiced from the first step of the collaboration. This makes it possible to design and to realize processes containing "real" and "virtual" communication and cooperation phases in a sense-making and effective synergy. One way to create a long-term, cross-cultural community linking conflicting interests is to start with a concrete short-term project realizing this methodology. In every phase of this work we use collaborative visualization. This visual practice is later the foundation for the continuing active life of the community which will be based on well known visual rituals for dialogue, sharing and co-creation.

2.3 A Short-Term Project – Useful Kick-Off for Building a "Virtual" Community

For example, in a project for developing a new product, different work phases are built on each other, overlapping from one to the next step.

The briefing in a face-to-face dialogue shows the visualization of the user requirements, the aims and strategies of the decision-makers as well as all necessary information about the context.

Starting with this step we construct a solid basis for the development process which contains early prototyping on many different levels. This is building a strong bridge to implementation of the new product and assures that it fits perfectly to the clients' and the users' needs as well as to the context.

After the successful implementation of the new product, clients often do not want to stop visual dialogue practice for being able to profit from its community building effect. They continue practising the visual rituals in a continuous improvement process.

Here a strong foundation for a long-term community has grown in a natural way. Thus a short-term project can be a kind of kick-off for the creation of a long-term community living beyond short-term projects.

2.4 From 300 to 30 000 Participants Through a Visual Dialogue

With virtual tools it is possible to reach a higher level and to make projects "real" on a bigger scale:

In a project for creating a new computer platform for 30 000 users working in different locations the aim was to facilitate all business processes of an organization. First a "real" community was set up inviting about 300 stakeholders, users, decision makers and developers to join a visual dialogue in face-to-face workshops. Participants said: "It is really great to participate in the creation of our new work processes and to contribute to the development of our new tools." Decision-makers later asked: "What a success we had in the dialogue with 300 people, but we have more than 30 000 users in different places. How do we have them participate in an interactive dialogue process with the same intensity and success?"

Here the idea of creating a "virtual" community was born. A "virtual" process was consequently constructed on the basis of the "real" experience. Thus a "real" and "virtual" participation process was realized for increasing the number of participants from 300 to more than 30 000 people.

The "virtual" knowledge space opened the possibility of sharing the experiences and materials, which were created during the face-to-face workshops, with a large number of people.

3 Result

The special quality of our processes is the consistent application and the continuous use of a common visual knowledge space. This structure offers places well known for the participants. They "have the power" over this space, being able to locate and to quickly find every knowledge element and every experience in a whole visible context while always seeing a bigger, sense-making picture. It is important that this structure is perfectly suited to the needs and fitting the work processes and the experiences of the community. This can become a symbol for strong identification of the members with their community. At the same time it is a success factor for the network to see this common knowledge space growing continuously. Its increasing value is not only due to the growing number of content elements, but first of all to various relationships and helpful connections between these elements within an intelligent network of knowledge. This and the high availability of experiences and contents for all the members of the community were often described by the participants as a very special value they were proud of. Thus all community partners were linked to the same common visible platform which perfectly represented the culture of the community.

At first this may seem to be a very formal structure, but this is only the view from the outside. In fact it is the perfectly fitting representation of a co-creation process for sharing even unfinished ideas and for giving the chance for others to build on these. This is the result of an active participation process where the presence for others and the visibility of all information at any time is practised. Trust, confidence and passion have been created. These are key factors for the new dimension of "virtual real" communities in which it becomes possible to create a common, cultural basis and to transform conflicts and different points of view into potential opportunities for synergy. Of course this needs facilitators with a lot of experience with "real" co-creation as well as with "virtual" collaboration and it challenges them and the participants to be continuously open to new views and to new situations in a flexible transparent way.

4 Conclusion

During the last years we have learned that we can successfully create novel, basic structures for new forms of communities. We are convinced that it is possible to develop "Virtual Real Communities" as a platform for working towards the vision of sustaining common, global responsibility beyond continents and beyond generations linking conflicting interests. This necessitates building the bridge of interaction between a "real" space of face-to-face work and a "virtual" space of remote collaboration. To make this connectivity happen we incorporated "real" and personal elements into the "virtual" space, and "virtual" and remote elements into the "real" work.

This is established with a comprehensive participation process creating a clear and consistent culture of dialogue. At the start, in a project based networking activity it is the first objective to meet the desires, requirements and needs of all involved stakeholders, the clients, the users, the decision makers as well as the clients of the client and those who are concerned with the network activity. Therefore all these different parties are brought together in an open and frank, visualized dialogue. The challenge for the facilitator is to encourage the participants to express their concerns in a positive way, even if these seem conflicting and to make these visible. Therefore, he has to have and use rituals for dealing with conflicting interests. Remaining neutral, he has to facilitate an atmosphere of good will and positive spirit. This creates an open platform for all different views and interests.

The involvement of peers of the different stakeholder groups helps to build a foundation for a common cause and vision. As with the whole process, key visual images are crystallising here through messages expressed by the participants in an early stage of the cooperation. This leads to high identification within the project community.

For implementing personal qualities into the virtual space several criteria are important for us:

- We want the users to have the overview over the whole information structure at all times with visibility of connections and relationships between content elements and the opportunity to share common clusters and patterns.

- This structure has to fit perfectly with the different cultures of the users focusing on natural, human perception.

- Navigation and interaction design are based on a methodology for situating and finding knowledge elements through their location in a space with qualities which are approved by the community members using a common code of different forms, colours, structures and sound tracks.

5 Ongoing Work

The next steps in this ongoing work are taking place on two levels:

On the technical side our next challenge is to represent a growing number of information elements created in ongoing long-term processes on the small computer screen without loosing the facility to see pattern in a complete overview over the whole big picture.

On the personal level we have to continue the work of developing more and more effective methodologies for implementing multicultural value structures and sense-making commitments into broad actions in reality, and to find ways to keep these structures open and flexible for unexpected situations and new joining partners with different views from cultures which are not yet represented in the network.

3D Visualization Method of Large-Scale Vector Data for Operation

Min Sun[1], Renliang Zhao[2], Junhong Hu[2], and Hui Guo[1]

[1] Institute of RS&GIS, Peking University, Beijing, China, 100871
[2] National Geomatics Center of China, Beijing, China, 100084
sunmin@pku.edu.cn

Abstract. In order to make fast 3D visualization and operation to be feasible for large-scale global vector data, in this paper, one method based on real-time simplification to vector data is presented. This method use a list of expression error limitation to simplify line objects in the iterative process, and the result is recorded by coding. In order to realize effective data organization, line objects are divided into different priority types according to its attributes and indexed with quadtree. In addition, proper original data with certain scales are suggested to select. At last, one demonstration is given, and the result shows that the method is efficient.

Keywords: cooperative visualization, geo-information, large-scale vector data.

1 Introduction

Sharing and cooperation to large-scale spatial information over internet becomes very important in geographic information system (GIS) field, one typical case is that many users try to access, browse and operate their interested data in different places on the globe, similar to utilities of query and browse function provided by Google Earth, Virtual Earth and so on systems. However, these systems do not provide operate function to vector data, which is very important in GIS field. So the main aim of our work is to resolve large-scale vector data visualization for operation, as visualization is the basis of sharing and cooperation to geo-information.

In order to realize fast 3D visualization of vector data, we use simplification method to vector data, it's similar to data generalization in cartography field. Many research works have been done in data generalization, e.g. Li-Openshaw algorithm and Daglaus-Peauker algorithm, while many improved works have been done for these algorithms. But the main aim of these algorithms is to resolve problems in cartography field, they are not suitable for fast visualization. In addition, data generalization methods orient to internet environment are also presented, as works state in literature [1][2], but they are also can't satisfy requirement to fast 3D visualization.

2 Real Time Simplification for Vector Data

In order to realize real time simplification to vector data, firstly we simplify the vector data, then record the result with coding. In the rendering time, different levels of detail is extracted and rendered with given expression errors. In order to simplify the problem, here we only discuss line objects.

Line simplification can be considered as a process of point elimination: e.g. assume {a b c} is a set of neighbor points on line l, if distances of ab and bc are less than one given error, then b is a point can be eliminated, otherwise calculate distance from point b to line ac, if this distance less than one given error, then b is a point can be eliminated. For a list of given expression error, eliminate points in such a way by an iterative process, and record the result by coding. For real time elimination, we developed a very fast algorithm, which could extract salient point in real time. The specific code method is (fig. 1): assume line l is composed of m points, and n times simplification are required, then one number with n bits length can be used to record each point state. If one point is eliminated in ith iterative process, then mark ith bit in the number to 1 otherwise to 0, when n < 4, then number 1 2 4 8 can be selected to record point state, and the whole line simplification result can be record with a code of length m.

The simplify process is controlled with a list of given expression errors, which can be determined by visualization process. Vector line expression error should be coincident with image resolution, so its value should take resolution of pyramid levels of the image, e.g. {0.5, 1.0, 2.0, 4.0, 8.0, ...}, assume image is divided into block with size of 512×512, then error list {L_i} can be calculated with formula:

$L_n = 2\pi R_E/(2^n×512×10)$ where R_E is radius of earth, if $n = 14$, $L_n = 0.477$m, i.e. the resolution is about 0.5 meter, and keep coincident with vector map scale 1: 5000. Considering specific hardware and software environment, the value of {L_i} can be relaxed to 2 or 3 times of ideal value.

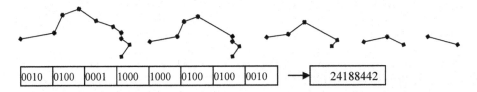

Fig. 1. Coding to data simplification result

3   Data Organize Strategy

Original vector data generally has certain scales, so select proper data is very important to real time data simplification and data organization. From many sides consideration, a scale series that could be selected is: 1:10,000, 1:100,000, 1:1,000,000, 1:10,000,000, and a series: 1;5000, 1:50,000, 1:250,000, 1:1,000,000, 1:10,000,000 can also be selected in practice if necessary.

In order to promote data operation efficiency, for each scale of original data, all line objects are divided into different types with its attributes, and assign different priorities, quadtree index is established to line objects with priorities. When data amount is too huge to realize real time visualization, only render visible objects with higher priorities.

4 Experiment and Conclusion

One vector data set including water network and county boundaries with scale 1:1,000,000 is rendered on 3D global surface (see fig. 2). 5 viewpoint distances to 3D global surface are selected, and cost time of rendering are respectively recorded for original data and simplified data, the result shows in fig.3. Low blue dot-dash line shows cost time for simplified data, while high red dot-dash line shows cost time for original data. Obviously, data simplification in far distance has great effect on high speed visualization. Fig.4 shows 5 pictures are copied respectively from 5 viewpoint distances to one area during viewpoint running towards 3D global surface, the distances are labeled on right up side of each picture. Data simplification effect from one picture to next picture is clear, while the changing is relatively smooth.

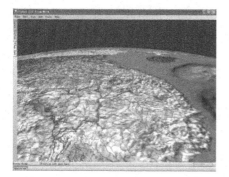

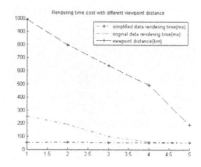

Fig. 2. Interface of experiment system

Fig. 3. Rendering time cost for simplified and original data in different viewpoint

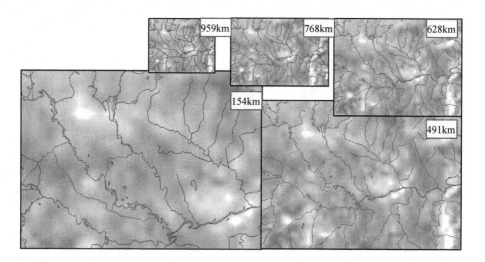

Fig. 4. The screen shot sequence in one area from different viewpoint distance to global surface

With the development of spatial information application towards internet environment, vector data visualization for operation becomes very important for far users cooperative works. Virtual Global is an ideal platform for such works, when large-scale vector data needs to be visualized, real-time simplification to line vector objects is one efficient solution to realize fast visualization. However, a good visualization method for large-scale vector data determines from several sides, in practice, many factors such as data scale selection, data preprocess are all very important.

Acknowledgement

The authors hereby deliver their thanks to National Science Foundation of China for its financial supports to this research work of project No: 40471104.

References

[1] Jones, C.B., Ware, J.M.: Map Generalization in the Web Age. International Journal of Geographical Information Science 19(8-9), 859–870 (2005)
[2] Harrower, M., Bloch, M.: MapShaper.org: A Map Generalization Web Service. IEEE Computer Graphics and Applications 26(4), 22–27 (2006)

Rule-Based Collaborative Volume Visualization

Yunhai Wang[1,2], Xiaoru Yuan[3], Guihua Shan[1,2], and Xuebin Chi[1]

[1] Computer Network Information Center, Chinese Academy of Sciences, Beijing, China
[2] Graduate University of Chinese Academy of Science, Beijing, China
[3] Department of Computer Science and Engineering, University of Minnesota, MN, USA
{wyh,sgh,chi}@sccas.cn, xyuan@cs.umn.edu

Abstract. Visualizing complex volume data sets often involves collaborative work of geographically distributed domain scientists and visualization experts. Integrating inputs from participants is critical to the success of such collaborative scientific visualization tasks. In this paper, we introduce a novel rule-based collaborative volume feature visualization system for sharing and integrating multiple users' knowledge in a collaborative environment. Our system is effective at combining multiple users' efforts on locating complex features.

1 Introduction

In large data visualization, locating underlying features often involves interaction among a team of geographically distributed collaborators. Such complex visualization tasks require supports of collaborative visualization environments. Brodlie [1] has given an overview about the distributed and collaborative visualization systems affiliating users to efficiently share and interactively adjust the rendering results.

In this paper, we introduce a collaborative volume visualization system based on Neural-Network. Rather than adjusting rendering results indirectly with non-intuitive transfer function parameters, our system allows multiple users to share their knowledge on data and tune rendering results directly in users' knowledge space. The proposed system is based on our previously developed volume visualization system [2] based on Adaptive Network based Fuzzy Inference System (ANFIS), which represents users' knowledge by fuzzy rules, shares and fuses multi-users' knowledge with neural network. Our system accepts inputs from multiple distributed users and integrates into a uniform result.

2 Collaborative Knowledge Visualization Based on ANFIS

Our system employs Adaptive Network based Fuzzy Interference System (ANFIS) [3] to integrate multi-users' knowledge into visualization and establish direct mapping relationship between knowledge and the rendering results. In this section, we discuss a few issues pertaining to our ANFIS based collaborative feature visualization system: representing and sharing users' knowledge, fusing multi-users' knowledge, and combining knowledge for collaborative visualization.

Y. Luo (Ed.): CDVE 2007, LNCS 4674, pp. 261–263, 2007.

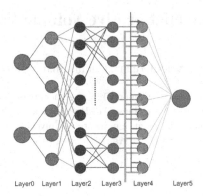

Layer0   Layer1   Layer2   Layer3   Layer4   Layer5

Fig. 1. The structure of ANFIS: the first layer is the input variables, the second layer is the input variables' membership functions, the third layer is the fuzzy rules, the fourth layer performs normalization for each rule, the fifth layer evaluates each rule's output, and the last layer calculates the output

2.1   Knowledge Representing and Sharing with Fuzzy Logic

Users' knowledge is usually vague and not straightforward to be expressed in a formal mathematical formula. As a solution for representing these uncertain knowledge, we propose to use fuzzy rules. In our system, we use the fuzzy rule proposed by Takagi and Sugeno [4], assuming output variables are generated by linear combination of input:

Rule 1.   IF the *scalar value* is *low* and the *gradient* is *high*,
THEN boundary's *probability* = $p \times scalar + q \times gradient + r$.

where *scalar value* and *gradient* are the input variables and *boundary* is the output variable, *high* and *low* are input variables' value evaluated by membership functions, and p, q, r are output variable parameters. Users can provide similar rules to the knowledge base for sharing, although membership functions and output variable parameters usually are unknown.

2.2   Knowledge Fusing by Neural-Network

We adopt Adaptive Network based Fuzzy Interference System (ANFIS) to compute aforementioned unknown parameters [2]. In addition, ANFIS has the capability of learning knowledge and fusing multi-users' knowledge. Figure 1 shows an example structure of ANFIS.

2.3   Knowledge Combination for Collaborative Visualization

After participants have obtained the visualization results, they submit their knowledge and the corresponding parameters to a knowledge base server. New users could either query the knowledge base, reuse previous knowledge and parameters based on ANFIS and linear combination, or define new knowledge and add it to the knowledge base.

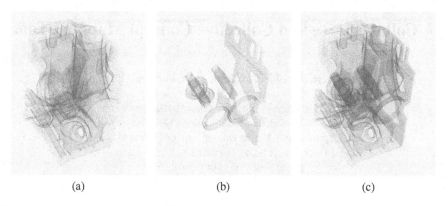

(a)   (b)   (c)

Fig. 2. Results of our collaborative volume visualization system. (a) The result of user I, (b) The result of user II, (c) A collaborative visualization result integrating inputs from user I and II.

We test our rule-based collaborative volume visualization system on a CT scanned engine. As shown in Figure 2, inputs are from researchers with emphasis on different interest features. In our case, Figure 2(a) emphasizes the outer surface of the engine while Figure 2(b) emphasizes the inner part. Note in each case, the transfer function is generated by our system based on the user input. The user does not specify any transfer function directly. With our collaborative volume visualization system, both features can be well depicted as illustrated in Figure 2(c). We are investigating the possibility of applying our system to other complex data set, such as fluid simulation data.

Acknowledgement

This work is supported by China 863 program Grant 2006AA01A116, the Ministry of Science and Technology of China Research Grant 2005DKA64002, and China 973 program Grant 2005CB321702.

References

1. Brodlie, K., Duce, D., Gallop, J., Walton, J., Wood, J.: Distributed and collaborative visualization. Computer Graphics Forum 23(2), 223–251 (2004)
2. Wang, Y., Yuan, X., Shan, G., Liu, J., Chi, X.: Rule-based volume visualization. In: The 2008 IEEE Pacfic Visualization Symposium (submitted)
3. Jang, J.: Anfis: Adaptive-network-based fuzzy inference system. IEEE Transactions on Systems, Man, and Cybernetics 23(3), 665–685 (1993)
4. Takagi, T., Sugeno, M.: Derivation of fuzzy control rules from human operator's control action. In: Proceedings of IFAC Symp. on Fuzzy Information, Knowledge Representation and Decision Analysis, pp. 55–60 (1983)

A Collaborative and Collective Concept Mapping Tool

Ivan Blecic, Arnaldo Cecchini, and Giuseppe A. Trunfio

LAMP – Laboratory of Analysis and Models for Planning,
Department of Architecture and Planning - University of Sassari,
Palazzo Pou Salit, Piazza Duomo 6, 07041 Alghero, Italy
{ivan,cecchini,trunfio}@uniss.it
http://www.lampnet.org

Abstract. This paper presents the general philosophy, features and few aspects related to the implementation and underlying technologies of MaGIA, an Internet-based multi-user system designed for a collective and collaborative construction of knowledge models represented as concept maps. The use of the system can cover a wide range of purposes, from a theoretical discussion and construction of formal models to a support for collective *brain-storming*. What makes MaGIA an interesting tool is the emphasis put on a *collective* construction of such maps. In fact, one of the distinctive features and objectives of the system is to offer an enabling tool for a multi-user, bottom-up construction, where users can intervene, freely contribute and extend concept maps and where collective and collaborative multi-user map construction can take place in asynchronous as well as in synchronous way.

Keywords: concept maps, multi-user collaborative design, Jabber.

1 Introduction

Concept maps are graphical representations of knowledge in the form of node-arc-node diagrams, where nodes represent concepts and arcs represent relationships between them. Concept maps were proposed in the 1960s and 70s by Novak [1] and since then they have been used in many educational contexts, as a knowledge-acquisition methodology and as a complement to natural language for representing and communicating knowledge. In many disciplines, various forms of concept map are used as formal methods of knowledge representation, such as semantic networks in artificial intelligence, bond graphs in mechanical engineering, Petri nets in communications, and category graphs in mathematics.

While concept maps were traditionally carried out by hand using a pencil and paper, with the development of specific software tools, they began to be enhanced and complemented by the use of hypertext, sounds, video and pictures. In general, information technology made construction, modification, maintenance and analysis of concept maps easier and more effective. Furthermore, thanks to the developments of network-based technologies, many researchers have explored the potential of collaborative construction of concept maps within such environments (e.g. [2]), offering synchronous and asynchronous communication and collaboration capabilities between

Y. Luo (Ed.): CDVE 2007, LNCS 4674, pp. 264–271, 2007.
© Springer-Verlag Berlin Heidelberg 2007

geographically distributed participants. Nowadays, there exist many tools offering advanced features for development, visualization and analysis of enhanced concept maps (e.g. GetSmart [3], CmapTools [4], Compendium [5] and Knowledge Manager [6]). Nevertheless, more research is needed to improve the support for- and to explore aspects of collaborative and multi-user construction of concept maps.

In this paper we present a multi-user software called MaGIA, designed for a collective and collaborative construction of knowledge models represented as concept maps. The system offers a series of functions and procedures, but does not preclude in any sense the type and the nature of themes and topics that can be treated. The use of the system can – in the line of principle – cover a wide range of purposes, from a theoretical discussion and construction of formal models (for example ontology models) to a support for collective *brain-storming*. Furthermore, it is of a particular interest the collective and "horizontal" nature of constructs obtained via the system.

2 Overview of MaGIA

The grounding information structure of any concept map are nodes (representing concepts) and arcs (representing links or relations between nodes). Generally, both nodes and arcs contain some additional information which further specify them: nodes may contain labels and descriptions, while arcs may contain propositions or linking phrases which specify the relationship between two concepts. In MaGIA, we have adopted a more elaborated internal data structure. In fact, both nodes and arcs can contain *(i)* textual descriptions or definitions provided by users, *(ii)* documentation and media content (files) that can be attached to nodes and arcs, and *(iii)* references (bibliographies and webiographies). As it will be explained more in detail below, MaGIA is a multi-user system where users can act upon nodes and arcs, and that is the reason why nodes and arcs may have multiple textual descriptions (one per user), and may contain multiple attached files and references. Furthermore, every entity of a map can receive users' "votes", expressing their rate of approval (agreement or opinion).

MaGIA allows many users to synchronously and asynchronously act upon and modify concept maps. This is obtained through a central server repository of maps which can be accessed with MaGIA client. Once authenticated and connected to the server infrastructure, users can access, view, modify and create new concept maps, based on the assigned privileges and general access-rights configuration of the server.

2.1 Map Definition and Creation

Users with map creating privileges can create new concept maps. Besides assigning a name, description and access rules and permissions, that includes also the decision about shapes and semantics of nodes and arcs whose use is to be permitted in the map construction. In other words, for a specific map, every allowed node shape (e.g. circle, rectangle, ellipsis, etc. in combination with a specific color) and every arc shape (e.g. plain line, one-directional arrow line, scattered line, etc.) can be assigned to a meaning or semantics (e.g. type of objects, processes, phenomena, etc.). On the other hand, it is possible to use and define map templates for specific purposes, containing possible node and arc shapes and semantics as well as eventual rules and constrains to be applied during the construction of the map. This templating system is useful when we need to construct a particular type of maps such as semantic networks, bond graphs, Petri nets, ontologies, and so on, which require the satisfaction of particular constraints and need to respect specific rules of composition.

2.2 Map Construction

The main MaGIA client workspace is the drawing canvas where users can add nodes and arcs, as well as modify and add their internal content. In particular, besides the possibility to draw nodes and arcs, through the "Object inspector" window (see on the right side of Fig. 1) users can add a definition (or a description) for nodes and arcs, insert bibliographical and web-biographical references, upload related files.

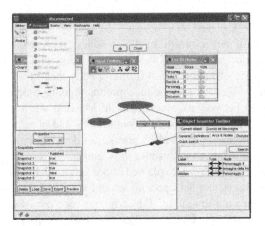

Fig. 1. Overview of MaGIA client user interface (left) and a detail of "Object inspector" (right)

But what, in our opinion, makes this software an interesting tool is the emphasis put on *collective* construction of concept maps. In fact, one of the distinctive features and objectives of the system is to offer an enabling tool for a multi-user, bottom-up construction, where every authorized user can intervene, freely contribute and extend concept maps. For this purpose, the system integrates an extensive voting and commenting system allowing users to express their opinion and vote on barely any entity of a map. In fact, users may express their vote – generally using a qualitative scale from -2 (with meanings "absolutely inadequate", "wrong", "incorrect", "strong disagreement") to 2 (meaning "completely adequate", "correct", "strong agreement") – on any entity in a map, be it a node, arc, definition, reference or a file. Votes expressed by users can subsequently be used as a ranking criterion for map's entities, and that permits the activation of filtering and analysis models based on users evaluations and map's structure.

2.3 Analytical and Visualization Tools

MaGIA offers a series of tools for analysis and graphical representation of concept maps. Several types of filters, visualization options and analysis tools allow:

- to visualize arcs between concepts where the "strength" (e.g. expressed in users' votes) of the connection exceeds a particular threshold value defined by user;
- to activate specific cluster analysis and research, based on a series of parameters and "nodes of aggregation" defined by user
- to visualize "hierarchies" between nodes, where the importance of a node depends on the number and the strength of connections with other nodes;
- to rearrange and to search for particular "geometries" in the map
- to view how the map has evolved with time and to visualize the map at any particular point in its history.

Of particularly interesting are also analytical tools that use and confront concept maps with the data related to users' activities. Such tools, besides providing usage statistics for users and groups of users, allow to confront the correspondence between clusters of nodes and clusters of users.

3 Collaborative Use Scenarios

3.1 Map Synchronization and Map Sharing

Since MaGIA operates as a client-server system, it allows various collaborative use scenarios. In MaGIA, concept maps are permanent entities stored on the server, and therefore both synchronous as well as asynchronous use scenarios are possible. In an *asynchronous collaboration*, users connect to the server and access and modify the same map at different times, without being simultaneously connected to the server. When a map gets modified by someone during a disconnection period, users will upon their new connection see the newly added nodes and arcs and will be able to inspect all the other added information. On the other hand, *synchronous collaboration* is also possible: here users are simultaneously connected to the server and concurrently act upon the map.

The way the collaboration is managed does not depend only on the above mentioned synchronism. In general terms, same nodes and arcs can be arranged and positioned differently on the drawing canvas. Since in some conceptions and uses of concept maps the arrangement of the map itself might be relevant (for instance, when different dispositions of the same map "communicate" and emphasize different points of view or perspectives of the knowledge represented by it). On that ground, one of the key aspects, and indeed a relevant feature which distinguishes it from some other tools like CmapTool, is that MaGIA offers two modes of map sharing: *(i)* unsynchronized and *(ii)* synchronized mode. *Unsynchronized map sharing* allows every user to preserve and work on his/her own visual organization of the map. This mode permits to different users to have and work on different arrangements of the map they are sharing and jointly working on. From the point of view of software functioning, if such an unsynchronized map sharing is activated, upon every addition of a new node by an user, other users will not immediately see the node *in* the map (i.e. on the drawing canvas), but rather the node will appear in a windows containing the *list* of newly added nodes. Users (except the one who have originally added the node in the first place) then have to drag-and-drop the node from that list onto the drawing canvas, deciding freely where to graphically position it in the concept map. Of course, if the dropped node has already some connection arcs to other nodes, these will automatically be drawn by the system upon the drag-and-drop procedure.

Since different arrangements of the same map are possible, and may be relevant as we said, MaGIA client offers the possibility to locally store such arrangements, called "map snapshots". Practically speaking, a snapshot is nothing more than a set of *x* and *y* coordinates for every node, determining the position of nodes on the drawing canvas. In this manner, users can save different arrangements of the same map. One useful feature of MaGIA is the possibility to share such map snapshots among users, with the possibility to preview, "download", and add other users' snapshots to ones own personal archive of snapshots and eventually adopt one such snapshot as a current map view. This snapshot publishing and sharing is managed on a pseudo peer-to-peer basis, meaning that single map snapshots are not stored on the central server, but only locally by each client, and sharing and transfer of snapshots occurs between clients.

Additionally, as we anticipated before, there is also the possibility to collaborate in a *synchronized map sharing mode*, where all users participating in such a collaboration session share the same map arrangement (in other words, they all see the same "drawing" on their drawing canvas). When users are simultaneously working on the same map they actually share the same drawing and "see" each others' actions in the real-time. Conversely, in asynchronous modality and upon every new logon, every user sees the map as it has developed since his/her last visit. The synchronized sharing mode is an on-demand feature, and every user can set up a working session which might be restricted only to a sub-groups of users, by eventually defining an access password for the session and by inviting users the session creator wishes to join in.

The above mentioned possible collaboration activities are further supported by the discussion forums present for every node and arc and by the chat and instant messaging infrastructure natively supported by the Jabber-based client and server technology. Table 1. summarizes the four possible collaboration use scenarios.

3.2 Maps Combination, Voting System and Conflict Resolution

Concept maps are representations which does not necessarily find an agreement among different people: for example two persons might have different maps about the same domain or issue being represented. This opens several issues about how to handle such conflicts in a multi-user context. In many multi-user systems, like Cmap-Tools and Compendium, there is really one single shared map, which implicitly means that the agreement is considered as reached and not managed by the software.

In our system, the extensive voting system mentioned before actually makes possible a different interpretation of results of users' behaviors, actions and collaboration. Indeed, with the possibility to vote for nodes and arcs, in addition to directly adding them to the map, one is essentially expressing his/her idea about the adequacy of entities (be it nodes or arcs) in the map. Consequently, it is possible to "distill" the specific map belonging to an user, based on his votes for nodes and arcs. As a matter of fact, we can conceptually even overturn the order and interpret the final overall map merely as an aggregation of individual users' maps.

This interpretation and the voting system opens the possibility for potentially massive multi-user concept mapping, but also offers perspectives to possible definition and development of analytical tools for comparing different users' maps and cluster analysis and their relation to possible interpretations of adherences or collisions among world views; topics our research efforts will be more focused in the future.

Table 1. Summary of four collaboration use scenarios, depending on the interaction sinchronism and on the map sharing mode

| | Interaction | |
Map sharing	Asynchronous	Synchronous
Synchronized	− all users share the same map arrangement − on-demand, sub-groups collaboration possible − forum discussion	− real-time − all users share the same map arrangement − on-demand, sub-groups collaboration possible − chat discussion
Unsynchronized	− every user works on a personal map arrangement − nodes added by others appear in a list and need to be drag-and-dropped on the canvas − forum discussion	− real-time − every user works on a personal map arrangement − nodes added by others appear in a list and need to be drag-and-dropped on the canvas − peer-to-peer snapshot sharing − chat discussion

4 System's Architecture

From the technical point of view, the MaGIA system is a client-server architecture based on Jabber XML streaming protocols and technology used for network interaction, data exchange and user management (see Fig. 2).

Jabber [7,8] is an open XML protocol for the real-time exchange of messages and presence between any two points or users in a Jabber network. There are various usage for the Jabber technology; however, the first application of Jabber technology is an asynchronous, extensible instant messaging (IM) platform, and an IM network that offers functionality similar to legacy IM systems such as AOL Instant Messaging (AIM) and Yahoo Instant Messaging. Jabber is based on a client/server architecture: all Jabber data sent from one client to another must pass through at least one Jabber server. In particular, a Jabber client connects to a Jabber server on a TCP socket connection which is "always-on" for the life of the client's session on the server. Any message intended for delivery to the client is immediately pushed out to the client messenger as long as the client is connected. The server keeps track of whether the client is online or not, and when the client go off-line it stores any messages sent to the client for delivery when he or she connect again. The advantage of Jabber is to move complexity from clients to the server. In practice, many of the low-level functions of the client (e.g., parsing XML and understanding the core Jabber data types) are handled by Jabber client libraries, enabling client developers to focus on the user interface. Besides, the Jabber protocol is open source and extensible since its relies on XML in every aspect of the communication. Thus, anyone can build or extend the Jabber protocol functionality without actually modifying the core protocol and still maintain core interoperability with other IM clients.

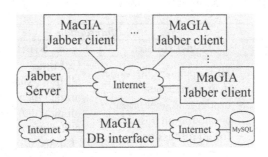

Fig. 2. The general architecture of MaGIA

All these advantages have induced us to build MaGIA on top of this set of protocols and technologies. In particular, MaGIA client, used for concept map design and drawing and for communication was developed as a plug-in extension of the BuddySpace Jabber client [9,10]. We have chosen BuddySpace as the starting point since it is an open-source instant messenger, built on Jabber and implemented in Java, which generalizes the concept of 'Buddy List' (popularized by tools such as AOL Instant Messenger, ICQ, MSN Messenger, and Yahoo Messenger) and provide multiple views of collaborative workgroups according to users' needs and tastes. BuddySpace is a cross-platform software, highly customizable and scalable and, more important for our purposes, it includes a plug-in architecture which means that additions and plug-in extensions can easily be implemented and integrated.

For the purpose of developing BuddySpace MaGIA plug-in, we have used the freely available JGraph library for map drawing and visualization. JGraph provides a range of graph drawing functionality and offers an effective API enabling to visualize, automatically layout and perform analysis of graphs. Besides, the JGraph API provides the means to configure how the graph or network is displayed and the means to associate a context or metadata with those displayed elements.

The MaGIA server architecture is based on a Jabber server. As explained before, Jabber is highly versatile in managing extensions of services and functionalities in the form of plug-ins. In fact, for MaGIA we have developed a Jabber server component ("MaGIA DB interface" in Fig. 2) that on one hand implements and manages an ad hoc Jabber XML protocol for handling concept maps and their construction which we have designed specifically for our purposes, and on the other hand interacts with the back-end database where concept maps, access privileges and other information are stored server-side. Potentially, all the mentioned components of the server architecture (core Jabber server, MaGIA DB interface and back-end database) can be distributed and hosted across the internet as well as can be installed on a single hosting server.

5 Conclusions

MaGIA has been used quite extensively in few experiences, ranging from public participation to teaching activities and to software modeling. It has proven to be a useful and effective tools for collaborative concept map building. However, there are still many areas for further developments, both in terms of general usability and user interface improvements as well as in terms of implementation of new features. Notwithstanding the fact that MaGIA is already a ready-for-use system with a small but consolidated user base, these developments will certainly be necessary to accomplish the intention to offer a fully-fledged and robust solution for a wide public adoption. We believe that MaGIA offers promising perspectives, also in the light of its distinctive characteristics with regard to other solutions, such as the richness and versatility of possible collaboration scenarios, different modes of map sharing and synchronization, the fact it has been developed around robust Jabber architecture which is part of main-stream technologies for on-line collaboration based on open standards and protocols.

References

1. Novak, J.D.: A Theory of Education. Cornell University Press, Ithaca, Illinois (1977)
2. Gaines, B.R., Shaw, M.L.G.: Collaboration through concept maps. In: Proceedings of Computer Supported Cooperative Learning Conference, October 1995, Bloomigton (1995)
3. Marshall, B., Zhang, Y., Chen, H., Lally, A., Shen, R., Fox, E.A., Cassel, L.N.: Convergence of Knowledge Management and E-Learning: the GetSmart Experience. In: Proc. Third ACM / IEEE-CS Joint Conference on Digital Libraries, Houston, May 27-31, 2003, ACM Press, New York (2003)
4. Cañas, A.J., Hill, G., Carff, R., Suri, N., Lott, J., Gómez, G., Eskridge, T.C., Arroyo, M., Carvajal, R.: CmapTools: a Knowledge Modeling and Sharing Environment. In: Proceedings of First International Conference on Concept Mapping, Pamplona, Spain (2004)
5. Compendium web site: http://www.compendiuminstitute.org
6. Knowledge Manager web site: http://www.knowledgemanager.eu
7. Shigeoka, I.: Instant Messaging in Java: The Jabber Protocols. Manning Publ. Co. (2002)
8. What is jabber, WWW page: http://www.jabber.org
9. Eisenstadt, M., Dzbor, M., Komzak, J., Vogiazou, I.T.: BuddySpace: Large-Scale Presence for Communities at Work and Play. In: International Conference on Communities and Technologies, Amsterdam, the Netherlands (2003)
10. Eisenstadt, M., Komzak, J., Dzbor, M.: Instant messaging + maps = powerful collaboration tools for distance learning. In: Proceedings of TelEduc03, Havana, Cuba (2003)

WSHLA: Web Services-Based HLA Collaborative Simulation Framework

Hengye Zhu[1], Guangyao Li[1], and Lulai Yuan[2]

[1] CAD Research Center, Tongji University, Shanghai 201804, China
[2] Key Laboratory of Embedded System and Service Computing of Ministry of Education,
Tongji University, Shanghai 201804, China
hengyezhu@gmail.com, lgy@mail.tongji.edu.cn, lulaiyuan@gmail.com

Abstract. Collaborative simulation technology is an important factor in improving the efficiency of complex product design. Although High Level Architecture (HLA)-based simulation technology can meet the needs for simulation in product design, it's also marked by many deficiencies. In this paper, we focus on the introduction of web services into HLA simulation system and propose a Web Services-Based HLA Collaborative Simulation Framework (WSHLA). The framework uses web services to encapsulate the invocations of HLA services and then make simulation system more interoperable and reusable. Firstly, the overall structure of WSHLA and the proxy, which acts on behalf of a federate and interacts with Runtime Infrastructure (RTI), are presented. Then, the detailed design and implementation process of WSHLA are discussed. Experimental results show that, using web services, the framework can make up for the deficiencies in HLA simulation system and ensure WSHLA-based collaborative simulation goes smoothly at the expense of some time.

Keywords: web services, high level architecture, collaborative simulation framework, complex product design, run time infrastructure.

1 Introduction

Complex product design involves the consideration of many interdependent factors and variables, which are too complicated for the human mind to cope with. Simulation is a powerful tool that provides the capability and allows designers imagine new systems, conduct experiments to observe behavior, predict and evaluate the results of alternative decisions.

High Level Architecture (HLA) is an advanced distributed simulation architecture, which can effectively integrate sub-models in different domains together to form a complicated simulation system for simulation analysis. However, there exist some deficiencies in HLA simulation system [1]. For instance, due to the characteristics of platform-specific and programming language-specific of Runtime Infrastructure (RTI), the interoperability between different RTIs is poor; HLA is also not compatible with the standards and technologies in other domains; HLA-based simulation may be

Y. Luo (Ed.): CDVE 2007, LNCS 4674, pp. 272–279, 2007.

blocked by firewall, which even makes simulation fail. The above deficiencies make it hard for HLA to get a deeper development in the field of collaborative simulation of complex product design. Therefore, HLA simulation system should adopt and assimilate related standards or technologies to achieve better development. Web services, using eXtensible Markup Language (XML) and HyperText Transportation Protocol (HTTP), represent a new distributed computing pattern, which allow applications to interact with each other in a platform-independent and programming language-independent manner. Introduction of web services can effectively make up for the deficiencies in HLA simulation system, greatly improve its interoperability, reusability, and then better support collaborative simulation of complex product design. However, web services and HLA are different standards for different purposes and domains, which makes the combination of the two difficult.

According to the characteristics of HLA simulation system and web services, we introduce web services into HLA simulation system and propose a Web Services-Based HLA Collaborative Simulation Framework (WSHLA). Firstly, we present the overall structure of WSHLA and a new object: proxy, which acts on behalf of a federate in interacting with RTI. Then, the detailed design and the implementation process of WSHLA are discussed in detail. Experimental results validate the framework and show that, using web services, the framework can make up for the deficiencies in HLA simulation system and ensure WSHLA-based collaborative simulation goes smoothly at the expense of some time.

The rest of paper is organized as follows: Section 2 presents some related works. Section 3 discusses the Web Services-Based HLA Collaborative Simulation Framework (WSHLA). Section 4 validates WSHLA through experiments and analyzes experimental results. Section 5 concludes the paper and gives the plan of future work.

2 Related Works

Andreas Wytzisk presents an initial solution that tries to bring HLA and web services together by creating a standard compliant bridging framework: "management federation", which can make HLA federations controllable from the World Wide Web without needing to extend current standard [2]. Katherine L. Morse uses Web Enabled RTI (WE RTI) libraries instead of standard RTI libraries to build federation. The goal of WE RTI is to enable a simulation to communicate with HLA RTI through web-based services. The long-term goal is to be able to have multiple federates that are able to reside as web services on Wide Area Network, permitting an end-user to compose a federation from a browser [3]. Paul Gustavson explores how Services-Oriented Architecture and supportive technologies, such as XML, Web Service Definition Language and Base Object Model, can begin to be applied to provide a loose coupling and better support distributed simulation and how this concept is being applied to support aggregation [4]. Katherine L. Morse proposes an approach that uses web services as basis for sophisticated Interest Management in real time distributed simulation and presents a Web Services Internet Management architecture designed to achieve these capabilities in a way that is compatible with simulations using HLA [5].

3 Web Services-Based HLA Collaborative Simulation Framework

In HLA, federates and RTI interact with each other directly by using the address and port specified in RID file, which is one of the reasons resulting in the above-mentioned problems in HLA simulation system. Introducing web services and then changing the manner of interaction are the key issues to be addressed in the paper.

Before presenting the overall structure of WSHLA, we give some definitions. In WSHLA, the computer where RTI and all necessary web services are deployed at is called "RTI side"; the computer where federates run at is called "client side"; the object, deployed at RTI side, which is on behalf of a federate in interacting with RTI, is called "proxy".

The overall structure of WSHLA is shown in Fig. 1:

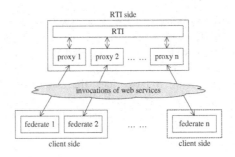

Fig. 1. Overall structure

RTI side and client side are two indispensable components of WSHLA. RTI side is the same with the RTI of HLA functionally. The functions of RTI side are to manage RTI, all necessary web services and proxies. The functions of client side are to provide special RTI ambassador interfaces, federate ambassador interfaces to users and to manage all federates. In WSHLA, each federate in client side has a corresponding proxy in RTI side, and federates and RTI interact with each other indirectly via their proxies by using web services. When joining a federation execution, a federate calls a web service to create a corresponding proxy in RTI side, and then the proxy not the federate joins the federating execution. When calling an RTI ambassador service, a federate calls a web service to send the request to its corresponding proxy, which will transfer the request to RTI. The process of calling a federate ambassador service is similar to the above.

3.1 Detailed Design

In HLA, RTI interacts with federates using RTI ambassador services and federate ambassador services (callbacks), which are specified in Interface Specification. However, in WSHLA, RTI interacts with federates indirectly via the proxy using web services. Therefore, we must design web services for the two categories of HLA services. Meanwhile, due to the introduction of web services, it's necessary to introduce some auxiliary functions, which are also needed to be designed as web services. In a word, the web services in WSHLA can be designed into three categories: web services designed for RTI ambassador services, web services designed for federate ambassador services and auxiliary web services.

(1) Web services designed for RTI ambassador services. RTI ambassador services, provided by libRTI, are stable and don't change with the change of federates. These characteristics simplify the design work of this category of web services. What we need to do is to use web services to encapsulate each RTI ambassador service and deploy these web services at RTI side. When calling an RTI ambassador service, users may call the corresponding web services directly. Of course, the invocation of these web services can be wrapped again for facilitating their usage.

(2) Web services designed for federate ambassador services. Compared with the previous work, it's hard to design web services for federate ambassador services. Because, it's users not libRTI who provide federate ambassador services for each federate running at different client sides. If we do the same job as we did in the previous design work, the web services designed for federate ambassador services must be deployed at different client sides, which will make it hard to design the proxy and to use WSHLA. (For example, in this circumstance, each client side must install web services container.) Therefore, we use another method. When a proxy receives a request for a callback, the proxy writes the information about the callback, such as function name, the number and content of parameters, etc, to a sharable file. In addition, we provide web services to parse the file. In client side, users may create a timer to call the web services. When a callback is called by RTI, client side will get the information about the callback by using the web services and then call the callback provided by users.

(3) Auxiliary web services. WSHLA also supports some auxiliary operations; therefore, we must design web services for these operations. Starting RTI: Before running a simulation, users call the web service to start RTI. Determining whether RTI is running in RTI side: Before starting RTI, users call the web service to determine whether RTI is running in RTI side or not. Shutting down RTI: After all simulations are end, users call the web service to shutdown RTI. Determining whether there are federation executions in RTI side: Before shutting down RTI, users call the web service to determine whether there are federation executions in RTI side or not.

The detailed class diagram of WSHLA is shown in Fig. 2.

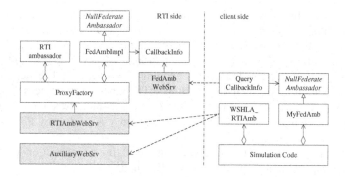

Fig. 2. Class diagram

(1) Detailed design of RTI side (six important classes)

FedAmbImpl: The class implements *NullFederateAmbassador*, and its main function is to receive the callback called by RTI and use *CallbackInfo* to record the information about the callback. *CallbackInfo*: The class writes the information about a callback to a sharable file. *FedAmbWebSrv*: The class can parse the sharable file created by *CallbackInfo* and provide web services to users. *ProxyFactory*: The class aggregates the two instances of *RTIambassador* and *FedAmbImpl*. Its main function is to manage the proxy, such as creating a proxy, destroying a proxy, etc. *RTIAmbWebSrv*: Containing an instance of *ProxyFactory*, the class provides web services for RTI ambassador services to users. *AuxiliaryWebSrv*: The class provides auxiliary web services, such as starting RTI, shutting down RTI, etc to users.

(2) Detailed design of client side (three important classes)

WSHLA_RTIAmb: Though users can directly call web services in their simulation code, it's inconvenient for users to use WSHLA. Therefore, we wrap the web services provided by *RTIAmbWebSrv* and *AuxiliaryWebSrv* and provide standard DMSO HLA interface to users. Hiding invocations of web services, the class makes programming much easier. The standard APIs also enable users to be more consistent with their programming habits and simplify the conversion from HLA-based simulation to WSHLA-based simulation. Due to the characteristics of platform-independent and programming language-independent of web services, different programming languages can be used to wrap these web services under different platforms to extend its application area. In our experimental prototype, Java and C# are used to wrap these web services. *QueryCallbackInfo*: The class uses a timer to call the web services provided by *FedAmbWebSrv* to get the information about a callback and then call the callback provided by the subclass of *NullFederateAmbassador*. Similarly, because the class is a wrapper of web services, the class also has the advantages of *WSHLA_RTIAmb*. *MyFedAmb*: The class implements *NullFederateAmbassador*. Users may override the callbacks according to their needs.

3.2 Implementation Process

The whole implementation process of WSHLA is as below:

(1) Start RTI: before running a simulation, users must start RTI first. (2) Create RTI ambassador and federate ambassador: instantiate *WSHLA_RTIAmb* and *MyFedAmb* at client side. (3) Create and join federation execution: two *WSHLA_RTIAmb* methods will be called at client side and translated into web services invocations to RTI side. Then, *ProxyFactory* creates a proxy and let it join federation execution. (4) Initialization, publish and subscribe. (5) Set time advance tactic: enable time constrained or time regulating if needed. (6) The step is the main body of simulation code, including calling RTI ambassador services and federate ambassador services. (7) Federates resign from federation execution. (8) Destroy federation execution and end a simulation. (9) Destroy RTI: destroy RTI if there are no federation executions in RTI.

Now, we will take the course of sending and receiving an interaction as example to illustrate the implementation process of WSHLA in detail.

(1) Simulation code in client side calls *WSHLA_RTIAmb.sendInteraction()*. (2) The request is send to the corresponding proxy, which calls *RTIambassador.*

sendInteraction() to interact with RTI. (3) Repeat Step 1 and 2 for *WSHLA_RTIAmb.tick()* and pass control to RTI. (4) RTI calls the *receiveInteraction()* of those federates whose proxy subscribes the interaction. When the proxy received the callback, it writes the information about the callback to a sharable file. (5) Simulation code executes the *receiveInteraction()* provided in *MyFedAmb*. (6) Repeat Step 5 and 6 for *timeAdvanceGrant()* callback. (7) When all callbacks are finished, the control is passed back to federates to resume simulation, which ends *tick()* method. (8) Simulation continues its execution.

4 Experiments and Analysis

Experiments are designed to validate WSHLA. Experimental environment is: Windows 2000 Professional, Java 1.4, C#, Pitch pRTI 1.3, Tomcat 4.1 and Axis 1.4. Tomcat, Axis and pRTI run at RTI side.

4.1 Experiments

In the first experiment, we create a federation that comprises two federates programmed with Java and C# language respectively. Running at client side 1 and client side 2 respectively, the two federates have the capability of sending/receiving interactions and updating/reflecting attributes.

We modify the benchmark program from DMSO HLA packet and focus on the latency benchmark. The latency benchmark program measures the elapsed time it takes for federates to send and receive an interaction or update and reflect an attribute. In the experiments, we measure the RO interaction latency, and the size of the interacted packet is 1024 bytes. We measure the elapsed time in LAN and WAN with firewall on and off. Meanwhile, we conduct the same experiment in the same circumstance using HLA instead for comparing the experimental results of WSHLA and HLA. The experimental result measured in LAN is shown in Fig. 3 and the experimental result measured in WAN is shown in Fig. 4.

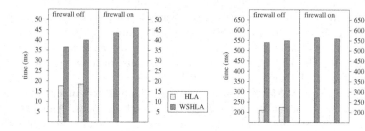

Fig. 3. Experimental result in LAN   **Fig. 4.** Experimental result in WAN

It's obvious that firewall exerts no influence on WSHLA, however firewall makes HLA-based simulation completely fail. However, in the same circumstance, WSHLA will cost much more time in these operations than HLA.

Then, we conduct the second experiment in complex product design. F14 fighter jet model, which comprises two sub-models: controller and dynamics, is used in this experiment. The model, built by using MATLAB/Simulink, analyzes how changing the gains used in the Proportional-Integral Controller affect the aircraft's angle of attack and the amount of G force the pilot feels. In our experiment, we focus on the angle of attack. We use MATLAB/RTW to turn the two sub-models into C++ code. Controller as one federate runs at client side 1 and dynamics as another federate runs at client side 2. We compare the experimental result conducted by using MATLAB and WSHLA respectively. The experimental result using MATLAB directly is shown in Fig. 5 and the experimental result using WSHLA is shown in Fig. 6.

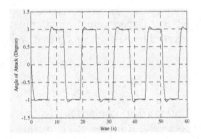 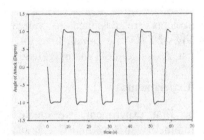

Fig. 5. Experimental result using MATLAB   **Fig. 6.** Experimental result using WSHLA

The experimental result shows that WSHLA, which also gets the right result, can be applied to the field of collaborative simulation correctly.

4.2 Analysis

We analyze the experimental results in the following aspects.

(1) In WSHLA, RTI and federates interact with each other indirectly via the proxy. The invocations of web services, which using XML and HTTP, won't be blocked by firewall. In addition, the proxy is located at the same computer where RTI located at, therefore the interaction between RTI and proxies won't be blocked by firewall either. In a word, WSHLA-based simulation won't be blocked by firewall at all. However, in HLA, RTI and federates interact with each other directly by using the address and port specified in RID file. Unfortunately, if simulation runs in network, the port is always blocked by firewall, which makes simulation fail.

(2) The second merit of WSHLA is that we can use the platform-independent and programming language-independent characteristics of web services. Any program language that can call web services can be used to program simulation code under different platforms. However, in HLA, only the language specified by RTI can be used to program under the specified platform. In the first experiment, the HLA/RTI in RTI side is pRTI 1.3, which only provides Java programming interface. However, the introduction of web services makes it available for us to use C# to program simulation code, which increases the flexibility of WSHLA greatly.

(3) Web services encapsulate the differences between RTIs and provide users the same programming interface, which increases the interoperability and reusability of

simulation codes. In addition, web services also make WSHLA more compatible with other related standards and technologies, which will expand the application area of WSHLA greatly.

(4) In WSHLA, RTI side may be considered as a public resource, which may be used by anyone and then decrease the expenses used to purchase RTI.

(5) Though WSHLA has a lot of merits, its efficiency is worse than HLA. Because, the size of soap packet used in WSHLA is much larger than the packet used in HLA. In addition, when a service is requested or responded, the necessary parameters will be marshaled or unmarshaled, which will decrease the efficiency of WSHLA. The above reasons increase the traffic of WSHLA and make the efficiency lower. However, it's an inevitable demerit of introducing web services to HLA.

5 Conclusions and Future Work

Introduction of web services can make up for the deficiencies in HLA simulation system. We propose a framework named WSHLA to build HLA collaborative simulation system based on web services. Using the framework, we can use web services to build a loose-coupling simulation system, which will increase the flexibility, interoperability and reusability of HLA simulation system. Experimental results, which validate the framework, show that the framework can resolve the problems in HLA simulation system at the expense of some time.

Though the introduction of web services into HLA increases the interoperability and reusability of HLA simulation system, it also reduces the efficiency of simulation system. So, we will consider in the future work how to increase the usage of WSHLA further on the premise of improving the efficiency of the framework, and then make it more compatible with more standards and technologies.

References

1. Brutzman, D., Zyda, M., Pullen, M., et al.: Extensible Modeling and Simulation Framework (XMSF) Challenges for Web-Based Modeling and Simulation. In: XMSF 2002 Findings and Recommendations Report: Technical Challenges Workshop and Strategic Opportunities Symposium, Monterey (2002)
2. Wytzisk, A., Simonis, I.: Integration of HLA Simulation Models into a Standardized Web Service World. In: Proceedings of the 2003 Europe Simulation Interoperability Workshop, Stockholm (2003)
3. Morse, K.L., Drake, D.L., Brunton, R.P.Z.: Web Enabling HLA Compliant Simulations to Support Network Centric Applications. Proceedings of the 2004 Symposium on Command and Control Research and Technology, San Diego, 2004.
4. Gustavson, P., Chase, T., Root, L., et al.: Moving Towards a Service-Oriented Architecture (SOA) for Distributed Component Simulation Environments. In: Proceedings of the 2005 Spring Simulation Interoperability Workshop, San Diego (2005)
5. Morse, K.L., Brunton, R.P.Z., Pullen, J.M., et al.: An Architecture for Web Services Based Interest Management in Real Time Distributed Simulation. In: Proceedings of the 8th IEEE International Symposium on Distributed Simulation and Real-Time Applications, Budapest, IEEE Computer Society Press, Los Alamitos (2004)

Cooperative Validation in Distributed Control Systems Design

Dariusz Choinski, Mieczyslaw Metzger, Witold Nocon, and Grzegorz Polakow

Faculty of Automatic Control, Electronics and Computer Science,
Silesian University of Technology,
ul. Akademicka 16, 44-100 Gliwice, Poland
{dariusz.choinski,mieczyslaw.metzger,
witold.nocon,grzegorz.polakow}@polsl.pl

Abstract. The team of engineers designing and implementing distributed control system software must communicate within a multidisciplinary environment. One of the main problems is the interaction between hardware and software solutions. Software project presumptions may not be based only on minimum hardware requirements and on technology rules. Modern distributed control systems embrace all aspects of a complex and widespread object. Hence, every modification within any discipline requires interference into the system and validation of its new features, which in turn constraints effectiveness of designing. This paper discusses how to increase effectiveness and speed up validation, in a standardised CAD environment, by using: Multi-Agent System in order to limit the number of interactions between particular subsystems, ontology for assisting topology description and properties of system entropy for assessment of introduced solutions. The proposed system was implemented and worked out in a biotechnological pilot plant.

Keywords: Collaborative design, multi-agent systems, knowledge ontology, web environment for collaborative working, multiple location collaborative design, industrial applications.

1 Introduction

Design of modern industrial plants creates problems because the control system running this plant needs to be taken into account. Such a system usually comprises a great amount of different components, such as control instrumentation, control software and communication networks. Design and integration of the control system are difficult tasks, both during operation of the process in normal condition and in emergency situations. Another problem arises from a significant difference in mean time between failures (MTBF) of the mechanical and electronic plant components (control and information devices should be frequently upgraded). Therefore, during normal exploitation of the plant, the control and information instrumentation should be redesigned. A multi-agent-based system for cooperative design, validation and operation of industrial processes proposed in the paper facilitates those tasks. The proposed system includes several modern ideas such as multi agent systems

Y. Luo (Ed.): CDVE 2007, LNCS 4674, pp. 280–289, 2007.

(MAS) – see for example [1], control algorithms of hybrid systems [2] hybrid I/O automata [3], knowledge ontology [4], cooperative systems for design [5],[6],[7],[8] as well as network-based collaborative design systems [9],[10].

2 Problem Under Consideration

Our research, using a biotechnological pilot-plant as an example [11], has proven that the control system may be represented by a hybrid system model. This system consists of an automaton having a finite number of states. Transition conditions between those states are described by two sets defining controllable and uncontrollable events. Control of a system modelled in this way is realized within MAS. The control agent tries to maintain the given state despite disruption caused by uncontrollable events, while the supervisory agent tries to change the current state into another desirable state, by applying a sequence of controllable events. Any transition functions that are missing or not specified, may by developed by an expert.

Because of technological constraints and limited capabilities of measurement, control and powering devices and also because of the information structure of the distributed communication equipment, the system has been divided into subsystems. This division is based on ontology that takes the semantics used in CAD systems into account. Apart from the subsystems, the system possesses defined functions, the taxonomy of which is based on phenomenological models. The main technological concepts are based on those phenomenological models. Architecture of the proposed system is presented in Fig. 1.

An impartial assessment of the distributed control system operation is very difficult and depends on the goal of this assessment. One of the important aspects is determination, whether the system's user, who is not familiar with control theory,

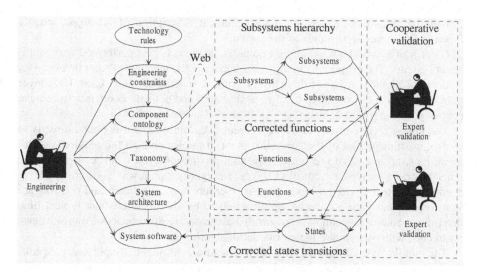

Fig. 1. Concept of the hybrid system

may utilize all the capabilities of the technological object. That is in relation to the possibility of access to different states by a minimum number of intermediate states and remembering the once-carried-out organization of subsystems. Such operations must be robust, with means avoiding the system to be moved into a state, from which the currently used controls may be insufficient to move the system into the previous state.

3 Developed System Description

As practice of automation of biotechnological [11],[12] processes shows, that automated plants may be represented as hybrid state machines [3] i.e. state machines augmented with sets of differential equations. Such hybrid systems are described with two sets:

- Ω – set of continuous state variables. Range of those variables depends on the specifics of the considered system i.e. process constraints, measurements, activator's capabilities, etc.;
- Φ – set of events conditions enabling transitions between states. The Φ set can be divided into two subsets:
  - Φ_u – subset of uncontrollable events – transitions caused by internal process behaviour or external environment, the control system can not prevent nor cause;
  - Φ_c – subset of controllable events – transitions which can be induced and/or prevented by the control system, so those transitions can be used to perform a control task.

Changes of system's state may occur as discrete events when certain conditions defined in Φ are fulfilled or as a continuous trajectory in a space state according to the differential equations (which are a mathematical description of an object-specific function f of inputs and outputs of the system).

Control of a hybrid automaton is a complex task and is best performed with multi-agent systems. The proposed structure of control agents, which proved to be effective, is hierarchical and consists of three layers: control, supervisory and expert. Each layer performs tasks at a designated level of abstraction, and actively cooperate to achieve control goal in a robust manner.

The lowest layer consists of Control Agents. A Control Agent is bound directly to control instrumentation of the controlled plant. It implements all the required control algorithms, takes care of presumed sequential production cycles and performs all the other functions of typical control task (e.g. emergency shutdowns). All control layer agents work in time-driven mode (that is, measurements are taken and controls are sent to actuators with a constant time period) to be able to implement typical time determined control algorithms. Uncontrollable events are disturbances Control Agents try to cope with by standard means of control algorithms.

The middle layer of the control system structure is formed by Supervisory Agents. Each agent supervises a number of Control Agents and monitors quality of control in a broader scope than Control Agents are able to. Supervisory Agents are capable of more advanced state recognition and trajectory planning, therefore in case of worsening control quality, a Supervisory Agent may decide that it is desirable to switch the system into some Ω_i state (or even through some Ω_i, ..., Ω_n states sequence planned ahead) to fulfil a given control task. The plan is then performed by the specific Control Agent as a proxy.

At last, the top layer contains Expert Agents. Expert Agents are a system's interface to external sources of knowledge such as human and/or artificial overseers and experts. Expert Agents' role is to supply Supervisory Agents with additional knowledge on processes in the system. Experts are able to serve their general knowledge to many physical instances of the class, if only Expert Agent supports data exchange with spatially distant location over long range communications link (including Internet network).

To make design, verification and maintenance phases of the system's cycle of work easier and more regular, all of the system elemental components should be logically grouped into subsystems. Such classification can be done according to the IEC 61346 standard, which defines rules for structuring system's components into hierarchical subsystems and referencing them. This standard proposes three kinds of hierarchies, according to components': function, location, and product. In effect, system's logical organisation consists of three different trees with system's components as vertices, where each of the components belong to each of the trees at the same time. Edges of the trees are designated by membership relations (smaller subsystems forming larger ones). In distributed control systems, usual function criteria are for technical reasons: power supply, process, and control task.

In a real complex control system many subsystems of varying complexity levels can be distinguished on various levels of abstraction. Additionally, each of the control instruments and each of the subsystems belong to many structures depending on the assumed grouping criterion. Independently of subsystems distinction, whole control system has some functions defined. Those functions are a consequence of control systems designed tasks and their taxonomy is determined by phenomenological models of processes in the specific controlled plant.

This structure of subsystems hierarchy taken together with boundary conditions of the systems' variables defines the system as a deterministic finite state automaton. On the other hand, the ontology is also taken into account when definition of functions taxonomy is built. Taxonomy of functions performed by the system is derived from phenomenological models of processes being automated. Finally, both state automaton definition and set of system's functionalities define the architecture of hybrid system which is the final product of the design process.

To make Web–based application capable of data interchange with industrial–grade software, a specialised application was developed. The self-organizing relational data base [13] is a data mining application actively probing the designed control system and storing the variables and their historical trends in Web-standards compliant MySQL-driven database. The database is accessed by a custom web server-side application, which transparently encodes and decodes incoming queries and outcoming replies using the XML notation. Such encoding enables quick and easy deployment of Webservices, enabling access to the control system's internal information. End client application for system–human expert interaction is developed using Flash technology and can be embedded in webpage and executed in nearly any

Web browser. The Flash application uses the Web service to communicate with the system (interface part of the expert's application is designated as a Mediator). The role of the remote expert is correction of the possible state transitions and correction of system's functions.

The structure of the presented system allows for easy and quick connecting of multiple remote experts. However, in case where multiple remote experts are employed in one control system, inter-expert cooperation becomes problematic. As Smith and Davis suggest [14], cooperative distributed problem solving consists of three steps: *problem decomposition, sub-problem solution*, and *solution synthesis*. In the system under consideration second and third steps are already implemented. *Sub-problem solution* consists of correcting states transitions sequences and functions by a remote expert, based on his knowledge, observed finite states, and functions (received from system's database). *Solution synthesis* is a simple process of storing corrected data in the database. However, the first step of *problem decomposition* requires additional effort. It is required to describe the control system in such way, so that each of the experts works in his own problem domain without interfering with other experts. Since natural division of problem in hybrid systems is into automaton's particular states, it is desired that each system's state is as independent from other states as possible. When this assumption is fulfilled, each of the experts may focus on a specific subset of the states space, and modify the subset without disturbing other experts. To enable this possibility and to maximise control capabilities of the system, innovatory definition of the control system's design and verification goals are introduced in the following section.

4   Ontology-Based Subsystem Topology Semantics

Even a simple system design has a multilevel tree of reference designations, which is usually incomprehensible without associated diagrams. The main aim of the proposed ontology is to make physical meaning of the subsystems as a collection of formal axioms based on primitive relation incorporated only in the reference designation tree and the distances in hierarchy.

The set of reference designations prepared in accordance with the IEC 61346 standard is a basis for the division into subsystems according to the component ontology. The mereology starts taking a relation 'Cx,y' to express that individuals x and y are connected, as was introduced by Clarke [15] as a Calculus. This Calculus may state ontology describing topology based on reference designation according to IEC 61346 [16].

The Fig. 2 presents an example of subsystem composition based on this ontology. For particular individuals with descriptions based on IEC 61346 (where superscript '*' is for all references designation, '-' is for subset of product, '+' is for subset of location, '=' is for subset of process function hierarchy and '==' is for subset of power supply function hierarchy respectively): we can present the following connections: **P**: 'x^* is a Part of y^*', **O**: 'x^* Overlaps y^*', **DR**: Independent functions: '$x^{==}$ is Discrete from $y^{==}$', **EC**: Connected to externally subsystem: 'x^+ is Externally Connected to y^+' or Remote subsystem function: '$x^=$ is Externally Connected to $y^{+=}$',

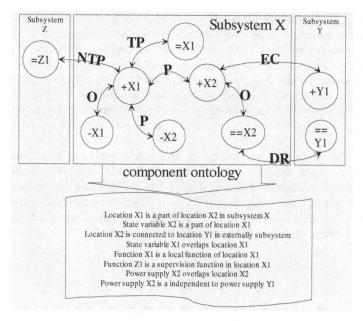

Fig. 2. Ontology based subsystem composition

TP: Local subsystem function: '$x^=$ is Tangential Part of y^+', **NTP**: Supervised function: '$x^=$ is Non Tangential Part of y^+'. The mereological definitions of presented connections can describe in open language sophisticated subsystem composition.

5 Entropy Functions-Based Validation

Variables characterizing the system in general and the individual subsystems in particular, may be divided into intensive variables and extensive variables. Extensive variables Ω^{ex} depend on the system' scale, while intensive variables Ω^{in} are independent of the system' scale. In other words, extensive variables are dependent on the size of the system (quantities of mass, heat etc., since dividing a given mass of substance into two subvolumes, naturally decreases quantities of mass in those subvolumes), while intensive variables are independent of the system's size (temperature, concentration etc., since, dividing a mass of substance having a certain temperature, into two subvolumes, will result in two subvolumes having exactly the same temperature as the original volume). Any subsystem state may be characterized by values of intensive variables that depend on each other. Balance equations that serve as a basis for phenomenological models describe fluxes of the extensive variables. Those fluxes are forced by the difference in intensive variables that are in this case the moving force of the process.

   In a controlled system, some intensive variables posses defined ranges of values, while other intensive variables with unspecified limits are observed or bindings of those variables with other intensive variables are known, usually by applying Le Chatelier-Braun principle. The relation between flows and forces characterizes the system kinetics. Conditions for reaching a steady state of the subsystem are specified by extensive variables bound with each other in balance equations. Because the intensive variables used in control of the process are independent of the system scale, only binding those variables with extensive variables enables the steady state of the system to be determined. It is especially important for biotechnological objects, where stable values of intensive variables (substrate concentration for example) may correspond to unstable values of extensive variables (biomass quantity for example). Any intensive variable acting between two subsystems must obviously posses the same value.

MAS for the hybrid control system enables determination of all reachable states. For every subsystem, the state is specified by the Ω set of extensive variables that are part of the state equations of the base class and by intensive variables with limits specified. For every subsystem a probability p_i of reaching the outcome of the state characterized by Ω^i *a posteriori* may be determined and the discrete form of Shannon information entropy function [21] my also be determined:

$$S(p) = -\sum_{i=1}^{N} p_i \log_2(p_i) \tag{1}$$

where: N – number of states for the subsystem, and $p=\{p_i\}$. A normalization condition is defined as:

$$\sum_{i=1}^{N} p_i = 1 \tag{2}$$

For an isolated subsystem, the possibility of reaching particular states with the same probability is connected to entropy maximization. In order to check the behaviour of the particular state i, minimization of partial Kullback-Liebler cross-entropy function is used.

$$D_i^{KL} = p_i \log_2 \frac{p_i}{q_i} \tag{3}$$

where: q_i is the *a priori* probability of income for state i.

Fig. 3 presents values of the D^{KL} function for particular states in case when reduction, maintaining and production takes place in the subsystem. In should be noted, that when entropy is maintained, the D^{KL} function has low values in a wide range of states. In addition, averaging values of states increases entropy. In case when entropy increases, it is possible to find a set of states in the region of minimal values of D^{KL}. This region however is divided by states with low probability of occurrence, hence finding such a minimum requires precise knowledge about constrains, because change in those constrains may be burden with a penalty for exceeding the regions with low probability of occurrence. Opposite situation occurs when entropy is reduced. In such a case, the region of high probability is very small, while the low probability region is large. Such situation may for example take place when fault or wrong state changing function is determined.

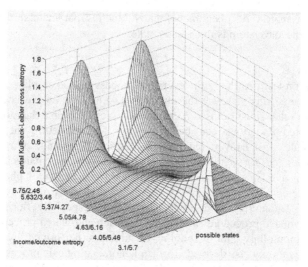

Fig. 3. Three dimensional plot of the partial Kullback-Leibler cross entropy used to examine the behaviour of each state of particular subsystem

For application of Kullback-Liebler [18] cross-entropy in the cooperative validation, on-line estimation of entropy value is necessary. When the Gaussian distribution of subsystem states probability is assumed, for the window of P observed income states $\{q_1,...,q_i,...,q_P\}$ enforced by Expert and outcome states $\{p_1,...,p_i,...,p_P\}$ realized by the control system, standard deviation μ can be estimated [19].

The cross-entropy is an unsymmetrical measure. Because subsystems have a variety of mutual interconnections that are dynamically changing during designing and validation, the estimator of entropy value is defined as follows:

$$\hat{D}_P^{KL} = \frac{\log_2\left(\frac{\hat{\mu}_p}{\hat{\mu}_q}\right)^2 + \left(\frac{\hat{\mu}_q}{\hat{\mu}_p}\right)^2}{2} + \frac{\log_2\left(\frac{\hat{\mu}_q}{\hat{\mu}_p}\right)^2 + \left(\frac{\hat{\mu}_p}{\hat{\mu}_q}\right)^2}{2} - 1 \qquad (4)$$

The system considered in this paper exchanges entropy with the surroundings in a necessary way. A system consisting of many mutually connected subsystems may serve as an infinite source of entropy for every subsystem. In such a case, entropy may be dissipated and the system may transit into a state of irreversible processes. In such a case it should be checked whether the subsystem is in a stable state with a concurrent minimization of the entropy value. Hence, despite decreasing the probability of particular states occurrence, the subsystem is in a steady state, in which there are bindings between different state variables. For this situation, a Onsager condition [20] may be used. If it is possible to find the following dependence, for the intensive variables moving forces and fluxes of extensive variables:

$$\Omega_i^{ex} = \sum_j L_{ij} \Omega_j^{in} \qquad (5)$$

where: L is a matrix of phenomenological kinetics parameters, than it may be assumed, that the subsystem is in a steady state, if:

$$L \cong L^T \qquad (6)$$

Such situation testifies that an irreversible process has taken place, hence is it not possible to change this state by the currently available intensive control variables. Cooperation of other subsystems is necessary in order to reverse the moving forces.

The presented equations can be used only for predicting the possibility of equilibrium state with irreversible process. During designing, process technology rules are elaborated for avoiding such states. However, dynamically configured subsystems can overlap state variables with symmetric matrix of phenomenological kinetics parameters. This requires very expensive validation of subsystem functions related to the technology rules. For that reason, especially during cooperative validation, automated procedures are advisable. Such automated procedures are based on component ontology and taxonomy of function performed by the particular subsystem. Taxonomy is derived from phenomenological process models and boundary conditions, both based on technology rules. Component ontology ensures description of multidimensional relationship subsystems describing mutual hierarchy of products, locations, process, power supplies, and controls.

6   Concluding Remarks - Application for the Biotechnological Pilot-Plant

For over three years, a biotechnological pilot-plant has been operated continuously at the Faculty of Automatic Control, Electronics and Computer Science. It serves as a platform for investigations regarding activated sludge processes in aquatic environment. One of the processes that may be investigated is bioaugmentation of biomass for different purposes. Hence, depending on the goal of research, the structure of the pilot-plant is changed.

Therefore, operation and maintaining of this pilot-plant is a difficult task, and participation of external experts is crucial. The proposed structure of the control system evolved to the presented form, based on experiences, trial-and-error changes and constant development. It is still being developed.

Acknowledgements. This work was supported by the Polish Ministry of Scientific Research and Information Technology.

References

1. Wooldridge, M., Jennings, N.R.: Intelligent agents: theory and practice. The Knowledge Engineering Practice 10(2), 115–152 (1995)
2. Leduc, R.J., Lawford, M., Dai, P.: Hierarchical Interface-Based Supervisory Control of a Flexible Manufacturing System. IEEE Transactions on Control Systems Technology 14(4), 654–668 (2006)
3. Lynch, N., Segala, R., Vaandrager, F.: Hybrid I/O Automata. Inf. and Comp. 185, 105–157 (2003)

4. Guarino, N.: Understanding, building and using ontologies. Int. J. Human – Computer Studies 46, 293–310 (1997)
5. Roller, D., Eck, O., Dalakakis, S.: Integrated version and transaction group model for shared engineering databases. Data & Knowledge Engineering 42, 223–245 (2002)
6. He, F., Han, S.: A method and tool for human-human interaction and instant collaboration in CSCW-based CAD. Computers in Industry 57, 740–751 (2006)
7. Anumba, C.J., Ugwu, O.O., Newham, L., Thorpe, A.: Collaborative design of structures using intelligent agents. Automation in Construction 11, 89–103 (2002)
8. Korba, L., Song, R., Yee, G., Patrick, A.: Automated Social Network Analysis for Collaborative Work1. In: Luo, Y. (ed.) CDVE 2006. LNCS, vol. 4101, pp. 1–8. Springer, Heidelberg (2006)
9. Huang, G.: Web-based support for collaborative product design review. Comp. Ind. 48, 71–88 (2002)
10. Zhao, G., Deng, J., Shen, W.: Clover: an agent-based approach to system interoperability in cooperative design systems. Computers in Industry 45, 261–276 (2001)
11. Choinski, D., Nocon, W., Metzger, M.: Real-time control strategy for sequentially operated continuous WWTP. In: Proceedings of the 10-th IEEE International Conference on Methods and Models in Automation and Robotics, Miedzyzdroje, pp. 451–456. IEEE Computer Society Press, Los Alamitos (2005)
12. Davidsson, P., Wernstedt, F.: Software agents for bioprocess monitoring and control. Journal of Chemical Technology and Biotechnology 77, 761–766 (2002)
13. Choinski, D., Nocon, W., Metzger, M.: Multi-agent System for Hierarchical Control with Self-organising Database. In: The 1-st KES Symposium on Agent and Multi-Agent Systems – Technologies and Applications, Wroclaw, May 2007. Springer Lecture Notes in Computer Science (to appear, 2007)
14. Smith, R.G., Davis, R.: Frameworks for cooperation in distributed problem solving. IEEE Transactions on Systems, Man and Cybernetics 11(1) (1980)
15. Clarke, B.L.: Individuals and Points. Notre Dame J. of Formal Logic 26(1), 61–75 (1985)
16. Choinski, D., Nocon, W., Metzger, M.: Application of the Holonic Approach in Distributed Control Systems Design. In: Mařik, V., Vyatkin, V., Colombo, A. (eds.) HOLOMAS 2007. LNCS(LNAI), vol. 4659, pp. 257–268. Springer, Heidelberg (2007)
17. Shannon, C.E.: A Mathematical Theory of Communication. The Bell System Technical Journal 27, 379–423, 623–656 (1948)
18. Niven, R.K.: The constrained entropy and cross-entropy functions. Physica A 334, 444–458 (2004)
19. Chendeb, M., Khalil, M., Duchêne, J.: The use of wavelet packets for event detection. In: Proceedings of the 13th European Signal Conference EUSIPCO, 4-8 September 2005, Antalya, Turkey (2005)
20. Tsirlin, A.M.: Optimal Processes in Open Controllable Macrosystems. Automation and Remote Control 67(1), 132–147 (2006)

A Two-Level Programming Method for Collaborative Scheduling in Construction Supply Chain Management

Xiaolong Xue[1], Chengshuang Sun[1], Yaowu Wang[1], and Qiping Shen[2]

[1] School of Management, Harbin Institute of Technology, Harbin 150001, China
[2] Department of Building and Real Estate, The Hong Kong Polytechnic University,
Hung Hom, Kowloon, Hong Kong, China
xlxue@hit.edu.cn, chshsun@hit.edu.cn, ywwang@hit.edu.cn,
bsqpshen@polyu.edu.hk

Abstract. There are increasing requirements for collaborative scheduling (CS) in supply chain management (SCM). CS in construction supply chain (CSC), which involves multiple partners, such as general contractor, subcontractors, and material suppliers, can be seen as a multilevel decision-making system with hierarchical structure. Adopting the decomposition-coordination thought of large scale system theory and using the multilevel programming theory, a two-level programming model for CS decision making is established to find satisfactory solution for every partner in CSC. This model has the merit of paying attention to the maximization of profit or minimization of cost of all partners located at different decision-making level in CS process. The algorithm of this model is provided, which is combined with the first level programming adopting simulated annealing algorithm and second level programming using discrete search algorithm. Finally, an illustrative example of CS in a CSC is presented. The two-level programming method provides a new way to improve collaborative decision making in CSC. This research makes a contribution to the body of knowledge of scheduling.

Keywords: Collaborative scheduling, Two-level programming, Supply chain, Construction industry.

1 Introduction

Effective supply chain management (SCM) has become a potentially valuable way of securing competitive advantage and improving organizational performance since competition is no longer between organizations, but among supply chains. Applications of SCM in manufacturing environments have saved hundreds of millions of dollars while improving customer service [1]. With the increasing interests in applying SCM principle, which focuses on collaborative decision-making in business operations, to the construction industry [2], [3], collaborative scheduling (CS), one of the crucial operation problems in construction supply chain (CSC) management, has become an emerging managerial demands beyond traditional construction scheduling method from an independent view of a firm.

Y. Luo (Ed.): CDVE 2007, LNCS 4674, pp. 290–297, 2007.
© Springer-Verlag Berlin Heidelberg 2007

Scheduling is concerned with the optimal allocation of scare resources to activities over time. It is very attractive for researchers, with an impressive amount of literature as the result, because it's obvious practical importance. However, scheduling problems, in general, are really challenging from a computational point of view with the increasing complexity of decision-making environment. In the construction community, a lot of attempts have also been made to solve the construction scheduling problem, for example the work carried out by [4], [5], [6], [7]. Most of the above models or methods can generally be called approach to classical resource-constrained project scheduling problem [8].

CSC is a construction business system involving multiple stakeholders [9]. Considering the constraints of capability and resource, CSC is not governance structure to autonomously pursue maximum benefit in global chain domain from the perspective of principle-agent theory. Coordination mechanisms should be applied to the operational process of CSC to achieve global optimization, which is a result in centralized decision-making [10]. This research adopts CS as a coordination mechanism to improve collaborative decision-making performance.

CS problem in CSC is a typical multiple level programming problem. Adopting the decomposition-coordination thought of large scale hierarchical system theory, a two-level programming model for CS decision making is established to find satisfactory solution for each partner.

2 Hierarchical Decision-Making in CSC

CSC consists of multiple decision units involved in the construction process, such as client/owner, designer, GC, subcontractor, and suppliers. CSC system is typical hierarchical system in which general contractor is located at the upper level (leader) and subcontractor or supplier is located at lower level (follower), as shown in Figure 1. The hierarchical decision-making characteristics of CSC are described as follows.

(1) CSC is organized in a 'taper' structure with multiple decision units including general contractor (GC), subcontractor (designer also can be seen as one kind of subcontractor), suppliers and suppliers' supplier.

(2) GC, subcontractor and supplier make decision in turn, especially in project scheduling, but subcontractor and supplier have considerable decision power independently.

(3) Information is exchanged between difference levels in CSC. But the information from upper level to lower level has priority. For example, GC's information is prior to subcontractors. Subcontractors should abide by GC's 'order' if possible.

(4) Decision maker is located at higher level more interesting to long time goal. GC firstly makes decision, for example making master project scheduling, then subcontractor or supplier makes decision on the condition of complying with GC's decision.

(5) CSC has the global goal systems, for example, quality, cost, time, safety, and environment. The goals of whole decision makers should be coordinated.

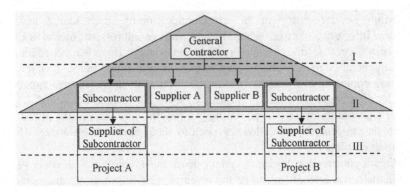

Fig. 1. Hierarchical decision-making structure of construction supply chain

3 Methodology

3.1 Hierarchical Two-Level Model of CS in CSC

In two-level programming problem, each decision maker in different level tries to optimize its own objective function(s) without considering the objective(s) of the other
partners, but the decision of each partner affects the objective value(s) of the other
partner as well as the decision space [11].

According to the principle of two-level programming technique, the two-level CS
model of CSC can be formulated as follows:

The upper level model (P1) is formulated as

$$P1 : \max F = \sum_{i=0}^{N} F_i(x^i, y^i)$$

$$\text{s.t.} \quad a^i \le x^i \le b^i$$
$$x^i \ge 0$$
$$i = 0, 1, 2, ..., N$$

(1)

where F is the total profit function of CSC, $F_i(x^i, y^i)$ is profit function of CSC
partner i, $i=0,1,2,...,N$, ($i=0$ stands for GC). x^i is the upper level (GC) decision variable and is a non-negative integer, and stands for the decision variable of construction
scheduling or procurement planning made by partner i, such as the duration of construction, the lead time of materials. $[a^i, b^i]$ is allowable change range of construction scheduling or procurement planning. y^i is the lower (subcontractor or material
supplier) decision variable and stands for subcontractor's construction duration or
material lead time of supplier.

The lower level model (P2) is formulated as

$$P2 : \max F_i(x^i, y^i) = \pi_i(x^i, y^i) - v_i(x^i, y^i)$$

$$\text{s.t.} \quad c^i \leq y^i \leq d^i$$

$$y^i \leq x^i \tag{2}$$

$$y^i \geq 0$$

$$i = 0,1,2,...,N$$

where $\pi_i(x^i, y^i)$ is the revenue function of partner i in CSC, and $v_i(x^i, y^i)$ is the cost function of partner i in CSC. Revenue function and cost function is nonlinear function, which is determined by upper level (P1) decision variable. They can be obtained through regression analysis of history data. $[c^i, d^i]$ is the change range of lower decision variable of partner i in CSC, which is determined by partner's resource constraints. $y^i \leq x^i$ denotes that lower level decision variable (construction duration or material lead time) is constrained by upper level decision variable.

3.2 Algorithm for CS in CSC

This research hybridizes simulated annealing and discrete search algorithm to find optimization solutions of the two-level programming model for CS. Simulated annealing algorithm is based on the principle of stochastic relaxation, which was introduced by Kirkpatrick et al [12] in the mid-1980s. Search algorithms intelligently guide the simulation model to a near-optimal solution. The process is initiated by the user entering the initial inputs for the design variable values. These values are sent to the simulation program. Running the program generates an output performance measure, which is evaluated by the search algorithm [13].

This paper adopts simulated annealing algorithm in upper level programming (P1) and discrete search algorithm in lower programming (P2) to solve the two-level programming model for CS. This hybrid algorithm starts from setting values of upper lever decision variables in P1, and selects an initial value x_0^i of in feasible region Ω.

And then put x_0^i into lower level programming (P2) and use discrete search algorithm to find optimal solutions. In turn, put optimal solutions into to upper levelP1 and use simulated annealing algorithm to find optimal solutions of P1. Through this replicating process find the global optimal solutions. The details of each algorithm are presented in appendix [12], [13], [14], [15].

4   A Briefly Calculated Example

The authors have applied the above model and algorithm to optimize a master construction scheduling and obtain a compromise and satisfactory construction scheduling to all partners. Suppose that a GC signed an EPC (Engineering, Procurement, and Construction) contract with an owner to construct an office building. The contract construction duration is 210 days and total price is $50 million. GC takes charge of procuring all materials, equipments and subcontracting. Considering the limits of paper pages of this conference, the detailed process is omitted. The initial master construction scheduling and the finally optimal construction scheduling are just shown in Figure 2. A note is that we suppose that start date of each subcontractor is decided by GC's lower-limit construction scheduling and cannot be changed in the final construction scheduling.

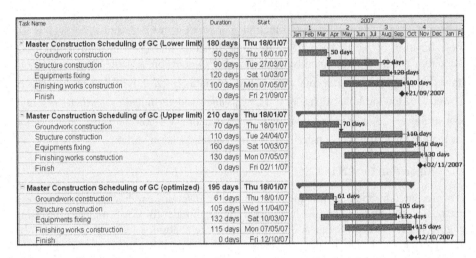

Fig. 2. Initial and optimal master construction scheduling

5   Conclusions

Collaborative scheduling (CS) has become an emerging managerial demand beyond traditional construction scheduling method from an independent view of a firm in CSC management environment. Adopting the decomposition-coordination thought of large scale system theory and using the multilevel programming theory, this paper provides a hybrid algorithm to find optimal solutions, which is a two-level nonlinear integer programming. Simulated annealing algorithm is applied at upper level programming (P1) and discrete search algorithm is used at lower level. The advantage of this hybrid method is that it can speed the research process in lower level and improve the efficiency to find effective approximate optimal solution.

Although there are many hypotheses when establishing model and applying algorithm, and also the example only focuses on a general master construction scheduling, the finally formed master construction scheduling provides a generally significant reference for GC when managing project, especially from strategy perspective. Also, the thought of two-level programming applying to CS in CSC management provides a valuable academic and practical reference for collaborative decision-making in business operation of other economic sectors, especially for project-based industry since most of hierarchical multiple level system can be seen the integration of many two-level subsystems.

Acknowledgement. The research was supported by the foundation under the grant of htcsr06t05 from National Center of Technology, Policy and Management, Harbin Institute of Technology. It was also funded by the Research Grants Council of the Hong Kong Special Administrative Region, China (PolyU 5252/05E and 5264/06E).

References

1. Arntzen, B.C., Brown, G.G., Harrison, T.P., Trafton, L.L.: Global supply chain management at Digital Equipment Corporation. Interfaces 25(1), 69–93 (1995)
2. London, K.A., Kenley, R.: An industrial organization economic supply chain approach for the construction industry: a review. Construction Management and Economics 19, 777–788 (2001)
3. O'Brien, W.J.: Construction supply-chain management: a vision for advanced coordination, costing, and control. In: NSF Berkeley-Stanford Construction Research Workshop, Stanford, California (1999)
4. Dzeng, R.J., Tommelein, I.D.: Product modelling to support case-based construction planning and scheduling. Automation in Construction 13(3), 341–360 (2004)
5. Chester, M., Hendrickson, C.: Cost impacts, scheduling impacts, and the claims process during construction. Journal of Construction Engineering and Management 131(1), 102–107 (2005)
6. Zhang, H., Tam, C.M., Li, H.: Multimode Project Scheduling Based on Particle Swarm Optimization. Computer-Aided Civil and Infrastructure Engineering 21(2), 93–103 (2006)
7. Hyari, K., El-Rayes, K.: Optimal planning and scheduling for repetitive construction projects. Journal of Management in Engineering 22(1), 11–19 (2006)
8. Zhu, G., Bard, J.F., Yu, G.A: Branch-and-Cut Procedure for the Multimode Resource-Constrained Project-Scheduling Problem. INFORMS Journal on Computing 18(3), 377–390 (2006)
9. Xue, X.L., Li, X.D., Shen, Q.P., Wang, Y.W.: An agent-based framework for supply chain coordination in construction. Automation in Construction 14(3), 413–430 (2005)
10. Sahin, F., Robinson, E.P.: Flow coordination and information sharing in supply chains: review, implications, and directions for future research. Decision Sciences 33(4), 505–536 (2002)
11. Roghanian, E., Sadjadi, S.J., Aryanezhad, M.B.: A probabilistic bi-level linear multi-objective programming problem to supply chain planning. Applied Mathematics and Computation (2006), doi:10.1016/j.amc.2006.10.032
12. Kirkpatrick, S., Gelatt, C.D., Cecchi, M.P.: Optimization by simulated annealing. Science 220, 671–680 (1983)
13. Lacksonen, T.: Empirical comparison of search algorithms for discrete event simulation. Computers & Industrial Engineering 40(1-2), 133–148 (2001)
14. Romeijn, H.E., Smith, R.L.: Simulated annealing for constrained global optimization. Journal of Global Optimization 5, 101–124 (1994)
15. Wu, Q., Xu, N.: A new method for solving a class of nonlinear integer programming problems. Control and Decision 12(2), 97–102, 108 (1997)

Appendix

Simulated Annealing Algorithm

Step 1. Set $x_0^i \in \Omega$. Let initial temperature $T_0 > 0$, integer $\sigma \geq 2$ and constant $\beta > 0$. Calculate $F(x_0^i, y^i)$. Given $X_0^i = x_0^i$, $x_{max}^i = x_0^i$, $F_{max} = F(x_0^i, y^i)$, and $k=0$.

Step 2. Get a random vector $\overline{Z}^k = (\overline{Z}_0^k, \overline{Z}_1^k, ..., \overline{Z}_N^k)$. Let

$$\overline{Z}_i^k = \text{sgn}(U_i) \cdot T_k \cdot \left(\frac{1}{|U_i|^\sigma} - 1 \right), \quad i=0,1,2,...,N \tag{1}$$

where $\text{sgn}(\cdot)$ is sign function and $U_0, U_1, ..., U_N$ is pair wise independence random variables on [-1, 1] uniform distribution.

Step 3. Using current replicated point X_k^i and random vector Z^k get a new feeler point I^k, where $I^k = X_k^i + Z^k$. And then calculate $F(I^k)$.

Step 4. If $I^k \in \Omega$, then turn to step 5, otherwise calculate

$$I^k = X_k^i + random\left[-\frac{1}{2}, \frac{1}{2} \right] \cdot Z^k \tag{2}$$

until $I^k \in \Omega$, where $random\left[-\frac{1}{2}, \frac{1}{2} \right]$ stands for a random number on uniform distribution $\left[-\frac{1}{2}, \frac{1}{2} \right]$. If $I^k \notin \Omega$ in limited replicated steps, then let $I^k = X_k^i$, and turn to step 5.

Step 5. Get a random number η on (0, 1) uniform distribution. Calculate acceptance probability of feeler point I^k, i.e.

$$P_a(I^k | X_k^i, T^k) = \min\left\{ 1, \exp\left[\frac{F(X_k^i) - F(I^k)}{\beta T_k} \right] \right\} \tag{3}$$

If $\eta \leq P_a(I^k | X_k^i, T_k)$, then let $X_{k+1}^i = I^k$ and $F(x_{k+1}^i, y^i) = F(I^k)$. Otherwise let $X_{k+1}^i = X_k^i$ and $F(x_{k+1}^i, y^i) = F(x_k^i)$.

Step 6. If $F(x_{k+1}^i, y^i) > F_{max}$, then let $X_{max}^i = X_{k+1}^i$ and $F_{max} = F(x_{k+1}^i, y^i)$.

Step 7. If meet the condition of ending replicating process, the algorithm is end, and X_{max}^i is seen as the approximate global optimal solution and F_{max} is the corresponding optimal value. Otherwise turn to step 8.

Step 8. According to the given temperature update function and get a new temperature T_{k+1},

$$T_{k+1} = \frac{T_0}{(k+1)^\sigma} \quad k=1,2,3,\ldots \tag{4}$$

Let $k=k+1$. Then turn step 2.

Discrete Search Algorithm

Definition

$$DA\varphi_{ij}(y^i) = \frac{\text{sgn}(A\varphi_{ij}^-(y^i)) - \text{sgn}(A\varphi_{ij}^+(y^i))\text{sgn}(A\varphi_{ij}^-(y^i))}{2} \cdot A\varphi_{ij}^-(y^i)$$

$$= \begin{cases} 0, & A\varphi_{ij}^+(y^i) \cdot A\varphi_{ij}^-(y^i) \geq 0 \\ A\varphi_{ij}^+(y^i), & other \end{cases} \tag{5}$$

$j=1, 2$

$$D_k^i = \max \left\{ D\varphi_{ij}(y^i), j=1,2 \right\} \overset{\Delta}{=} \left| D\varphi_{id}(y^i) \right|, d=1\,2 \tag{6}$$

The steps of discrete search algorithm are presented as follows:

Step 1. Given a discretionary start point y_0^i as integer vector, where precision is constrained to $0 < \varepsilon << 1$. Let $k=0$.

Step 2. Calculate $DA\varphi_i(y^i)$. If $\|DA\varphi_i(y^i)\| \leq \varepsilon$, then turn to step 5.

Step 3. According to equation (6), calculate D_k^i.

Step 4. Calculate t_d^k with constraint $\min_{t_d^k} \varphi_i \left(y_k^i - \left\langle t_d^k \cdot \frac{D\varphi_i(y_k^i)}{D_k^i} \right\rangle \right)$. If $t_d^k \neq 0$, then

let $y_{k+1}^i = y_k^i - \left\langle t_d^k \frac{D\varphi_i(y_k^i)}{D_k^i} \right\rangle$. Otherwise calculate t_d^k with con-

straint $\min_{t_d^k} \varphi_i \left(y_k^i - t_d^k \cdot \text{sgn}(D\varphi_i(y_k^i)) \right) \cdot e_d^i$. Let $y_{k+1}^i = y_k^i - t_d^k \text{sgn}(D\varphi_i(y_k^i)) \cdot e_d^i$ and $k=k+1$. Then turn to step 2.

Step 5. Test the optimal property of y_k^i. If find a point y_{k+1}^i excels y_k^i, then let $k=k+1$ and turn to step 2. Otherwise y_k^i is the optimal solution, and calculate end.

A Particular Approach to the Analysis of Manufacturing Process Rhythmicity

Edmundas Kazimieras Zavadskas, Valentinas Podvezko, Algirdas Anriuskevicius, and Leonas Ustinovichius

Vilnius Gediminas Technical University, Saulėtekio al. 11, LT-2040 Vilnius, Lithuania
Edmundas.Zavadskas@vtu.lt

Abstract. Steady pace (rhythmicity) of work is a relevant parameter reflecting the performance of production systems. A coefficient (index) of the steady pace is used for quantitative evaluation of a production system's performance. Various rhythmicity indices often yield different and even conflicting results. The application of logically consistent axioms to a set of indices allows us to identify indices accurately describing a steady pace of production. A case study of rhythmicity of suspended aluminium ceilings' manufacture at one of the enterprises over the period of 5 years divided into quarters and months is provided.

1 Introduction

Steady pace (rhythmicity) of work is a relevant parameter reflecting the performance of production systems. A coefficient (or index) of the steady pace is used for quantitative evaluation of production system performance. Several methods of determining rhythmicity indices can be found in the literature [1-5].

Various rhythmicity indices yield different and often conflicting estimates of the same statistical data [5]. Axiomatic methods used to check the effectiveness of the above indices help to determine how precise they are in assessing the actual pace of work.

2 The Requirements to Rhythmicity Indices and Axioms Used for Their Determination

The assignment is to compare the pace of work of a particular enterprise in different periods of time or of a team of workers or mechanisms. This problem consists in comparing the objects: $x = (x_1, ..., x_n); \ y = (y_1, ..., y_n)$,

where $x_i \geq 0, \quad y_i \geq 0, \quad (i = 1, ..., n), \quad \sum_{i=1}^{n} x_i = 1; \quad \sum_{i=1}^{n} y_i = 1$, where x_i, y_i indicate

products manufactured by the 1st and the 2nd manufacturers in the i-th subperiod.

The whole period is subdivided into n parts. This means that the preference order should be defined, i.e. a binary relationship R with the properties described below

Y. Luo (Ed.): CDVE 2007, LNCS 4674, pp. 298–300, 2007.
© Springer-Verlag Berlin Heidelberg 2007

should be established. For any pair x *and* y the following statements hold: 1) xRy or yRx, or both are valid; 2) it follows from xRy and yRz that xRz. The relationship R should be interpreted as 'more rhythmic than'.

It is clear that the preference order R should be established as follows: first, some more important indicators of enterprise performance should be defined, and the relationship between work rhythmicity and the variation of these indicators should be established. Second, R should be specified so that xRy, if the vector x correlates with a higher value of an indicator.

This method is, however, rather complicated and can hardly yield a 'universal' estimate of work rhythmicity. It may be specified by a set of two axioms.

Axiom 1. Let $(i_1, i_2,...,i_n)$ be an arbitrary rearrangement of numbers $(1, 2, ... , n)$. Then, any $(x_1, x_2, ... , x_n)$ and $(x_{i_1}, x_{i_2}, ..., x_{i_n})$ are related to the same pace of work. The axiom states that the pace of work of two enterprises is considered to be equally steady if the vectors of their production in the particular periods of the year (e.g. quarters) may be obtained by rearranging the components of the vectors corresponding to each enterprise.

If axiom 1 is assumed, then, any vector x may be reduced to the following form by rearrangement: $x_1 \leq x_2 \leq x_3 \leq ... \leq x_n$. In specifying the equalization procedure and maintaining the order of the components (EPMOC), it is assumed that x is obtained from y using EPMOC or $x=E(y)$. If for any pair i, j $(j > i)$ and $h > 0$, we get:

1) $x_k = y_k$ for $k = 1,2,...n$; $k \neq i, k \neq j$; 2) $x_i = y_i + h$; $x_j = y_j - h$,

where $h \leq 0{,}5(y_j - y_i)$, if $j = i+1$; $h \leq \min\{y_{i+1} - y_i; y_j - y_{j-1}\}$, if $j > i+1$.

Axiom 2. Let $x_1 \leq x_2 \leq x_3 \leq ... \leq x_n$ and $y_1 \leq y_2 \leq y_3 \leq ... \leq y_n$. If $x=E(y)$, then, xRy.

The following example describes the meaning of the axiom. Let work rhythmicity of a production system during a year be expressed in the following shares of the annual production falling to particular quarters: $y=(0{,}1; 0{,}1; 0{,}2; 0{,}6)$. Let us apply the equalization procedure $x=E(y)$ to $i=2$ and $j=3$; $h \leq 0{,}5(0{,}2-0{,}1)=0{,}05$. Then, $x=(0{,}1; 0{,}1+0{,}05; 0{,}2-0{,}05; 0{,}6)=(0{,}1; 0{,}15; 0{,}15; 0{,}6)$.

Evidently, the latter expression (x) may be assumed to describe more rhythmical work of the production system than the former (y).

A large number of various estimates $f(\cdot)$ satisfy the axioms 1 and 2.

It may be demonstrated that the following rhythmicity estimates satisfy the axioms 1 and 2:

1. Variability coefficient: $C = \sqrt{n \sum_{i=1}^{n} \left(x_i - \frac{1}{n} \right)^2}$,

2. Atkinson's coefficient [2]: $A = 1 - n^{\frac{\varepsilon}{1-\varepsilon}} \sum_{i=1}^{n} x_i^{\frac{1}{1-\varepsilon}}$, $\varepsilon > 1$,

3. Theil's index [1]: $T = \ln n + \sum_{i=1}^{n} x_i \ln x_i$.

It is clear that the values of expressions are not dependent on the rearrangement of components x_i of vector x. Therefore, the conditions of axiom 1 are satisfied. The calculations show that, when the values of vector x are changed according to axiom 2 to increase the rhythmicity of a manufacturing process, the values of C, A and T are decreased.

The Djini's coefficient offered in [2], $G = -1 - \dfrac{1}{n}(1 - 2\sum_{i=1}^{n} i \cdot x_i)$,

is clearly dependent on the positions of components x_i, and the conditions of axiom 1 are not satisfied. This conclusion is confirmed by actual calculations.

The evaluation of rhythmicity of suspended aluminium ceilings' manufacture at one of the enterprises in 2000-2004 conducted by the authors has confirmed that production rhythmicity can be assessed by verbal indices.

3 Conclusions

A unified *axiomatic approach to defining the requirements* to rhythmicity indices of manufacturing processes has been developed. It has been found that some currently used indices do not satisfy the suggested axioms. These axioms are satisfied by variability coefficients, Atkinson's coefficient and Theil's index, which may be recommended to determining the rhythmicity and smoothness of manufacturing processes.

The data obtained show that the most rhythmic manufacturing could be observed in 2002, when calculations were made on the monthly basis. The minimum values of the main characteristics C, A and T were found for that year. The calculation on the quarterly basis yielded the best results for 2000, when the values of the main characteristics were minimal. The results obtained in the present research can be successfully used as the initial data in pace analysis aimed work to identify factors preventing to achieve smooth and rhythmic manufacturing.

The developed approach may be used in simulating any manufacturing process. Special computer programs have been developed for this purpose.

References

1. Andruškevičius, A., Sadauskas, V., Tamošaitis, R., Zavadskas, E.K.: Raising steady pace of work of construction organizations. Vilnius, LitNIINTI (1989)
2. Djini, C.: Average values, Moscow, Statistics (1970)
3. Theil, H.: Economic forecasts and policy. Second revised edition, North-Holland publishing company, Amsterdam (1965)
4. Ustinovichius, L.: Determination of Efficiency of Investments in Construction. International Journal of Strategic Property Management 8(1), 25–44 (2004)
5. Zavadskas, E.K., Kaklauskas, A., Ginevičius, R.: Raising the effectiveness of construction projects. In: Proceedings of International Symposium "Modern Project Management", Saint Petersburg, pp. 337–339 (1995)

A Study Upon the Architectures of Multi-Agent Systems for Petroleum Supply Chain

Jiang Tian[1], Huaglory Tianfield[2], Juming Chen[1], and Guoqiang He[1]

[1] School of Management, University of Electronic Science and Technology of China
Chengdu, 610054, P.R. China
tianj@uestc.edu.cn
[2] School of Computing and Mathematical Sciences, Glasgow Caledonian University
70 Cowcaddens Road, Glasgow, G4 0BA, UK
h.tianfield@gcal.ac.uk

Abstract. In system development, the crucial step is the architecture design. This paper proposes a multi-agent based architecture for petroleum supply chain. The nested architecture can encapsulates the complex system, and number of supply chain partners can effectively interact through communications between agents.

Keywords: multi-agent system, architecture, petroleum supply chain.

1 Introduction

Generally, an agent is defined as a physical or logical entity with social ability, autonomy, reactivity and granularity degrees properties. An agent is an autonomous entity which contains all the required resources for its execution. An agent can allow encapsulation and communication of heterogeneous software components. An agent is also a software program, which performs a given function automatically or semi-automatically by communicating with other agents, programs or human agents [1].

Multi-agent system (MAS) can refer to systems composed of multiple (semi-) autonomous components. MAS can be viewed as systems in which large numbers of agents process tasks by interacting with each other. MAS may be envisaged as a software system, which is known as a set of actions that are carried out, and each action has an associated precondition [2, 3, 4].

MAS have wide applied in various domains, such as manufacturing, e-commerce and military domains. In the development of MAS, the main challenge is the architecture design of the system. Architectures decide not only what functions are provided by this system, but also how intelligent this system is, how this system adapts its environment, and how this system can integrate with the other systems.

The architecture of a system specifies its components, the relationship among components, and its mechanism for working. Architectures can describe the software system at a macroscopic level in terms of a manageable number of subsystem/components/modules inter-related through data and control dependencies [4, 5]. Architecture design involves the description of components, from which systems are built, interactions among those components, and patterns that guide their composition and constraints on those components.

Y. Luo (Ed.): CDVE 2007, LNCS 4674, pp. 301–303, 2007.

The conventional architectures of MAS can include control-oriented architecture, role-oriented architecture, and information-oriented architecture. The dominative architectures of MAS are role-oriented architecture which depends on the domain knowledge and thus they are lack of reuse and compatibility with other system. Control-oriented architecture not only matches human society, but also possesses the general characteristics of system architectures. Control-oriented architecture can conquer the large complex system. Information-oriented architecture only reflects the information interaction and communication so it is not completed [3, 4, 5].

2 A Multi-Agent Based Architecture for Petroleum Supply Chain

The petroleum supply chain is very complex which spans a long distributed supply tiers and involves many related industries. Usually, the petroleum supply chain comprises six tier, i.e., customer, petroleum products distribution, refining, transportation, and exploration and exploitation tiers [6]. Based on the complexities of petroleum supply chain, a nested architecture is proposed for petroleum supply chain, where the higher levels are nested by a cluster of agents, as depicted in Fig 1.

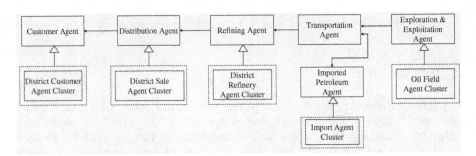

Fig. 1. The multi-agent based architecture for petroleum supply chain

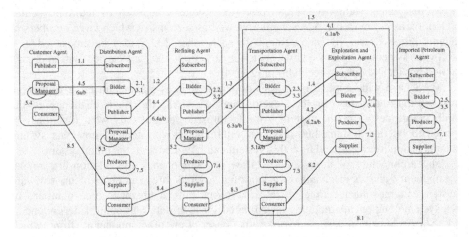

Fig. 2. Interactions between agents for petroleum supply chain

Interactions between agents in the system can be depicted as the interactions between these roles played by different agents, as shown in Fig 2, where arrows represent the speech acts of interactions between the agents, respectively.

3 Conclusion

In system development, the crucial step is the architecture design. Although there are numerous architectures, a nested MAS architecture is proposed for petroleum supply chain, which can encapsulate complexities of the system and reflect the mutual interactions between up-stream and down-stream partners in the supply chain.

Acknowledgement. This paper is supported by The Development and Research Center for Petroleum and Natural Gas of Sichuan Province (Grant No. SK06-11).

References

[1] Dumond, Y., Roche, C.: Formal specification of a multi-agent system architecture for manufacture: the contribution of the π–calculus. Journal of Materials Processing Technology 107, 209–215 (2000)

[2] Yamamoto, G., Nakamura, Y.: Architecture and performance evaluation of a massive multi-agent system. In: Proceedings of Autonomous Agents 1999, Seattle WA USA, pp. 319–325 (1999)

[3] Debenham, J.: A multi-agent architecture for process management accommodates unexpected performance. In: Proceedings of SAC, 2000, Como, Italy, pp. 15–28 (2000)

[4] Paderewski-Rodríguez, P., Rodrígez-Fortiz, M.J., Parets-Llorca, J.: An architecture for dynamic and evolving cooperative software agents. Computer Standards and Interfaces 25(3), 261–269 (2003)

[5] Kolp, M., Giorgini, P., Mylopoulos, J.: Organisational multi-agent architectures: A mobile robot example. In: Proceedings of AAMAS, Bologna, Italy, pp. 94–95 (2002)

[6] Tian, J., Tianfield, H.: Multi-agent modelling and simulation for petroleum supply chain. In: Huang, D.-S., Li, K., Irwin, G.W. (eds.) ICIC 2006. LNCS (LNAI), vol. 4114, pp. 496–501. Springer, Heidelberg (2006)

Multidisciplinary Knowledge Modeling and Cooperative Design for Automobile Development

Jie Hu and Yinghong Peng

Institute of Knowledge Based Engineering, School of Mechanical Engineering,
Shanghai Jiao Tong University, 800 Dongchuan Road, Shanghai, 200240, P.R. China
hujie@sjtu.edu.cn

Abstract. The paper presents a cooperative design approach based on multi-disciplinary knowledge modeling for automobile development. The design knowledge from multidisciplinary domain is obtained to establish multidisciplinary knowledge model. Then multidisciplinary cooperative design method allows multidisciplinary designer to synthetically coordinate and design considering multidisciplinary knowledge. The method described in this paper was used to develop knowledge driven multidisciplinary cooperative design system, which is applied to automobile development processing.

Keywords: Cooperative design, multidisciplinary, knowledge modeling, automobile.

1 Introduction

The need to remain competitive for survival in the current world market has led design and manufacturing firms to consider the low cost and high quality of product, moreover, a large-scale product design activity requires the cooperation of multi-disciplinary teams of individuals who are both geographically and organizationally distributed. Thus, designers should consider not only manufacturing and assembly process but also the requirement of multi-disciplinary teams. Many researchers paid attention to the modeling for multidisciplinary cooperative design. Sky et al. [1] proposed an integrated conceptual model of the product life cycle, and a virtual collaborative environment to support concurrent engineering. Xue and Xu [2] introduced a new approach for web-based collaborative concurrent design. Li [3] presented a satisfaction-driven, multifunctional team approach with application to concurrent product design. Lee et al. [4] presented the approach that combines the current feature-based modeling technique with distributed computing and communication technology for collaborative design activities over the network.

2 Multidisciplinary Knowledge Model and Cooperative Design

The overall performance of a complex product generally depends on a number of specifications distributed in various disciplines, such as mechanics, cybernetics,

Y. Luo (Ed.): CDVE 2007, LNCS 4674, pp. 304–306, 2007.
© Springer-Verlag Berlin Heidelberg 2007

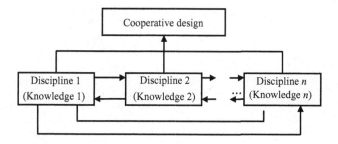

Fig. 1. Knowledge flow between multiple disciplines

dynamics and so forth. In a typical multidisciplinary optimization problem, the information flow between multiple disciplines could be represented by Fig. 1.

The model for multidisciplinary cooperative design based on knowledge network is formulated as

Given p and the tolerance of x and p: $t_{x_1}, t_{x_2}, t_{p_1}, t_{p_2}$, find x

$$
\begin{aligned}
&\min \ \varphi(x,p) = \sum_{i=1}^{q} w_i \left[\alpha \frac{\mu_{y_i}}{\mu_i^*} - (1-\alpha) \frac{\sigma_{y_i}}{\sigma_i^*} \right] \\
&\text{s.t.} \quad g_i(x,p) = 0, \ i = 1, \cdots, l \\
&\quad h_{j,\text{new}}(x,p) = h_j + \sum_{k=1}^{n} \left| \frac{\partial h_j}{\partial x_k} \right|_x \cdot \Delta x_k + \sum_{k=1}^{s} \left| \frac{\partial h_j}{\partial p_k} \right|_x \cdot \Delta p_k \le 0, \ j = 1, \cdots, m \\
&\quad x \in \left[x^L, x^U \right]
\end{aligned}
\tag{1}
$$

where $x = \{x_1, \cdots, x_n\}$ is a vector of design variables and $p = \{p_1, \cdots, p_s\}$ is a vector of design parameters whose values are fixed as a part of the problem specifications. $[x^L, x^U]$ are consistent intervals. $t_{x_1}, t_{x_2}, t_{p_1}, t_{p_2}$ are tolerance of design variables and design parameters respectively. $y = y(x,p)$ is a vector of the system performance. μ_y, σ_y are the mean value and the standard deviation of y respectively. μ^*, σ^* are the expected mean value and the expected standard deviation. α is weight factor. $g_i(x,p)$ and $h_{j,\text{new}}(x,p)$ are constraints, where $\Delta x = t_{x_1} - t_{x_2}$, $\Delta p = t_{p_1} - t_{p_2}$.

The above multidisciplinary cooperative design model can be solved by Genetic Algorithm.

3 An Example of Automotive Engine Design

Following is an example of automotive engine design to illustrate the method to multidisciplinary cooperative design. There are four disciplinary knowledge models: 1) design knowledge model from assembly; 2) Design knowledge model from

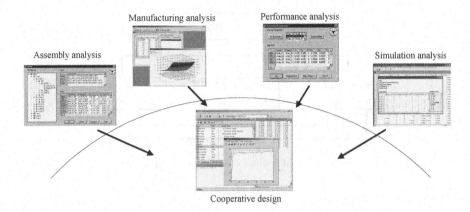

Fig. 2. Multidisciplinary design process for automotive engine design

manufacturing cost; 3) Design knowledge model from performance; 4) Design knowledge model from simulation. The multidisciplinary design process is shown in Fig. 2.

4 Conclusions

This paper presents an approach based on knowledge network to support multidisciplinary cooperative design for automotive engine design. First, the method of knowledge network-based multidisciplinary cooperative modeling is presented. Then, the illustration of automotive engine design, which include design knowledge model from assembly, manufacturing cost, performance and simulation, is presented to familiarize the reader with the application of the new method.

Acknowledgments. This research is supported by the National Natural Science Foundation of China (No. 50575142 and 60304015) and the Shanghai Committee of Science and Technology (No. 055107048 and 04ZR14081).

References

1. Sky, R.W.E., Buchal, R.O.: Modeling and implementing concurrent engineering in a virtual collaborative environment. Concurrent Engineering Research and Applications 7, 279–289 (1999)
2. Xue, D., Xu, Y.: Web-based distributed system and database modeling for concurrent design. In: Proceedings of the ASME Design Engineering Technical Conference, vol. 1, pp. 547–556 (2001)
3. Li, C., Li, S.: Modeling concurrent product design: A multifunctional team approach. Concurrent Engineering Research and Applications 8, 183–198 (2000)
4. Lee, J.Y.: A Web-enabled approach to feature-based modeling in a distributed and collaborative design environment. Concurrent Engineering 1, 74–87 (2001)

Integrating Domain Dependent Tools in Artificial Bone Scaffolds Design

Yanen Wang[1,2], Shengmin Wei[1], Xiutian Yan[2], and Qingfeng Zeng[2,3]

[1] Mechatronic Engineering School, Northwestern Polytechnical University,
Xi'an, China, 710072
[2] Department of Design, Manufacture and Engineering Management,
The University of Strathclyde, Glasgow, UK, G1 1XJ
[3] Material School, Northwestern Polytechnical University, Xi'an, China, 710072
yanen.wang@strath.ac.uk

Abstract. This paper proposes a systematic approach to integrate domain-dependent design tools in artificial bone scaffolds process. Integrated solution of CAD modelling and properly analysis of biomedicine knowledge are utilized to design complicated bone scaffolds. FEA and CFD are comprehensively analyzed for the mechanical and internal micro circulation properties. A case study of a successful artificial bone scaffolds model demonstrates that the cooperative design methodology can facilitate the design in the multi-physics domain substantially.

Keywords: Integration, domain dependent tools, artificial bone scaffolds.

1 Introduction

Advances in biomaterials science, computer aided engineering techniques, applied mechanics, physics, and biomedicine offered new opportunities for bone tissue engineering. Bone scaffolds design has been developed separately by Computer Aided Design (CAD), Finite Element Analysis (FEA), Computational Fluid Dynamics (CFD) and Material Computation (MC). Such a separation makes it cumbersome and complex for designers to exchange the necessary information in the design process. CAD tools provide bone scaffolds conceptual models with special internal microstructure. Most researchers who want to know biocompatible, mechanical properties of those models must go through the FEA and CFD tools[1].

In 1892, Wolff first demonstrated that relationship between bone cells growth ratio and the mechanical strength. Since then, many biological and physical scientists illustrate that interstitial fluid flow stimulates bone cells diffusion from piezoelectricity, and investigated the steaming potential, mechanical strain and fluid shear stress[2-4]. Researchers also indicated that complex and interconnected microstructure in natural bone can maintain the blood circulation, metabolism, nutrition transfer and bone's growth and reconstruction[5]. Based on these studies, the diameter of micro holes in current artificial bone scaffolds is set to be between 200 µm to 800 µm and micro holes of these sizes facilitate the micro circulation of bone nutrients in artificial bone scaffolds. These mechanical properties have guided the

Y. Luo (Ed.): CDVE 2007, LNCS 4674, pp. 307–314, 2007.

design of artificial bone structures, enable the construction of biomimetic internal structure of any artificial bones and facilitate the flow of the nutrient fluid and the growth of natural bones.

Due to continuing development of new bioactive material, new biodegradable three-dimensional porous scaffolds have now been fabricated to cure bone disease and they have gained great success in recent years. Present study revealed the potential of biomimetic constructs play critical role in osteoinduction. Researchers have also found that Bone Morphogenetic Protein (BMP) and Growth Factors (GF) can induce osteoblast-like cells to adhere to scaffolds.

Dawn of a new era of bioactive bone scaffolds is approaching. This is due to the fact that biodegrade bioactive artificial bone scaffolds can now be possibly developed by using advanced techniques such as CAD, FEA, CFD and MC. In the past, MC design, CAD modelling, FEA and CFD of artificial bone scaffolds are generally regarded as separate domains of interest and speciality in CAD, Computer Aided Engineering (CAE) and biomaterial communities. Such a separation of CAD, FEA, CFD and MC of bone scaffolds design makes it cumbersome and complex for designers to exchange the necessary information in the entire design process. Therefore, applications in all domains are impeded and consequently the numbers of biocompatible artificial bone scaffolds are limited.

This paper describes a systematic approach to integrate these domain-dependent design tools in supporting the design and evolution of artificial bone scaffolds in research at the University of Strathclyde and the Northwestern Polytechnical University (NPU). The complex and bio-oriented geometries of bone scaffolds and internal microstructures are modelled in CAD tools Pro/E and UG and relevant data from MC and CAD tools is transferred to FEA software system ANSYS and CFD system Fluent for design evaluation and validation of mechanical and fluid dynamic prosperities. A successful artificial bone scaffold model case study demonstrated that this collaborative design method involved multidisciplinary can facilitate the design of multi-physics domain in a systematic plan.

2 Motivation and Integration Model

Developing a good biocompatible artificial bone scaffolds should abide by the strict requirements and rules from clinicians and material scientists. The conflicting requirements for strong, yet porous bio-material structures always pose challenges for researchers. The important characteristics of these structure lies in the material selection, determination of pore sizes and suitable manufacturing methods and techniques for a designed structure. Research work is in fluid dynamics as well. These work[6, 7] showed partially satisfactory results in their work, but it is clear that a holistic design approach is needed to design scaffolds from system points of view. The deficiency of current design approach and opportunity to integrate the design tools available from multi-disciplines motivated this research to develop a holistic design and research approach. The research aims to investigate and generate a framework to support the collaboration of multidisciplinary design team members in their design and development of a suitable artificial bone scaffold structures.

2.1 Motivation of Integration of Computer Aided Techniques for Bone Scaffolds

Critical to bone tissue researchers are the development of new scaffolds structure with new biomaterials to improve the characteristics of bone scaffolds: namely, strength, porosity, biodegradability and compatibility with patients. The current research focuses on the first two characteristics by developing complex porous structure. Such the aforementioned complex and interconnected bone scaffolds microstructure plays critical roles in ensuring the blood circulation and nutrition transfer to allow the normal growth and reconstruction natural bone. Structural and biological analyses by scanning samples using an electron microscopy revealed that high porosity and big pore diameter of an artificial bone will facilitate nutrient, blood and oxygen flow in the artificial bone scaffolds. The Haversian and Volkman's canals have showed to be good connection style in designing internal micro structure of artificial bone scaffolds. Based on this, an ideal artificial bone scaffolds microstructure should have two micro circulation systems in addition to the biomimetic microstructure.

Current CAD tools allow designers to create the internal microstructure in the artificial bone scaffolds, but most of them don't support modelling of mechanical, nutrient fluid dynamics properties and some biochemical behaviour of bone scaffolds. The modelling of these prosperities requires further research. Most of these discussed CAD modelling methods provide capabilities in representing diverse bone scaffolds with proper CAD models and offering intuitive modelling tools for scaffolds construction, visualization and manipulation. However, with these CAD tools only, the researchers are still uncertain whether the designed scaffolds can really meet the requirements on structural, fluid and biological properties. In order to describing these properties, the FEA and CFD tools have been employed in this research to demonstrate an integrated and the additional support in design and evaluating some scaffold concepts. The bone scaffolds' strength, strain and stress could be properly generated and analysed by FEA software. Transportation of nutrients, blood and metabolize products are designed to flow through micro channels. The interstitial fluid flow in micro-holes of artificial bone scaffolds[8] can be visualized analyzed by CFD tools. Using the biological vitro or inside organisms' experiments to validate these fluid shear stress, piezoelectricity, and steaming potential to stimulate osteoblast-like cells growth. From the above of brief review, it can be seen that CAD modelling and FEA/CFD of artificial bone scaffolds are generally regarded as separate domains of interest in CAD, CAE and CFD communities. They do possess the potential to produce an integrated support for scaffold design and evaluation.

Motivated to overcome the aforementioned limitations and span the gap between CAD modelling and FEA/CFD of artificial bone scaffolds, this paper presents a systematic approach to integrate these independent tools in artificial bone scaffolds research. The schematic structure is established on a reference model of collaborating to research artificial bone scaffolds at the both Universities in UK and China[9].

2.2 Integrated CAD, FEA, CFD Model

Different from traditional separated view of the MC, CAD, and FEA/CFD of engineering design process. The optimization tools, FEA and CFD, should be used to

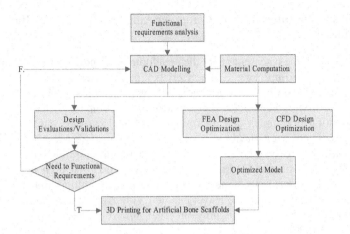

Fig. 1. A collaborative model to support an integrated design of artificial bone scaffolds using MC, CAD, and FEA/CFD

integrate the MC and CAD design activities. Fig. 1 demonstrates the entire integrated procedures. This cooperative conceptual design research methodology is furthered on the similar methodology in multidisciplinary developing 3D printer nozzle at both institutions. Readers can find all details about methodological models in [9].

In order to integrate domain dependent design tools, a specification of requirements derived from concurrent engineering principles and best practices is essential. It is therefore necessary to establish a systematic methodology to integrate the domain design tools based on four models described in[9]: integration framework reference model, efficiency collaborative activities model, technical system model, and multidisciplinary collaborative information model. Here, the artificial bone scaffolds development was a good example to the application of cooperative and integrated domain design tools approach in material, biomechanics structure, and fluid dynamics domains. The design and manufacture of such scaffolds presents challenge for the collaboration partners distributed in China and UK. At the same time, engineers and designers come from different background with different expertise and vocabulary. It is therefore a big and important task on developing a collaborative support to facilitate the data exchange and communication among domain dependent design users and tools for artificial bone scaffolds.

3   Systematic Integration for Artificial Bone Scaffolds

For multidisciplinary research, it is common but complex for different domains users to use various special tools. So at the beginning of project, it is necessary to define the four integrated models[9] and clarify the data communication standard or format about different technical tools. A design and fabrication research project for artificial bones is supported and cooperated by specialists in MC, Biomedicine, CAD, FEA, and CFD etc.. The cooperative methodology was represented in section 3.1 and all details techniques followed it. Section 3.2 focus on MC computing synthetic reaction equation about Hydroxaptite (HAP) powder and designing HAP micro spheres for controlling micro holes in artificial bone scaffolds. The results will export to expert database and store for FEA/CFD and CAD tools. Section 3.3 describes the proposed scheme for the integrated CAD modelling of bone scaffolds shape and micro channels for transporting blood, nutrient fluid and oxygen. MC and CAD data communication with FEA/CFD are also illustrated. The comprehensive mechanical and fluent properties of porous bone sample are discussed in section 3.4.

3.1 The Methodology for Cooperation in Artificial Bone Scaffolds Design

During the research process of artificial bone scaffolds, MC models of these scaffolds are constructed with the MC designer developed by authors. The material data about HAP micro spheres is exported into this bespoke special database. The geometries of Haversian channels developed in Pro/E are converted into a neutral file and then exported to Fluent, commercial fluid dynamics software. The Gambit of Fluent interprets the geometric data and converts neutral format file into Fluent computation module. It is then used to simulate the behaviour of nutrient fluid and the simulation results can be used to determine which conceptual model a designer should use and be exported into FEA module to compute the stress and strain. In order to get more suitable micro structure, the modified model will be redesigned by the CAD modeller. CFD and FEA systems are used to continue to validate the modified design until all results are accepted by the designer. Fig.2. illustrates those finite element analyses supporting the collaboration of a CAD based designer, material scientist, and analyst.

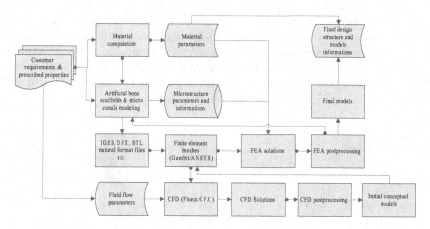

Fig. 2. The mechanism of integrated MC, CAD and CFD/FEA of artificial bone scaffolds

3.2 Material Computation Design HAP Micro Spheres

The biomaterial play important role in artificial bone scaffolds research process, so the purity of HAP will be calculated by special material computations software developed by the authors at Department of Design, Manufacture & Engineering

Management, University of Strathclyde. The chemical reaction equation was provided by thermodynamic calculations as follows:

$$5Ca(OH)_2 + 3H_3PO_4 \rightarrow Ca_5(PO_4)_3OH + 9H_2O \qquad (1)$$

The high purity HAP biomaterial has gotten through chemical synthesis method under 85^0C water bath. In order to fabricating 3D artificial bone scaffolds and controlling the pore size and porosity, four mass patterns have been proposed shown as Fig. 3 from MC work team at Material Engineering School, NPU. And all material parameters exported to a shared database for FEA and CFD.

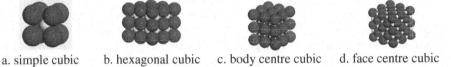

a. simple cubic   b. hexagonal cubic   c. body centre cubic   d. face centre cubic

Fig. 3. Hydroxyaptite micro sphere mass pattern. This shows four different mass patterns.

3.3 Integrated CAD Modelling of Micro Channels in Artificial Bone Scaffolds

CAD modelling primarily deals with representing the geometry and topology of artificial bone scaffolds with computer models. There have been a lot of conceptual models developed by the CAD designers for this research as shown in Fig. 4. All models have been generated on CAD platform. These can then be passed to Fluent and ANSYS for further analyses. In order to providing models with same topological structure but different Haversian systems' parameters for fluid dynamic and mechanical analyses. The authors used C++ language to develop a software module for designing micro channels on Pro/E platform collaborative the PDM technique. All computer models have be converted to those standard file formats (e.g. DXF, IGES or STL), and it is important to ensure that finite element software systems have the correct translators and interface for standard data file formats.

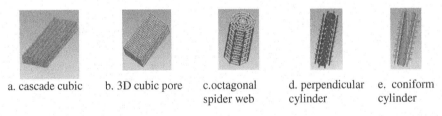

a. cascade cubic   b. 3D cubic pore   c.octagonal spider web   d. perpendicular cylinder   e. coniform cylinder

Fig. 4. Haversian systems' five current conceptual models

3.4 Integrated CFD/CAE of Artificial Bone Scaffolds

This section further presents the methodologies and results of using the finite element method to analysis these bone scaffolds under multi-physics and multi-phase conditions. It is difficult for current artificial bone scaffolds to transport the nutrient, blood and oxygen into the interior of scaffolds, owing to its variable pore sizes, low porosity, low pore interconnectivity based on the current manufacture techniques. Therefore, fluid flow analysis is a key part to design internal structure of bone scaffolds. With support from Fluent dynamics analysis, a biologists can be supported in collaboration with a fluid analyst to choose the most suitable Haversian micro channels shown as figure 5.

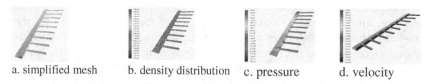

| a. simplified mesh | b. density distribution | c. pressure | d. velocity |

Fig. 5. multi-phase fluid flow analysis contours based on 1/16 simplified model of 75^0 angle between Haversian and Volkman micro-channels

The mechanical properties simulation analysis ascertains the Haversian and Volkman's channels structure parameters via FEA. Exception for substitute's biocompatibility, stress and strain should be similar to the natural bone. Because if the substitute toughness is stronger than natural bone, the bone closed to graft scaffolds will be weak and easily cause fracture for natural bone's automatic biodegradation. A general outline of all technology integration is given on section 3.1 and Fig. 2. Readers can also refer to literature 9 providing methodology details.

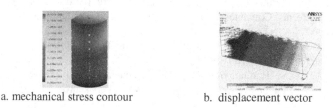

| a. mechanical stress contour | b. displacement vector |

Fig. 6. Mechanical analysis contour and vectors based on 1/4 artificial bone simplified model with 75^0 angle Haversian system

4   Conclusion

In this paper, a systematic approach of integrating domain dependent design tools to help designers, material scientists, analysts and medical researcher to improve the quality of artificial bone scaffolds. The integrating methodology is based on three partial models developed[9] in the research, namely the activity model, technical system model, and the information model. The biomaterial research work are carried out by MC and formed into micro spheres. All material information and geometry parameters are transferred to bone scaffolds designers. The designed geometries and internal microstructure are represented by CAD models and further exported to a CFD and an FEA tool for design evaluation and validation. By integrating such domain-dependent design tools, artificial bone scaffolds, which are difficult to design using the traditional methodology, can be intuitively modelled and analyzed; the designer's intention can be properly captured.

Five different Haversian micro channels have been modelled and compared in terms of fluid flow property, multi-phase density distribution, and pressure distribution. The proposed model proves to have good and more uniform shear stress distribution. This design based on Haversian system was then modelled and developed into artificial bone scaffolds. The Von Mises stress value can then be revalidated. Through these examples, one can clearly see the benefits of the proposed methodologies with possibilities for transferring and feeding back information were deployed to support the main research objectives which are to rapidly design and analyse a new solution and increase the flexibility of the approach. Results show that such a solution can take advantage of the designer's experiences in the design process and provide a mechanism to exploit existing potential for increasing the quality of new multidisciplinary product design and manufacturing.

Acknowledgments. The authors would like to acknowledge of the support from an Asia-Link project, funded by the European Commission with a contract number: ASI/B7-301/98/679-09 and Doctorate Foundation of Northwestern Polytechnical University (CX200509).

References

1. Rifai, S.M., et al.: Automotive design applications of fluid flow simulation on parallel computing platforms. Computer Methods in Applied Mechanics and Engineering 184(2-4), 449–466 (2000)
2. Gunaratne, G.H., et al.: Model for Bone Strength and Osteoporotic Fractures. Physical Review Letters 88(6), 068101-1-068101-4 (2002)
3. Rubin, C., Judex, S., Hadjiargyrou, M.: Skeletal adaptation to mechanical stimuli in the absence of formation or resorption of bone. Musculoskel Neuron Interact 2(3), 264–267 (2002)
4. Thomas, G.P., Haj, A.J.E.: Bone Marrow Stromal Cells are Load Responsive. Vitro. Calcified Tissue International 58(2), 101–108 (1996)
5. Werner, J., et al.: Mechanical properties and in vitro cell compatibility of hydroxyapatite ceramics with graded pore structure. Biomaterials 23(21), 4285–4294 (2002)
6. Sigmund, O.: Design of multiphysics actuators using topology optimization - Part I: One-material structures. Computer Methods in Applied Mechanics and Engineering 190(49-50), 6577–6604 (2001)
7. Huang, J., et al.: Bi-objective optimization design of functionally gradient materials. Materials & Design 23(7), 657–666 (2002)
8. Guest, J.K., Prevost, J.H.: Optimizing multifunctional materials: Design of microstructures for maximized stiffness and fluid permeability. International Journal of Solids and Structures 43(22-23), 7028–7047 (2006)
9. Wang, Y.E., et al.: Integration of collaborative design and process planning for artificial bone scaffold 3D printer nozzle. Cooperative Design, Visualization, and Engineering, Proceedings pp. 132–140 (2000)

An Integrated Multiplatform Travel Service System

Antoni Bibiloni, Yuhua Luo, Miquel Mascaró, and Pere A. Palmer

University of Balearic Islands, 07122, Palma de Mallorca, Spain
{toni.bibiloni,dmilyu0,mascport,pere.palmer}@uib.es

Abstract. Recently an integrated multiplatform system aiming at offering travel service over several communication channels is under development. A set of cooperating systems in completely different platforms will work together to provide integrated services to the clients anywhere and anytime. The structure, communication environment, some special issues and implementation of the system are discussed in the paper.

Keywords: cooperative applications, integrated services.

1 Introduction

As an important industry, tourism has been growing rapidly. The demand of the clients becomes more and more specific while the competition of this sector is getting higher. A better service providing all the possible resources to the clients anytime and anywhere is becoming an urgent need for the clients and the service providers.

On the other hand, travel resources are complicated to be integrated and provided to the clients due to a series of challenges. The challenges from a global view include the cross-industry needs and relationships, lack of general-purpose XML infrastructure, the key players acting individually, the need of legacy standards organizations, conflicts between the service speed and the range of resources, and the distance among service suppliers etc. From a technical point of view, the services so far have been limited to certain traditional channels. The Open Travel Alliance white paper [6] describes the former situation where each travel supply had only a single distribution channel, the travel agency and its Global Distribution System. To provide a solution to all these challenges, large scale cooperative effort becomes necessary. The Topshop project is consequence of the efforts of some travel companies and Spanish Government agencies, to join all the travel information services in a cooperating multiplatform system.

The objective of the project is to develop a complete integrated multiplatform system to offer the travel resources and personal travel packages to the clients in a comfortable, simple and efficient way. The basic solution lies on both sides of the integration of all the available travel resources and facilitating the service to the clients.

From the resource supply side, the project combines all the existing travel resources of the different platforms into an integral system that can manage all the user transactions in real time. The XML standard of the *OpenTravel* Alliance is used

Y. Luo (Ed.): CDVE 2007, LNCS 4674, pp. 315–322, 2007.
© Springer-Verlag Berlin Heidelberg 2007

to obtain multi-industrial shared information. The project integrates all the different systems into a single platform to make the cooperation possible for different environments and companies. The resource providers can therefore achieve their business goal to offer all the available resources anytime and anywhere the clients need.

On the service side to the clients, two major efforts have been made. The first is to extend the service to much more channels. The system covers the most basic and typical human communication platforms currently available: the mobile phone, personal computer via TCP-IP, interactive TV, and www support. The second is to improve the way to serve the final clients using the dynamic packaging scheme. Instead of serving the client item by item, the system will help the clients to make their own travel package according to their preferences and economical constraints. The clients can reserve and pay flights, cruisers, cars, hotels, etc. in one package.

The following will describe the designed solutions on both the resource supply side and the client service side. Some implementation issues on mobile phone and DTT platforms will also be discussed.

2   The System Structure

The system structure can be seen in and Fig. 1 and Fig. 2. As we can see, it is a centralized server based system. The whole system is built on top of a TCP/IP network as indicated in Fig. 3.

The centralized server (Fig. 2) receives travel resources from all related service providers and integrates it into a uniform, easy to retrieve format. Such resources

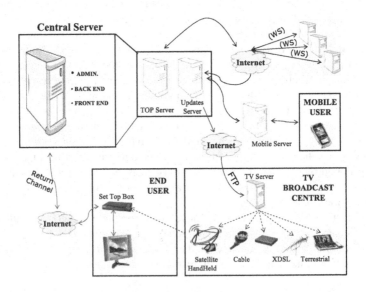

Fig. 1. The system structure

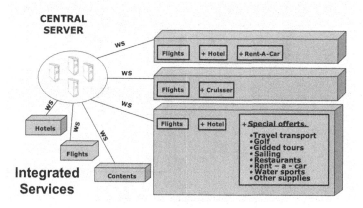

Fig. 2. The central server structure

include hotels, flights, car rentals, cruses and other services worldwide. Whenever a client requests travel resources, the server will use the dynamic packaging scheme to produce proper travel packages dynamically for the client.

The server application and all the final service terminals are built on top of the TCP/IP network.

As indicated in Fig. 3 the final service terminals include all the currently available human machine communication platforms: tourist agency workstations, computers, individual final client personal computers, lap-tops, mobile phones and a new type of terminal, the digital home and mobile television receiver.

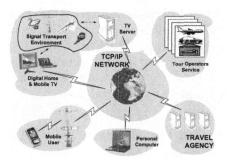

Fig. 3. The communication environment

3 The Dynamic Packaging Scheme

Whenever a client wants to request a travel service, they can look for whatever terminal that has the network coverage at that location, mobile phone, or a TV with interactive service and connect to the service center. The transport channel will drive the transactions to the *Dynamic Packaging Service*.

The *Dynamic Packaging Service* is a system that integrates all the travel offers of all the available agencies and resource providers in a single access point (see Fig. 4).

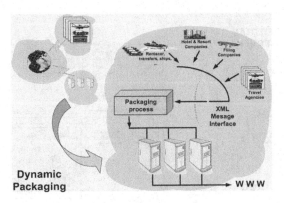

Fig. 4. The dynamic packaging scheme

The users can make their own trip package according to their preferences and economical constraints.

The implementation of the dynamic packaging lies on the successful XML representation of the information coming from all travel resource providers. The *OpenTravel* Alliance has been working on an XML specification (tags, DTDs, infrastructure etc.) for the use across the widely-defined travel industry. Several political, organizational, and technical challenges were overcome. Working with over 100 member organizations, airlines, hotel chains, travel agencies, Global Distribution Systems, software companies, companies with large numbers of 'managed' travelers, etc the dynamic packaging now becomes available. With this as a base, the project implements the dynamic packaging into DTT–MHP platform. When the system receives a client's request, it will choose the services the client selected. In the case of a multiple-service request, it will apply pre-compiled business rules to choose the available suppliers. It then decides on the possibility of packaging the specific services as an integrated package and sells to the client as a single unit. The result will be offered in XML, without taking the presentation layer into account. Services will be made available through all the media in real-time.

4   The DTT Integrated Travel Service Sell-Out Sub-system

DTVi[1] is a feature of Digital Television with interactive possibilities that allows viewers to interact with an advertisement, program or service on their television set via a set-top box (STB) and remote control. Digital interactive TV systems use the familiar remote control and potentially to reach a wider audience than the Internet. Companies gain access to a wider audience, covering all age groups, socio-economic categories and individuals who are uncomfortable using PC technology or do not have access to the Internet. Television is a more trusted source than the Internet because people are familiar with it and feel that TV is still subject to government regulation.

---

[1] Digital Interactive TV (DTVi).

Of course MHP applications can be viewed and information possessed with STB's that don't include a return channel, but everything remains static and monologue as with the analogue television's teletext. A return channel is a necessity in order to create an interaction between the digital television set and the spectator. The return path is used to establish a two-way communication link back to the service provider.

The Return channel in this project will be used to accept the user's choices of application navigation and also personal details to be sent back to providers. Not all STB's come with return channels but for the purpose and the full effects of the TOPshop it will be necessary for the spectator to have one installed. There is the possibility of two types of TOPshop application: STB with return channel and without it.

For digital television sets without a return channel, the idea is to display a phone number and package code to the viewer so that once they have selected and mounted their chosen package holiday, they can call the displayed number and make the reservation by phone with the travel agency or intermediary tour operator. However, in the case that the user's digital television set has a return channel, this is where the interactive experience with the TOPshop becomes complete through the possibility or completing reservations and purchasing the selected holiday packages.

This project will implement and is implementing the use of return channel which can be made possible through a number of ways including: ASDL, modem and Ethernet. The target STB receivers will obviously need to come with return channel that has the necessary ASDL, Modem and Ethernet interfaces implemented.

The return channel runs on the same basic principal as that of the internet, receiving information through one channel and sending information through another.

As a fist take of contact with the DTT environment an experimental application to sell travel cruiser was developed called LOGITRAVEL. With this application users can see the especial offers in pleasure cruisers and make reservations and pay travel packages. Using LOGITRAVEL, users can see in an interactive mode the aspect of the ship berths, the different prices of the resources, the cruiser travel route and the services on the cruiser.

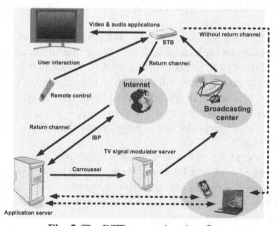

Fig. 5. The DTT transaction data flow

The contents of the telecast as well as the available resources get up-to-date periodically, being modified according to the information provided by the dynamic packaging. The modifications make changes in the carrousel of the TV emission and come to effect periodically (approximately each 30 minutes), not to count the service speed of TV's broadcasting system. Using the DTT input interface (the TV remote control) users can make the reservation and pay for it. If client has a return channel at in the STB he can confirm and pay his reservation on line. System offers the users without a return channel a code to confirm and pay his reservation via internet or via SMS by mobile phone channel. All transactions are managed concurrently in a real time by the agency server and data updates in a dynamic packaging system are made. The data transaction flow of the sub-system can be seen in Fig. 5.

5   The Mobile Phone Travel Service Sell-Out Sub-system for Large Number of Users

Mobile phone module offers the users the possibility of making dynamic package reservations using a mobile phone interface in real time. The application is developed on the J2ME[2] platform. Using the mobile application based on J2ME API, mobile phones can connect to the dynamic packaging service on our server. Once the TCP connection is established, users can make their transactions in a similar way as they can do in a browser on computers.

In order to guarantee that the application runs in a massive number of terminal mobiles, a low cost RAM application has been developed. The major problem was the XML interpreter. Most of mobile phones accept only applications smaller that 128 KB. The minor standard XML API has 87 KB and it is too much for this application. To solve this problem we have developed a miniXML J2ME API (SAX based) required only 3.5KB.

The transaction dataflow between the mini mobile application and the dynamic packaging is realized in the following steps:

1. The client inputs a set of personal requirements such as number of passengers, age, etc.. All the data will be encrypted in XML form and sent via TCP-IP to the central server.
2. When the central server receives the information it will ask the Dynamic Packaging Server about the available flights according to the user's requirements.
3. The response of the dynamic packaging server is put into an XML format and sent back to the mobile phone. This information is basically a set of available choices. The choices may be a set of flights according to the user's request, or only one way flight or two way flights etc.
4. In mobile phone user select the desired option (or flights) and sends this selection to the central server.
5. Once the client's reply is in the central server, the availability of the requirements will be checked again by the Dynamic Packaging Information. If the result of the check is affirmative, then an identification number is generated and the package reservation takes place. Finally a confirmation message with an identification number will be sent back to the client.

---

[2] J2ME: Java 2 Micro Edition. Java Api for microdevices.

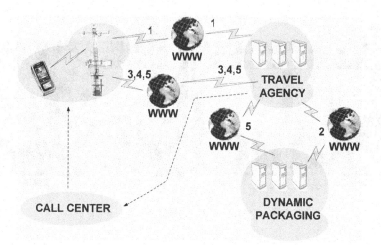

Fig. 6. Mobile phone transaction data flow

The real payment of the reservation was in some of the options that the client sent to the agency during the reservation process. It can be paid through the call center, by phone or direct charged for the registered clients. The whole process can be followed in Fig. 6.

6 System Evaluation

In our experimental application to sell cruiser travel packages, our first test with the DTT environment LOGITRAVEL, the result is positive. The users can see the normal and especial offers of the cruisers and make reservations and pay them. Using LOGITRAVEL, users can see the aspect of the ship interactively and the prices of different choices. They can also see the cruiser travel route and the services on the cruiser. The response from the users on this experimental environment is positive.

In order to check the usefulness of the Graphic User Interface, we evaluated the application by a group of users that usually use internet systems to deal with their travel supplies. Each one of them has searched his desired offer and bought it. The conclusion is that the access to the catalog of the cruisers is lineal, instead of the internet non lineal access. But their general opinion is that the DTT application is very user friendly and usefully.

Another aspect to take into account is the hardware features of several STB. We tried the DTT application using five different STB´s. And we noted that the behavior of the application showed some differences running on different STB, most of them on RAM and CPU speed aspects. But these differences are not critical and do not disturb the normal use of the application. Fig. 7 shows some screen shots during the testing.

There are many issues that need further research and development. As the project is still going, we will attack these issues step by step.

Fig. 7. Some DTT application screenshots

7 Conclusions

The paper presented an integrated travel service system which integrates both the resource supply side and the client service side. It opens a completely new possibility to provide the travel services anytime and anywhere. The system is both integrated and cooperative. Massive amount of different types of travel service resources is integrated by the system. The system provides an easy-to-operate way for a large number of resource providers to work cooperatively and efficiently. It provides anytime and anywhere simultaneous access to huge number of clients by integrating most popular access communication means into the access platform. New access methods for travel services including DTT interactive services and mobile phone are also implemented. Future research topics include finding new return paths for Digital Interactive TV Systems and new user interfaces on mobile phones.

References

[1] Eureka Tourism Secretariat, Europe Community (2007), http://www.eurekatourism.eu
[2] Mascaró, M., Estrany, B., Luo, Y.: Design of a cooperative working environment for mobile devices. In: Luo, Y. (ed.) CDVE 2005. LNCS, vol. 3675, pp. 111–118. Springer, Heidelberg (2005)
[3] Lefevre, L., Pierson, J.M.: Just in time Entertainment Deployment on Mobile Platforms. In: Proceedings of the Advanced International Conference on Telecommunications and International Conference on Internet and Web Applications and Services (AICT/ICIW 2006)
[4] Gilbert, A., Sangwan, S., Mai Ian, H.: The OoBE dynamics of mobile data services markets. Springer London, vol. 9(4) (July 2005) ISSN: 1617-4909 (Print) 1617-4917 (Online)
[5] Van Setten, M., Pokraev, S., Koolwaaij, J.: Context-Aware Recommendations in the Mobile Tourist Application COMPASS. In: De Bra, P., Nejdl, W. (eds.) AH 2004. LNCS, vol. 3137, pp. 235–244. Springer, Heidelberg (2004)
[6] The Open Travel Alliance white paper http://www.OpenTravel.org
[7] The Digital Video Broadcasting Project, http://www.dvb.org/

Cooperative Mobile Healthcare Information Support System Using Web Services over Wireless and Wired Network

Ho Hyun Kang[1], Sung Rim Kim[2], Kee-Deog Kim[3], Dong Keun Kim[1],
and Sun K. Yoo[4,5,6]

[1] Graduate Program in Biomedical Engineering, Yonsei Univ.,
134 shinchon-dong, Seodaemun-Ku, Seoul, Korea
[2] Dept. of Internet Information, Seoil College,
49-3, Myonmok-dong, Jungrang-Ku, Seoul, Korea
[3] Advanced general dentistry, Yonsei University College of Dentistry
[4] Department of Medical Engineering, College of Medicine Yonsei University
[5] Center for Emergency Medical Informatics, Human Identification Research Center
[6] Brain Korea 21 Project for Medical Science, correspondence,
Yonsei University College of Medicine, Seoul, Korea
sunkyoo@yumc.yonsei.ac.kr

Abstract. Mobile computing system using mobile Web Services now supports advanced methods for application integration through the Internet at distributed computing environments. Mobile Web Services on mobile networks is the foundation for ubiquitous healthcare that gives patients better medical services anytime and anywhere. However, available existing web contents are mainly used for desktops on wired networks, but are not yet compatible with mobile Web Services. In this paper, we suggested the cooperative mobile healthcare information support system. The designed system can achieve the advanced inquiring manner of medical information for collaborate diagnosis at both desktop and mobile machines, and also afford to support wider accessibility of users over wireless and wired network environments.

Keywords: Mobile Healthcare Information System, Mobile, Web Services, Cooperative design.

1 Introduction

Providing healthcare and related services through the web, or e-healthcare, is an emerging phenomenon. Wireless personal computing devices are finding a niche in the healthcare communities, promising point-of-care access to medical records and information ranging from patients to drug libraries. And they will help healthcare institutions build a real-time care process, provide a continuous patient record across the continuum of care, and improve outcomes by creating an environment where clinicians can make evidence based decisions [10].

Quickly becoming significant technology in the evolution of the Internet are Web services, a set of standards that can interconnect systems over a variety of networks. It

Y. Luo (Ed.): CDVE 2007, LNCS 4674, pp. 323–330, 2007.
© Springer-Verlag Berlin Heidelberg 2007

is an open XML-based technology providing a generic data exchange format and has been rapidly adopted by many vendors. Web services can easily be built upon existing applications, no matter what the underlying technology is. Because they are expected to have a growing familiarity and acceptance among many users and offer great technological promises, Web services are an interesting subject for the investigation of their possible application in the healthcare service platform [4].

The provision of mobile web services is an important issue in ubiquitous healthcare due to the growth of web services and wireless networks, and the increased usage of mobile devices. Mobile web services have the following attributes: interoperability of web services for desktop, internet compatibility, convenient use with small mobile devices, and mobility. Therefore, mobile web services on wireless networks are the foundation for ubiquitous healthcare that gives patients quality medical care services anytime and anywhere.

Today, healthcare services can access all of a patient's total information unified into the hospital information system. Recently many researchers have tried to integrate HIS with both wired and wireless networks. Patient satisfaction increases because of faster access to accurate healthcare information [5].

In recent years, we have seen an increasing trend in the use of small mobile devices, such as cell phone and PDAs, to access the Internet. However, these devices differ from powerful desktop computers in significantly many ways. In particular, their processor power, bandwidth and display sizes all put constraints on properly representing web content that is originally designed for desktops. To solve these problems, we need to adapt content to meet the constraints mentioned above in small mobile devices. Existing web contents are only used for desktops on wired networks but are not yet compatible with mobile web services [3, 4].

In this paper, we suggest a healthcare information system that provides healthcare information on both wired and wireless networks with the following functions. First, the system provides medical information used for desktops on wired networks. Second, the system has a mobile context server that reconfigures web contents according to the mobile device. The mobile context server applies context to the contents by using styles, a property override, and templates according to the resources of a given mobile device. In this way the system serves reconfigured web contents to the mobile device.

The rest of the paper is structured as follows: In section 2 we review several existing approaches. In section 3, we describe a healthcare web service processes. In section 4, we describe a designed system and several experiments. Finally, we conclude our paper in section 5.

2 Related Works

The mobile devices have been widely used to provide ubiquitous access to the web content. However, due to screen size limitations, it is inconvenient to browse most of the websites that are traditionally designed for desktop PCs. Therefore, developing automatic adaptation techniques to render and squeeze web content into small mobile devices become critical to Internet Service Providers.

Recently, several research projects initiated the investigation for solutions to the constraint of limited screen size. These techniques are referred as page layout adaptation [7]. In general, there are three categories of methods that have been proposed and deployed.

The simplest adaptation technique is to not change the original page in any way, but let the user navigate. Given a single web page, the user needs to interactively navigate by using the scroll bars at the edges of the display area. This approach is adapted by most of the industrial PDA web browsers. Though simple to implement, client side navigation requires frequent interactions between the users and the devices.

Manual authoring also refers to device-specific authoring. The content provider, who is typically a professional in web design, has customized the web content for each individual device. Most of the interface design decisions have been made to compromise the screen size and input facility limitations of small devices. In the most part, this method provides the best user experiences for mobile device users. However, due to mass manual labor work involved, this technique can only apply to small set of websites [8] and hence is limited in scalability.

Automatic authoring usually relies on proxy-like trans-coders that render and filter useful contents and transforms them for browsing on devices with small display. In general, this method requires minimum user intervention. In addition, it can take arbitrary web documents and generate adapted version on-the-fly [8]. Therefore, it has the most potential for widespread use.

3 Cooperative Mobile Healthcare Information Support System Using Web Services

In recent years, the Web Services [15] technology has been emerged as a set of standards for publishing, discovering, and composing independent services in an open network. Web Services are a family of XML based protocols to achieve interoperability among different networked applications. The benefits of Web Services include loose coupling, ease of integration and ease of accessibility. Web Services involve three interactions, namely publishing, finding and binding. In the publishing operation, the service provider publishes the service to a service registry in order to make it possible for a service requestor to find and access it. A UDDI registry is normally used for this purpose. In finding operation, the service requestor retrieves a service description by inquiring the service registry. A WSDL(Web Service Description Language) documents is used for this purpose. In the binding operation, the service requestor uses the binding details in the service description to locate, contact and invoke the service at runtime. All these transport function are performed using SOAP.

Figure 1 shows the overview of proposed system architecture. The designed system is conceptually composed of five main components: the web server, medical information database, mobile context server, mobile user, and desktop user. The web server served medical information for mobile devices on both wired and wireless networks using WSDL to describe functions and protocols. The web server then transmits to the mobile devices. The user binds the web server and the WSDL. This enables the web service to be used by correspondence using SOAP [13, 14]. The medical information database consists of patient information, patient lists, symptoms, prescriptions, and diagnosis including related patient images. The medical information database consists of patient information, patient lists, symptoms, prescriptions, and diagnosis. Patient information consists of the patient's name, age, sex, address, insurance company, and insurance number. The patient list contains the date, patient name, and chart number. The symptom and prescription consist of name, symptom, prescription, progress, and patient image. The diagnosis list consists of patient's name, code, prescription type, prescription, medication, medication method, and medication due. The mobile context server applies context to the contents by using styles, an attribute override, and templates according to the resources of a given mobile device.

Desktop users can ask for services after checking the WSDL of the service from the web server. A desktop on wired networks can be used to browse full contents on one screen shot because of the wide screen used, and it can also provide users with information quickly because of its highly efficient resources. When a user requests medical information through a wired network, the web server serves the information by connecting to the databases of the web server.

Mobile devices are small and are also internet friendly, by having an internet browser. However, each mobile device may have a different screen size, input method, color, or mark-up language, which can affect internet browsing. For these reasons, this system requires a mobile context server. The mobile context server optimizes web contents according to the type of mobile device.

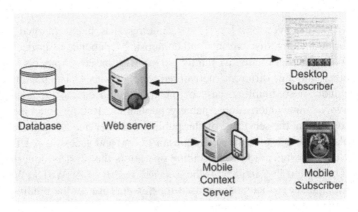

Fig. 1. The overview of proposed system architecture

The mobile context server was developed by Microsoft Mobile Internet Toolkit. The Mobile Internet Toolkit filters mobile devices and creates "DeviceSpecific /Choice" structure. The toolkit also applies a property override, style sheets, and a template for mobile devices. The Device Specific/Choice filter can describe a style according to the browser type by using style sheets [12]. Pseudo-code 1 shows a DeviceSpecific/Choice of the mobile internet toolkit.

```
Mobile StyleSheet Begin
    ...Stylesheet Property Define
    <mobile:Form runat="server">
        ...... Property Define for mobile form
    <mobile:Image runat="server"
        AlternativeText="text..."
        ImageUrl="image.jpg"
        <DeviceSpecific>
            <Choice Filter = "isPocketIE">
            ...... Property Define for choice Device
            </Choice>
            <Choice Filter = "deviceFiltername>
            ......
            </Choice>
        </DeviceSpecific>
    </mobile:image>
    </mobile:Form>
Mobile StyleSheet End
```

Pseudo-code 1. DeviceSpecific/Choice of mobile internet toolkit

In our proposed system, a page is divided and made up of the select/result structure. That is, on the first page a user selects a patient list by date. On the second page a patient is chosen by the reference item. On the next page, the divided medical care information is shown.

The proposed system is not based on loose coupling [15] that is open to UDDI (Universal Description Discovery and Integration) sending and receiving SOAP messages, but rather a tight coupling of a client and server. Using a tightly coupled application development approach provides certain safeguards from quality-of-service, security, privacy, data integrity, and complex transaction processing perspectives as compared to web services architecture [15]. After the system evaluates mobile device's computing capacity, the system serves the web contents based on the context chosen by the mobile context server.

When a user requests medical information through a wireless network, the mobile context server divides the content pages according to the screen size of the mobile device. It also filters the pages according to mobile devices and then browses the adopted contents from the context server to the mobile web browser. The mobile context server reconfigures contents offered by the web sever.

4   Experiments

We experimented with the PDA application and the desktop application. The web server was using Microsoft IIS 5.1 on Microsoft Windows XP Professional. Server application was implemented by Microsoft ASP.NET based on C# [9]. The medical information database was served by Microsoft SQL-SERVER 2000. The context server connected to the web server acted as IIS as the web server. The user system served on the wired network was browsed by Microsoft Internet Explorer 6.0. The mobile web browsers used in the wireless network were a Microsoft MME 3.0 emulator, Microsoft Pocket PC 2003 PDA, HP iPAQ H2200, or HP RW6100.

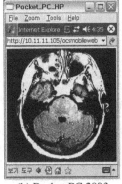

Fig. 2. Discharge web page on the Order Communication System

Figure 2 shows discharge information that is displayed on the web browser using a wired network in the Severance Hospital in Korea. The desktop shown have an adequate screen size, so web contents can be displayed on one screen. In this case, the content of discharge information consists of patient number, duration in hospital, doctor, final diagnosis, medical history, inspection view, and patient images, etc.

Figure 3 shows the patient image displayed on a MME 3.0 emulator and Pocket PC 2003. The system can display optimized contents on mobile devices determined by the context server. Our system divides the discharge web page (Fig. 2) into one "choose" page and eight "result" pages for mobile web browser. Figure 4 shows the discharge mobile web pages displayed on a HP RW6100. Figure 4(a) shows the list of patients order by date and Figure 4(b) shows MRI image of patient.

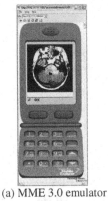

(a) MME 3.0 emulator   (b) Pocket PC 2003

Fig. 3. Patient image page of various mobile browsers

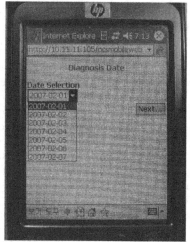 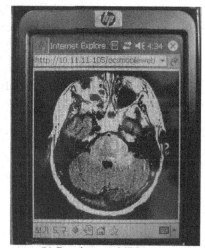

(a) Choose page: diagnosis date selection   (b) Result page: MRI image

Fig. 4. Discharge mobile web pages on a mobile device

5 Conclusion

The mobile devices have been widely used to provide ubiquitous access to the web content. However, due to screen size limitations, it is inconvenient to browse most of the websites that are traditionally designed for desktop PCs. We presented an cooperative mobile healthcare information support system using Web services over wired/wireless integrated services according to the resources of given devices both desktop and mobile devices through the optimizing web contents according to both desktop and mobile user's browser resources. The web service is internet friendly, inter-operational, and compatible with fire walls. To develop this system from a prototype to a total healthcare system, additional patient information and research is needed, and a greater compatibility with divisions in dynamic web pages.

Acknowledgment

This study was supported by a grand of the Korea Health 21R&D project, Ministry of Health & Welfare, Republic of Korea (A020608).

References

[1] Andrade, R., Wangenheim, A., Bortoluzzi, M.K.: Wireless and PDA: a novel strategy to access DICOM-compliant medical data on mobile devices. International Journal of Medical Informatics 71, 157–163 (2003)

[2] Hung, K., Zhang, Y.: Implementation of a WAP-Based Telemedicine System for Patient Monitoring. IEEE Transaction on Information Technology In Biomedicine 2003 7(2), 101–107 (2003)

[3] Hwang, Y.H., Kim, J.H., Seo, E.K.: Structure-Aware Web Transcoding for Mobile Devices. IEEE Internet Computing, 14–21 (2003)

[4] Knikker, R., Guo, Y., Li, J.L., Albert Kwan, K.H., Yip, K.Y., Cheung, D.W., et al.: A Web Services choreography scenario for interoperating bioinformatics applications. BMC Bioinformatics 5, 25 (2004)

[5] Li, X., Zhang, Y.: Bioinformatics data distribution and integration via Web Services and XML. Genomics Proteomics Bioinformatics 1(4), 299–303 (2003)

[6] Mendonca, E.A., Chen, E.S., Stetson, P.D., Mcknight, L.K., Lei, J., Cimino, J.J.: Approach to mobile information and communication for health care. International Journal of Medical Informatics 73, 631–638 (2004)

[7] Mohommed, I., Chin, A., Chengming, C.J., Delara, E.: Community Driven Adaptation: Automatic Content Adaptation in Pervasive Environment. In: 6th IEEE Workshop on Mobile Computing Systems and Applications (WMCSA), English Lake District, UK,

[8] Schilit, B.N., Trevor, J., Hilbert, D.M., Koh, T.K.: Web interaction using very small internet devices. In: Proc. Of the 7th Annual Int'l Conf. on Mobile Computing and Networking, July 2001, Rome, Italy (2001)

[9] Short, S.: Building XML Web Services for the Microsoft. NET Platform. 1st edn. Washington; Microsoft Press, pp. 16–26 (2002)

[10] Intille, S.S.: A New Research Challenge: Persuasive Technology to Motivate Healthy Aging. IEEE Transactions on information technology in Biomedicine 8(3) (September 2004)

[11] Tachakra, S., Wang, X.H., Istepanian, R.S., Song, Y.H.: Mobile e-health: the unwired evolution of telemedicine. Telemed. J. E. Health 9(3), 247–257 (2003)

[12] Wigley, A., Roxburgh, P.: Building.NET Applications for Mobile Devices. 1st edn., pp. 235–276. Microsoft Press, Washington (2003)

[13] Available at: http://www.w3.org/TR/2004/NOTE-ws-arch-20040211/ (Accessed January 11, 2005)

[14] Available at: http://www.w3.org/TR/2002/WD-ws-desc-reqs-20020429/ (Accessed January 11, 2005)

[15] "WEB SERVICE GOTCHAS", Available at: http://www-306.ibm.com/ software/ solutions/webservices/documentation.html

Resource Sharing and Remote Utilization in Communication Servers

Guofeng Qin[1,2], Qiyan Li[1,2], and Xiuying Deng[1,2]

[1] The CAD Research Center, Tongji University, Shanghai 200092, P.R. China
[2] The Chinese National CAD Application Technology Training Center for Engineering Design,
Shanghai 200092, P.R. China
gfqing@yahoo.com.cn, qylcad@sina.com

Abstract. The communication cluster servers require many key technologies in an information integration platform. In order to improve dependability, scalability, and other QoS features, we design a system structure to meet these requirements. The resource sharing and remote utilizing are applied to resolving the dynamical resource dispatch and the tasks distribution. The thread model and mechanism of the thread pool in the Non-blocking Input/Output (NIO) are created which include a case trigger mechanism. The system successfully resolves thousands of terminals connected to the information integrated platform. Messages, files, data, and other information can transport among the platform, the clients and the terminals.

Keywords: Cooperative server cluster, resource dispatch, concurrent processing, real time systems.

1 Introduction

Due to heavy use of web information systems, network transmission bandwidth and servers must meet the rapid increase of the internet traffic of large amount of clients and server nodes with dependability, scalability, and other QoS[5] features. So it is necessary and important to solve the problems of adaptive resource sharing and remote utilizing.

The communication servers must have strong CPU and I/O process capabilities because of the large amount of data transportation and the requirement of Qos character in network services. A cluster server system is a good solution which can meet the requirement of net parallel computing and increase of communication services. In this paper, resource sharing and remote utilizing for a cluster server system is studied. Thread and thread pool issues are also discussed in the paper.

2 The System Structure

2.1 The System Structure of the Information Integration Platform

The information integration platform consists of the intelligent mobile terminals, software systems, integrated GPS(Global Position System), GPRS (General Packet

Y. Luo (Ed.): CDVE 2007, LNCS 4674, pp. 331–339, 2007.

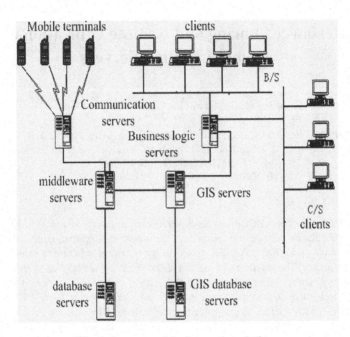

Fig. 1. Structure of the integration platform

Radio Service) or CDMA (Code Division Multiple Access), Internet (Intranet) and M-DMB(Mobile Digital Multimedia Broadcasting) networks.[1] more details can be seen in Fig. 1.

The communication server setup many imports and exports for messages, data, files and stream multimedia in the integration platform. Their functions are to receive the data packages from the mobile terminals and the middleware servers; and build a message sharing pool to hold up the data packages. At the same time, the communication servers transfer the bidirectional message packages between the middleware servers and the terminals in the message sharing pool.

2.2 Formulas

There are a message receive module, a message send module, a receive pool and a send pool in the communication servers. The received and sent messages are both in the message sharing pool. Our design is based on the principle of Non-blocking Input/Output(NIO), which utilizes a case trigger mechanism. The components structure can be seen in figure 2.

In the thread pool, there are read threads, working threads and write threads. The read threads deal with the read operation in thread pool. A read thread is in charge of read message packages from the message pool; a write thread is responsible for writing the message packages into the message pool; the working thread is in charge of the cooperative work between the read thread and the write thread, including import, export and holdup for the message packages in the message pool. Each selected operation only deal with one case by each case trigger, which is a switch and

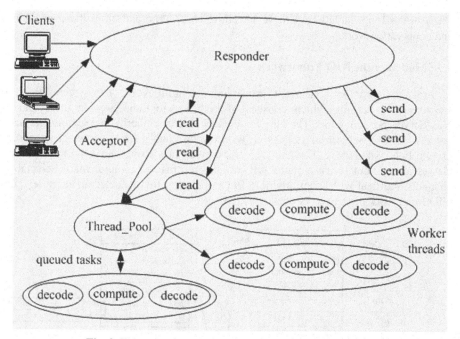

Fig. 2. The component structure in the communication server

gives an "enable" signal to activate to active the threads. When the operation ends, the channel will be changed; the case sequence number will be fed back in order to monitor the status of the case.

The write threads will find the channel of the client in IP address table, and change the channel status into writable status in the communication server. When the working threads receive information from a buffer pool, the middleware servers will be informed automatically to deal with the information. The message package will be sent to the message pool using the RMI from the middleware servers. The parser module will then analyze the message package and feedback the information. In this process, the working threads monitor the cooperative work between the read threads and the write threads in message pool. They deal with reading, writing and holding up the message packages.

3   Thread Model and Mechanism

The NIO uses multiplexing to deal with many sockets in one selector, and get the readable and writable channels to operate input/output of the messages.

Because of bandwidth of network, the reading or writing operations often take place in waiting status. We use threads to deal with the waiting messages in network parallel computing method. This can improve the system capacity and Qos. The reading and writing threads pool can improve the data transfer ability substantially. Based on the case trigger mechanism in the servers, the triggers can deal with the cases in the loop, including setup connection, read, write and close the connection, and cooperative work.

3.1 Modeling the NIO Framework

In order to improve concurrent processing capabilities for the system, a NIO framework is set up, which consists of both a Nio_Echo_Session class and a Nio_Server_Session class. The Nio_Echo_Session class inherits three public classes, namely, a NIO_Session class, a NIO_Worker class and a Echo_server class, and a private Echo_state class. The Nio_Server_Session class also inherits the three public classes and a Shut_down module. NIO applies a thread to monitor many selectable channels and deal with many multiple I/O's operation by one selector in circle. The NIO framework model can be seen in Fig. 3.

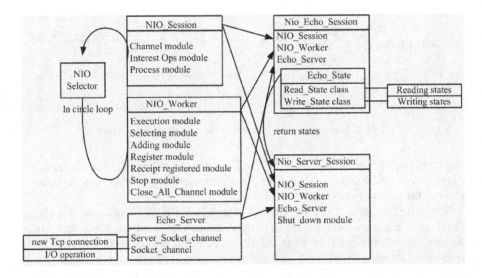

Fig. 3. The NIO framework model

In the NIO, the selecting operations are always realized in circles by the clients. After each selecting operation returns, the clients can catch many required selectable channels by a selector to copy them one by one. In order to simplify some problems, the channel and its I/O are enveloped.

The NIO supports a group of general API for the NIO_session class, which is enveloped software, which includes a channel module, an interest Ops module and a process module. The channel module will return the object of Selectable Channel in the NIO_Session; and the interest Ops module will receive the object of selectable channel. If a channel is registered, it will return a registration message. The process module is a kernel in the NIO_Session API, which enveloped the logical process for Selectable Channel. It gets the Selection Key of the registered channel from the interest Ops module and sends the message to the NIO_Worker class.

The NIO_Worker class supports a group of executable API's, including interfaces for an execution module, a selecting module, an adding module etc. The execution module will copy the select logical operation. In the NIO framework, the selecting module is always executing in circle. Every correspondent Selection Key will be acquired and utilized by the process module.

Each service in NIO_Worker will be registered into the selecting module by the adding module in circle. When the registration is successfully, the Receipt Registered module will be called. The adding module is utilized to add a service into the NIO_Worker, and makes the current selected operation wakeup. The stop module will halt the execution module for the current service in the NIO_Worker. The close_All_Channels module will close the current registered channel, and release the I/O resource, which is not used in NIO_Worker any more.

In the Echo_Server class, a Server_Socket_channel is used to create a new TCP connection, which is respondent for a Socket_channel to deal with its I/O operation. There are many other modules that cooperating to perform the operations in the Nio_Echo_Session and the Nio_Echo_Server together, including the Echo_state class which monitors reading state or writing state of the Nio_Echo_Session and is in charge of reading data or writing data.

Finally, the Nio_Echo_Server is will start and close a TCP Server, its execution module is used to start an Echo Server; its shut_down module is used to close this Echo_Server, and returns the current service sequence number to the NIO_Worker.

3.2 The Resource Dispatching Algorithm of NIO Multiple Thread Servers

Resource dispatching and sharing of NIO by multiple thread servers is the key technical solution in our communication servers.

Hypothesis N is the number of computer process units in the communication server. E is the whole time cost without loader in one unit. L is the loader of only one unit. The work load of the others is 0. If the communication server can be paralleled, the time cost is E/N without loader in the system [7-8]. If there is a loader L in one unit, then its computing ability is 1/L, so if loader 1 is added to the unit, its computing ability will be 1/(L+1), then the whole time cost C is as follows:

$$C = \frac{E}{(N-1)+\dfrac{1}{1+L}} = \frac{E(1+L)}{NL+N-L} \tag{1}$$

The formula (1) is in a theoretical condition. In fact, the whole time cost C' can approximately be expressed in load balanced condition as follows:

$$C' = C + \delta(N) + T_{comm}(N) \tag{2}$$

$T_{comm}(N)$ is the whole communication time, which can be determined by experience, $\delta(N)$ is the estimated number of units. The details of resource dispatching algorithm of NIO can be expressed as follows.

Algorithm:

Input : Graph $G(V,E)$ and its sub-graph $G_{cluster}(V_{clusterp}, E_{clusterp})$, where V are LPs, the E's are empty links, $V_{clusterp}$ is the set of LPs assigned to all processors, $s \in$ $Cluster_p$, and $E_{clusterp}$ is the set of empty links belonging to each processor or $q \in$ $Cluster_p$; $Cluster_p$ is the set of neighbor-processors to p, LST_v, T_{minu}, $Ts_{minu,v}$, $T_{w,u}$ such that $u \in Cluster_p$, $v \in V$ and $w \in E(V-V_{clusterp})$.

Output: time-of-next $T_{u,v}$ and a selected LP to process a new event

Begin

PQ is initial and empty /*PQ is the priority queue, a data structure*/

For all (u,v) $u \in V_{clusterp}$, $v \in (V-V_{clusterp})$ do $T_v=0$;

For all $v \in V_{clusterp}$ do

Temp = $Minw \in E(V-V_{clusterp})(T_{minv}, T_{w,u})$;

$T_v=Max(Temp, LST_v)$; $T_u=Minv \in PQ(T_v)$; /*LST is the stimulated time, T is the min timestamp of LP */

Insert(v,PQ);

Endfor;

While (Not finished) do

If (Non-blocking(Pr_j)) /*unblock any process in Pr_j*/

Select an LP to process a new event   /*setup a logic processor to process a new event */

Endif

Endwhile;

4 Mechanism for Case Trigger

The trigger is an important element and a driver unit for service in the system. It can give an "enable" signal to activate the NIO server. Its basic function is to trigger the correspondent cases if it receives a service request, including read, process, write, and close a TCP connection. The case process modules will respond to the corresponding cases, and finish the business logic process from the clients. In the model, the basic cases are defined, including on_Accept, on_Accepted, on_Read, on_Write, on_Closed, and on_Error cases. The details can be seen in Fig. 4.

The on_Accept module will be triggered when the servers receive the service request from the clients. The server will know a new client is trying to link, and control a loader; for example, if the service request is out of the servers' capacity, the new TCP connection will be refused.

The on_Accepted module will be triggered after the servers receive the requests from the clients. The case expresses the new client has connected with the servers, and record the IP address of the client, then start the next service.

The on_Read module will be triggered after the control thread has read the data from the client, and notify the case process module to deal with the received data. The on_Write module will be triggered after the clients start to receive the data from the servers.

The on_Closed module will be triggered when the connection between the clients and the servers is closed. The on_Error module will be triggered when the errors and

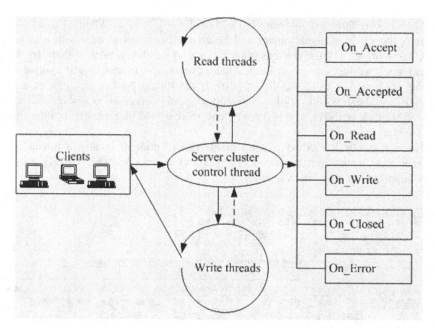

Fig. 4. Case trigger mechanism of NIO multiple threads servers

impediments occurred in the whole connection including the read, process, write, and close TCP connection.

The receipt mechanism of the cases is very important in the model. The submission of the cases utilizes the broadcast method, namely, all case process modules can get the case notice. The different character business logic process will be realized by different process module, and all process modules will be classified and simplified. In the case model, there are a server_listener, an event_adapter, a handler, and a notifier.

The server_listener is an interface for defining the monitored server cases, and can be extended as necessary. The event_adapter is an event adapter for the server_listener interface. The benefit is that the process module only needs to copy the correspondent cases. The notifier will notify the servers to respond the triggered case, and control the cases for the servers using a singleton method, in order to avoid any confusion.

5   Mechanism for Case Trigger

The thread pool consists of a thread manager, working threads, task queue and interface, and an execution module. When a thread pool is created, it contains an interface for the thread_pool_worker. At first, if a task is laid in the thread pool, a free thread_pool_worker will be used to deal with it. After it is finished, its result will be laid in the thread pool.

The execution module in the thread pool will utilize the process function in the thread_pool_worker to take the thread into the Handoff Box. The thread will be copied in circle.

The working thread is an object in the thread_pool_worker. When a thread pool is created, the working thread object will be created; in order to deal with a task, the executable object will use the execution module in the thread pool. If there are some thread_pool_worker to be used, the execution module will move the thread_pool_worker from the thread pool. If the thread pool is free, the execution module will be blocked, until a new thread_pool_worker is available. When the executable task is finished, this thread_pool_worker will be returned into the thread pool again.

The active object method is used in the thread pool. It creates a thread as an internal class, and starts the thread internally. Of course, the object FIFO queue is very important for the system security.

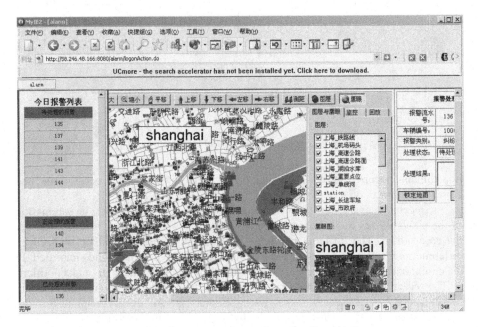

Fig. 5. The task requests from the clients

For security reason, some tables are used to record the information of the clients, including the information channels, the clients IP addresses, and so on. The communication server cluster utilizes the network paralleled computing method to deal with massive data, including service support for multitudinous clients and terminals. The details of the service requests from the clients can be seen in Figure 5.

6 Conclusion

In order to improve dependability, scalability, and other QoS features of the communication server, we designed some dynamic dispatching and arrangement strategy and implemented in our system. The resource sharing and remote utilization technologies are applied to resolve the dynamical resource dispatching and tasks distribution. The thread model and mechanism of the thread pool in NIO framework are discussed, including the case triggering mechanism. There are two problems should be investigated in the future: one is to lower down the cost for the dynamical resource dispatch and the tasks distribution; the other is the evaluation of the capability of the communication cluster servers.

Acknowledgments

This work is funded partly by the Young Talent Fund from Shanghai P.R. China.

References

1. Qin, G., Li, Q.: An Information Integration Platform for Mobile Computing. In: Luo, Y. (ed.) CDVE 2006. LNCS, vol. 4101, pp. 123–131. Springer, Heidelberg (2006)
2. Mohan, C.: Application servers: Born-Again TP monitors for the Web. In: SIGMOD (ed.) Proceedings of 2001 ACM SIGMOD International Conference on Management of Data, 622, ACM Press, New York (2001)
3. Object Management Group. The common object request broker: architecture and specification.2.4 ed (2000), http://www.omg.org/docs/ptc/96-03-04.pdf
4. Sun Microsystems Inc. Java remote method invocation specification (RMI) (1998), http://java.sun.com/products/jdk/1.2/docs/guide/rmi/spec/rmi-title.doc.html
5. Kindel, C., Booch, G.: Essential COM, 2nd edn. Addison-Wesley, Reading (2001)
6. Othman, O., O'Ryan, C., Schmidt, D.C.: An efficient adaptive load balancing service for CORBA.IEEE Distributed Systems Online 2(3) (2001) http://www.computer.org/dsonline
7. Boukerche, A., Tropper, C.: Parallel Simulation on the Hypercube Multiprocessor. Distributed Computing (1995)
8. Fujimoto, R.M.: Parallel Discrete Event Simulation. Communications of the ACM 33, 30–53 (1990)

A Proxy Based Information Integration System for Distributed Wireless Sensor Networks

Li Li, Yuan'an Liu, and Bihua Tang

Wireless Communication Technology & EMC Laboratory,
Beijing University of Posts and Telecommunications
lili66@bupt.edu.cn

Abstract. This paper proposes a novel information sharing system architecture to integrate the distributed and various WSNs together to make their resources more sharable, based on Peer to Peer (P2P) network and the technologies of web service and middleware.

Keywords: WSN, architecture, integration, distributed system, P2P.

1 Architecture Introduction

In this paper, we propose a novel network architecture to integrate the widely distributed and diversified WSNs together to form an uniform, efficient and feasible information sharing system. The architecture is shown in Fig.1. It utilizes distributed proxies to constitute the backbone of the system as well as interface the WSNs and users to this system. Each proxy with its underlying WSNs and combined users acts as a client as well as a server to the system, which can be looked as a node in P2P network or a sub-computational system in the grid. The architecture and its components are different from former works[1][2][3][4].

2 Framework of the Proxy

The software framework of the proxy is shown in Fig.2. It is constituted by three layers, *User Interface, Service Coordinating Platform (SCP)* and *Middleware*.

User interface is based on web services and XML language. It includes two modules, *XML Scheme* and *XML Paser*. XML Scheme defines the standards of the web services and XML Paser interprets the incoming packets and packaging the outgoing packets according to defined XML Scheme.

Middle layer, SCP, is the core component in the framework. It provides system information to users, responds to users'request, allocates the demanded information and actuates the underlying WSNs.

There are three memory components in SCP. The index of the system resources is stored in *Index Database*. Using this information, SCP can find the destination WSN who holds the data requested by users. The latest or most popular news are listed on *Bullitin Board*, which is actively pushed to users

Y. Luo (Ed.): CDVE 2007, LNCS 4674, pp. 340–342, 2007.

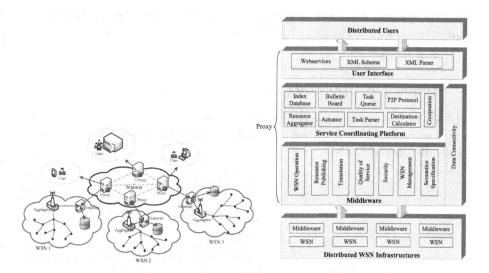

Fig. 1. Network Architecture   **Fig. 2.** The framework of the proxy

when they connected to the proxy, making them familiar with the system. *Task Queue* is a first-in-first-out queue, used to store the tasks to be handled and can be scheduled based on QoS service.

P2P Protocol is the core application protocol, through which the distributed SCPs are able to cooperate together to search and share information. *Resource Aggregator* is used to decrease the data redundancy before saving them into the Index Database. *Actuator* is in charge of interacting with the middleware, to create and send requests or instruction to the underlying WSNs. *Task Paser* analyzes the user requests and pases them into simple instructions. Sometimes one request needs the actions of several WSNs. *Destination Calculator* is like an engine, responsible to find the WSNs with the highest possibility to hold the required data. These modules may run together, so *Cooperation* is needed to cooperate them.

The lowest layer is the middleware, which acts as the interface for SCP to talk to distributed WSNs, eliminating the diversities of underlying WSNs and executing the management and security functions to them. *WSN Operation* receives the instruction from SCP, parses it to sensor network command primitives and operates the WSN to do appropriate actions. *Resource Publishing* is used to create the resource index information and upload it to SCP. *Translation* fulfills the transform functions between sensor network standards and universal internet standards. *Quality of Service* sets the QoS scheme for the WSNs. *Security* includes the firewall function as well as the certification function. *WSN Management* keeps key state information of the underlying WSNs, and cooperates with other modules. *Semantic Specification* defines the specific protocol rules or data formats used by underlying WSNs, which is the basis for *Translation*. When the WSNs upload the data responding to the user' requirement, *Data Connectivity* provides the direct path to user interface without the interference of SCP.

3   Request Responding Cycle

The work mode of the system is presented by one request responding cycle, which is shown in Fig. 3. Note, here SCP means the platform composed by all of the distributed SCPs.

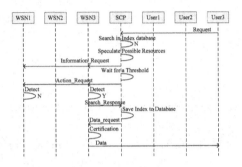

Fig. 3. Request Responding Cases

4   Conclusion and Future Work

In this paper, we propose a proxy based information integration system architecture for widely distributed WSNs and SCP is the core component of it. Now we are setting up the testbed for the system. Next step work is to evaluate the system performance by physical experiments.

References

1. Hasiotis, T., Alyfantis, G., et al.: Sensation: A Middleware Integration Platform for Pervasive Applications in Wireless Sensor Networks. In: Proceeedings of the Second European Workshop on Wireless Sensor Networks, 2005., 31 January-2 February 2005, pp. 366–377 (2005)
2. Madden, S.R., Hellerstein, J., Hong, W.: TinyDB: In-Network Query Processing in 'TinyOS, Version 0.4 (September 2003)
3. Lim, H.B., Teo, Y.M., et al.: Sensor Grid: Integration ofWireless Sensor Networks and the Grid. In: Proceedings of the IEEE Conference on Local Computer Networks 30th Anniversary
4. YuJie, Y., Shu, W., Zhao, H.: MPAS: a Connecting Platform for Integrating Wireless Sensor Network with Grid. In: 2005 Asia-Pacific Conference on Communications, 3-5 October 2005, Perth, Western Australia (2005)

Using Ontological Slicing to Construct Semantic Context Facades for Mediating Collaboration

Ruliang Xiao

State Key Lab of Software Engineering, Wuhan University, Wuhan 430072, China
Department of Information & Management, Hunan Finance & Economics College,
Changsha 410205, China
xiaoruliang@163.com

Abstract. Available ontologies of different information sources are often heterogeneous. It is critical to find an effective solution for many problems of collaborative environment. This paper presents a novel approach to completing heterogeneous collaboration environment that offers a means for developers to describe context essentials with intent-extent of context, to construct context facades using ontological slice, and to implement mediating collaboration based on the context facades.

Keywords: mediating collaboration, ontological slice, context intent-extent, context structure, shallow context façade.

1 Introduction

Recently, we are facing many problems of semantic heterogeneity between information sources in the collaborative environments. Such problems are commonly context-aware, and reliant on different information sources. Available ontological technologies are increasingly demanded to provide a feasible base of the software architecture for it. A lot of efforts in the ontology-based collaborative field such as C-OWL [1], ε-connections[2] have been done. In this paper, we present a novel approach to completing heterogeneous collaboration environment by describing context essentials. We also propose new ideas about context ontology slice, combing iterative intent-extent of contexts, to construct semantic context facades for implementing the mediating collaboration environment.

2 Context Essentials

General speaking, each conception, and each relation between the conceptions means them in possession of a concrete environment, which is usually called a context [4]. A context is a network concerning a set of concepts and relations. We also associate the characters of program slicing, which is a method for decomposing programs by analyzing their data and control flow [3]. We formalize the ontology slice as follows:

Definition 1 (Ontology Slice). An ontology slice is a triple form $\gamma=<\mathbb{C},\mathbb{R},\mathbb{F}>$, $\mathbb{C}$ as a collection of conceps (objects) in the description logics (DL), denoted by $A,B,C \ldots$; $\mathbb{R}$

Y. Luo (Ed.): CDVE 2007, LNCS 4674, pp. 343–345, 2007.

as a collection of relations (roles or attributes)(arrows) in the DL, denoted by $R, S, \ldots$; $\mathbb{F}$ as a set of morphisms, any element f in $\mathbb{F}$ means that a concept holds some attributes. Therefore, once an individual "a" should be represented as a concept $\{a\}$, all the elements in the set $\mathbb{R}$ show concept inclusion relations.

If we begin to trace a concept posed in a certain scenario, then there exists a concept-based context corresponding to a concept ontology slice, and we call the concept "seed" of the ontology slice. Because of assuming the individual "a" is concept $\{a\}$, we don't consider such an ontology slice of individual instance.

Definition 2 (Concept-Based Ontology Slice). All the concepts and Attributes (roles) directly or indirectly connecting a given "seed"—concept in a certain scenario construct a ontology slice, just because the mini ontology started with a given seed concept, we call it concept-based ontology slice. In a word, this given concept A is a "seed" of this concept-based ontology slice. If we use γ_A to represent a concept -based ontology slice, γ_A must be a subset of a certain ontology slice γ, i.e. $\gamma_A \subseteq \gamma$.

Definition 3 (Attribute-Based Ontology Slice). Similarly, as well as the definition 2 before, an attribute-based ontology slice starts with a given "seed"—attribute. We use γ_R to represent an attribute-based ontology slice, γ_R must be a subset of a certain categorial ontology slice γ, i.e. $\gamma_R \subseteq \gamma$.

From the above two definitions, this character embodies two factors of a concept or an attribute: intent and extent. We use A_{intent} to denote the intent of concept A, and A_{extent} to denote the extent of concept.

Definition 4 (Concept Intent and Extent). Assume that a form $\gamma_A = <\mathbb{C}, \mathbb{R}, \mathbb{F}>$ denotes a based on concept A ($A \in \mathbb{C}$) ontology slice, then, within this γ_A, all attribute-based ontology slices that directly connect concept A build a new set A_{intent},

$$A_{intent} := \{ \gamma_P \mid \gamma_P \subseteq \gamma_A, P \in \gamma_A.\mathbb{R}: \forall f \in \gamma_A.\mathbb{F}, f: A \to P \}.$$

All concept-based slices that directly connect concept A build a new set A_{extent},

$$A_{extent} := \{ \gamma_C \mid \gamma_C \subseteq \gamma_A, C \in \gamma_A.\mathbb{C}: \forall C \subseteq A \}.$$

In the following definition, we use R_{intent} to denote the intent of attribute R, and R_{extent} to denote the extent of attribute.

Definition 5 (Attribute Intent and Extent). Assume that a form $\gamma_R = <\mathbb{C}, \mathbb{R}, \mathbb{F}>$ denotes a based on attribute R ($R \in \mathbb{R}$) ontology slice, then, within this γ_R, all attribute-based ontology slices that directly connect attribute R build a new set R_{intent},

$$R_{intent} := \{ \gamma_S \mid \gamma_S \subseteq \gamma_R, \forall S \in \gamma_R.\mathbb{R}: S \subset R \}.$$

Within this γ_R, all concept-based ontology slices that directly connect attribute R build a new set R_{extent},

$$R_{extent} := \{ \gamma_A \mid \gamma_A \subseteq \gamma_R, \forall A \in \gamma_R.\mathbb{C}, \forall f \in \gamma_R.\mathbb{F}, f^{-1}: R \to A \}.$$

According to definition 4 and definition 5, whether concepts or attributes in an ontology, their *intent* or *extent* itself is an ontology slice. By far, we can consider categorial context structure from the point of view of categorial context essentials.

Definition 6 (Context Sructure). A context structure of concept A which acts as a part of concept-based ontology slice, is an intent-extent pair (A_{intent}, A_{extent}). Similarly, a context structure of attribute R which acts as an attribute-based ontology slice, is an extent-intent pair (R_{intent}, R_{extent}).

3   Shallow Context Facade and Mediating

If the context ontology slice is too large, the directed graph will be too complex to be understood by agents. We must consider how to meet the necessary granularity and capture an appropriate context ontology slice. We take the top level nodes out of A_{intent} and A_{extent} to construct a crosstable: $\mathbb{C} \otimes \mathbb{R} = \{(C,R) \mid C \in \mathbb{C}, R \in \mathbb{R}\}$. We know there is three such shallow context crosstables: $\mathbb{C} \otimes \mathbb{C}$, $\mathbb{R} \otimes \mathbb{R}$, $\mathbb{C} \otimes \mathbb{R}$.

Context scene of collaboration constructs an ontology slice which is given by a triple form $\gamma = <\mathbb{C}, \mathbb{R}, \mathbb{F}>$, $\mathbb{C}$ as a set of concepts, $\mathbb{R}$ as a set of relations, and $\mathbb{F}$ as a set of morphisms. Suppose that C denotes the center element of γ, context structure of C can be denoted as an extent-intent pairs (C_{intent}, C_{extent}), let set $\mathbb{A}$ indicates top concepts in C_{intent}, set $\mathbb{S}$ indicates top attributes in C_{extent}, then we call the triple form $<\mathbb{A} \otimes \mathbb{A}, \mathbb{S} \otimes \mathbb{S}, \mathbb{A} \otimes \mathbb{S}>$ a **Shallow Context Facade**.

A given *"seed"* out of the scenes facilitates generating context ontology slices. It is sure that there exist many centered concepts and relations and help refine the shallow context facades from these slices.

By far, shallow context facade pattern, using a simpler interface, efficiently wraps the complicated context of the session scenes and provides a unified mediating interface to a set of interfaces in a context. This facade model provides a mechanism for dynamically mediating semantic collaboration to complete mediating heterogeneous data sources in the collaborative environment.

4   Conclusion

Our method offers a means for developers to describe context essentials with intent-extent of context, to construct context facades using ontological slices. This can be used to implement the mediating collaboration based on the context facades.

Throughout this paper, we always emphasize a so-called semantic cognitive structure—shallow context facades. This is an intermediate result of our ongoing work. We will continue implementing the architecture and further, to validate and test our approach in the collaborative domain of virtual crawlers.

References

1. Bouquet, P., Giunchiglia, F., van Harmelen, F., et al.: C-OWL: Contextualizing Ontologies. In: Fensel, D., Sycara, K.P., Mylopoulos, J. (eds.) ISWC 2003. LNCS, vol. 2870, pp. 164–179. Springer, Heidelberg (2003)
2. Kutz, O., Lutz, C., Wolter, F., Zakharyaschev, M.: E-connections of abstract description systems. Artificial Intelligence 156(1), 1–73 (2004)
3. Tip, F.: A Survey of Program Slicing Techniques. Journal of Programming Languages 3, 121–189 (1995)
4. Schmidt, A.: Ontology-Based User Context Management: The Challenges of Imperfection and Time-Dependence. In: Meersman, R., Tari, Z. (eds.) On the Move to Meaningful Internet Systems 2006: CoopIS, DOA, GADA, and ODBASE. LNCS, vol. 4275, pp. 995–1011. Springer, Heidelberg (2006)

A Design of Personal Window Knowledge Capsule Based on Data Warehousing Concept

JeongYon Shim

Division of General Studies, Computer Science, Kangnam University
San 6-2, Kugal-ri, Kihung-up,YongIn Si, KyeongKi Do, Korea
Tel.: +82 31 2803 736
mariashim@kangnam.ac.kr

Abstract. Based on Data warehousing concept Personal Window Knowledge Capsule is Designed. This knowledge capsule has learning, perception Inference, knowledge structuring and Knowledge retrieval functions. Especially it provides multiple aspects of personal windows assembling the selected necessary functional module and personal viewpoint of Knowledge network flexibly. We applied this system to the virtual memory and test with sample data.

1 Introduction

As the computer technology and information society develop rapidly, information environment is encompassing with a huge amount of data. Because of dynamic complex characteristics as well as a huge amount of data,It is essential to develop more efficient intelligent system. This system has to not only encompass maximum amount of data and functions but also provide the variable aspects of this system appropriate to the personal purpose flexibly. In the recent researches,the concept of Data Warehousing is supporting these requirements.

For providing the personal aspects, Personal Window Knowledge Capsule based on Data Warehousing concept was designed in this study. Personal Window Knowledge Capsule is Designed. This knowledge capsule has learning, perception Inference, knowledge structuring and Knowledge retrieval functions. Especially it provides multiple aspects of personal windows assembling the selected necessary functional module and personal viewpoint of Knowledge network flexibly.

2 Personal Window Knowledge Capsule Design

Knowledge Capsule has a hierarchical structure consisting of Memory ,Knowledge processing engine such as a learning engine, various functional modules, Data Warehousing module,personal windows and I/O Interface as shown in Figure 1. The functions of Learning and Knowledge Construction module take charge of storing the knowledge in memory in a top down direction. The knowledge is obtained by Learning engine. Learning engine has two typed methods of

Y. Luo (Ed.): CDVE 2007, LNCS 4674, pp. 346–348, 2007.

Neural network and symbolic conceptual learning. BP algorithm is used for the Neural network learning process and Knowledge Network Structure was made for Symbolic conceptual learning. Knowledge retention and modification are performed Knowledge construction module. After Learning and Knowledge Construction process, Perception Inference and Knowledge Retrieval process can be performed in a bottom up direction from the Memory. Memory consists of Short term memory and long term memory, Learning memory by neural network and memory by symbolic learning. Data Warehousing module makes Personal Windows to be composed of selected modules and reconfigured knowledge network retrieved from memory.

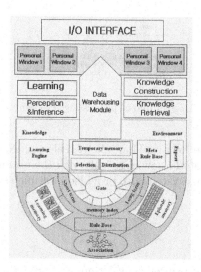

Fig. 1. The structure of Knowledge capsule

If the function of Decision making and explanation process in the personal point of view is necessary, Data warehousing module compose Personal window by selecting Perception Inference and Knowledge Retrieval module. If it is necessary to make a retention of memory, Personal Window is composed of Learning and Perception Inference module. For the data extracting process, personal window includes Knowledge Construction module for making personal knowledge network and Knowledge Retrieval module. The mechanisms of functional modules are described in the previous papers in detail[1][3]. As described, Data Warehousing module can make various personal Windows with multiple aspects reflecting the personal purposes.

3   Experiments

This system was applied to the Virtual memory and experimented with sample data. As shown in figure 2,one personal window composed of Perception/Inference

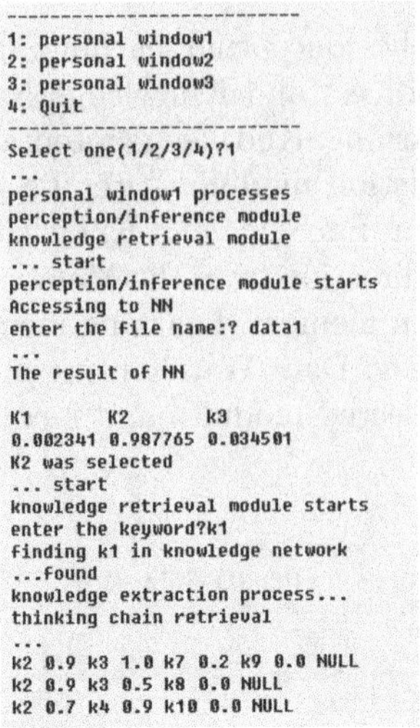

```
--------------------------------
1: personal window1
2: personal window2
3: personal window3
4: Quit
--------------------------------
Select one(1/2/3/4)?1
...
personal window1 processes
perception/inference module
knowledge retrieval module
... start
perception/inference module starts
Accessing to NN
enter the file name:? data1
...
The result of NN

K1        K2        k3
0.002341 0.987765 0.034501
K2 was selected
... start
knowledge retrieval module starts
enter the keyword?k1
finding k1 in knowledge network
...found
knowledge extraction process...
thinking chain retrieval
...
k2 0.9 k3 1.0 k7 0.2 k9 0.0 NULL
k2 0.9 k3 0.5 k8 0.0 NULL
k2 0.7 k4 0.9 k10 0.0 NULL
```

Fig. 2. An example of processing a personal window

module and Knowledge Retrieval module was selected. NN memory was accessed for perception, the related knowledge cells with the obtained data,k2, were successfully extracted. This system also provided multiple aspects of other personal windows.

4   Conclusion

For making more efficient intelligent system and providing multiple personal aspects, Knowledge Capsule with personal windows was designed.This knowledge capsule has learning, perception Inference, knowledge structuring and Knowledge retrieval functions. The personal windows were designed for reflecting the multiple aspects by assembling the selected necessary functional modules. By designing Personal Windows, more efficient process and more satisfied services focusing on the particular purpose can be provided to the customer of this system.

References

1. Shim, J.-Y.: Knowledge Retrieval Using Bayesian Associative Relation in the Three Dimensional Modular System. In: Yu, J.X., Lin, X., Lu, H., Zhang, Y. (eds.) APWeb 2004. LNCS, vol. 3007, pp. 630–635. Springer, Heidelberg (2004)
2. Anderson, J.R.: Learning and Memory. Prentice Hall, Englewood Cliffs
3. Shim, J.-Y., Hwang, C.-S.: Data Extraction from Associative Matrix based on Selective learning system. In: IJCNN'99, Washongton D.C. (1999)

Dynamic Resource Dispatch Strategy for WebGIS Cluster Services

Guofeng Qin and Qiyan Li

The CAD Research Center, Tongji University, Shanghai 200092, P.R. China
The Chinese National CAD Application Technology Training Center for Engineering Design,
Shanghai 200092, P.R. China
gfqing@yahoo.com.cn, qylcad@sina.com

Abstract. In order to meet the requirements of massive data processing and high quality of service, a WebGIS(Web Geographic Information System) cluster system has been developed which has the capability of balancing resources between servers. This cluster system includes three parts: a load balancer, a GIS server cluster, and a database of spatial and geographic information. The strategy of dynamic dispatch and the algorithm of adaptive load balancing service are presented in the paper.

Keywords: cooperative GIS, cluster services, load balancing strategy, concurrent processing.

1 Background

Generally, middlewares such as JAVA RMI[2]□CORBRA[3]□COM[4] are often used to balance the loaders by Web application servers. With the development of Internet and WebGIS application, GIS is used widely nowadays. There are massive number of users that retrieve and analyze the WebGIS spatial data and graphics data at the same time. This raises a very special problem in the cooperative visualization of the WebGIS. With more and more data transportation in WebGIS servers, the bandwidth of network transmission and capability of servers are required more strictly. WebGIS servers must meet the rapid increase of the number of the internet clients and server nodes with high dependability, scalability, and other QoS[5] features. To solve this special problem, an adaptive WebGIS server cluster system is under study about its adaptive load balance and dynamic resource dispatch to meet the requirement of massive data transportation, QoS and net parallel computing.

2 Components of the WebGIS Server Cluster System

In order to transmit requests from the clients to different severs properly, IP load balancing and dynamic feedback mechanisms are utilized in our cluster server system. The hot plug-in servers are used as a solution. The load balancer in the cluster system can shield the impedimentary servers automatically and add new GIS servers into the register. The whole server cluster has a high capability to deal with the dynamic

Y. Luo (Ed.): CDVE 2007, LNCS 4674, pp. 349–352, 2007.

loader change. An additional virtual server can be added by the load balancer when necessary. Therefore, the data transmission and information process are completely transparent to the clients. The whole system includes the load balancer, the GIS server cluster and the database servers for spatial information and geography properties.

2.1 The Load Balancer

A balancer , a monitor and a register make up a load balancer[1]. The load balancer will be in charge of monitoring the load situation of each server dynamically dispatching suitable GIS servers for the request tasks. It maintains a server table, which contains registered address, scale weight and loader of registered GIS server in the dispatcher. Once the balancer receives a request from clients, it will appoint the lightest loaded GIS server to respond to the tasks according to the information and dispatch algorithm in the server table. The monitor has two tasks. One is to keep watching if each GIS server has impediments. If yes, the server will be removed from the server table to prevent dispatching tasks to the wrong GIS servers. The other is to collect the load information periodically, and renew the server table in order to adjust parameters of the dispatch algorithm in time. The register receives the register request from GIS servers, and searches their information in server table. If their information is contained in the table that means the GIS server has been registered in the cluster system successfully. If there is no information, the server will be added into the server table.

It is necessary to have an assistant load balancer to backup the information of the chief load balancer to avoid the whole system failure when the chief load balancer has impediments. The chief load balancer、the assistant load balancer and the GIS server cluster are connected by internet or intranet. The problem in the single joint impediment has been overcome using integrated dispatching. We have added an assistant load balancer to the whole WebGIS cluster system. As a result, the whole cluster system increased greatly its stability and reliability.

2.2 The GIS Server Cluster

The GIS Server Cluster is in charge of dealing with the client requests, sending the results to the clients. Each GIS server contains five modules, including a Receive module, a GIS module, a Sent module, a Load feedback module, and a Register module. The Receive module receives the package requests from the clients, parses them, and sends the parsed result to the GIS module. The GIS module retrieves spatial data, operates the geography property database and packs the result data into a XML data stream. The Sent module delivers the XML data stream on parsed IP address from the Receive module. The Load feedback module records the load condition of its GIS server. It must be informed in order to renew its load parameter while the Receive module sends a resulted XML data stream. It will feedback the parameters to the balancer according the requirement. The Register module is responsible for sending registered request to the load balancer. If it registers successfully, the GIS servers will be initialized, and server table in the load balancer will be updated.

3 Dispatch Algorithm of the Cluster System Load

A load dispatch algorithm with minimal connected scale weight is implemented in the cluster system. Each server has a scale weight to express its capacity with a default value 1. The scale value can be dynamically set.

Hypothesis the cluster server is presented by : $S=\{S_1, S_2, \ldots\ldots, S_n\}$. $W(S_i)$ is a scale value of a server S_i. $C(S_i)$ is the number of connection in sever S_i. SUM is the sum of connections in the cluster, namely, SUM= $\sum C(S_i)$. Because the divide circle time is longer than multiplication, and $W(S_i) \neq 0$, $C(S_i) \neq 0$, the problem can be simplified as :

$$C (S_i) \bullet W (S_{-i}) > C (S_i) \bullet W (S_i) \qquad (1)$$

Algorithm:
(1) Start the balancer;
(2) Start the registration thread, the load feedback thread and the monitor thread in parallel method. After the registration thread begins, execute(3). After the load feedback thread begins, execute (5). After the monitor thread begins, execute (6);
(3) Initial the WebGIS server table and the server weight table, and set the default value of the server weight table;
(4) Receive the registration request from the WebGIS servers; query the WebGIS server table, if the server exists in the table, it has registered; else it must be checked in and added into the table; then send the default scale weight to it; arrange some tasks;
(5) Receive the load feed scale weight from the WebGIS server, and update the WebGIS server table and the server weight table in circle.
(6) Receive the application tasks, and search the server weight table, query both $W(S_j)$ and $C(S_j)$ values of every server S_j in the cluster, and compute their $W(S_j)*C(S_j)$; check out the minimum value $W(S_j)*C(S_j)$. If yes, then the server S_j has the minimum tasks, and the task from the message pool is dispatched to server S_i in FIFO, and the $C(S_j)$ value is increased by 1.
(7) If a task is finished in one server S_m, then its $C(S_m)$ value is decreased by 1, waiting for the result of computing and comparing its $W(S_m)*C(S_m)$. Wait for new task, go to (6).

4 The WebGIS Cluster System

When the load balancer starts running, the WebGIS cluster system will display the "No server" information. That means there is no server in the cluster system. When a server starts the register function, the balancer will indicate that a new server is requesting to add into the cluster system and apply registration.

If the cluster receives requests from the clients, its balancer will start to dispatch these tasks, and transmit the tasks to the WebGIS servers, including indicating the connected number and scale weight of every WebGIS server, choice of the best server for the task with the dispatch algorithm. If the balancer finds a WebGIS server is wrong, the server will be removed from the cluster system, and its current task will be distributed to the other servers. After every WebGIS server receives a dispatch task, the cluster must re-compute its load, send the feedback message to the load balancer, and update the weight table. By the end of the task, it returns the results to the client, and notifies the load balancer and the client.

5 Conclusion

In order to meet the requirements of massive data processing and high quality of service for WebGIS servers, a cluster system with capability of balancing resources between servers has been implemented. The strategy of dynamic dispatch and the algorithm of adaptive load balancing service are described. The strategy includes the dynamic load feedback, hot plug-in, load balancing and the mechanism for failure backup. There are two problems must be further studied in future, one is to lower the cost for balancing load; the other is to make up an evaluation system for ability of the GIS servers.

References

1. Qin, G., Li, Q.: An Information Integration Platform for Mobile Computing. In: Luo, Y. (ed.) CDVE 2006. LNCS, vol. 4101, pp. 123–131. Springer, Heidelberg (2006)
2. Mohan, C.: Application servers: Born-Again TP monitors for the Web. In: SIGMOD (ed.) Proceedings of 2001 ACM SIGMOD International Conference on Management of Data, p. 622. ACM Press, New York (2001)
3. Object Management Group. The common object request broker: architecture and specification.2.4 ed. (2000), http://www.omg.org/docs/ptc/96-03-04.pdf
4. Sun Microsystems Inc. Java remote method invocation specification(RMI) (1998), http://java.sun.com/products/jdk/1.2/docs/guide/rmi/spec/rmi-title.doc.html
5. Kindel, C., Booch, G.: Essential COM, 2nd edn. Addison-Wesley, Reading (2001)
6. Othman, O., O'Ryan, C., Schmidt, D.: An efficient adaptive load balancing service for CORBA.IEEE Distributed Systems Online, 2(3) (2001), http://www.computer.org/dsonline

Leveraging Single-User Microsoft Visio for Multi-user Real-Time Collaboration

Kai Lin[1], David Chen[1], Chengzheng Sun[2], and Geoff Dromey[1]

[1] School of Information and Communication Technology,
Griffith University, Brisbane, QLD 4111, Australia
{K.Lin,D.Chen,G.Dromey}@griffith.edu.au
[2] School of Computer Engineering, Nanyang Technological University, Singapore, 639798
CZSun@ntu.edu.sg

Abstract. Microsoft Visio is one of the most prevalent commercial single-user graphic editing systems, which can be used to create a wide variety of business and technical drawings. It is desirable to leverage single-user Visio system for multi-user real-time collaboration. One feature that distinguishes Visio from other graphic editing systems is that *formulas*, a type of constraint, are defined in Visio to express the attributes of each graphic object, and the relationship between different Visio graphic objects. The ability to describe shapes with constraints opens many possibilities for making shapes behave in complex and sophisticated ways, but satisfying constraints in the presence of concurrency in collaborative systems is a challenge. In this article, we introduce a collaborative Visio system, called CoVisio, which enables a group of users to view and edit the same Visio documents at the same time from different collaborating sites. The methods applied to develop CoVisio are generic and can be adopted to leverage other single-user systems that support constraints, such as Microsoft Excel, for multi-user collaboration.

Keywords: Collaborative Visio, Consistency maintenance, Constraint satisfaction.

1 Introduction

With the increasing importance of using computers to support collaborative work, it is natural to expect existing single-user computer applications to play an important role in supporting collaboration. Leveraging single-user commercial systems for real-time multi-user collaboration has been a popular research topic for many years. So far, pioneer researchers have successfully enriched Microsoft Word and PowerPoint with collaborative functions, without modifying the source code of MS Word and Power-Point [6], [9]. This is achieved through the use of MS Word/PowerPoint's API (Application Programming Interface), to combine Word/PowerPoint with collaboration features.

Microsoft Word and PowerPoint represent two types of well-known single-user computer applications: text editing and presentation. Another type of popular computer applications is graphic editing that provides both generic and comprehensive graphic manipulation functions. Microsoft Visio is one of the most prevalent

Y. Luo (Ed.): CDVE 2007, LNCS 4674, pp. 353–360, 2007.

commercial single-user graphic editing systems, which can be used to create a wide variety of business and technical drawings. It is desirable to furnish single-user Visio system with multi-user collaborative functions, so that users can work collaboratively in groups to improve productivity.

One feature that distinguishes Visio from other graphic editing systems is that *formulas* are defined in Visio [4]. Visio *formulas* are constraints that determine how Visio shapes look and behave on a drawing page. Visio users can precisely control the appearance and behavior of Visio shapes by editing *formulas*. The ability to describe shapes with constraints opens many possibilities for making shapes behave in complex and sophisticated ways, but satisfying constraints in the presence of concurrency in collaborative systems is a challenge [3].

This paper presents a collaborative Visio system, called CoVisio, which extends single-user Microsoft Visio for multi-user collaboration based on Visio API, so that a group of users can view and edit the same Visio documents at the same time from different sites. Both constraints and consistency are maintained in CoVisio.

The rest of this article is organized as follows. Section 2 introduces Visio *formulas*, which distinguish Visio from other graphic editing systems. CoVisio system is described in section 3, including CoVisio components, architecture and how to maintain both constraints and consistency in CoVisio. The major contributions and future work of our research are summarized in the last section.

2 Visio Formulas

An attribute of a graphic object, called a *cell* in Visio, is expressed by a *formula*. A *formula* is an expression that can contain constants, operators, and object attribute references. Microsoft Visio evaluates a *formula* to a result and then converts the result to the appropriate units for the attribute that contains the *formula* [4]. Some *formulas* consist of a single constant, but all *formulas* go through this evaluation and conversion process. In a Visio *ShapeSheet* window, a user can display *cell* contents as either *values* or *formulas* by clicking the appropriate command on the **View** menu.

Visio *formulas* may define the relationship between graphic attributes of a single graphic object. For example, the X and Y coordinates of the top-right vertex of a rectangle are defined by two *formulas*, *width×1* and *height×1*, respectively. Therefore, each time a user resizes the rectangle (i.e. changes the *width* or *height* of the object), the *formulas* defining the coordinates of the vertex will be reevaluated, so that the position of the vertex will be changed accordingly.

On the other hand, a Visio *formula* may define the relationship between graphic attributes of different objects. For example, when a user connects the *begin point* of a line to a *connection vertex* of a rectangle, the *formula* defining *begin point* of the line is automatically changed to something like `PAR(PNT(Rectangle! Connections.X1, Rectangle!Connections.Y1))`, which means the *begin point* of the line should have the same coordinate as the *connection vertex* of the rectangle. Therefore, even if a user moves or resizes the rectangle, the *begin point* of the line still glues to the *connection vertex* of the rectangle.

It is worth to point out that users could not change the value of an attribute directly in Visio, as a value is always evaluated from a *formula*. Each time a user updates the attributes of graphic objects, he/she directly changes the *formulas* expressing these attributes. There are three ways to change *formulas*: (1) Through Visio drawing pages by mouse/keyboard operations. For example, when a user moves a shape with the Pointer tool, Visio changes and then reevaluates the *formulas* that define the shape's center of rotation, or pin, on the drawing page, because those *formulas* determine the shape's location on the page. (2) Through Visio *ShapeSheet* window where users can edit *formulas* directly. A *ShapeSheet* window gives users more precise control over the appearance and behavior of an object. (3) Through Visio API, where developers can modify *formulas* by program.

Visio *formulas* are constraints. Constraints are adopted in a wide variety of single-user commercial systems, such as AutoCAD, Rational Rose, Microsoft Excel, etc., to automatically enforce semantic rules and properties. To leverage these systems for multi-user collaboration, it is important to investigate constraint maintenance in collaborative environments.

3   CoVisio

CoVisio is built by extending single-user Microsoft Visio into a multi-user collaboration application, so that a group of users can use MS Visio to view and edit the same Visio documents at the same time from different sites. It is implemented in the programming language C# based on Visio API without knowing or modifying Visio source code. The interface of CoVisio is shown in Fig. 1.

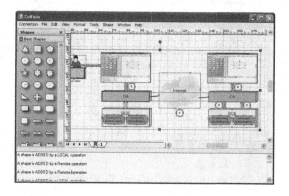

Fig. 1. The Collaborative Visio (CoVisio) interface

3.1   CoVisio Architecture and Components

To meet the requirement of high responsiveness in the Internet environment, replicated architecture is adopted in CoVisio. Shared Visio documents are replicated at the local storage of each collaborating site, so that operations can be performed at local sites immediately and then propagated to remote sites [1], [5]. A collaborative Visio application may span many collaborating sites. At each site, a CoVisio instance is composed of three components:

The first component is a Single-user Application (SA), i.e., Microsoft Visio, which provides the conventional single-user functionalities and interface features. A local user can manipulate the shared documents via SA's user interface. SA's API functions are used to intercept local user's operations and replay operations generated at remote sites. For example, once a user updates the color of object A to *red* at a site, the operation semantic will be intercepted by Visio API functions, and marshaled into a message sent to remote sites. Once the message arrives at a remote site, it is unmarshaled and a Visio API function will be invoked to color the replica of A at the site to *red*.

Another component is Generic Collaboration Engine (GCE), which provides application-independent collaboration capabilities. This component is fully collaboration-aware, but completely unaware of the single-user application. Two crucial functions of GCE are consistency maintenance and constraint satisfaction, which will be addressed in detail in the next subsection.

GCE is generic, but SA is application-specific. They may define different data and operation models. Therefore, the third component, Collaboration Adapter (CA), is implemented to adapt application-specific SA to generic GCE. CA provides application dependent collaboration capabilities and is aware of both the single-user application and multi-user collaboration.

The interactions among the three components in processing an editing operation can be illustrated briefly based on the following simple scenario in a CoVisio application, as shown in Fig. 2.

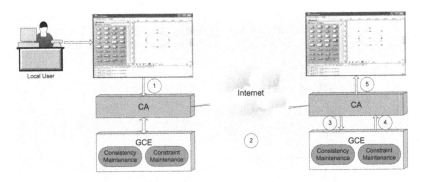

Fig. 2. The interactions between CoVisio components

Suppose a user uses the keyboard and/or mouse to edit a graphic object in a shared Visio document, the following events shall occur at the local site:

(1) Once the operation is performed on the local document, the operation semantic is sent to CA via SA's API. Then it is translated into a GCE recognizable operation by CA.
(2) The GCE recognizable operation is propagated to remote sites by CA.
When the operation arrives at a remote site, the following shall happen:
(3) The received operation will be passed to GCE.

(4) The operation is processed by GCE for consistency maintenance and constraint satisfaction. After that, the processed operation is passed to CA.

(5) A suitable SA's API function will be invoked by CA to replay the remote op eration at the site.

3.2 Maintaining Formula Consistency

The concurrent execution of user operations in CoVisio may result in divergence. For example: suppose that user-1 and user-2 simultaneously color object *A* to *red* and *white* respectively from different collaborating sites in a CoVisio application. At the site of user-1, the color of *A* will be changed to *red* first by user-1. When the operation of user-2 arrives and is executed at the site of user-1, the color of *A* will be changed to *white*. For the same reason, the color of *A* will be *red* after the executions of the two operations at the site of user-2. Obviously, the colors of *A* are different at different sites, so that divergence occurs.

Consistency maintenance in replicated collaborative systems has been investigated for decades, and many approaches have been proposed. Among them Operational Transformation (OT) is an innovative and well-known technique. The basic idea of OT is to transform (or adjust) the parameters of operations according to the effects of previously executed concurrent operations so that the transformed operations can achieve the correct effects and maintain document consistency [5], [7]. Due to the space limitation, we will not describe OT in detail in this paper (please refer to [5], [7] to find the detailed information of OT). Two advantages of OT are worth of notice: (1) OT is a generic strategy, which can maintain consistency in a wide variety of collaborative systems, and (2) OT ensures document consistency independent of the execution orders of concurrent operations, which makes OT an efficient method as it will not undo/redo operations to ensure the same execution order of concurrent operations at different collaborating sites.

OT is adopted in CoVisio for maintaining *formula* consistency. As described in the previous section, each time a user updates the attributes of graphic objects in a CoVisio application, he/she directly changes the *formulas* expressing these attributes. Therefore, OT ensures that after the same set of operations has been executed at different collaborative sites of a CoVisio application (concurrent operations can be executed in arbitrary order at each site), (1) the same set of graphic objects is maintained at each site, and (2) the *formulas* defining the same graphic attribute of the same graphic object are identical at all the sites.

3.3 Value Propagation

As the existence of *formulas* in CoVisio, the change of one *cell*'s value may propagate to the values of other *cells*. For example, suppose there is a *cell C* defined by *formula*, *A+B*, so that the value change of either *A* or *B* will result in the value change of *C*. Moreover, if there are other *cells* defined by *formulas* where *C* is a referenced parameter, then the value change of *C* will in turn be propagated to the values of these *cells*, and so on.

OT ensures *formula* consistency, but it does not guarantee concurrent operations be executed in the same order at different collaborating sites. This may result in different value propagation paths at different sites. For example, suppose that initially *cell C* is defined by *formula, A+B*. Two users concurrently modify *formulas* from different sites. One makes *C* be defined by *formula B+D*, and the other changes the *formula* defining *A*. The operation changing the *formula* defining *A* will result in the value change of *A*. If this operation is executed before the other operation at a site, the value change of *A* will be propagated to *C*, as *C* is still expressed as *A+B*. On the other hand, if the operation updating the *formula* of *C* is executed first at another site, the value change of *A* will not be propagated to *C*, as *C* is defined as *B+D*, when *A* changes value.

If value propagations are performed in different orders and paths at different sites, consistent propagation effects must be maintained in CoVisio, so that after the same set of user operations and the value propagations triggered by these operations have been performed, the document states are identical at all the collaborating sites.

We have proved that if no cycle exists in any propagation path, *formula* consistency ensures consistent propagation effects in CoVisio, which can be curtly explained as follows:

We can use a constraint graph to express the relationship between different graphic attributes (i.e. *cells*) of graphic objects in a Visio document. In a constraint graph, a circle represents a *cell*, a triangle a constant, and a square expresses a *formula*. We use the directed edges connecting *cells*, constants and *formulas* to express the constraint propagation paths. For any *formula, f*, in a Visio document, add a directed edge from *f* to the *cell* it defines. Moreover, for any *cell* reference or constant which *f* contains, add a directed edge from the referenced *cell* or constant to *f*. As a *cell* can be constrained by exactly one *formula*, each *cell* is pointed to by one directed edge. For example, suppose that *cell S* is defined by *formula, (width+height)/2*, and *width* and *height* are defined by *formulas, 50* and *60*, respectively. The constraint graph representing the relationship of the three *cells* is shown in Fig. 3.

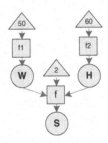

Fig. 3. A constraint graph, **W** and **H** represent *Width* and *Height*, respectively

If a *cell* is defined by a *formula* containing only constant input(s), such as *width* and *height* in the above example, Visio can calculate the value of the *cell* directly. On the other hand, if a *cell* is constrained by a *formula* containing some *cell* references, such as *S* in Fig.3, Visio has to calculate the value of the *cell* indirectly according to the values of the referenced *cells*. Therefore, the value of *S* should be calculated according to the values of *width* and *height*. Moreover, if the value of either *width* or *height* changes, the value of S will be changed accordingly as a result of constraint propagation.

Each time a user updates a Visio document, the constraint graph expressing the relationship of graphic objects in the document will be changed accordingly to reflect the effects of the user operation. For example, once the *formula* constraining S is changed from f to f', this change should be reflected in the graph, so that all the directed edges from and to f, and f itself should be deleted from the graph. Moreover, f' and new directed edges from and to f' should be added into the graph.

If two collaborative sites maintain the same constraint graph and no cycle exists in the graph, the document states at the two sites must be the same [2], [8]. Here, two identical constraint graphs ensure that: (1) the same set of *cells* is contained in each graph, and (2) the *formulas* defining the same *cell* are identical at different constraint graphs. OT ensures that after the same set of concurrent operations has been executed at all the collaborating sites of a CoVisio application, each site maintains the same constraint graph. Therefore, if no cycle exists in the constraint graph, consistent propagation result is maintained.

Constraint Maintenance (CM) component is implemented in GCE for constraint satisfaction. This component maintains system consistency based on OT's *formula* consistency maintenance result. It propagates value changes according to the user operations, which update Visio *formulas*, and the constraint graph expressing the relationship of graphic objects in a local Visio document. CM performs constraint propagation efficiently. For example, suppose that C is defined by *formula*, $A+B$, and two users concurrent update the *formulas* defining A and B, which result in the value changes of both A and B. CM is able to propagate the value changes of both A and B to C by one value propagation, rather than change the value of C twice, one for propagating A's value change to C and the other is for propagating the value change of B. This can improve system performance. Another functionality of CM is to prevent cyclic propagation path from occurring. Concurrently updating *formulas* in CoVisio may result in cyclic value propagation path. For instance, two users concurrently update the *formulas* defining A and B, so that A is confined by $B+C$ and B is confined by $A-C$. Cyclic propagation path must be prevented as it makes propagation cannot stop without outside interference. CM ensures acyclic propagation path based on our algorithm introduced in [3]. Due to the space limitation, these functionalities of CM will not be discussed in detail.

4 Conclusions and Future Work

Microsoft Visio is a well-known single-user commercial graphic editing application. It is desirable to leverage single-user MS Visio for multi-user real-time collaboration, so that users can work collaboratively in groups to improve productivity.

This paper addressed the key issues in developing CoVisio, especially, how to maintain both constraint and consistency in concurrent environments. We have proved that without cyclic propagation path, *formula* consistency ensures consistent propagation effects in CoVisio. This conclusion can be applied directly to leverage other commercial single-user applications, which support *formulas*, such as Microsoft Excel, for multi-user collaboration.

CoVisio adopted the architecture applied in both CoWord and CoPowerPoint. A CoVisio instance is composed of three components: SA, GCE and CA. GCE functionalities are extended in CoVisio by including constraint maintenance component. This component is responsible for maintaining constraints based on OT. Moreover, it prevents cyclic propagation path and efficiently propagates value changes. The constraint maintenance method implemented in CoVisio is generic and can be adopted by other collaborative systems that support *formulas*.

CoVisio has not extended all the Microsoft Visio functions for multi-user collaboration. For example, CoVisio users cannot execute self-designed programs, add-in, to perform complicated graphic manipulation functions. How to enrich CoVisio with sophisticated graphic manipulation functions has been investigated and will be reported in our further publications.

Over the last fifteen years, real-time collaborative systems have moved from being prototypes in laboratories to becoming usable commercial systems and also freeware. With the investigation of enriching single-user commercial systems that support constraints with collaborative functions, we hope to make real-time collaboration even more efficient and productive.

References

1. Begole, J., et al.: Resource Sharing for Replicated Synchronous Groupware. IEEE/ACM Transactions on Networking 9(6), 833–843 (2001)
2. Borning, A., et al.: Constraint Hierarchies. Lisp and Symbolic Computation 5(3), 223–270 (1992)
3. Lin, K., Chen, D., Sun, C., Dromey, R.G.: Maintaining Constraints in Collaborative Graphic Systems: the CoGSE Approach. In: Proceedings of 9th European Conference on Computer-Supported Cooperative Work (ECSCW05) (September 2005)
4. Microsoft, Developing Microsoft Visio Solutions, http://msdn2.microsoft.com/en-us/library/aa245244(office.10).aspx
5. Sun, C., et al.: Achieving Convergence, Causality-Preservation, and Intention-Preservation in Real-Time Cooperative Editing Systems. ACM Transactions on Computer-Human Interaction (TOCHI) 5(1), 63–108 (1998)
6. Sun, C., et al.: Transparent Adaptation of Single-user Applications for Multi-user Real-time Collaboration. ACM Transactions on Computer-Human Interaction (TOCHI) 13(4), 531–582 (2006)
7. Sun, D. et al.: Operational Transformation for Collaborative Word Processing. In: ACM Conference on CSCW, November 6–10, Chicago, USA (2004)
8. Zanden, B.: An Incremental Algorithm for Satisfying Hierarchies of Multi-way Dataflow Constraints. ACM Transaction on Programming Languages and Systems 18(1), 30–72 (1996)
9. Xia, Q., et al.: Leveraging Single-user Applications for Multi-user Collaboration: the Co-Word Approach. In: ACM Conference on CSCW, Chicago, USA, November 6-10, 2004, pp. 162–171 (2004)

Lattices and the Collaborative Design in Shipbuilding

Maryna Z. Solesvik[1], Sylvia Encheva[1], and Sharil Tumin[2]

[1] Stord/Haugesund University College, Bjørnsonsg. 45, 5528 Haugesund, Norway
mzs@hsh.no, sbe@hsh.no
[2] University of Bergen, IT-Dept., P.O. Box 7800, 5020 Bergen, Norway
edpst@it.uib.no

Abstract. The paper is devoted to application of formal concept analysis and collaborative design in shipbuilding. Sourcing and shoring strategies of a Norwegian multinational design company is illustrated by a concept lattice.

Keywords: multiple location collaborative design applications, virtual organizations, shipbuilding.

1 Introduction

The modern globalization trends together with computer, information and communication technologies have great influence on the collaborative nature of a ship design. A few decades ago collaborating partners in the ship design process such as shipyards, shipowners, designers and suppliers were mainly located in one country. Nowadays they operate all over the globe. Collaborative processes inside participant organizations are also becoming much more complicated. On the one hand, the number of subcontractors has increased during the last thirty years. Enterprises tend to concentrate on their core competencies and outsource a number of operations that have been made in-house earlier. This concerns, first of all, shipyards. On the other hand, all collaborative participants in the shipbuilding try to minimize their expenses by offshoring activities, partly or entirely, to other countries. This lead to creation of virtual organizations which became popular among firms of different sizes during the last decade. The establishment of virtual organizations is a response to new business environment conditions. Formation of virtual organizations gives participants benefits of large organizations without disadvantages appropriate to complicated organizations [5]. The nature of the ship design work is favorable to the emergence of virtual enterprises in this area. The technical work is greatly computer-assisted. Information is produced in electronic form (such as, drawings and specifications). This gives a possibility of virtual working. Ship designers benefit from standardization. Standard software is used around the world to make drawing.

It is a very common situation in the modern shipbuilding when the shipowner is, for example, from the Great Britain, a designer is from Norway, the shipyard

Y. Luo (Ed.): CDVE 2007, LNCS 4674, pp. 361–368, 2007.

is situated in China, and suppliers are from all over the world. Globalization tendencies, tough competition, geographical and cultural remoteness demand high level of inter-enterprise and intra-firm collaboration during the ship design process.

The objective of the paper is to investigate the possibility of application of the formal concept analysis in the area of virtual organizations. The methodology of this paper uses concept lattices as a tool for the formalization and integration of concepts in the shipbuilding process and relationships encoded in different domain-specific concepts, to reveal their association and interaction. Sourcing and shoring strategies of a multinational design company are illustrated by a concept lattice.

The rest of the paper is organized as follows. Related work and statements from formal concept analysis may be found in Section 2. The main results of the paper are placed in Section 3 and Section 4. The paper ends with a conclusion in Section 5.

2   Related Work

Formal concept analysis [9], [16] started as an attempt of promoting better communication between lattice theorists and users of lattice theory. Since 1980's formal concept analysis has been growing as a research field with a broad spectrum of applications. Various applications of formal concept analysis are presented in [10]. A technical oriented application field of formal concept analysis is the area of production planning where the concept lattices are used to partition the products into disjoint groups during the optimization of the production cost [16].

A *context* is a triple (G, M, I) where G and M are sets and $I \subset G \times M$. The elements of G and M are called *objects* and *attributes* respectively [7]. The set of all concepts of the context (G, M, I) is a complete lattice and it is known as the *concept lattice* of the context (G, M, I).

For $A \subseteq G$ and $B \subseteq M$, define

$$A' = \{m \in M \mid (\forall g \in A) \ gIm\}, \quad B' = \{g \in G \mid (\forall m \in B) \ gIm\}$$

so A' is the set of attributes common to all the objects in A and B' is the set of objects possessing the attributes in B. Then a *concept* of the context (G, M, I) is defined to be a pair (A, B) where $A \subseteq G$, $B \subseteq M$, $A' = B$ and $B' = A$. The *extent* of the concept (A, B) is A while its intent is B.

The structure of a concept lattice is represented with a Hasse diagram. The Hasse diagram is a special directed graph, where the nodes are the concepts and the edges correspond to the neighborhood relationship among the concepts. The Hasse diagram of a concept lattice is used to describe the concepts hidden in the underlying data system.

3   Virtual Organization Concept

Virtual organization concept was first proposed in [8]. Virtual organization can be defined as "one to which different people contribute, from the strategic apex to the operational level, and do not necessarily coincide on time or space" [11]:242. Since then different impacts were explored by researchers: social, psychological, information and communication technology (ICT), and others. The bulk of research in the area of virtual organizations is devoted to ICT aspects. The use of sophisticated information technologies in modern virtual organizations is an important issue and is considered as a source of competitive advantage [13]. ICT is a source of extra margin for virtual enterprises [6]. These tools include collaboration software, internet, intranet, electronic mail, databases, groupware, and the like. However, not all virtual organizations depend on the electronic collaboration tools. Some industries, such as film-making enterprises, are essentially project oriented, but the collaboration process in this type of virtual organizations consists mainly in socialization processes rather than electronically based tools [1].

In fact, it is much easier, quicker, and cheaper to move information in electronic form than traditionally paper based information exchange and relocate people [12]. But the success of virtual enterprises depends greatly not only on ICT tools used, but on focusing on common goals and peoples dynamics [2]. At the same time there is a stresses on importance of the exploration of information and communication tools used in inter-firm collaboration since it sheds light on the nature of virtual organizations' operations [2].

Emergence of virtual organizations may lead to a principally novel manner of doing business [14]. Virtual organizations make it possible, first, for business units with limited resources to realize projects that would be impossible to accomplish for them alone, [3]. Second, powerful businesses also benefit from virtual organizations by more rational utilization of their core competencies. Virtuality here refers to "ability of an enterprise to offer customers a complete product or service, with the enterprise itself having only a few proprietary competencies while remaining required competencies are achieved through cooperation" [3]:213. According to [6] there are three important problems in virtual organizations - cooperation, coordination, and change. The members of virtual organization are connected with the common goals. Cooperation here is referred to the task of goal aligning [6].

4   Internal and External Collaborative Process in the Vessel Design

There are two directions in collaborative ship design. First, there is collaborative design work between all participants of the shipbuilding chain: the shipping company and its customers, the hull and outfitting yards, ship designers, suppliers of materials and equipment, and others. This is an external collaboration. It is necessary to consider customer's requirements, technical possibilities of manufacturers, delivery times, and economic efficiency of single operations and chosen options. Moreover, the preferred design must be in compliance to technical and safety rules of classification societies which control the design documentation, national maritime authorities, and international maritime conventions.

Second, internal collaborative processes inside the contributing organizations are important for the whole ship design progression. For instance, large and medium-sized ship design companies are not confined inside a single office or the same country. They actively participate in international business and become multinational. Many design firms have moved their businesses closer to the leading shipbuilding destinations and try to produce vessel drawings in lower-cost countries. The most advanced design companies tend rather to manage drawing production from the home country than to make drawing themselves. It does not mean that the quality suffers or firms exploit labour in lower-cost regions, just the price of consumption basket is minor there.

We must admit that effective insourcing and outsourcing is a vital part for those companies that want to compete effectively in the present and in the future. The offshoring theory defines six main strategies

- onshore insourcing (Ion),
- onshore outsourcing (Oon),
- nearshore insourcing (In),
- nearshore outsourcing (On),
- offshore insourcing (Ioff), and
- offshore outsourcing (Ooff).

They are derivatives of sourcing policies and subcontractors' geographical location. For example, the main sourcing strategies may be divided in insourcing (that is when the work is performed by company's department or subsidiary) and outsourcing (the case when the job is done by a third-party vendor). From the geographical point of view, strategies are categorized to onshoring (the executor is situated inside the client's home country), nearshoring (the internal or external subcontractor is located abroad, but geographically close, often in the same or nearby time zone), and offshoring (the piece of work is done far away from the domestic territory).

Let us illustrate these strategies by looking at a transnational virtual enterprise - a ship design group. The VS Group has several branches in Norway, Poland, Serbia, China, India, and Brazil, (see Table 1). The headquarters is situated in Norway. The VS Group optimally combines insourcing and outsourcing strategies. Such a policy is called "flexible sourcing" [4]. The company's management redistributes works that should be done among the VS subsidiaries. Sometimes VS uses vendors for some kinds of job or attract third-party firms in order to complete the tasks on time. Typically this takes place during the shipbuilding boom periods when the number of design orders exceeds existing capacities.

The ship design work is not homogeneous. There are usually four alternatives.

- *To design a sister vessel*: that is to copy a design of an existing ship. That is often a case of duplicating the success design that has proved to be reliable and effective in the sea operations.
- *To design a similar vessel with minor changes*: regular practice in the maritime business to make changes in the vessel design to follow the regulations

Table 1. Design based on Insourcing and Outsourcing

	Insourcing			Outsourcing		
	Onshore	Nearshore	Offshore	Onshore	Nearshore	Offshore
Norway	Skipskonsulent AS (Bergen) El-Design AS (Omastrand) VS Industrial Design AS (Fitjar) Omega Technology AS (Ålesund)			Albatross Services AS (Stavanger) East European Consulting (Austevoll)		
Poland		Vik-Sandvik Poland Ltd (Gdynia)			Navicentrum (Wroclaw)	
Serbia		Albatros DO (Novy Sad)			Infinity Craft Ltd. (Belgrade)	
China			SK Shanghai			DF-Marine Dalian
Brazil			Vik-Sandvik Brazil			PROJEMAR (Rio de Janeiro)
India			Vik-Sandvik Design India Pvt Ltd			
Ukraine					Sudomarket Ltd (Nikolaev)	
Italy					Gloss Design (S.Giovanni Teatino)	

of the state flag, port states, or satisfy owner's and customers demand. That is especially actual in the case of long-time charter (ten years and longer), when the shipping company only owns and carries out daily management of the vessel following directions of the industrial customer.

It is notably that the price for the set of classification drawings in the first and the second cases is only 20-25% lower than for a new design.

- *To design a new design*: the design process takes longer time and suits for shipping companies with special requirements.
- *To have a fundamentally novel design*: that is a situation when the ship owner has a policy of keeping modern vessels, concerns about the environment and aims to employ power saving technologies. From the recent novel designs examples we can mention gas-driven ferries and platform supply vessels. Such vessels have significant advantages compared to traditional ships that use diesel and marine oils as a fuel. Gas-driven ships allow achieving higher speed and saving considerably on fuel.

The first two options are comparatively easy to perform and the work does not require a very high qualification. This core work may not easily be sourced out either to subsidiaries or third-part collaboration partners.

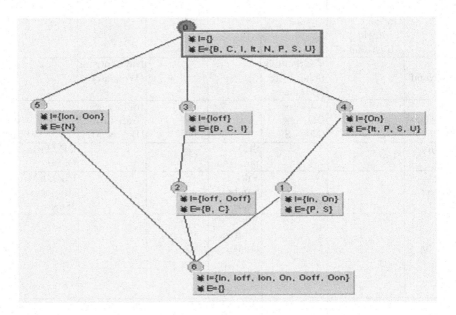

Fig. 1. Concept lattice

A formalization of the semantic basis of the shipbuilding process concepts consists of two parts: the extension and the intension. The extension includes the instances, which belong to the concept, whereas the intension represents its intrinsic meaning and is usually described in terms of discriminating properties, criteria or conditions. The method can achieve the integration of different components in the shipbuilding process, exhibiting differences in application context and thematic resolution. Related categories can be associated with subtype, supertype or overlapping relationships. Formal concept analysis is further applied to combine different categories and generate a corresponding concept lattice.

The concept lattice on Fig. 1 facilitates information exchange between ship owner, design agent, shipyard/s, classification society, suppliers, model basin, etc.

All concepts are presented by the labels attached to every node of the lattice. The meaning of the used notations is as follows.

- Node number 2 has a label $I = \{Ioff, Ooff\}, E = \{B, C\}$. It means that some activities are insourced and outsourced offshore to Brazil and China only.
- Node number 4 has a label $I = \{On\}, E = \{It, P, S, U\}$. It means that some activities are outsourced nearshore to exactly four countries - Italy, Poland and Serbia and Ukraine.
- Node number 5 has a label $I = \{Ion, Oon\}, E = \{N\}$, and it means that Norway is the only country in this example with activities that are insourced nearshore and outsourced offshore.

5 Conclusion

Key features of the virtual organizations are goal orientation, temporary character, flexibility, geographical dispersion, and cultural differences. All these factors stipulate massive and complicated information flow between agents. The enormous information flow in a shipbuilding design process requires an effective system for collaboration. The methodology of this paper uses concept lattices as a tool for the formalization and integration of concepts in the shipbuilding process concepts and relationships encoded in different domain-specific concepts, to reveal their association and interaction.

References

1. Beckett, R.C.: Determining the Anatomy of Business Systems for a Virtual Enterprise. Computers in Industry 51, 127–138 (2003)
2. Beckett, R.C.: Exploring Virtual Organizations Using Activity Theory (2004)
3. Bremer, C.F., Michilini, F.V.S., Siqueira, J.E.M., Ortega, L.M.: VIRTEC: An Example of Brazilian Virtual Organization. Journal of Intelligent Manufacturing 12, 213–221 (2001)
4. Chakrabarty, S.: Making Sense of the Sourcing and Shoring Maze: Various Outsourcing and Offshoring Alternatives. In: Kehal, H., Singh, V. (eds.) Outsourcing and Offshoring in the 21st century, pp. 18–53. Idea Group Publishing, Hershey London Melbourne Singapore (2006)
5. Collins, P.: Virtual and Networked Organizations. Capstone Publishing, Oxford (2002)
6. Corvello, V., Migliarese, P.: Virtual Forms for the Organization of Production: A comparative Analysis. International Journal of Production Economics (2007), doi:10.1016/j.ijpe.2007.02.006
7. Davey, B.A., Priestley, H.A.: Introduction to lattices and order. Cambridge University Press, Cambridge (2005)
8. Davidow, W., Malone, M.: The Virtual Corporation. Harper Collins, New York (1993)
9. Ganter, B., Wille, R.: Formal Concept Analysis - Mathematical foundations. Springer, Heidelberg (1999)

10. Ganter, B., Stumme, G., Wille, R.: Formal Concept Analysis - Foundations and Applications. In: Ganter, B., Stumme, G., Wille, R. (eds.) Formal Concept Analysis. LNCS (LNAI), vol. 3626, Springer, Heidelberg (2005)
11. Gil-Estallo, M.-D.-A., Celma-Benaiges, M.D., Aparicio-Valverde, M., Ferruz-Periz, M., Escardibul-Ferra, B.: The New Organizational Structure and its Virtual Functioning. International Advances in Economic Research 6(2), 241–248 (2000)
12. Negroponte, N.: Being Digital. Knopf, New York (1995)
13. Potpcan, V., Dabic, M.: The Virtual Organization from the Viewpoint of Informing (2002)
14. Taylor, R., Peltsverger, B., Vasu, M.: The Nature of Virtual Organizations and their Anticipated Social and Psychological Impacts. Education and Information Technologies 2, 347–360 (1997)
15. Wille, R.: Concept lattices and conceptual knowledge systems. Computers and Mathematics with Applications 23(6-9), 493–515 (1992)
16. Wille, R.: Formal concept analysis as mathematical theory of concepts and concept hierarchies. In: Ganter, B., Stumme, G., Wille, R. (eds.) Formal Concept Analysis. LNCS (LNAI), vol. 3626, pp. 1–3. Springer, Heidelberg (2005)

Web-Based Engineering Portal for Collaborative Product Development

Shuangxi Huang and Yushun Fan

Department of Automation,
Tsinghua University, 100084 Beijing, P.R. China
{huangsx,fanyus}@tsinghua.edu.cn

Abstract. Nowadays, collaborative product development has become a strategic necessity to develop high quality products at low cost and with quick response time to market demand. Past decades have seen significant advances to collaborative product development. However, Enterprises are still confronted with some problems. Firstly, the research in strategic level of collaborative product development is lacking. There are no formal processes and models for collaborative product development. On the other hand, the full alignment between information system and collaborative business is still missing. The information system cannot adapt to the fast changed business. This paper aims to provide the strategy and reference business model for collaborative product development. And then, to support the implementation of strategy and model, a workflow and web service based engineering collaboration portal is developed. The workflow is used to model and execute the collaborative product development processes, and the web service is the implementing technology of the portal. The combination of workflow and web service can fit the gap between business and information system and achieve on-demand business.

Keywords: Web-based, portal, collaborative product development, web service.

1 Introduction

The advancement of information technology, dynamic market, and global environment has set a new stage for manufacturing. In order to remain competitive and to maintain their competitive advantage, enterprises must be able to 1)manage increasing product complexity and product innovation from market demands, 2) have faster and more flexible product development cycle, and 3) control globally distributed/outsourced operations[1]. One strategy for enterprises to succeed in this environment is Collaborative Product Development (CPD). Several similar terms already exist in the literatures, such as collaborative engineering [2], collaborative design [3], and collaborative product commerce [4]. Each term emphasizes different aspects and applications. In this paper, CPD is defined as: "an Internet based computational architecture that supports the sharing and transferring of knowledge and information of the product life cycle amongst geographically distributed companies to aid taking right decisions in a collaborative environment" [5]. The main goal of CPD is to integrate and leverage knowledge, technologies, and resources

Y. Luo (Ed.): CDVE 2007, LNCS 4674, pp. 369–376, 2007.

among all the collaborators through the full life cycle of product development. In the last decades, significant efforts have been made in the research of CPD. Most of them have been focused on enhanced collaboration by leveraging information technologies, such as how to develop a collaborative information platform [6], what is an acceptable standard for information/knowledge exchange and presentation [7], what is an efficient information/knowledge schema to be shared among collaborators [8], how to improve detailed functionalities of the CPD system [9].

However, technology is not the whole of CPD anyway. Regarding collaboration processes between dislocated partners, collaborating companies still manage their product development processes in a highly inconsistent and inefficient way because there is no common model to specify the collaborative process to be shared in partners especially in cultural backgrounds (language, education, rules of behaviour etc.).

The past studies pay more attention to the research of theories and technologies. There have been very few reports concerning the best practices and the reference processes of CPD deployment in industry settings, especially inter-organization and cross-culture collaborations. Due to lacking knowledge of deploying CPD in current industrial settings, the research efforts may thus fail to fulfill practical needs [10].

On the other hand, in IT perspective, although numerous IT technologies and tools have been developed to facilitate the collaborative product development, they are simply the fraction of the software functions required to enable the collaboration process in the full lifecycle of CPD. Most of them focus on the engineering development, which is in the later phase of CPD. Few technologies and tools are developed to facilitate the early phase of CPD, such as contact initiation and collaboration establishment.

Furthermore, the alignment between business processes and supported IT system is largely missing. The current CPD system can not adapt to the fast changed requirements and business processes due to the architecture, implementation technologies, and control mechanism of the system. How to align the CPD requirements and processes with the supported IT systems is one of the key challenges of CPD.

In order to solve the above mentioned difficulties, in this paper, a web-based engineering portal is developed and implemented to enable value-added collaboration between European and Chinese partners by providing new technical solutions, best practices, and collaboration tools. The Engineering Portal represents a virtual, process-driven and service-oriented integration platform accessible to the involved companies within a heterogeneous IT-infrastructure.

The paper is organized as follows: In section 2, a structural top-down analysis approach is used to derive all the necessary business objectives and processes that must be achieved in CPD. Based on reference model, the strategy of CPD is proposed. In section 3, the development and implementation of a web based engineering portal for CPD is discussed. The web service is used to wrap all the components of the portal into services. Different services are provided by the portal to facilitate the full life cycle processes of CPD. In section 4, the scenario validation of the portal is described. The contributions of the portal in this scenario are introduced. Finally, the conclusions of the paper are summarized in section 5.

2 Reference Model and Strategy for CPD

In order to derive all the necessary business objectives that enterprise users must achieve in CPD processes, a structural top-down analysis approach is used. The approach started with the overall objective of CPD, i.e. to collaborate with other enterprises based on core competence and economic benefit, therefore, to be able to quickly delivery high quality product to customers with low cost. In general, the objectives of enterprises utilizing CPD fall into three categories: seeking collaboration opportunities by publishing their products and/or services, outsourcing some engineering tasks by selecting suitable collaboration partners, and performing engineering collaboration with the partners. From the perspectives of enterprises, the overall objective is broken into more tangible objectives that can be realized in certain stages of the whole collaboration process. Within this paper, the overall objective is realized in two stages, i.e. the earlier phase of the collaboration process and the later phase of the collaboration process. The respective objectives of the two stages are:

- To facilitate the establishment of OEM-supplier or joint venture collaborative relationships
- To facilitate collaborative product development

The two stages are referred to as the medium-level objectives in the structural analysis approach. The medium-level objectives are further broken into detailed-level objectives, which can be realized through the execution of the respective business processes. The reference model for CPD is illustrated in figure 1.

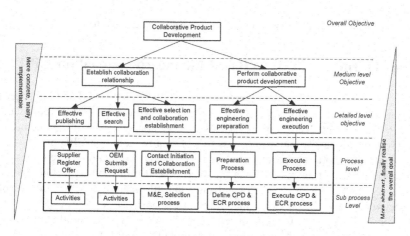

Fig. 1. The reference model for CPD

In order to support the implementation of the above mentioned objectives, the strategy for CPD is proposed to provide an overall framework to enable common, tightly integrated product development processes between distributed companies based on given IT-technologies and software tools as well as Internet technologies

[11]. Figure 2 shows the conceptual architecture of the strategy. Five basic requirements in CPD were addressed in the strategy:

1) Locate collaboration partners in markets, to initiate contact and to establish a collaboration,

2) Support the dynamic integration of development processes based on consistent information models,

3) Support the handling, visualization and validation of product data,

4) Facilitate a requirement driven product development process, and

5) Identify and solve problems caused by cultural differences.

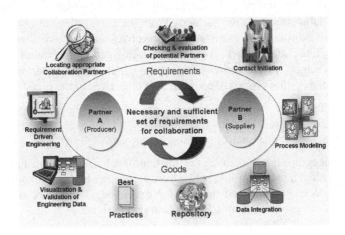

Fig. 2. Strategy for collaborative product development

3   Implementation of Web Based Engineering Portal for CPD

In this paper, a web based engineering portal for CPD is developed and implemented. The engineering portal represents a process- and service-oriented integration platform accessible to the involved companies within a heterogeneous IT-infrastructure. The portal serves as a central point of access to a (virtually) common CPD process model and allows collaborating partners to share product information stored in various application systems transparently via the Web. The use of modern technologies, i.e. web service and workflow, enables not only the information collaboration from IT perspective, but also the process collaboration from business perspective [12].

As shown in figure 3, four major layers are identified in the portal's architecture: application service layer, infrastructure layer, collaboration service layer, and UI (user interface) service layer.

1) The application service (AS) layer provides functionalities to access proprietary information sources of the enterprises involved in a collaboration, like PDM-systems, ERP-systems, etc. The connection between portal and the application systems is realized with SOAP. Therefore an adapter must be

implemented for every application, which assumes the mapping between the enterprises' applications and SOAP.

2) The Infrastructure Service (IS) layer: The infrastructure layer provides the basic data service and integration service for CPD. All data flows within portal are supported by the infrastructure. The data service manages distributed data sources and offers a transparent view on the data for the portal services. The integration service provides the interaction mechanism between portal components. In order to provide these functionalities, the infrastructure has to provide functions/services to manipulate the data. These services could either rely directly on the meta data model or use a more high level business context. The Integrated Domain Data Models are derived from the meta data model and contain the data object types which are required by the business services provided by the components. The infrastructure provides the basic access function to data and components according to the meta data model and/or according to the integrated domain data model. The meta data model interface and the integrated domain data model interface together represents the data interface. This interface is accessible through Web Services.

3) The collaboration service layer provides the specific collaboration services. According to the CPD strategy mentioned in section 2, five basic collaboration components are provided by the portal in form of service:

(1) Request & Navigation Component (RNC): The Request and Navigation Component offers functionalities to find a relevant partner, initiate contact with the found partner, and establish collaboration by defining universal conditions and arranging competences and responsibilities.

(2) Check of Collaboration Partners Component (CCP): The Check of Collaboration Partner component is utilized to support the collaboration initiation phase of CPD. It is divided into three services: partner matching, evaluation of Matching Results, and evaluation of Offers during Negotiation.

(3) Process Management Component (PMC): The Process Management Component provides functionalities for modeling and executing the CPD processes. The process models are saved in the portal in a certain process definiton format, which can be interpreted by the workflow engine, which coordinates the execution of these business processes.

(4) Specification Modeler Component (SMC): The Specification Modeler Component lets users define and manage a necessary and sufficient subset of product requirements. It further provides functionality for the checking of consistency and completeness of requirements and product properties. It is also involved in the early phases, when initial product requirements are formulated and when requirements on potential partner companies are defined. The data is only shared by involved partners.

(5) Visualization & Validation Component (VVC): The Visualization & Validation Component allows users to define different views on engineering data and to validate the data. The data is only shared by involved partners.

(6)   Cultural Repository Component (CR): In order to override the problems in collaborative processes between distributed companies caused by different cultural backgrounds and differences in language and education, a cultural repository is foreseen. Its functionality is going beyond simple request-based advisory systems and literature databases. It also intends to survey ongoing processes on the portal and intervene when necessary.

4)   UI service layer: In portal, the service-specific UI service and generic UI service will be provided for browsing available information resources or navigating through networked data structures. The UI services interact with the other services via HTTP or SOAP.

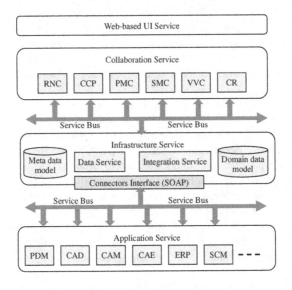

Fig. 3. The Architecture of engineering portal

4   Scenario Validation for Engineering Portal

The scenario selected in this paper is about the collaborative development of a new variant of a car in Mercedes-Benz. There is an existing type: Mercedes-Benz "A-Class A 210". The new variant should be bullet proofed. Only parts, concerning the bullet resistance have to be modified. In this scenario only the left rear door is modified. The scenario demonstrates the whole development process beginning with the search for a new supplier for a window motor and ending with a certified prototype of a bullet proofed. Table 1 shows the stakeholders in this scenario.

The scenario contains the following general steps:

1)   User login and registration,
2)   Search for a new supplier, matching of possible suppliers,
3)   Sign the contract,
4)   Define a new product by using a template,

5) Definition of initial requirements,
6) Consistence check,
7) Start of the development process
8) Definition of detailed requirements,
9) Consistence checking, CAD visualization
10) Data exchange (using the security tool for CAD data, DMU, simulation)
11) Testing, release,
12) End of development project

Several components of the portal are used to support the implementation of the scenario. Table 2 shows the contributions of the portal components in the scenario.

Table 1. Stakeholders in the scenario of Mercedes-Benz

Shortcut	Name	Description
OEM	Mercedes-Benz	Development of the whole car, management of the suppliers and development partners.
SUP 1	Car Engineering Solutions	Development (design) of the modified door, including the window glass.
SUP 2	Electric-Motor-Corporation	Supplier of the window motor.
BOA	Shelling Office	Official institution, tests the new guard variant, before it gets the sign of authorization to be called "bullet proofed". They also provide guidelines to reach the authorization.

* OEM: Original Equipment Manufacturer. SUP: Supplier. BOA: Official Board.

Table 2. The contributions of the portal components

Name	Phase	Description
IS, UI	SP, CE, CPD	Showing and handling of the distributed data (Requirements, CATIA V5-files, pictures, "pdf" and "Word"-documents). Integration of the portal components.
RNC	SP, CE	Search for a new supplier for the window motor.
CCP	SP, CE	Locating of a new supplier for the window motor.
PMC	CPD	Modelling and Management the development processes between the project partners.
VVC	SP, CE, CPD	Visualisation of the CAD model and data (product requirements, pictures, "pdf"- and "Word"-documents).
SMC	SP, CE, CPD	Definition of the initial (process and product) and detailed requirements, use of templates, consistency check of the requirements including an automated generating of new requirements, interactions between OEM and Supplier according the requirements.
CR	SP, CE, CPD	Notification of the users about differences between some countries according norms and laws.

* SP: Searching Partner, CE: Collaboration Establishment, CPD: Collaborative Product Development.

5 Conclusions

Enterprises are driven by the world market to seek global engineering opportunities, which can be for example joint ventures, subsidiaries or relations with foreign suppliers. In order to ensure an efficient and reliable partnership with cooperators in distributed environments, the common processes of collaboration must be modeled and controlled, and the necessary information to be passed between business partners must be defined and provided. The research results of this paper enable the collaborative product development by providing the common CPD processes and the new technical solutions for the engineering portal. The activities and business processes supported by the engineering portal cover the full life cycle of CPD, from the searching of potential partners, establishing collaboration to the engineering development of product. Through the scenario validation, the portal can effectively support the whole processes in CPD. Both manufacturer and supplier are enabled to collaborate via the portal.

Acknowledgments. The research of the paper is supported by the National Natural Science Foundation projects of China under Grant No. 60504030, the National Basic Research Program of China under Grant No. 2006CB705407 and the European Commission FP6 project ImportNET.

References

1. Hong, S.J.: Web service oriented collaborative workflow management for design and manufacturing, Master Thesis, Michigan State University (2004)
2. Cutkosky, M.R., Tanenbaum, J.M., Glicksman, J.: Made fast collaborative engineering over the Internet. Commun. ACM 39, 78–87 (1996)
3. Li, W.D., Lu, Y.Q., Lu, W.F., et al.: Collaborative Computer-Aided Design: Research and Development Status. Computer Aided Design and Applications 2, 127–136 (2004)
4. Morris, A.: The Challenge of Collaborative Commerce. IEE Rev. 48, 33–37 (2002)
5. Rodriguez, K., Al-Ashaab, A.: A review of internet based collaborative product development systems. In: Proceedings of the International Conference on Concurrent Engineering: Research and Applications, Cranfield, UK (2002)
6. Li, W.D., Qiu, Z.M.: State-of-the-art technologies and ethodologies for collaborative product development systems. International Journal of Production Research 13, 2525–2559 (2006)
7. Teresa, W., Nan, X.: Design and Implementation of a Distributed Information System for Collaborative Product Development. Journal of Computing and Information Science in Engineering 12, 281–293 (2004)
8. Lihui, W., Weiming, S., Helen, X., et al.: Collaborative Conceptual Design: A State-of-the-Art Survey. In: Proceedings of CSCWD2000, Hong Kong, pp. 204–209 (2000)
9. Karina, R., Ahmed, A.: Knowledge web-based system architecture for collaborative product development. Computers in Industry 56, 125–140 (2005)
10. Chu, C.H., Chang, C.J., Cheng, H.C.: Empirical Studies on Inter-rganizational Collaborative Product Development. Journal of Computing and Information Science in Engineering 6, 179–187 (2006)
11. DRAGON Consortium, (2006) available at, http://www.dragon.uni-karlsruhe.de
12. Jae, Y.L., Lee, S., Kwangsoo, K., et al.: Process-centric engineering Web services in a distributed and collaborative environment. Computers & Industrial Engineering 51, 297–308 (2006)

Application of Paraconsistent Logic in an Intelligent Tutoring System

Sylvia Encheva[1], Sharil Tumin[2], and Maryna Z. Solesvik[1]

[1] Stord/Haugesund University College, Bjørnsonsg. 45, 5528 Haugesund, Norway
sbe@hsh.no, mzs@hsh.no
[2] University of Bergen, IT-Dept., P. O. Box 7800, 5020 Bergen, Norway
edpst@it.uib.no

Abstract. Experience shows that testing students' understanding of new concepts immediately after they have been introduced considerably improves the learning process. In this work understanding of a concept is assumed to take place if a student can provide reasonably correct answers to questions requiring application this concept. A possible solution to the problem of how to determine whether students actually understand a concept is to give them tests. Such tests, being a part of an intelligent system, provide inconsistent information to intelligent agents, facilitating the tests evaluation process. This happens because the degree of a student's understanding varies a lot depending on factors like time and the way questions are formulated. Since classical logic fails to draw conclusions in the presence of inconsistencies we propose application of paraconsistent logic.

Keywords: intelligent infrastructures and automated methods, logic.

1 Introduction

Many philosophers have been questioning the "ex contradictione quodlibet" rule in classical logic. The rule states that in the presence of inconsistency, anything, and thus nothing useful at all, can be inferred as an answer to any given problem. However, the majority of today's information systems produce quite meaningful answers despite receivel of inconsistent information.

Russell and Whitehead's logicism, Hilbert's formalism and Brouwer's intuitionism [9] represent different approaches of building contradiction-free logic foundation of mathematics. The first two are based on classical logic while the third one is questioning the law of excluded middle (tertium non datur), which states that a statement is either true or false. Brouwer's intuitionism was first presented by axioms in [10].

In this paper we propose use of paraconsistent logic for assessing learner's understanding of a concept employing an intelligent tutoring system. An important advantage of using such a system is that problems with inconsistent and/or incomplete input can be resolved. In addition, using automated tests reduces

Y. Luo (Ed.): CDVE 2007, LNCS 4674, pp. 377–384, 2007.

the problem of evaluating learner's understanding to that of making a decision based on a limited number of alternatives. The applied system logic is very useful if incorporated in a multiple user system. This approach can facilitate both cooperative learning and cooperation of tutors.

The rest of the paper is organized as follows. Related work and supporting theory may be found in Section 2. The model of the proposed system is presented in Section 3. The system architecture is described in Section 4. The paper ends with a conclusion in Section 5.

2   Related Work

Paraconsistency is considered to be a way to reason in the presence of inconsistency [7]. Paraconsistent logic suggests a solution by disregarding the law of double negation and the law of contradiction [4].

The field of paraconsistent logic was independently established by Jaskowski [8] and da Costa [2]. Paraconsistency, many-valued logic, query answering systems and higher order logic are discussed in [15].

Lukasiewicz has devised a three-valued calculus whose third value, $\frac{1}{2}$, is attached to propositions referring to future contingencies [11]. The third truth value can be construed as 'intermediate' or 'neutral' or 'indeterminate' [14].

Let P be a non-empty ordered set. If $sup\{x, y\}$ and $inf\{x, y\}$ exist for all $x, y \in P$, then P is called a *lattice* [3].

The epistemic value of formula when it is known that the formula may take on the truth value true is denoted by unknown_t and by unknown_f when it is known that the formula may take on the truth value false, [5].

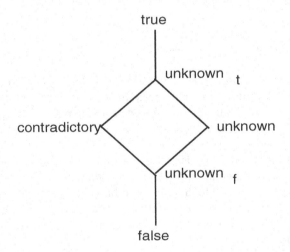

Fig. 1. Degree of truth

The epistemic value of formula when it is known that the formula may take on the truth value true is denoted by unknown$_t$ and by unknown$_f$ when it is known that the formula may take on the truth value false, [5].

The meaning of the used truth values is:

- true - it is possible to prove the truth of the formula (but not its falsity)
- false - it is possible to prove the falsity of the formula (but not its truth)
- unknown - it is not possible to prove the truth or the falsity of the formula (there is not enough information)
- unknown$_t$ - intermediate level of truth between unknown and true
- unknown$_f$ - intermediate level of truth between unknown and false
- contradiction - it is possible to prove both the truth and the falsity of the formula

A lattice showing a partial ordering of the elements false, unknown$_f$, contradiction, unknown$_t$, contradiction, true by degree of truth is presented in Fig. 1. The logical conjunction is identified with the meet operation and logical disjunction with the join operation.

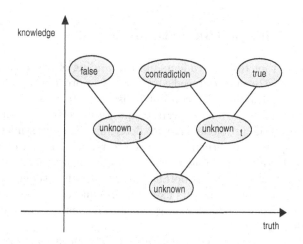

Fig. 2. Knowledge lattice

A lattice showing a partial ordering of the elements false, unknown$_f$, contradiction, unknown$_t$, contradiction, true by degree of knowledge is presented in Fig. 2. The knowledge lattice illustrates how the truth value of a formula that has a temporary truth value can be changed as more knowledge becomes available. Suppose a sentence has a truth value unknown$_f$ at one point of time and false at another. Its truth value is then determined as false, i.e. the system allows belief revision as long as the revision takes place in an incremental knowledge fashion.

Relationships among the described truth values are given in Table 1.

Table 1. Truth table

$\wedge$	true	false	contra-diction	unknown$_t$	unknown$_f$	unknown
true	true	false	contra-diction	unknown$_t$	unknown$_f$	unknown
false	false	false	false	false	false	false
contra-diction	contra-diction	false	contra-diction	contra-diction	unknown$_f$	unknown$_f$
unknown$_t$	unknown$_t$	false	contra-diction	unknown$_t$	unknown$_f$	unknown
unknown$_f$	unknown$_f$	false	unknown$_f$	unknown$_f$	unknown$_f$	unknown$_f$
unknown	unknown	false	unknown$_f$	unknown	unknown$_f$	contra-diction

3   Testing Concept Understanding

Experience shows that testing students' understanding of new concepts immediately after they have been introduced considerably improves the learning process. In this work understanding of a concept is assumed to take place if a student can provide reasonably correct answers to questions related to this concept. A possible solution to the problem of how to determine whether students really understand a concept is to give them tests. Such tests, being a part of an intelligent system, provide inconsistent input to the intelligent agents, facilitating the tests evaluation process. This happens because the degree of a student's understanding varies a lot depending on factors like time and question types. Since classical logic fails to draw conclusions in the presence of inconsistencies we propose use of paraconsistent logic.

We consider testing students' understanding of concepts introduced in a lecture. After the first concept being presented students are suggested to take a test with few questions that require skillful application of that concept. Based on student's responces an intelligent agent will recommend the student to proceed working with the next concept or to read some explanations related to his/her misconceptions and/or mistakes and then take a new test. Every following test contains new questions similar to the contents and level of difficulties of the previous one. The student is strongly advised to go back and work more on the presented learning materials about that concept if the third test still indicates lack of understanding of that concept. In the model for automated

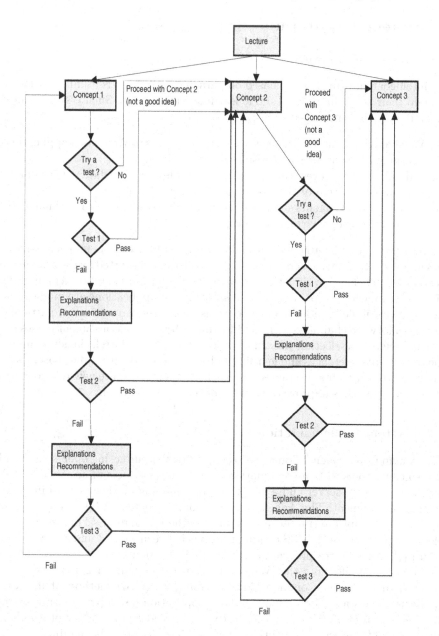

Fig. 3. Testing concept understanding

evaluation of concept understanding, shown on Fig. 3, we propose use of short tests. The decision making process is based on paraconsistent logic.

4   System Architecture

4.1   System Framework

An intelligent tutoring system based on paraconsistent logic is useful to students who do their study in a mixed mode learning environment. Such a system must support the following sub-systems:

1. Web based user interfaces for students and teachers to Web based applications
2. Learning objects, tests and results driven tutoring rules.
3. A database that stores students identity, profile and state data which support the implementation of the system as shown in Fig. 3
4. Intelligent multi-agents sub-system that provide students with optimal learning path for every particular concept.

Initially the system is provided with all relevant learning objects for each particulars line of study. The teachers responsible for subjects supported by the system are also responsible for providing the system with contents and meta-data of learning objects. For each concept thought in a subject, test applications are made to assess students' understanding. A test contains a small set of questions. A particular test has a forward chaining to the next learning object in case a student passes the test and refers to a selection of learning objects otherwise. The relationships among the test, results references and learning's objects are stored in the database. Using feedback from students responces, the teachers can incorporate new relationships at any time and thus improve the quality of the tutoring system.

4.2   System Implementation

The system is implemented on a Web server infrastructure using open source and free software tools. It is a combination of free software tools of an Apache Web server, a database server and a scripting programming platform on a Linux operating environment. The Apache server is complemented with security module mod_ssl and script interpreter module mod_python. The mod_ssl makes it possible to support secure HTTPS communications between a client and a server. The mod_python facilitates program applications in Python language. Since the interpreter is compiled into the Web sever, mod_python handler is hundreds time faster than the using Common Gateway Interface (CGI) method of invoking application softwares. Using mod_python, application developers have powerful development tools in their disposition. Python provides powerful set of standard libraries like for example networking and database connectivity modules.

The deployed Web application server is made of:

1. an Apache front end Web server
2. a Python based Web application middle-ware for dynamic content, data integration and user interface to software agents
3. a back end PostgreSQL database server for data store of both static and dynamic data.

Behind this traditional three-tiers Web deployment are service support subsystems. Communication framework based on XML-RPC is used to connect together the Web application middle-ware and the intelligent tutoring sub-system. The separation of these two software service units makes it possible to modularly design and implement the system as loosely couple independent sub-systems.

The Web application middle-ware and the software agents run independently of each other. As such, they can be situated on different servers. The middle-ware implement the Web side of the system while the software agents implement the logical side of the intelligent tutoring side of users, learning a particular subject. Given a certain result at a particular student learning state, what best action can be taken to increase the probability that the student will assimilate a piece of knowledge related to a particular learning process? This optimal learning path is provided by the intelligent tutoring agent.

5 Conclusion

Building computer systems based on classical logic requires data consistency and in real life a logical data consistency is almost impossible. Thus we come to the idea of proposing a model for an intelligent system using paraconsistent logic. The applied system logic is very useful if incorporated a multiple user system. This approach can facilitate cooperative learning as well as cooperation of tutors and cooperation of students. Furthermore, the system is able to provide distinctive characteristics of different degrees of students' concept understanding in the process of learning.

References

1. Belnap, N.J.: How a computer should think. In: Contemporary Aspects of Philosophy, vol. GB, pp. 30–56. Proceedings of the Oxford International Symposia, Oxford (1975)
2. da Costa, N.: On the Theory of Inconsistent Formal Systems. Notre Dame Journal of Formal Logic 15(4), 497–510 (1974)
3. Davey, B.A., Priestley, H.A.: Introduction to lattices and order. Cambridge University Press, Cambridge (2005)
4. Decker, H.: Historical and Computational Aspects of Paraconsistency in View of the Logic Foundation of Databases. In: Bertossi, L., Katona, G.O.H., Schewe, K.-D., Thalheim, B. (eds.) Semantics in Databases. LNCS, vol. 2582, pp. 63–81. Springer, Heidelberg (2003)
5. Garcia, O.N., Moussavi, M.: A Six-Valued Logic for Representing Incomplete Knowledge. In: Proceedings of ISMVL, pp. 110–114 (1990)
6. García-Duque, J., López-Nores, M., Pazos-Arias, J., Fernández-Vilas, A., Díaz-Redondo, R., Gil-Solla, A., Blanco-Fernández, Y., Ramos-Cabrer, M.: A Six-valued Logic to Reason about Uncertainty and Inconsistency in Requirements Specifications. Journal of Logic and Computation 16(2), 227–255 (2006)
7. http://plato.stanford.edu/entries/logic-paraconsistent/
8. Jaskowski, S.: Propositional Calculus for Contradictory Deductive Systems. Studia Logica 24, 143–157 (1969)

9. Kneale, W., Kneale, M.: The Development of Logic. Clarendon Press (1962)
10. Kolmogorov, A.N.: O principie tertium non datur. Matematiceskij Sbornik (Recueil Mathematique) 32 (1924/25)
11. Lukasiewicz, J.: On Three-Valued Logic. Ruch Filozoficzny, 5, (1920), English translation. In: Borkowski, L. (ed.) 1970. Jan Lukasiewicz: Selected Works, North Holland, Amsterdam (1920)
12. Priest, G.: An Introduction to Non-Classical Logic, Cambridge (2001)
13. Prior, A.N.: A Statement of Temporal Realism. In: Copeland, B.J. (ed.) Logic and Reality: Essays on the Legacy of Arthur Prior, Clarendon Press, Oxford (1996)
14. Sim, K.M.: Bilattices and Reasoning in Artificial Intelligence: Concepts and Foundations. Artificial Intelligence Review 15(3), 219–240 (2001)
15. Villadsen, J., Andreasen, T.: Paraconsistent Query Answering Systems. In: Andreasen, T., Motro, A., Christiansen, H., Larsen, H.L. (eds.) FQAS 2002. LNCS (LNAI), vol. 2522, pp. 370–384. Springer, Heidelberg (2002)

Novel Collaborative Automated Testing Framework Using DDF*

Songwen Pei, Baifeng Wu, Qiang Yu, and Kun Zhu

Department of computing and information technology, Fudan University,
Shanghai 200433, P.R. China
061021045@fudan.edu.cn

Abstract. Collaborative testing is an effective way of distributed interoperability in pursuit of automated testing. In this paper, a novel collaborative testing approach named Collaborative Automated Testing Framework (CATF) which meets the requirements of not only automated testing but also collaborative operation is proposed. Through the abstract analysis in terms of extended dynamic dataflow (DDF) model's viewpoint incorporating with UML2.0 profile of MDA, we design the framework with an automated engine working as a Finite State Machine (FSM). Particularly, as a approach to collaborative testing at a system level, CATF is implemented with component modules based on J2EE and verified to be of efficiency.

1 Introduction

Collaborative working on software is a critical and perpetual issue. As a consequence, the issues about collaborative developing and collaborative testing are surging out. In particular, automated and collaborative testing oriented to distributed systems and its applications is essential in effective development of reliable software. It is a hotspot not only in the domain of industrial application but also in the research field focusing on computer aided design, software development, etc. [1, 2]. Unfortunately, the dramatic expansion of software complexity and the shorter time-to-market become the strongest pressure and bring critical challenges to the research and industrial communities.

There has been lots of research referring to collaborative testing. However, scarcely has any approach to automated testing system-level model involved abstract dataflow model so far. Hence, we focus on this issue with an improved and integrated abstract testing approach based on dynamic dataflow (DDF) not only catering for collaborative operations but also meeting automated testing requirements. The separation of various aspects of concerns allows more effective exploration of alternative solutions, particularly the separation of function from architecture and the extraction of dataflow and control flow from system. In the Collaborative Automated Testing Framework (CATF), an extended dynamic dataflow corresponding to partitioned role relationships is considered, and a system-level Finite State Machine (FSM) is adopted in automated testing engine so as to guarantee a dynamic balance between input and output dataflow in the whole of testing system. All the testing operations through web interface are

Y. Luo (Ed.): CDVE 2007, LNCS 4674, pp. 385–395, 2007.

decompounded by DDF model and the role compatibility of various operations is guaranteed by the role interface algorithm.

Under the guide of the concept of dynamic dataflow, we have implemented the automated testing engine with distributed functions aiming at collaborative and concurrent testing using J2EE [3] model. The testing framework is modeled in terms of Model-View-Control (MVC) principle. It consists of five modules as a whole: Web Interface, Queue Pool, Dynamic Scheduler, Resource Manager Module and Test Result Module. The Web Interface module is a part of View in the MVC, and Queue Pool and Dynamic Scheduler model is corresponding to the Control in the MVC. Besides, the Execution Server in test engine is implemented by java beans or enterprise java beans to accomplish the tasks of Model in the MVC. Among others, the Resource Manager and Test Result module are supplements for advancing the efficiency and the quality of testing and fixing the bugs of tested functions.

The rest of this paper is organized as follows: In Section2, we review the related work about collaborative testing. The abstract analysis based on DDF will be discussed in Section 3. In Section 4, the critical models of CATF that are job scheduler and state transfer of FSM are expatiated on respectively. The novel collaborative automated test framework (CATF) is proposed in Section 5. At last, we conclude in the final section.

2 Related Work

The typical approach to depicting collaborative working depends on the Collaboration State Chart of UML. Therefore, modeling software system with UML testing profile is a predominant approach in the domain of collaborative working currently [4]. The main idea of Model Driven Architecture (MDA) is using UML to specify both the static interfaces and the dynamic behavior of the components in Platform-Independent Models (PIMs). Additionally, it defines rules so that PIMs can be mapped into a number of Platform-Specific Models (PSMs). Therefore, the MDA strengthens the concepts of portability and interoperability due to the transformation between PIMs and PSMs. Raul Silaghi, et al. [5] introduced the abstract and distributed realization profile oriented to MDA, but they didn't solve the collaboration issues existing in the distributed system. TPTP-based tools are not only interoperable but also tightly integrated with the Eclipse Platform-based development tools [6], but it can't accomplish automated testing directly. Recently, Pyxis Technologies has launched their testing product GreenPepper which is a platform intended to improve collaboration between business experts and software developers [7], but it cannot support automated testing among several testers. Petrenko, A.[8]proposed a queued-quiescence testing framework based on input-output transition systems, and it applied inputs via a queue to an implementation under test (IUT) and detected outputs from IUT. However, it lacks an effective mechanism to detect deadlocks occurred in queue. Jan Tretmans et al. [9, 10] designed an automated model based testing called TorX which is based on the ioco-test theory. In contrast with the framework of Torx, we intend to execute test cases and test suite automatically and collaboratively. However, they focus on how to generate test case and suite automatically.

Starting from a high-level of abstract about collaborative testing, with the capability of partitioning roles compatibly and decompounding functions properly using extended

DDF [11], the CATF becomes a system level solution for distributed collaborative testing. Songwen Pei et al. [12] introduced the main functions of Automated Testing System (ATS) based on J2EE that is similar to CATF, but without considering the effect of dataflow module throughout the whole system implicitly and analyzing the collaborations among different roles. In this paper, we focus on this issue to meet the collaborative testing based on the theory of DDF model.

3 Abstract Analysis Based on DDF

The two basic nodes: SWITCH node and SELECT node in Dynamic Data Flow (DDF) [13] model are shown in the Fig.1. The SELECT node corresponds to decision-making node of communication diagrams in UML, and the SWITCH node can accomplish the task of integration ability for sub-workflows. DDF is an extension model of Boolean-controlled Data Flow (BDF) that introduces dynamic nodes that may consume and produce varying numbers of data samples in an execution. Such an extension makes DDF possess the ability to represent data dependent on iterations such as "FOR" iterations conveniently. At the point of the high-level abstract, a simple DDF graph is depicted in Fig.2. It is a typical instance in DDF to express iteration structure.

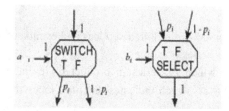
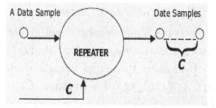

Fig. 1. SWITCH and SELECT node   **Fig. 2.** Simple DDF graph

As shown in the Fig.2, DDF graph is a directed graph containing nodes and edges in which the nodes of the graph can be viewed as processes that run concurrently and exchange data over the arcs of the graph and edges between nodes corresponding to data flows among computations. The simple DDF can be formally defined as a triple $D_f = < In, Out, R >$ such that:

In is the set of input dataflow,

Out is the set of output dataflow,

R is the set of relations between input and output dataflow.

DDF is an ideal model for common balance system currently. However, it is seldom applied in the field of automated testing. We have implemented a collaborative automated testing framework under the detail analyses about collaborative testing based on DDF in the following sections abstractly.

The function and object models in CATF reflect the dataflow and data respectively. Therefore, the most two important issues about collaborative automated testing base on

DDF, in the view of us, are roles compatibility and automated engine. With respect to roles compatibility, it guarantees the collaborative relationships on the operational layer and accomplishes the functions of communication diagram. As far as automated engine is concerned, it is the core unit of collaborative implementation and distributed execution in the CATF. On the high level viewpoint of CATF, the role compatibility corresponds to the function of PIMs, and the automated engine looks like the PSMs in MDA. We assumed that DDF had been transformed from UML successfully in this paper, and the following researches are based on the DDF model.

3.1 Roles Compatibility

Role interfaces compatibility is the capability of various role interfaces to exchange messages consisting with their interaction policies without exceptions and deadlocks. In order to implement collaborative work among test engineers, roles compatibility is essential to guarantee the actions among testers without confliction on the operational level.

Therefore, for discussing simply and formally, the finite state model denoting each role interaction policy is defined formally as a four tuple $RC = (Q, \Sigma, C, q_0)$, such that:

Q is the finite set of states,

Σ is the finite alphabet denoting the provided and required services and events, of which performance on the operational layer is series of actions,

C presents the set of transition relation which is Cartesian product represented as $C \subseteq Q \times \Sigma \times Q$. For instance, $C(\alpha, \beta) = \alpha'$ which indicates that after receiving an action β, the interaction finite state model transfers the state from α to α'.

q_0 is the initial state.

Definition: Let P be a set of states, $S(P) = \{a \in \Sigma \mid \exists p, p' \in P, p \rightarrow a.p'\}$ is in the interaction policy rules. That is $C(p, a) = p'$. I, I_c, I', I_c' are the sets of intermediate states while computing. And A is the set of actions while transiting states.

Algorithm of Role Compatibility is as below:

Input: $RC = (Q, \Sigma, C, q_0)$ and $RC_c = (Q_c, \Sigma_c, C_c, q_c)$
Output: TRUE if the roles are compatible; FALSE, otherwise.
Algorithm:
1 $RC = \varnothing$;
2 **If** $[(\Sigma_{in} \neq \Sigma_c^{out}) or (\Sigma_{out} \neq \Sigma_c^{in})]$ **then**
3   **return** FALSE;
4 **If** $(S_{in}(q_0) \subset S_{out}(q_c)) or (S_{in}(q_c) \subset S_{out}(q_0))$ **then**
5   **return** FALSE;

6 $RC = RC \cup [\{q_0\}, \{q_c\}, S(q_0)]$;

7 Repeat

8 $u = [I, I_c, A]$ where $A \neq \varnothing$ and choose an action $a \in A$

9 $RC = RC - u$;

10 $RC = RC \cup [I, I_c, A - \{a\}]$;

11   Compute I' and I_c' where $I_c \rightarrow a.I_c'$ and $I \rightarrow a.I'$

12   **If** $[I', I_c' \notin A'] \notin RC$ for some A' **then**

13   **If** $[(S_{in}(I') \subset S_{out}(I_c')) or (S_{out}(I') \subset S_{in}(I_c'))]$ **then**

14   **return** FALSE;

15   **If**

   $not (\forall p \in I_c', \exists p' \in I, S_{in}(p) \supseteq S_{out}(p'))$ and $(\forall p' \in I', \exists p \in I_c', S_{in}(p') \supseteq S_{out}(p'))$

16   **then return** FALSE;

17 $RC = RC \cup [I', I_c', S(I')]$;

18 **until** $\forall [X, Y, ActionSet] \in RC, ActionSet = \varnothing$

19 return TRUE

The algorithm ensures that the role interfaces are compatible. Because, it determines that the role interfaces define the expected input and output data and instructions, decides that initial interaction states are compatible beforehand, and assures that every state transformation is compatible and reachable. Therefore, role compatibility ensures that the associated roles are interaction consistent. Levent Yilmaz[14] proposed another refined algorithm that is similar to the algorithm of role compatibility. Although the refined algorithm guarantees the role compatibility by safe role refinement, the computational complexity is increased explosively. Besides, the role compatibility algorithm is suitable for analyzing the compatibility of system-level actions based on DDF model enough.

Because the DDF with iteration operation imports the conception of constraints, comparing with simple DDF model, we especially extend DDF formally with a four tuple $D_f = <In, Out, R, B_s>$ which is corresponding to the four tuple of the role interaction policy. B_s is defined as a synchronous barrier set based on the condition of data-dependences constraints. The constraints are implicit barrier sets in the DDF model, which contain the SELECT and SWITCH nodes in the inner or outer loop iterations inherently.

3.2 Automated Engine

The automated engine is designed by the decomposability of DDF graph considering the subdivision of functions and the implement of collaborative operations. When various input dataflow under the different constraints are surging into automated engine, an effective scheduler with resource management and state transition

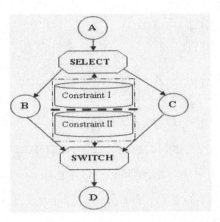

Fig. 3. Abstract decomposition of DDF

management functions is indispensable to implement collaboration and distributed execution. The abstract decomposition of DDF is depicted in the Fig.3.

As shown in the Fig.3, we decompose the DDF into two sub-DDF graphs according to the constraint sets of critical resource. The figure is the simplest decomposition of DDF applied in the automated testing without considering REPEATER node. However, we can partition abstract DDF graph into sub-DDF graphs depending on specified constrained conditions of corresponding testing. The constraints are not only existing in the dataflow, but also including environment constraints such as critical physical devices, self-defined system constraints and so on. We have implemented the prototype of automated engine, especially, the scheduler which is the key unit of automated engine. The Finite State Machine (FSM) of the scheduler will be expanded in the next section.

However, it is not enough at the abstract level design for collaborative automated testing framework due to the constraints introduced. As a result, we extend the dataflow equation formula with constraint relations as below:

$$Q_p * P_c = Q_c * C_c, \text{ where}$$

Q_p is the number of firing of actor producer,

Q_c is the number of firing of actor consumer,

$P_c = \sum_{i=1}^{n} (R_p \mid C_i)$ is the sum of produce rate R_p under the condition of constraints

$$\sum_{i=1}^{n} C_i,$$

$C_c = \sum_{i=1}^{n} (R_c \mid C_i)$ is the sum of consume rate R_c under the condition of constraints

$$\sum_{i=1}^{n} C_i.$$

The extended dataflow equation demonstrates that the input and output dataflow must be kept in a dynamic balance state due to the complex constraints. Only if the automated testing system is built on a balance system, the collaboration and stability can be guaranteed and the benefits of automated testing system designed on DDF can be acquired enough. Extended dataflow equation is the theoretical fundament of decomposing DDF by various constraints correctly.

4   Collaborative Automated Testing Framework

Based on the analyses above, we have designed a collaborative automated testing framework which is depicted in the Fig.4. As shown in the Fig.4, it consists of three sub-systems including input dataflow system on the left hand, automated engine in the middle, and output dataflow system on the right hand.

Input dataflow system contains test case library and the web interface operated by different test roles. Test case library is built in terms of different characters of Devices Under Testing (DUT) and the constraint relationships between input dataflow and critical resources. All tester assigned a unique role can work independently, and in the view of a single role, the constraint relationships and the role compatibility is opaque. That is, automated testing system is a black box for a single role. Because the method of partitioning tasks guarantees the role compatibility, collaborative testing can be implemented by web interface programmed in Java script language. Besides, the input dataflow and requests would be queued in a queue pool and be extracted by the rule of FIFO Pool.

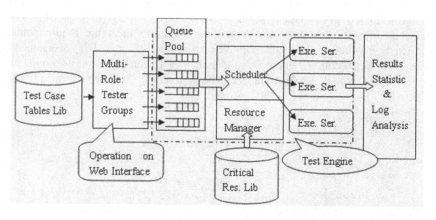

Fig. 4. Collaborative automated testing framework

As shown in the Fig.4, automated testing engine including a Queue Pool, Scheduler, Resource Manager, and distributed Execution Servers, which is marked with a broken rectangle. And various collaborative testing dataflow are surging into testing engine, which are firstly buffered in the Queue Pool. The queues are arranged in a group by the execution priority of dataflow and the constraint resource. However, as to a single queue, the dataflow and requests are organized by the time of firing and abided by the

FIFO principle. Resource Manager is responsible for managing critical resources stored in the critical resources database, which eliminates the conflicts existing among the critical resources and ensures the testing to be executed automatically. The Scheduler combing with Resource Manager as an integrated unit which selects the corresponding dataflow buffered in the Queue Pool under the idle state or suspended state of critical resource managed by Resource Manager. Executable dataflow is then dispatched by scheduler to corresponding Execution Server. Apparently, Execution Server is controlled by scheduler in a distributed way.

The testing results are collected and classified according to testing business. After that, the traced logs are analyzed with charts and plots. The framework of collaborative automated testing is implemented in the light of MVC pattern basically. The user interface is programmed in Java script language, the scheduler and the message passing system are programmed in Java language, and the execution server is implemented in Tcl script language in our prototype of automated testing system.

5   Scheduler and State Transfer

In the CATF, the dynamic scheduling between roles is the critical task. How to record the state of roles and control the state transfer safely and reliably is also the key component of CATF. Firstly, we partition various testing tasks into Cases or Suites which are relative fine granularity tasks. Then the Suites or Cases will be integrated into Job at a coarse granularity viewpoint. The scheduler of CATF only cares the Job states, and schedules different ready Jobs to accomplish their tasks in distribution way according to the current state of Job. The Job scheduling process is depicted in Fig.5. As shown in the Fig.5, Client sends a Job Control request to Controller which dispatches Jobs in different Suite Execution Server to meet the requirements of distributed execution and collaborative operation. If the Job dispatched in corresponding Execution Server is validated, it will comply with its Finite State Machine (FSM) model. All these states will be presented on JSP web interface to tester.

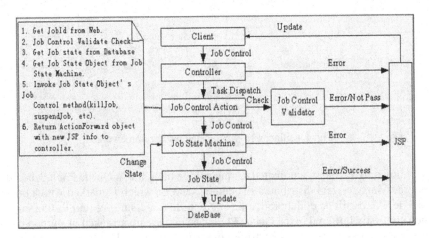

Fig. 5. Job scheduling process

However, as a general user, he can only control his own jobs. The Job Control Action invokes the Job Control Validator to check whether the user is the role owning the priority to control the job as shown in the Fig.5. If the role of the user is under the priority, an error JSP page will be produced and sent to Client. If the user has such role, the Action will read the job's state from Database and then find a Job State Object from JobStateMachine for this state and invoke the Job State Object's job control method (such as killJob, suspendJob, resumeJob, etc).

Among others, Job Control requests include "kill job", "suspend job", "retry job", "resume job", etc. Fig.6 shows how this kind of request is handled in FSM and the process of state transfer. The context contained in rectangle linked by broken line tell us that why job's state is transferred from one to another. In order to bind jobs' states with corresponding operations and to discriminate from the same or similar operations occurring in other states, the state pattern [15] is adopted to deal with these problems according to the theories of design pattern.

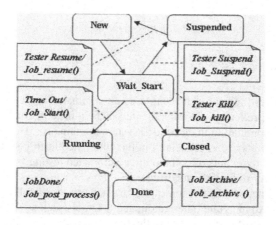

Fig. 6. State transfer process

As a consequence, we design a JobStateMachine class to drive the transition of job's states. The class holds its instance all the time, which is designed in accordance with skeleton pattern. JobStateMachine stores all states and other information of jobs into database. Besides, we design a basic class JobState. Several subclasses are derived from it to handle various jobs' operations such as Kill Job, Suspend Job etc. Another duty of the Job Controller is to retrieve a corresponding Execution Server according to the respective configure file information of Jobs. In particular, Job Controller and Execution Server run on different servers simultaneously through RMI communication bridge, as a result, CATF can work in a distributed mode naturally. The Job State Machine stores a job state map, which is used to map a job state to a job state object. Fig.7 shows Job State class diagram, which has some job control methods such as killJob, suspendJob and resumeJob. They are used to handle the job control request. After that, the methods will change job state machine's state and update the related information to database.

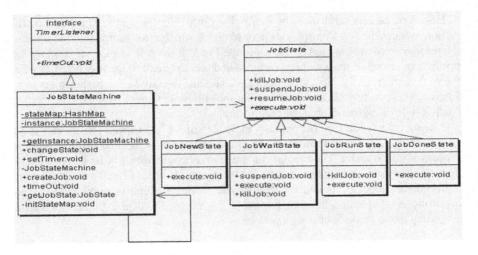

Fig. 7. Job state class diagram

6   Conclusions

The collaborative testing approach to building an automated testing model is designed by DDF model theoretically and implemented in Java in terms of MVC pattern. The DDF model is predominating in embedded system domain [16]. However, it is seldom adopted in the testing system, especially in the automated testing system. We manage to implement the core models of collaborative automated testing framework and make the greatest endeavor to improve its efficiency.

Although the functional extension of this framework is not full enough right now, we are considering to integrate other automated test tools such as WinRunner [17] into CATF by extending 3rd part interface in the future and advancing the capability of log trace and log analysis.

Acknowledgements

We would like to thank the anonymous reviewers for insightful feedbacks that improve the quality of this paper. This work was partially funded by the AMD's University Cooperation Program.

References

1. Heckel, R., Lohmann, M.: Towards Model-Driven Testing. In: TACoS - International Workshop on Test and Analysis of Component Based Systems, Warsaw, in conjunction with ETAPS 2003 (2003)
2. Blanc, M., et al.: A collaborative approach for access control, intrusion diction and security testing. In: International symposium on collaborative technologies and systems, pp. 270–277 (2006)

3. http://java.sun.com/javaee/ (available March 24, 2007)
4. List, B., Korherr, B.: A UML 2 profile for business process modeling. In: Akoka, J., Liddle, S.W., Song, I.-Y., Bertolotto, M., Comyn-Wattiau, I., van den Heuvel, W.-J., Kolp, M., Trujillo, J., Kop, C., Mayr, H.C. (eds.) ER 2005 Workshops. LNCS, vol. 3770, pp. 85–96. Springer, Heidelberg (2005)
5. Silaghi, R., et al.: Towards an MDA-oriented UML profile for distribution. In: 8th IEEE international proceedings of the enterprise distributed object computing conference, 227–239 (2004)
6. http://www.eclipse.org/tptp/ (available March 23, 2007)
7. http://www.pyxis-tech.com/en/produits/green-pepper/ available May 20, 2007
8. Petrenko, A.: Testing transition systems with input and output testers. In: International conference on testing of communicating systems, May 2003, pp. 129–145 (2003)
9. Tretmans, J.: Testing concurrent systems: a formal approach. In: 10th international conference on concurrency theory, pp. 46–65 (1999)
10. Tretmans, J., Brinksma, J.: TorX: automated model based testing. In: proceedings of the 1st European conference on model-driven software engineering (2003)
11. Jiao, Y., Guo, C., Wu, B., Luo, H.: Extended-DDF modeling embedded system design: adapting to IP technology. In: The fifth international conference on computer and information technology, September 2005, pp. 829–833 (2005)
12. Pei, S., Wu, B., et al.: Novel software automated testing system based on J2EE. In: CFTC 2007. Tsinghua Science and Technology (accepted, 2007)
13. Choi, C., Ha, S.: software synthesis for dynamic data flow graph. In: The 8th international workshop on rapid system prototyping proceedings, June 1997, pp. 72–79 (1997)
14. Yilmaz, L.: specifying and verifying collaborative behavior in component-based systems (Ph.D.Dissertation), Virginia Polytechnic institute and state university, Balcksburg, VA (March 2002)
15. Gamma, E., Helm, R., Johnson, R., Vlissides, J.: Design patterns elements of reusable object-orientd software. Addison-Wesley, MA (1995)
16. Wu, B.F., Peng, C.L.: A concurrent design approach for data flow dominated embedded systems. In: The 8th International conference on computer supported cooperative work in design proceedings, May.2004, vol. 1, pp. 3–7 (2004)
17. http://www.mercury.com/ (available March 30, 2007)

IT Services Design to Support Coordination Practices in the Luxembourguish AEC Sector

Sylvain Kubicki[1], Annie Guerriero[1,2], Damien Hanser[1], and Gilles Halin[2]

[1] Centre de Recherche Public Henri Tudor. 29, avenue JF Kennedy
L 1855 - Luxembourg-Kirchberg
[2] MAP-CRAI - Research Centre in Architecture and Engineering.
2, rue Bastien Lepage. 54001 Nancy, France
{sylvain.kubicki,annie.guerriero,damien.hanser}@tudor.lu,
gilles.halin@crai.archi.fr

Abstract. In the Architecture Engineering and Construction sector (AEC) cooperation between actors is essential for project success. The configuration of actors' organization takes different forms like the associated coordination mechanisms. Our approach consists in analyzing these coordination mechanisms through the identification of the "base practices" realized by the actors of a construction project to cooperate. We also try with practitioners to highlight the "best practices" of cooperation. Then we suggest here two prototypes of IT services aiming to demonstrate the value added of IT to support cooperation. These prototype tools allow us to sensitize the actors through terrain experiments and then to bring inch by inch the Luxembourgish AEC sector towards electronic cooperation.

Keywords: AEC, Cooperation Process, Coordination practices, IT services.

1 Introduction

Cooperation between actors is essential for the success of a construction project. The short-lived groups of actors, heterogeneity of stakeholders and intern strategies of their firms are the main specificities of the AEC[1] sector. In opposition to other industries the rationalization of work processes and their computerization are still low developed in the construction of buildings sector.

However this is not due to a delay or an archaism of the sector compared to "leading edge industries". Indeed, the diversity of projects and architectural realizations is added to the complexity of groups of actors and relations between them. In this context, the change of work method takes time, and stakeholders able to impose it don't exist. The Luxembourguish construction sector is not an exception and presents the same particularities as those of its European neighbours.

Then, the cooperative processes could be improved. In fact, delays and building defaults regularly appear on building construction sites. They are notably due to dysfunctions in cooperative processes that actors perform. These processes have to be

---

[1] Architecture Engineering and Construction.

Y. Luo (Ed.): CDVE 2007, LNCS 4674, pp. 396–403, 2007.

improved in order to limit these risks. IT innovation is a way to support these changes in professional practices.

In Luxembourg the Information Technology Resources Centre for Building (CRTI-B[2]) is an inter-professional organization, created in 1990. At the national level, the CRTI-B aggregates the main actors of the building sector: owners, architects, engineers, contractors etc. This organization supports integration of new Information and Communication Technologies in the building sector through innovation R&D projects. The overall objective of these projects is to lead tasks as closely as possible to the sector in order to propose concrete solutions (methods and tools software) to coordination needs of professionals coming from this working field (architects offices, design offices, home-building companies...). The primary goal of the Build-IT project is to enhance the competitiveness and the quality of the production process in the building sector by the use of ICT. Within the framework of this project, we focus on the practices of the exchange and the share of information that will ensure the interoperability between the actors of the Luxembourguish building sector. The Build-IT project encompasses a variety of research and development initiatives, most of which involve practitioners.

This article describes the first results of this project. First on a theoretical plan we address an analysis of actors' organizations in order to characterize coordination practices in building project. We present then two developments of IT services responding directly to the problems observed with practitioners, and the first validation elements. Finally, we conclude through opening future ways of actions to develop in the next stages of the project.

2 Cooperation Processes in AEC Projects

The terrain action carried out in the framework of the Build-IT project is completed by a theoretical background. Academic PhD works[3] reinforce this approach by characterizing and modelling cooperation and coordination processes in AEC.

2.1 Organization of Actors and Coordination Mechanisms

In AEC projects, cooperation is extremely important because projects bring together numerous independent actors during short periods. Their activities are low predictable and they very often have to adapt their tasks and decisions to the specific problems they have encountered. Organization of actors takes different forms in this evolving context [1]. It is "hierarchical" when an actor is responsible of the work of the others [2,3] (i.e. building construction coordinator). We call it "adhocratic"[4] when actors are grouped in an informal way to solve a specific problem, punctual and unanticipated.

These two fundamental forms of actors' organizations coexist during the design and building construction phases.

---

[2] http://www.crtib.lu

[3] Three PhD theses are and have been achieved in the Architecture and Engineering Research Centre (CRAI) at the Architecture School of Nancy, France (http://www.crai.archi.fr).

Coordination of activities depends on these organization forms. In the "hierarchical organization" a coordinator monitors tasks progression, anticipates problems and organizes their solving. His work is based on specific documents and tools [5] helping him to diffuse coordination information, such as construction planning or meeting report. In "adhocratic organization", coordination is essentially informal, based on awareness of the others and situated action [6]. It is an essential coordination mode, e.g. during the building construction activity. It ensures adaptability of the actions to the unpredictability of the activity and to frequent changes. In this coordination form, documents given by hierarchy don't serve directly the actions of the actors. They provide contextual information that actors need to adapt their decisions.

2.2 Cooperative Processes and Practices

We have described the actors' organizations and coordination mechanisms associated existing in construction projects. Then coordination tasks are essential activities. Indeed, the AEC sector involves heterogeneous teams and activities not really predictable. Cooperative processes realized in a construction project are not precisely defined. However, a certain number of practices exist and assist the cooperation between actors.

So, our approach doesn't consist in defining unique processes, repeatable or standardized. To the contrary, we try, with professionals, to highlight daily practices that can encourage and improve the cooperation in the construction projects.

In this approach, we inspire about methods of processes assessment and continuous improvement in the organizations, such as ISO 15504 (SPICE[4]). An ISO 15504 assessment consists in selecting a certain number of business processes (Process Assessment Model) in order to evaluate their maturity with people implicated in their realization. Each process is analyzed according to the "base practices" that allow its accomplishment. We suggest to apply this processes/practices division in order to tackle the cooperation from a "business" viewpoint. That is why we identify practices during interviews with professionals of the construction sector from Luxembourg.

We will see now that cooperation practices are directly linked with organizational configurations and also, coordination mechanisms.

2.3 IT Services Supporting These Practices

Many IT tools exist and assist actors during the execution of these cooperative practices. To manage coordination, the coordinator uses planning tools. The building construction meeting report informs about the state of the construction activity at a given moment. It is written after each meeting and regroups in a document, which will be validated by all the participants, all the decision taken, identified problems (more and more often illustrated with some pictures), state of the progress and other pieces of information [7]. More recently 4D CAD tools consist in an interface that shows relation between the 3D mock-up and the execution planning [8, 9]. The objective of such tools is to simulate the state of the construction activity. Moreover, it improves considerably communication with the owner and it allows to ripen the execution planning.

---

[4] SPICE project official website: http://www.sqi.gu.edu.au/spice/

These tools, which we have identified above, have a real utility in the construction activity coordination. They inform about the construction process, about the state of the activity and its execution. However, their use is not really common. A certain number of blocking factors explain it (e.g. tools appropriation, changes relative to the method of work, organizational changes, etc.). In the Luxembourguish construction sector, this problem exists like elsewhere. The privileged place of the CRTI-B allows us to regroup numerous actors representing the different professions of the construction sector around the Build-IT project, and to think together about real needs of the digital cooperation.

2.4 Problem and Hypotheses

In the framework of the Build-IT project, we focus on the identification of the essential cooperative processes and on their explaining with the professionals themselves during "Working Groups". This "applied approach" finds its origin in different works relative to the organizations and the coordination mechanisms. The identification, with the actors, of coordination practices (essential or problematic) allows us to suggest IT services supporting business needs formulated by the sector practitioners. Table 1 suggests a synthetic and non-exhaustive view of this approach. It puts in relation organizations and coordination mechanisms with the coordination practices identified as essential and IT services that we suggest to support them.

Table 1. Organization, coordination practices and IT services

Configuration of the organization	Coordination mechanism	Coordination practices	Associated IT service
Hierarchical configuration	Direct supervision	Meeting report writing	Meeting report management service
		Meeting report consultation	
		Reaction on a remark	
		Plans structuring	Plans management service
		Plans update	
		Plans annotation	
		Notification of published plan	
		Diffusion monitoring	
		Exchange traceability	
Adhocratic configuration	Mutual adjustment	Awareness practices	Context perception support service
		Consultation of various documents	

3 IT Services Development to Support Coordination Practices

The underlining of the cooperation practices, and the development of a model of the cooperation context [10] lead us to envisage their support in the form of a coherent set of IT services adapted to the needs of practitioners.

These needs often relates to the projects, their sizes, characteristics of the teams, types of the contract, etc. Our approach consists in considering modular services (one independent from each other) and in managing the exchange of information between service-specific HCI (Human-Computer Interfaces).

3.1 Meeting Report Writing and Consultation Service

The first Build-IT service[5], developed in the Build-IT project, is intended to manage exchanges around the meeting report. Then it supports direct supervision in hierarchical organizations. It is a typical situation of construction activity, where the coordinator writes a meeting report describing particular points to be adjusted.

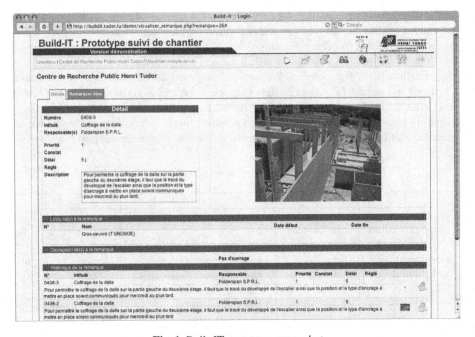

Fig. 1. Built-IT prototype screenshot

Our analysis of building activity meeting report and processes linked to this document allowed us to identify firstly, components of the meeting report (e.g. Presence and diffusion list, progress, list of remarks, etc.) and secondly, to determine services associated to the business practices.

The meeting report prototype integrates three services. *Writing service* covers functionalities intended to the writer. The prototype guides the writing by using forms. These forms correspond to generic components of meeting reports identified during the analysis phase. *Dynamic consultation service* covers functionalities of search. The tool offers the possibility to combine information filters to find easily information the user needs (filter on responsible people, lots, building elements...).

---

[5] http://buildit.tudor.lu/demo - Login: "demo" - Password: "demo".

Moreover, the search in three levels allows to restrict gradually the field of search: a first search level within various current construction sites, a second search level inside a construction site and finally, the last one, inside the meeting report. Finally *reaction service* covers functionalities intended to react to a remark. The tool allows the reader to react to a remark if he feels that its content is erroneous or requires further information. The centralization of information and the traceability of exchanges linked to the meeting report inside the tool is a way, on one hand, to enhance coordination between various contributors and on the other hand, to identify more easily the source of problems.

Currently, the experiment of this tool is in progress. It is used in 8 real construction projects. The experiment will allow us to verify the relevance of the tool in real situations of building activity, the consistency of visualized data, the usability of end-users interfaces and the appropriation of the tool by practitioners.

3.2 Bat'iViews: A Context Perception Support Service

Information related to coordination is represented in numerous views attached to documents, coordination tools or communication tools. Present practices consist in finding related pieces of information in the diverse useful documents, i.e. meeting report, planning and others. In terms of coordination, the need is to support practices of mutual adjustment. These practices are observed in unanticipated situations, in which the actors have to auto-coordinate. Concretely, the quality of this coordination depends on the capacity to obtain a global vision of the problem to be resolved, and to envisage risks that some potential solutions present. To improve context comprehension by the actors we think it is necessary to provide a representation, showing relations existing between the different elements of the context.

Bat'iViews prototype [11] suggests to make use of views manipulated everyday by the construction stakeholders and to integrate them in a navigation tool showing relations existing between content elements of each one. We choose 4 dynamic coordination views to develop the prototype: meeting report view, planning view, 3D mock-up view and a view of all remarks in all meeting reports. In order to show relations between elements of different views, the tool is based on the multi-visualization principle [12, 13]. It provides different views' arrangements to the user allowing him to navigate in the project context. The concepts to link through the views depend on the model of each view: i.e. meeting report displays "remarks" concerning "actors" and "building element", planning shows "tasks" and 3D mock-up represents "building objects". User-interaction is generated by the selection of one of these elements in each view. It consists in finding the corresponding concepts in the other views models and to highlight them. We call it a "free navigation": each view can generate interaction.

Figure 2 illustrates an arrangement in Bat'iViews[6]. It is composed of three views: 3D mock-up, planning and meeting report. An element selected in the 3D mock-up (here the main wall in red) is linked with related concepts in the planning (construction task of this wall) and a remark in the meeting report (e.g. There is a problem of synchronization between wall construction and roof frame construction).

---

[6] http://www.crai.archi.fr/bativiews

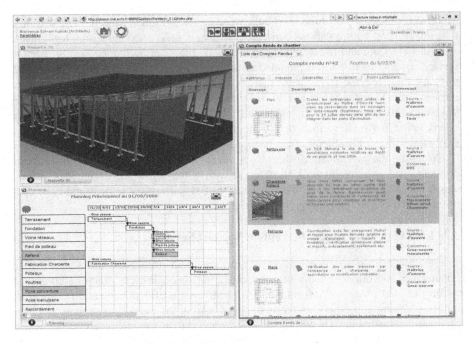

Fig. 2. Bat'iViews prototype screenshot

4   Conclusion and Future Works

The works presented here take place in the Build-IT project, which aims at guiding the Luxembourguish construction sector towards digital cooperation. The hypothesis that we argue is that numerous IT tools exist but their use is weak. The reasons are multiple: these tools are not really adapted to the needs of a particular industrial sector, and even more the actors don't see a real value-added in their use. In this context, the objective of the project is to lead actions of sensitization and service developments. This article describes the first steps of this action. We highlight potentialities of services managing coordination information about the building construction activity (meeting report service) and also services improving information understanding (contextual multi-visualization service). The experiments realized with those tools reinforce the hypothesis that if they are designed in collaboration with professionals, their appropriation and transfer to the sector is easier.

The next step is relative to the processes of plans exchange. It is about processes implicating the totality of stakeholders of the project, because sending and reception of documents concern everybody. So, we consider them like being essential in the hierarchy as in the adhocracy, and their coordination recovers from direct supervision and also from mutual adjustment. We have currently identified some base practices through a set of interviews with professionals (Cf. Table 1). We are now generalizing them to all the actors. Working Groups allow us to discuss and exchange with the professionals in order to highlight a set of "best practices". They will lead us then to suggest a set of IT services in the form of a prototype implementing these best practices. This demonstrator will allow itself to generalize the sensitization actions for the sector. The future steps of the Build-IT project are just drafted in the form of coordination scenarios. Beyond the management of documents of the project, the sector is going towards the "common and shared object" artefact. That will proceed certainly at first by the introduction of a common reference ontology, enabling to describe building elements through daily documents. This step will be followed by the generalization of the Building Information Model describing geometrically building elements and allowing everyone to add information in function of his particular point of view.

References

1. Mintzberg, H.: The structuring of organizations: A synthesis of the research. Prentice-Hall, Englewood Cliffs, NJ (1979)
2. Fayol, H.: Administration industrielle et générale, Editions, D.(ed.), Paris (1918)
3. Taylor, F.W.: Scientific Management, Row, H.(ed.) (1911)
4. Toffler, A.: Future Shock, House, R.(ed.), New York (1970)
5. Schmidt, K.: The problem with "awareness": Introductory remarks on "awareness in CSCW. The Journal of Collaborative Computing 11(3-4), 285–298 (2002)
6. Suchman, L.A.: Plans and situated action: the problem of human-machine interaction, Pea, R., Brown, J.S. (ed.) Cambridge University Press (1987)
7. Grezes, D., et al.: Le compte-rendu de chantier. Rapport final de recherche, Architecture, P.C.e. (ed.), Grenoble (1994)
8. Sadeghpour, F., Moselhi, O., Alkass, S.: A CAD-based model for site planning. Automation in Construction. 13, 701–715 (2004)
9. Chau, K., Anson, M., Zhang, J.: 4D dynamic construction management and visualization software. Automation in Construction 14, 512–524 (2005)
10. Kubicki, S., et al.: Assistance to building construction coordination. Towards a multi-view cooperative platform ((Special Issue "Process Modelling, Process Management and Collaboration Katranuschkov, P(ed.)). ITcon Electronic Journal of Information Technology in Construction 11, 565–586 (2006)
11. Kubicki, S.: Assister la coordination flexible de l'activité de construction de bâtiment. In: Une approche par les modèles pour la proposition d'outils de visualisation du contexte de coopération, CRAI. Université Henri Poincaré, Nancy (2006)
12. North, C., Shneiderman, B.: A taxonomy of multiple window coordinations. Human Computer Interaction Lab, University of Maryland. Tech Report HCIL-97-18 (1997)
13. Wang-Baldonado, M.W., Woodruff, A., Kuchinsky, A.: Guidelines for Using Multiple Views in Information Visualization. AVI - Advanced Visual Interfaces. Palerme, Italy (2000)

Expansion of Telecommunication Social Networks

Przemysław Kazienko

Wrocław University of Technology, Institute of Applied Informatics,
Wybrzeże S. Wyspiańskiego 27, 50-370 Wrocław, Poland
kazienko@pwr.wroc.pl
http://www.zsi.pwr.wroc.pl/~kazienko

Abstract. A social network, in which nodes represent humans and weighted ties reflect relationships between them, can be formed in an automatic way based on the data about customers of a telecommunication company as well as their communication activities. The expansion of a telecommunication social network can be supported with one of three main approaches that have been considered in this paper: existing group conjunction, internal expansion of groups, and transfer of external relationships.

Keywords: social networks, integration of networks, network expansion.

1 Introduction

A social network is the network of nodes – actors (individuals, organizations, organizational units) with ties i.e. social relationships linking pairs of actors [10]. The nodes and ties are usually represented by graphs or matrices. In social networks that are supported by computer or telecommunication networks, the mutual communication is crucial stuff in creating and maintaining personal relationships. Moreover, these relationships tend to change over the course of time: people establish new relations and neglect or discontinue the old ones. The evolution of a social network depends on mutual experience, knowledge, relative interpersonal interests, and trust of human beings [4, 8] as well as their social capital [7] and social position. The last ones describe importance and social statement of an individual within a social network. Some cohesive social subgroups can be recognized and extracted from a social network using clustering methods [11]. Building new or strengthening the existing relationships can benefit both individuals and entire social groups. The number of relationships can be increased by bonding or bridging [9]. The goal of the former is the interconnection of two or more homogeneous and similar but separate groups whereas in the latter the different heterogeneous groups are linked. Usually, the joined groups are internally very close. Both bonding and bridging enable the group to become a larger community in which the associations between humans are permanent. Another approach is to stimulate new relationships within groups. In this way the social network contains many disconnected but internally very coherent groups of members that know one another very well. Practically, the creation of new relationships can be stimulated by various types of recommendation systems [7, 8].

Y. Luo (Ed.): CDVE 2007, LNCS 4674, pp. 404–412, 2007.

Computer and telecommunication networks can not only reinforce but also help to expand existing social networks especially within a geographical community [5].

2   Telecommunication Social Network, Relationship Extraction

A telecommunication social network is the network created upon the interactions (calls) between customers of a single telecom provider. A telecommunication social network $TSN=(H,R)$ consists of the set of members H (humans) and the set of durable relationships between pairs of members $R=H{\times}H$ (see Fig. 1). Relationships are automatically mined from the data about phone calls that are performed within the network. Note that a network member is practically an owner and user of a single phone number.

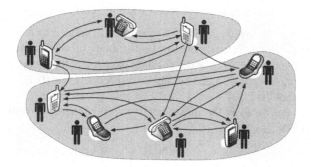

Fig. 1. Telecom network with two social groups. Edges reflect relationships between members.

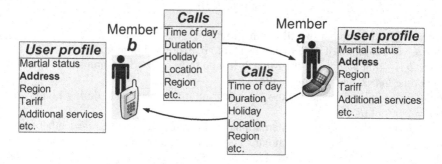

Fig. 2. Components used for relationship extraction

Social relationships that exist between telecom users can be extracted based on the data available from telecom companies with the certain probability, especially: user profiles that contain information from the contract and information about calls derived from the billing system (Fig. 2). People with the same or adjoining address live together or close to each other (neighbors), so they are in a common relationship even though they do not call each other. Nevertheless, performed calls are the most significant indicator of a relationship. However, a single call from member a to member b is not sufficient evidence of a durable social relationship from a to b. Thus, we can create a set of rules that indicate a durable relationship:

- longer calls are good indicators of a relationship (use the proper threshold),
- calls made at night and in the evening are a better indicator (use appropriate weights),
- calls performed on holidays are good indicators,
- international calls are good indicators [2],
- duration since the last call may indicate the durability of relationship: if the last call was made a long time ago, the relation may not be active any more,
- recent calls are more important than the older ones.

Based on the above general rules, the relationship function $rel(a,b)$ that reflects the relationship from member a to b can be proposed:

$$rel(a,b) = \alpha \cdot match(a,b) + calls(a,b) + \beta \cdot calls(b,a) \tag{1}$$

where: $match(a,b)$ – the value of similarity between member a to b derived from user profiles, $match(a,b)=match(b,a)$; $calls(a,b)$ – the value of all call indicators for calls initiated by member a to b; α, β – the constant parameters that denote how important is profile matching or calls initiated by others, respectively; $\alpha \in [0,1]$; usually α should be closer to 1 rather than 0.

Call function $calls(a,b)$ is the most significant component of relationship estimation. It is calculated as follows:

$$calls(a,b) =$$

$$\left(\sum_{i=1}^{n_{ab}} dur(a,b,i) \cdot tod(a,b,i) \cdot hol(a,b,i) \cdot reg(a,b,i) \cdot \frac{1}{t(a,b,i)} \cdot \frac{1}{rec(a,b,i)} \right) \tag{2}$$

$$- \gamma \cdot \min_i (t(a,b,i))$$

where: n_{ab} – the number of calls from a to b;
$dur(a,b,i)$ – duration of the i-th call from a to b, expressed in minutes;
$tod(a,b,i)$ – time of day for the i-th call from a to b; for working hours $tod=1$, for evening time $tod=2$, and for night calls $tod=4$;
$hol(a,b,i)$ – indicates whether the i-th call from a to b was made during holiday time ($hol=2$) or not ($hol=1$);
$reg(a,b,i)$ equals 2 for favors international and long distance calls, $reg=1$ otherwise;
$t(a,b,i)$ – indicates how many months ago the i-th call from a to b was made; $t=1$ for the recent month, $t=2$ for the previous one, $t=3$ – two months ago, etc.; it is possible to apply another period instead a month;
$rec(a,b,i)$ – refers to teleconference calls initiated by a, i.e. with more than one receiver (participant); note that b could be only one of them; for regular calls $rec=1$; for calls directed to two receivers $rec=2$, etc.;
γ – constant that denotes the importance of the lack of communication since the last call; its value depends on the typical number of calls between a pair of network members;

Values of *calls* function and in consequence values of *rel* function should be periodically recalculated: best once a month. Note that *rel* function is not symmetric and $rel(a,b)$ not necessarily $rel(b,a)$.

3 Network Expansion – Recommendation of Humans

The general idea of telecommunication network expansion is to stimulate new relationships between network members based either on links existing within the telecom network or relationships derived from external sources. It may be achieved by suggesting new communication to not yet known humans. For that reason, a separate recommendation list should be created for each of the selected network members. The recommendation of new acquaintances may be an additional service provided by the telecom company and available for open-minded people who seek new contacts. Three main approaches to network expansion have been considered: existing group conjunction, internal expansion of groups, and transfer of external relationships.

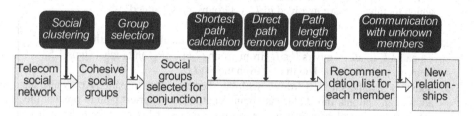

Fig. 3. Expansion based on group conjunction

3.1 Group Conjunction

Network expansion consists of several steps (Fig. 3). Social group conjunction requires the cohesive social group extraction to be performed before. This may be achieved by using any of the existing clustering solutions [11]. However, this process should respect some social aspects, in particular relationships between network members (see sec. 2). Thus, the relationship function $rel(a,b)$ (1) may be utilized as the similarity function necessary for clustering. It appears reasonable, to apply the appropriate minimum threshold to the relationship function rel which would help to exclude rather occasional, accidental and invalid communication, i.e. weak interpersonal ties. The value of the threshold has to be neither too high nor too low. At the threshold which is too high, we could have a network with a very small number of relationships. There are also some other parameters that help to adjust the density of the network: α, β from (1), and γ from (2).

After clustering, two groups assigned for conjunction have to be selected. The selection condition may be e.g. the greatest or the smallest average distance between both group members depending on general network expansion strategy.

Based on a calculation of lengths of the shortest paths, a ranking list can be created separately for each member from both groups. In other words, we seek members from the list of the closest members from the second group who could be suggested to a first group member h_1. Obviously only those second group members are accepted that are not yet in a direct relationship with h_1. If the member h_1 initiated some calls to any recommended member from the second group, then we could possibly manage to stimulate a new relationship between two input groups and finally join them both.

Note that due to necessity of shortest path calculations, there has to exist at least one path between both joining groups. Otherwise, the lengths of all paths would be infinite. This limitation may usually be overcome by the proper assignment of the minimum threshold as well as relationship parameters: α, β, and γ.

The entire process of recommendation list creation is the algorithm SNEC.

Algorithm SNEC

Input: $TSN=(H,R)$ – telecommunication social network

Output: $TSN=(H,R)$ with recommendation lists L_i assigned to each member i from two selected cohesive social groups

1. Perform clustering in $TSN=(H,R)$, i.e. split TSN into K cohesive social groups G_k, $k=1, 2, ...K$, $G_k=(H_k,R_k)$, $H_k{\subset}H$, $R_k{\subset}R$, and R_k is the set of all relationships in which members H_k are involved in TSN. Groups are separated.
2. Select a pair of groups $G_1=(H_1,R_1)$ and $G_2=(H_2,R_2)$ to join.
3. For each member $h^1_i{\in}H_1$ from group $G_1=(H_1,R_1)$ calculate the lengths of the shortest paths L_i to all members $h^i_j{\in}H_2$ from group $G_2=(H_2,R_2)$ and repeat steps 4-5.
4. Remove paths with the length of 1 from the list L_i.
5. Select M members $h^i_j{\in}H_2$ from L_i with the shortest length of paths. Apply also an additional, optional threshold: maximum length of the shortest path to prevent the recommendation of people who are too far. The result list L^M_i is simultaneously the recommendation list for the member h^1_i and the telecommunication company can suggest all the members from list L^M_i to contact the member h^1_i.
6. Proceed all lists L_i obtained in steps 3-5 to achieve equivalent recommendation lists L_j for each member $h^2_j{\in}H_2$ from the second group.

Constraint of separation for any two groups $G_i=(H_i,R_i)$ and $G_j=(H_j,R_j)$ in step 1 means that only their member sets are disjointed:

$$(\forall\ 1{\leq}i{\leq}K,\ 1{\leq}j{\leq}K)\ i{\neq}j \Leftrightarrow R_i{\cap}R_j=\varnothing; \tag{3}$$

while their relationship sets can overlap, i.e. R_i and R_j can have common relationships. This refers to direct links between $h_i{\in}H_1$, $h_j{\in}H_2$.

Note that since shortest paths are symmetrical, for each item from a list L_i obtained in step 4, we can create a new equivalent item in list L_j and this is the point of processing in step 6. Of course we can also consider directed shortest paths. In this case, we would need to compute the reverse shortest paths separately (step 6). It is possible

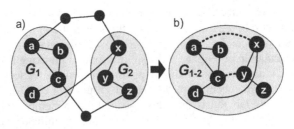

Fig. 4. Two social groups selected for conjunction (a) and the new merged group created owing to new relationships marked with dotted line (b). Undirected edges correspond to the existence of a relationship in any two directions.

to apply an additional threshold in step 5: the maximum length of the shortest path. In this case, some members from L_i may be excluded due to the paths being too long.

For two groups for conjunction from Fig. 4a, the algorithm SNEC creates the following list of humans and for $M=2$ (step 5) the following final recommendation lists:

$$L_a = ((x,3), (y,4), (z,3)) \qquad\qquad L^M_a = (x, z)$$
$$L_b = ((x,3), (y,4), (z,3)) \qquad\qquad L^M_b = (x, z)$$
$$L_c = ((x,2), (y,3), (z,2)) \qquad\qquad L^M_c = (x, z)$$
$$L_d = ((x,1), (y,2), (z,3)) \qquad\qquad L^M_d = (y, z)$$
$$L_x = ((a,3), (b,3), (c,2), (d,1)) \qquad L^M_x = (a, c)$$
$$L_y = ((a,4), (b,4), (c,3), (d,2)) \qquad L^M_y = (c, a)$$
$$L_z = ((a,3), (b,3), (c,2), (d,3)) \qquad L^M_z = (c, b)$$

If we managed to encourage member a to talk with member x (not only once) and member y to c, then we would be able to create new relationships (dotted lines in Fig. 4b) and in consequence to join both groups G_1 and G_2 into the larger G_{1-2} (Fig. 4b). Note that member a could have already talked with member x but their mutual relation was rather weak. In this case, the new communication stimulated by recommendation can simply strengthen the neglected relationship.

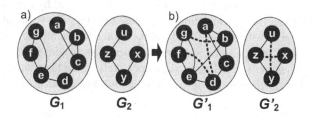

Fig. 5. Two social groups (a) which have been internally expanded (b)

3.2   Internal Expansion of Social Groups

In the internal expansion approach, social groups are extended by stimulation of new relationships between pairs of members from the same coherent group. As a result, we obtain groups that are more consistent and with higher density. Density is the measure which denotes what percentage of all possible relations is really maintained [12]. All possible relations within group $G=(H,R)$ means every group member with every other group member and its quantity is $0.5 \cdot \text{card}(H) \cdot (\text{card}(H)-1)$.

Ranking lists of humans are based on the lengths of shortest paths within the group. Similarly to the SNEC algorithm, ranking list L_i for member i consists of the same group member to which the length of the shortest path is the smallest. For groups from Fig. 5a, $M=3$, and the maximum length for the shortest path equals 2, we have the following recommendation lists: $L^M_a=(d, e)$, $L^M_b=(d, f)$, $L^M_c=(e)$, $L^M_d=(a,b)$, $L^M_e=(a,c)$, $L^M_f=(b,d)$, $L^M_g=(b,d)$, $L^M_u=(y)$, $L^M_x=(z)$, $L^M_y=(u)$, $L^M_z=(x)$. Having these lists the system can suggest the new contacts with the appropriate group members and as a result some new relationships may appear, e.g. $a-d$, $g-b$, $f-d$, $u-y$, $x-z$ (Fig. 5b).

3.3   Transfer of Relationships from External Social Networks

Telecommunication companies have also recently been involved in some other services which are external to traditional cable or mobile phone calls like news portal, email service, blogs, instant messenger, VoIP, etc. Additionally, specialized internet social network systems are available like *Friendster*, *LinkedIn* or *academici*, which Golbeck has named web-based social networks [4]. Based on a social network extracted from such an external system, some of its relationships can be transferred into the telecommunication network in the same way as group conjunctions, i.e. by recommendation of new relationships (Fig. 6).

There are two main difficulties in the transfer of relationships: member identification and the access to external data. Some telecom companies possess their own external systems which are restricted only to their customers, e.g. mailbox service in which a user is identified by their phone number. In this case both these problems do not occur. If the external social network is managed by another company, then member identification can be performed either based on phone numbers that have been delivered directly by members of the external network or according to their personal data like names and addresses. In any case, the privacy protection problem should be solved [3, 6], e.g. by the introduction of a special assent signed by the telecom user.

For the example telecommunication social network (Fig. 6), we are able to identify corresponding users in the email social network only for members *c*, *d*, and *e*. New contacts between *e* and *c* as well as *e* and *d* that are equivalent to relationships *e'-c'* and *e'-d'* from the email social network, respectively, have been suggested. This results in new relationships in the telecommunication social network (dotted lines in Fig. 6b).

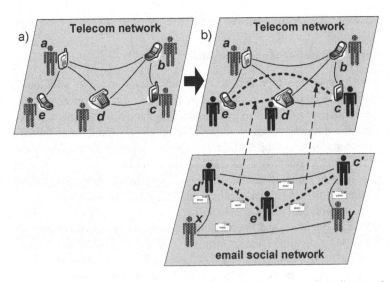

Fig. 6. Extension of telecommunication network based on external email network

3.4 Other Approaches to Network Expansion

Some other approaches to telecommunication network expansion can also be considered. Members can be placed in the recommendation lists of the given user a based on the similarity of their profile maintained by the telecom company to user a – component $match(a,b)$ in (1). This is a kind of simple demographic filtering. In yet another approach, members are matched according to their common activities like co-authorship, comments to the same blogs, watching the same pictures or movies, etc. In collaborative filtering method the closeness measure between people is based on the similarity of ratings made by the users [1]. All of these other approaches may suffer from the difficulty of access to the appropriate data as well as the identification problem (see sec. 3.3).

4 Conclusions and Future Work

It is possible to create a social network describing relationships between customers from the data available for the telecom company in an automatic way. Having this data, we can build a recommendation system that could help to develop the obtained social network by stimulation of new communication between its members as well as by strengthening the existing weak relationships. In consequence, communication traffic may grow. In the group conjunction method (sec. 3.1) and the method of internal expansion of groups (sec. 3.2), only the communication data is utilized while other approaches (sec. 3.3 and 3.4) require cooperation with an external data provider.

Future research will focus on the introduction of the maximum flow value known from the transport networks instead of the length of the shortest paths.

Acknowledgments. This work was partly supported by The Polish Ministry of Science and Higher Education, grant no. N516 037 31/3708.

References

1. Adomavicius, G., Tuzhilin, A.: Toward the Next Generation of Recommender Systems: A Survey of the State-of-the-Art and Possible Extensions. IEEE Transactions on Knowledge and Data Engineering 17(6), 734–749 (2005)
2. Barnet, G.A.: The social structure of international telecommunications. Progress in Comm. Sciences, Advances in Telecommunications, Indiana University, vol. XV (1999)
3. Directive on privacy and electronic communications. Directive 2002/58/EC of the European Parliament and of the Council of 12 July 2002 concerning the processing of personal data and the protection of privacy in the electronic communications sector (2002)
4. Golbeck, J.A.: Computing and applying trust in web-based social networks. Ph.D. Thesis, University of Maryland (2005), http://trust.mindswap.org/papers/GolbeckDissertation.pdf
5. Kavanaugh, A., Patterson, S.: The Impact of Community Computer Networks on Social Capital and Community Involvement. American Behavioral Scientist 45, 496–509 (2001)
6. Kazienko, P., Adamski, M.: AdROSA - Adaptive Personalization of Web Advertising. Information Sciences 177(11), 2269–2295 (2007)

7. Kazienko, P., Musiał, K.: Social Capital in Online Social Networks. In: Gabrys, B., Howlett, R.J., Jain, L.C. (eds.) KES 2006. LNCS (LNAI), vol. 4252, pp. 417–424. Springer, Heidelberg (2006)

8. Kazienko, P., Musiał, K.: Recommendation Framework for Online Social Networks. In: AWIC 2006, Studies in Computational Intelligence, vol. 23, pp. 111–120. Springer, Heidelberg (2006)

9. Putnam, R.D.: Bowling Alone: The Collapse and Revival of American Community. Simon & Schuster, New York (2000)

10. Scott, J.: Social network analysis: A handbook. SAGE Publications Inc., London (2000)

11. Tan, P.-N., Steinbach, M., Kumar, V.: Introduction to Data Mining. Ch. 8 & 9, pp. 487–649. Addison-Wesley, Reading (2006)

12. Wasserman, S., Faust, K. (eds.): Social network analysis: Methods and applications. Cambridge University Press, New York (1994)

Knowledge-Based Cooperative Learning Platform for Three-Dimensional CAD System

Jie Hu and Yinghong Peng

Institute of Knowledge Based Engineering, School of Mechanical Engineering,
Shanghai Jiao Tong University, 800 Dongchuan Road, Shanghai, 200240, P.R. China
hujie@sjtu.edu.cn

Abstract. Cooperative learning is a social interaction that involving a community of learners and teachers, where members acquire and share experience or knowledge. Recently, researchers have initiated studies that explore which factors are relevant to learner satisfaction or education effectiveness in a cooperative learning environment. However, little research effort for developing a cooperative learning platform for information system training, such as three-dimensional CAD system training. Thus, our study aims to narrow these gaps. We present the cooperative learning platform for 3D CAD system. This approach can be helpful for better establishing cooperative learning for information system training. We introduce a case involving three-dimensional CAD training with the web-based cooperative learning platform in China. This research is specifically related the context of a state-of-the-art cooperative learning platform that is based on network technology for real-time interaction amongst users, instructor, and the cooperative learning system itself.

Keywords: Cooperative learning, Three-dimensional CAD, Knowledge management.

1 Introduction

E-learning and cooperative learning is a social interaction that involving a community of learners and teachers, where members acquire and share experience or knowledge. Learning is no longer viewed as an individual process, but a social one in which knowledge and skill are discovered and built via interaction with instructor and other learners. The success of e-learning and cooperative learning activities requires the constant generation, transfer, and understanding of knowledge, making collaboration an essential and highly valued process. E-learning applications may appear with different forms of designation such as web-based learning, virtual classrooms, and digital collaboration [1],[2], which is conducted using the Internet (or Intranet/Extranet) and web technologies. Many researchers paid attention to e-learning and collaborative learning system. Wang [3] argued that current models for measuring user satisfaction and learners' evaluation of teaching effectiveness are inapplicable to the e-learning environment. The results of his work showed that a total of 17 items applicable to measuring e-learner satisfaction could be classified into the following dimensions: content, personalization, learning community and learner interface. Volery and Lord [4] developed instruments for measuring learner satisfaction with asynchronous e-learning systems. Koschmann [5] studied the web-based collaborative learning systems in the

Y. Luo (Ed.): CDVE 2007, LNCS 4674, pp. 413–419, 2007.

CSCL paradigm, which has been built upon a rich history of cognitive science research about how students learn. Essentially, web-based collaborative learning can be described as a context where the computer, information, and network technology facilitates interaction among learners for acquisition or sharing of knowledge. Dewiyanti *et al.* [6] presented that learners' satisfaction with collaborative learning can be described as the degree to which a learner feels a positive association with his/her own collaborative learning experiences. Scardamalia and Bereiter [7] presented web-based collaborative environments allow equal opportunities for learners to participate without the limitation on knowledge levels. Kagan [8] stated that learners' characteristics might promote or enhance their participation in the collaborative learning. Baker [9] presented that effective knowledge management within the context of ongoing educational processes can lead both to the successful development of learning improvement and the creation of more stable communities' relationships based on knowledge sharing.

The problem with these researchers is that few papers have addressed the cooperative learning for 3D CAD training. In this paper, 3D CAD cooperative learning or training system is presented. Then, we introduce a case involving 3D CAD training with a web-based cooperative learning system.

2   Knowledge-Based Cooperative Learning System

The knowledge based cooperative learning system consists of three layers: client layer, application layer and server layer. Fig. 1 shows the framework of our cooperative 3D CAD learning or training system.

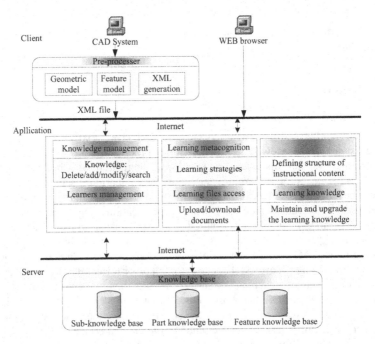

Fig. 1. The framework of our cooperative 3D CAD learning system

The 3D CAD Training System is developed to support web-based cooperative learning. The system is developed based on Web client-server architecture with server-based learning. Both learning activities and course instructional content run on servers. Individual computers are used as Web browsers. This means that learners have more chances to communicate with other learners or instructors through server computers. The Web offers interactive communication and creates a potentially cooperative learning environment. With hypermedia binding an online system, this multi-user network presents great possibilities for cooperative learning.

The proposed system is based on timely and accurate provision of knowledge, which in turn supports the cooperative learning applications. Hence, the need to have knowledge management applications is to control knowledge access, maintain the knowledge and manage the geographically distributed cooperative learners.

2.1 Server Layer of Cooperative Learning System

1. Knowledge management module includes: sub-knowledge base management, part knowledge base management, and feature knowledge base management.

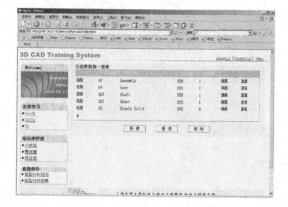

Fig. 2. The interface of sub-knowledge base management

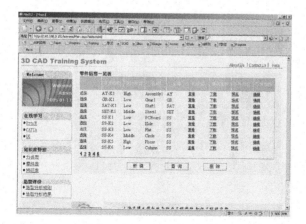

Fig. 3. The interface of part knowledge base management

a) Sub-knowledge base management

Knowledge base includes many sub-knowledge bases. Knowledge manager can add, delete, modify, and search knowledge by knowledge manage platform. Fig. 2 shows the interface of sub-knowledge base management.

b) Part knowledge base management

Part knowledge base management includes part coding, part search, part edit, learning file download. Fig. 3 shows the interface of part knowledge base management.

c) Feature knowledge base management

Feature knowledge base management includes feature tree modeling, reviewing and using. Fig. 4 shows the interface of feature knowledge base management.

2. Cooperative learning and evaluating management

The aim of cooperative learning and evaluating management is to evaluate the learning process. Fig. 5 shows the interface of cooperative learning and evaluating management.

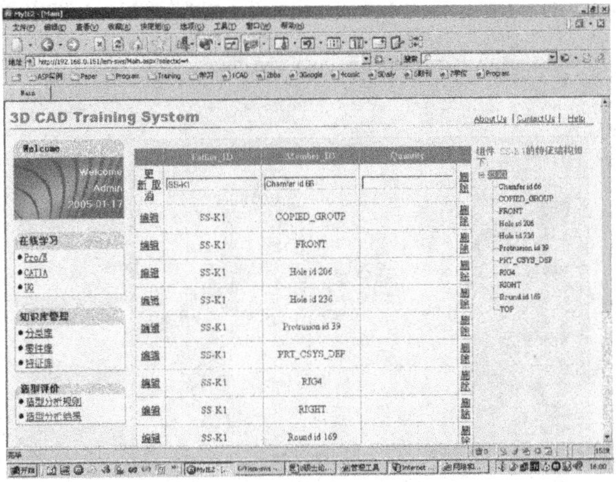

Fig. 4. The interface of feature knowledge base management.

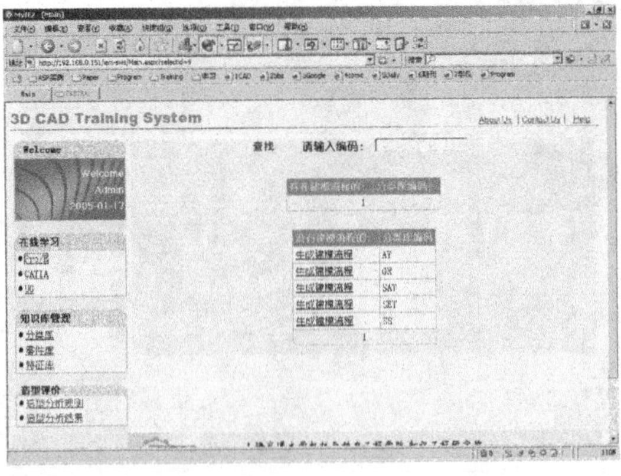

Fig. 5. The interface of cooperative learning and evaluating management

2.2 Application Layer of Cooperative Learning System

This application layer provides a range of key learning applications that need to be preformed in a cooperative manner. This research is concerned with the cooperative learning; and the proposed applications include knowledge management and inference engine applications:

1) Learning model application. This application is concerned with modeling the 3D CAD feature based on XML and OWL. In addition, learning to solve 3D CAD modeling problems requires the acquisition and refinement of many learning principles and procedures, which in turn that make it possible to devise and execute learning activities or solutions.

2) Learning metacognition applications. This application is concerned with defining learning strategies. Learning strategies are based on individual knowledge concerning cognitive processes and results.

3) Instructional structure applications. This application is concerned with defining structure of instructional content. Learning performance is influenced not only by the nature of the perceptual stimuli but also by the nature of individuals' expectations based on prior knowledge and past experience.

4) Learners management application, to capture learners' data, responsibilities, expectations and their right to access the different elements of the system.

5) Learning files access application, to upload/download documents from within the learning model.

6) Learning knowledge application, for the administrator to maintain and upgrade the learning knowledge model.

2.3 Client Layer of Cooperative Learning System

Fig. 6 shows the interface of client layer of cooperative learning system for 3D CAD software: Pro/ENGINEER™.

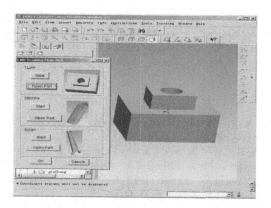

Fig. 6. The interface of client layer of cooperative learning system for 3D CAD software: Pro/ENGINEER™

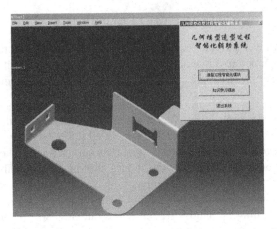

Fig. 7. The interface of client layer of cooperative learning system for 3D CAD software: CATIA^{TM}

Fig. 7 shows the interface of client layer of cooperative learning system for 3D CAD software: CATIA ^{TM}.

3 Conclusions

An approach for knowledge-based cooperative learning for 3D CAD training is presented in this paper. The 3D CAD Training System is developed to support web-based cooperative learning. The system is developed based on Web client-server architecture with server-based learning. The cooperative learning system is developed to support 3D CAD training, such as Pro/ENGINEER^{TM} and CATIA^{TM}. The proposed method has addressed the knowledge management and cooperative learning simultaneously to improve the 3D CAD training system.

Acknowledgments. This research is supported by the National Natural Science Foundation of China (No. 50575142 and 60304015) and the Shanghai Committee of Science and Technology (No. 055107048 and 04ZR14081).

References

1. Kaplan-Leiserson, E.: e-Learning glossary (2000) Available from
    http://www.learningcircuits.org /glossary.html
2. Khalifa, M., Kwok, R.C.-W.: Remote learning technologies: effectiveness of hypertext and GSS. Decision Support Systems 3, 195–207 (1999)
3. Wang, Y.-S.: Assessment of learner satisfaction with asynchronous electronic learning systems. Information & Management 1, 75–86 (2003)
4. Volery, T., Lord, D.: Critical success factors in online education. The International Journal of Educational Management 5, 216–223 (2000)
5. Koschmann, T.: CSCL: Theory and practice of an emerging paradigm. Lawrence Erlbaum Associates, Mahwah (1996)

6. Dewiyanti, S., Brand-Gruwel, S., Jochems, W., Broers, N.J.: Students' experience with collaborative learning in asynchronous computer-supported collaborative learning environments. Computers in Human Behavior 1, 496–514 (2007)
7. Scardamalia, M., Bereiter, C.: Computer support for knowledge-building communities. The Journal of the Learning Science 3, 265–283 (1994)
8. Kagan, S.: Cooperative learning. Wee co op: Resources for Teacher, Inc. (1994)
9. Baker, P.: Knowledge management for e-learning. Innovations in Education and Teaching International 2, 111–121 (2005)

Modeling the Metropolitan Region Cooperative Development Based on Cooperative Game Theory*

Jianrong Hou, Fanghua Wang, and Dan Huang

Antai College of Economics & Management, Shanghai Jiaotong University,
Shanghai, China, 200052
htt2000@hotmail.com

Abstract. A collaborative development mechanism model of regional economic system in metropolitan region is presented in this paper. The factors of accomplishing collaboration balance and development in metropolitan regions economic system are discussed.

Keywords: metropolitan region, co-operative game, collaborative envelopment.

1   Introduction

The emergence of the metropolitan region is an inevitable outcome of many mixed conditions such as the economic environment, geographic position and the development stage of the economy[1,2]. The development goal of a metropolitan region is to make a coordinative and efficient economic system by linking all the cities in the region together. This can help the region to achieve efficient resource allocation and continuous economic development. Regional collaborative development can be regarded as the coupling results of all the member sub-regions involved. It can reflect the dynamic co-promotion relations and reciprocities among the subsystems.

Behind the great trend of regional economic integration presently, there are a lot of political regional phenomena happening among member cities in the great metropolitan regions recently. These phenomena include: the unnecessary repeated constructions of production systems, separations of markets, separations of basic facilities, separation of government political protections, the discriminations caused by the internal and external regional memberships, competition disorders for investments etc.. These phenomena will restrict the development of metropolitan region seriously. As a new regional economic organization form, how can a metropolitan region achieve its continuous development based on synergistic cooperation? There are few literatures concerned about theoretical foundations for economic and strategic regulation decision-making of metropolitan regions.

This paper intends to put forward some necessary theoretical foundations for the development and regulation of Chinese metropolitan regions by analyzing the collaborative development mechanism of the metropolitan system based on modern cooperative game theory.

---

* Supported by Metropolitan Region Development and Management Foundation of China. The authors thank Mr. Yuhua Luo for his correction of this paper.

Y. Luo (Ed.): CDVE 2007, LNCS 4674, pp. 420–422, 2007.

2 Analysis of the Collaborative Mechanism of Economic Development in Metropolitan Region Based on Cooperative Game

In the realization process of metropolitan regional economic system integration, there are both competition and cooperation. For the success of the cooperation and efficient negotiation among the regional members it is necessary to realize promissory agreements by all regional parts[3,4,5].

For simplification, let us assume that the cooperative action between the members within the region has no effect on the outsiders, and the policy of regional members to the non-regional members is kept consistent.

We can define the following characteristic function to model the alliance relationship among member regions:

$$v(S) = \sum_{i \in s} \left\{ \alpha_o^i + \sum_{j \in N} \beta_j^i - \sum_{j \notin s} \theta_j^i + \sum_{j \notin s} \pi_j^i \right\} \tag{2.1}$$

where in (2.1), $v(S)$ denotes the maximum assured benefit achieved by alliance S by coordinating the strategies of other regional members, and $v(\Phi) = 0$, α_o^i is the conservative utility of each regional member before the cooperation. $\sum_{j \in N} \beta_j^i$ is the sum of benefit of all the regional members in alliance S after the formation of alliance N.. $\sum_{j \notin S} \theta_j^i$ is the benefit loss made by the members that are not in alliance S to alliance S. $\sum_{j \notin S} \pi_j^i$ is the possible benefit of members in alliance S if they cooperate with the members who are not in alliance S but are still in region alliance N.

The benefit allocation value $\varphi_i(N, v)$ of regional economic cooperation game (N, v) can then be given by the following:

$$\varphi_i(N, v) = \alpha_O^i \sum_{j=1}^n \beta_j^i + \frac{1}{2} \sum_{j=1}^n \left[\left(\pi_j^i - \theta_j^i \right) - \left(\pi_i^j - \theta_i^j \right) \right], i = 1, 2, \cdots, n \tag{2.2}$$

When all the members participate the cooperation, the benefit allocation vector lying in the center gives each regional member some benefit compensation value as follows:

$$\Delta_i = \frac{1}{2} \sum_{j \neq i}^n \left[(\pi_j^i - \theta_j^i) - \left(\pi_i^j - \theta_i^j \right) \right], i = 1, 2, \cdots, n \tag{2.3}$$

where $\Delta_i \geq 0$, which is the sum of the differences between the total net benefit of i and other cooperative members. If $\Delta_i < 0$, the region which gains more benefit without cooperation) needs the benefit compensation from the ones which gains less benefit without cooperation, the result goes against the goal of regional economy unification.

From the analysis above, we can have the following three conclusions:

① In the metropolitan region economy, all the members of the cooperation should establish efficient negotiation mechanism and the corresponding compensation mechanism according to the difference in the degrees of benefit obtained by each member.

② It is not necessary for the income transfer between those regions that have the same development level or even nearly the same level when they implement regional cooperation.

③ The striking point to achieve the collaborative equilibrium of a metropolitan regional economic system is the flow of commodities and factors between the areas in the metropolitan region.

3 Conclusions

Through our analysis, we can conclude that the cooperation in the economic system of metropolitan region can be a good incentive for the members in the economic system to give up their own present short-term interest to obtain their long-term benefit. Furthermore, all the members in the region should form some efficient negotiation mechanism among them. This is the precondition for collaborative development of the economic system in the metropolitan regions.

References

1. Tihua, J.: The Report of the Chinese Regional Development (2003-2004), the Social Science Press (2004)
2. Guowen, W.: Studies on Theory and Method, pp. 227–233, Chinese Economy Press (2000)
3. Arin, J., Inarra, E.: A Characterization of the Nucleolus for Convex Games. Games and Economic Behavior 23, 12–24 (1998)
4. Shapley, L.S.: A Value for n-Person Games, Contributions to the Theory of Games, pp. 307–317. Princeton University Press (1972)
5. Panayotou, T.: Green Markets. In: The Economics of Sustainable Development, ICS Press (1993)

Efficient Blind Signatures from Linear Feedback Shift Register*

Xiangxue Li[1,2], Dong Zheng[3], and Kefei Chen[3]

[1] School of Information Security Engineering, Shanghai JiaoTong University
[2] State Key Laboratory of Information Security(Institute of Software of Chinese Academy of Sciences), China
[3] Department of Computer Science and Engineering, Shanghai JiaoTong University

Abstract. Linear feedback shift register(LFSR) sequencces can be used to shorten the representation of the elements of a finite field. We employ n-stage LFSR sequence to construct an efficient blind signature scheme where main computation operations are performed in $GF(q)$ and there do not need any exponentiation in its extension field $GF(q^n)$.

Keywords: Linear Feedback Shift Register, Blind Signature.

For many practical usages or resource-limited environments, it is often desirable to speed up the cryptosystems without any security lost. Indeed, this is a very challenging task for researchers in order to meet the requirements of various security strategies. At least three issues are involved in this aspect, *i.e.*, communication overhead, computational cost and security level. On the one hand, in wireless environments, it is quite significant to reduce communication overhead due to bandwidth limitation. Traditional methods such as ElGamal *etc*, have to choose large security parameters to strengthen their securities. For applications where bandwidth is limited, this is undesirable. On the other hand, we always hope that the security level of the system be as high as possible and the computational costs as low as enough. All measurements are welcome to enhance the security of the system, and meanwhile to maintain low computational costs.

Recently, to shorten the representations of finite field elements, a class of key agreement and signature schemes are designed[1] from linear feedback shift register(LFSR)[2]. Let q be a prime or a power of prime, $f(x) = x^n + a_1 x^{n-1} + a_2 x^{n-2} + \ldots + a_n, (a_i \in GF(q))$ be an irreducible polynomial over $GF(q)$ with α a root of order P in the extension $GF(q^n)$. A sequence $s = \{s_k\}$ over $GF(q)$ is said to be an LFSR sequence generated by $f(x)$ if $s_{k+n} = a_1 s_{k+n-1} + a_2 s_{k+n-2} + \ldots + a_n s_k$, for all $k \geq 0$. We denote $\bar{s}_i = (s_i, s_{i+1}, \ldots, s_{i+n-1})$ the i-th state of the LFSR sequence. For states of an LFSR, we have two sequence operations that can be efficiently performed[3]: (i) SO1: Given states $\bar{s}_k$ and $\bar{s}_l (k, l \in \mathbb{Z}_P)$, to compute $\bar{s}_{k+l}$; and (ii) SO2: Given $\bar{s}_1$, $\bar{s}_k$, and $l(k, l \in \mathbb{Z}_P)$, to compute $\bar{s}_{kl}$.

State based discrete logarithm problem(S-DLP) is defined as, given $(q, n, P, \bar{s}_1, \bar{s}_k)$, to compute k. And state-based discrete logarithm assumption(S-DLA) says that S-DLP problem is hard to solve.

---

* Supported by NSFC(60573030,60673076) and NLMCSFC(9140C1103010602).

Y. Luo (Ed.): CDVE 2007, LNCS 4674, pp. 423–425, 2007.

Efficient electronic payment systems are an important prerequisite for electronic commerce. On one hand, the customer's privacy cannot be compromised by the bank or by the payee. On the other hand, there is a trusted third party, called the judge, which can in cooperation with the bank remove the anonymity of a transaction if the system is being misused by criminals.

Blind signatures[4] can be used to design electronic payment systems that allow participants to remain anonymous during a transaction. A blind signature scheme is always a cooperative protocol and the receiver of the signature provides the signer with the blinding information. Using a blind signature protocol a user can obtain from a bank a digital coin, that is a token properly signed by the bank. The goal of blind signature protocols is to enable a user to obtain a signature from a signer so that the signer does not learn information about the message it signed and so that the user cannot obtain more than one valid signature after one interaction with the signer. Combining the concepts blind signature and linear feedback shift register to realize "LFSR-based blind signature" is the focus of current work as summarized below.

Setup: Given the security parameter 1^λ, the algorithm Setup generates the domain parameters: $q, d, P, \bar{s}_1$. Moreover, to produce a blind signature on an arbitrary message m, one cryptographic hash function $H : \{0,1\}^* \longrightarrow \mathbb{Z}_P^*$ is also required.

KeyGen: To obtain his secret key and corresponding public key, one randomly chooses $\omega \in_R \mathbb{Z}_P$, and computes $\bar{s}_\omega$. The signer's key pair is $(\omega, \bar{s}_\omega)$. He keeps ω secret, while $\bar{s}_\omega$ may be made public by the trusted entity CA.

Sign: Suppose that m is the message to be signed, the cooperative process between the user and the signer is as follows. If all steps below are performed successfully, the user will obtain a valid signature (c, σ) on message m.

User	**Signer**
	$k \in_R \mathbb{Z}_P^*$
	compute $\bar{s}_k$
	$\xleftarrow{\quad \bar{s}_k \quad}$
$\gamma, \delta \in \mathbb{Z}_P^*$	
compute $\bar{s}_{k+\gamma+\delta\omega}$	
let $c = H(m\|\bar{s}_{k+\gamma+\delta\omega})$	
set $c' = c - \delta$	
$\xrightarrow{\quad c' \quad}$	
	compute $\sigma' = k - c'\omega$
$\xleftarrow{\quad \sigma' \quad}$	
$\sigma = \sigma' + \gamma$	
output (c, σ)	

1. (Commitment) The signer picks randomly a number k ($0 < k < P$), computes and forwards $\bar{s}_k$ to the user as a commitment.

2. (Blinding) The user randomly chooses γ and $\delta (0 < \gamma, \delta < P)$ as blinding factors. More concretely, he computes $\bar{s}_{k+\gamma+\delta\omega}$ from $\bar{s}_k$, $\bar{s}_\gamma$, $\bar{s}_\omega$ and δ using SO1 and SO2, sets $c = H(m||\bar{s}_{k+\gamma+\delta\omega})$, and sends the signer c' by computing $c' = c - \delta$.
3. (Signing) The signer returns σ' to the user, where $\sigma' = k - c'\omega$.
4. (Unblinding) The user computes $\sigma = \sigma' + \gamma$, and outputs (c, σ) as the blind signature on the message m.

Verify: Giving a purported signature (c, σ) and a message m, the verifier computes $\bar{s}_{\omega c}$ from $\bar{s}_\omega$ and c using SO2, determines $\bar{s}_{\omega c+\sigma}$ from $\bar{s}_{\omega c}$ and $\bar{s}_\sigma$ using SO1, and accepts the signature iff. the equation $c = H(m||\bar{s}_{\omega c+\sigma})$ holds.

Above-mentioned algorithms make an intact blind signature scheme. It is clear that if there is a probabilistic polynomial time algorithm that can solve S-DLP problem, then there exists an efficient algorithm which can break the scheme. Thus we can gain some confidence on the LFSR-based blind signatures.

Clever readers can note that the proposed scheme may be attacked just as well as the Schnorr blind signature scheme. The attack will be successful if so-called the *ROS*-problem is solvable, and indeed, a solution was shown[5]. We address that, to be resistant against this potential attack, q^n as a whole in our scheme, may need to be at least 1600 bits long, which means that the value q need not be too large. This attack just reflects by contrast the advantages of our method, that is, we can adaptively get balance between the base q and the power n according to our need. Indeed, the proposed scheme enjoys at least the following attractive features: i. *security properties rely on S-DLA* as defined above; and ii. *main computation operations are performed in* $GF(q)$. In fact, besides hashing and addition/multiplication(mod P), only multiplications of elements in $GF(q)$ are involved in our scheme. This *particularly* produces a fast construction. Due to the fact that the complexity of breaking S-DLA is computationally equivalent to that of solving traditional DLP in $GF(q^n)$ [6], the proposed scheme successfully *enhances the securities of the systems, at the same time, with low computational costs*. In other words, *to get a system equivalent to one based on the multiplication group $GF(q^n)$, there is no need to compute any exponentiation in $GF(q^n)$*. All these make our scheme more flexible.

References

1. Giuliani, K., Gong, G.: New LFSR-based cryptosystems and the trace discrete logrithm problem (Trace-DLP). In: Helleseth, T., Sarwate, D., Song, H.-Y., Yang, K. (eds.) SETA 2004. LNCS, vol. 3486, Springer, Heidelberg (2005)
2. Golomb, S.: Shift register sequences. Aegean Park, Laguna Hills, CA (1982)
3. Li, X., Zheng, D., Chen, K.: LFSR-based signatures with message recovery. Intenational Journal of Network Security 4(3), 266–270 (2007)
4. Chaum, D.: Blind signatures for untreaceable payments. In: Crypto 82 (1982)
5. Wagner, D.: A generalized birthday problem. In: Yung, M. (ed.) CRYPTO 2002. LNCS, vol. 2442, pp. 288–303. Springer, Heidelberg (2002)
6. Tan, C., Yi, X., Siew, C.: On the n-th order shift register based discrete logrithm. IEICE Transaction on Fundamentals E86-A, 1213–1216 (2003)

A Relative Entropy Method for Improving Agent-Based Negotiation Efficiency of Collaborative Working in Construction Projects

Xiaolong Xue[1], Jinfeng Lu[1], Yaowu Wang[1], and Qiping Shen[2]

[1] School of Management, Harbin Institute of Technology, Harbin 150001, China
[2] Department of Building and Real Estate, The Hong Kong Polytechnic University, Hung Hom, Kowloon, Hong Kong, China
xlxue@hit.edu.cn, lujf@hit.edu.cn, ywwang@hit.edu.cn,
bsqpshen@polyu.edu.hk

Abstract. This research presents a relative entropy method for improving agent-based multi-attribute negotiation efficiency (REAMNE) of collaborative working in construction projects (CWCP). This method aggregates preference information of negotiators of CWCP in two steps. Firstly, compromise group preference order is ascertained by using preference information, which is newly provided by negotiators, and compromise preference information, which is formed in previously agent-based automatically negotiation process and calculated by using a compromise preference model. Secondly, group preferences are aggregated by using a relative entropy model, which is established based on entropy theory meanwhile considering the multiple attributes in negotiation of CWCP. The method of REAMNE has the merit of fulfilling the necessary requirement of group decision making (GDM), i.e. maximizing preference consistency of GDM and keeping minimum gap of negotiators' utility and group preference.

Keywords: Collaborative working, Agent, Negotiation, Relative entropy.

1 Introduction

Construction is a collaborative teamwork process with successful projects dependent upon a strong weave of owner, architect, engineer, contractor, and supplier into a collaborative team. Negotiation is a very popular decision-making behavior in collaborative working in construction projects (CWCP). Recently, although various agent-based negotiation mechanisms have been developed and investigated [1], agents' abilities in dealing with the changing environments during negotiation are still very limited and need to be studied further to enhance negotiation efficiency [2]. Decision-makers (negotiator) have requirement to man-made termination of negotiation and find other methods to quickly search accepted solution by negotiators when there is yet being utility gap among them. This research presents a relative entropy method for improving agent-based multi-attribute negotiation efficiency (REAMNE) of CWCP. We employ

Y. Luo (Ed.): CDVE 2007, LNCS 4674, pp. 426–428, 2007.
© Springer-Verlag Berlin Heidelberg 2007

the concept of relative entropy to aggregate group preference in agent-based negotiation of CWCP when negotiation is failed or stopped.

2 Methodogy

The choice of solutions after negotiation is failed or stopped is a typical group decision making (GDM). The nature of GDM is a process of preference aggregation, which goal is to maximize consensus of group preference, i.e. to find a solution on which the gap of preference utility value between group and individual is minimum. Entropy based optimization theory as an effective tools has great successful in decision analysis area [3]. The general process steps of REAMNE are shown in Fig 1. REAMNE mainly includes three decision processes: calculating CGPO, transformation CGPO to utility value, and confirming group preference vector of negotiators using relative entropy aggregation optimization model.

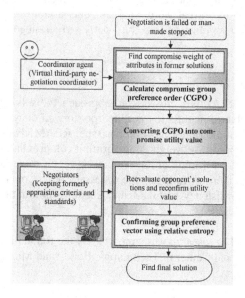

Fig. 1. Process steps in REAMNE

Step 1: Using the preference order which is formerly formed in negotiation process of CWCP to find compromise weight (CW) of decision-making attributes, which is accepted by decision-makers. Note that, to a negotiator, the former negotiation solution is better than next negotiation solution of next loop [4]. And then, to confirm the group priority order of former negotiation solutions according to CW. This kind of group priority order can be seen as compromise group preference order (CGPO) of a third-party virtual 'negotiation coordinator'.

Step 2: Converting CGPO into compromise utility value

Step 3: Aggregating final group preference relations of negotiation solutions in three-party GDM environment by using relative entropy preference aggregation model. The definition of relative entropy is given as follows.

Suppose that $x_i, y_i \geq 0, i = 1, 2, \ldots, n$ and $1 = \sum_{i=1}^{n} x_i \geq \sum_{i=1}^{n} y_i$, we call that

$h(X, Y) = \sum x_i \log \frac{x_i}{y_i} \geq 0$ is the relative entropy of X relative to Y, where

$X = (x_1, x_2, \ldots, x_n)^T$, $Y = (y_1, y_2, \ldots, y_n)^T$. Minimum relative entropy is obtained when two discrete variables X and Y have the same distribution. So we can use relative entropy to measure the consensus degree.

In step 3, negotiators in real world reevaluate their opponent's negotiation solutions in negotiation process and reconfirm utility of these solutions on their own abiding formerly appraising criteria and standards. This can keep the continuous consensus of decision-making preference. Then a three-party GDM model is formed, which includes two kinds of negotiators in real word, such as general contractor and subcontractor, general contractor and supplier, and the third-party virtual 'negotiation coordinator'.

3 Conclusions

The hybrid method REAMNE provides an approach for solving GDM problem of CWCP when agent-based negotiation is failed or stopped or when they can not efficiently get optimal solution on a negotiation issue. REAMNE mainly includes three steps: calculating compromise weight, transforming compromise preference orderings into utility value, and confirming group preference vector of negotiators. The method of REAMNE has the merit of fulfilling the necessary requirement of GDM, i.e. maximizing preference consistency of GDM and keeping minimum gap of negotiators' utility and group preference.

Acknowledgement. The research was supported by the foundation under the grant of htcsr06t05 from National Center of Technology, Policy and Management, Harbin Institute of Technology.

References

1. Bussmann, S., Muller, H.J.: A negotiation framework for co-operating agents. In: Proceedings of CKBS-SIG, Dark Centre, University of Keele, pp. 1–17 (1992)
2. Cheng, C.B., Chan, C.C.H., Lin, K.C.: Intelligent agents for e-marketplace negotiation with issue trade-offs by fuzzy inference systems. Decision Support Systems 42, 626–638 (2006)
3. Qiu, W.H.: Management Decision and Entropy Theory, pp. 290–293. China Machine Press, Beijing, China (2002)
4. Darling, T., Mumpower, J.: Modeling cognitive influences on the dynamics of negotiations. In: Proceedings of the 23rd Annual International Conference on Systems Science, pp. 128–135. IEEE Computer Society Press, Los Alamitos (1990)

Author Index

Lecture Notes in Computer Science

Sublibrary 3: Information Systems and Application, incl. Internet/Web and HCI

For information about Vols. 1– 4276
please contact your bookseller or Springer